ROGET'S
21st CENTURY™
THESAURUS

S0-BSZ-237

NELSON REGENCY
A Division of Thomas Nelson, Inc.

Published in Nashville, Tennessee, by Thomas Nelson Publishers.

Library of Congress Cataloging-in-Publication Data

Roget's 21st century vest-pocket thesaurus.
   p. cm
  ISBN 8407-6827-3 (PB) :
   1. English language—Synonyms   I. Title: Roget's
twenty-first century vest-pocket thesaurus.
PE1591.R718 1993
423'.1—dc20   93–3096
                                            CIP

1 2 3 4 5 6 7 8 — 98 97 96 95 94 93

Publisher's Preface

Leap into the future with Thomas Nelson's *Roget's Vest-Pocket Thesaurus*. Our concise, modern edition is an abridged version of Roget's original work published in 1852. With more than 1,000 entries, this powerful reference is an essential part of every school, home and office library. Included is a "plan of classification" (following Roget's original format) and a tabular synopsis of categories to aid you as you search for the perfect synonym. To assure clarity, all antiquated and duplicated entries have been removed.

The publishers are certain that you will find this resource both beneficial and enlightening as you use it to explore the depths of the English language.

How to Use Roget's Thesaurus

PETER MARK ROGET (1779—1869) was a British lexicographer and physician. *Roget's Thesaurus,* a standard reference work for over a century, represents his highly personal view of how the English language reflects the structure of the universe. In some ways, that view is dated today; but the complex structure and breadth of the thesaurus still prove surprisingly helpful to the modern user.

For most users, the key to the synonyms in the body of the book lies in the alphabetical listing in the index. The uniqueness of Roget's original plan of classification provides the user with access to related words and requires nothing more than a near-synonym to help locate the word sought. *Roget's Thesaurus* is more than simply a synonym dictionary—both in the lists following individual headwords and in the grouping of headwords under the various sections, it is a diverse collection of associated and related words and phrases.

For example, suppose you are looking for a synonym for *lull:* a check in the index yields the reference number, 403;

turning to that entry provides the synonyms *silence, stillness, quiet, hush, peace.*

But, suppose you are trying to find a verb meaning 'to feel very dissatisfied' and the synonyms listed under *discontent* are not "strong" enough for your purpose. A brief check of the related, contiguous headwords will lead you to the entry for *regret* which provides the synonyms *lament, deplore, bemoan, bewail, rue.*

This edition of *Roget's Thesaurus* has a number of other special features. Dictionaries of synonyms, unless they are of considerable size, rarely provide alphabetical listings of all the words in the book. In this edition, you will find every word listed in the index.

Larger books may provide more synonyms, but the user of a thesaurus is rarely looking for a rare or unusual word: he wants an equivalent word that is part of everyday language. This edition is the only abridged *Roget's Thesaurus* available. While retaining the original structure and all the 1,000 headwords, all antiquated words and phrases have been removed. In addition, the book has been modernized to include the most current usage and the newest developments in language.

In this abridgment, many duplications have been omitted to save space. For maximum usefulness, the user should look through other associated parts of speech for the word he is seeking, for adjectives and verbs can yield nouns and adverbs, and vice versa. For example, adverbs can be formed by adding *-ly* to some adjectives and nouns by adding *-ness* to some adjectives.

The Publisher

Caution: If the word selected is not completely familiar, check its meaning and usage in this volume's dictionary before risking its use in an incorrect or unidiomatic context.

The words shown in **boldface** *in the index indicate they are the title or heading of a category.*

Plan of Classification
(following the original Roget plan)

Tabular Synopsis of Categories

Class I. ABSTRACT RELATIONS
I. EXISTENCE

1. existence
2. nonexistence
3. substantiality
4. unsubstantiality
5. intrinsicality
6. extrinsicality
7. state
8. circumstance

II. RELATION

9. relation
10. nonrelation
11. consanguinity
12. correlation
13. identity
14. contrariety
15. difference
16. uniformity
16a. lack of uniformity
17. similarity
18. dissimilarity
19. imitation
20. nonimitation
20a. variation
21. copy
22. prototype
23. agreement
24. disagreement

III. QUANTITY

25. quantity
26. degree
27. equality
28. inequality
29. mean
30. compensation
31. greatness
32. smallness
33. superiority
34. inferiority
35. increase
36. decrease
37. addiction
38. deduction
39. adjunct
40. remainder
40a. decrement
41. mixture
42. simpleness
43. junction
44. disjunction
45. link
46. coherence
47. incoherence
48. combination
49. decomposition
50. whole
51. part
52. completeness
53. incompleteness

234. front	235. rear
236. side	237. opposition
238. right	239. left

III. FORM

240. form	241. formlessness
242. symmetry	243. distortion
244. angularity	
245. curvature	246. straightness
247. circularity	248. convolution
249. rotundity	
250. convexity	
251. flatness	252. concavity
253. sharpness	254. bluntness
255. smoothness	256. roughness
257. notch	
258. fold	
259. furrow	
260. opening	261. closure
262. perforator	263. stopper

IV. MOTION

264. motion	265. rest
266. journey	267. navigation
268. traveler	269. mariner, flier
270. transference	
271. carrier	
272. vehicle	273. ship
274. velocity	275. slowness
276. impulse	277. recoil
278. direction	279. deviation
280. precedence	281. sequence
282. progression	283. regression
284. propulsion	285. traction
286. approach	287. recession
288. attraction	289. repulsion
290. convergence	291. divergence
292. arrival	293. departure
294. ingress	295. egress
296. reception	297. ejection
298. eating	299. excretion

III. ORGANIC MATTER

xii

Class V. VOLITION
I. INDIVIDUAL VOLITION

Class VI. AFFECTIONS
I. AFFECTIONS IN GENERAL

II. PERSONAL AFFECTIONS

III. SYMPATHETIC AFFECTIONS

ROGET'S THESAURUS

Class I

Words Expressing Abstract Relations

I. Existence

1 existence n being, entity, subsistence, reality, actuality, presence, fact, matter of fact, truth, science of existence: ontology.

v exist, be, subsist, live, breathe; occur, happen, take place; consist in, lie in; endure, remain, abide, survive, last, stay, continue.

adj existent, extant; prevalent, current, afloat; real, actual, true, positive, absolute; substantial, substantive; well-founded, well grounded.

adv actually, in fact, in reality.

2 nonexistence n inexistence; insubstantiality, nonentity; blank, *tabula rasa*, void, emptiness, nothingness; potential, possibility; annihilation, extinction, obliteration, total destruction.

v not exist; pass away, perish, die, die out, disappear, dissolve; annihilate, destroy, obliterate, wipe off the face of the earth; nullify, void; take away, remove.

adj nonexistent, inexistent; blank, void, empty; unreal, baseless, unsubstantial, intangible, ineffable, spiritual, spectral; unborn, uncreated, unbegotten, unconceived; potential, possible; exhausted, gone, lost, departed, extinct, defunct; fabulous, visionary, imaginary, ideal, conceptual, abstract.

3 substantiality n materiality, corporality, tangibility, material existence, bodiliness, matter, stuff; creature, being, person, body, flesh and blood, substance; thing, object, article.

adj substantive, substantial, corporeal, material, bodily, physical, concrete, tangible, palpable, corporal, materialistic.

4 unsubstantiality n nothingness; nothing, naught, nil, nullity, zero; shadow, phantom, apparition, dream, illusion; fallacy, inanity, frivolity; hollowness, blank, void; flimsiness, thinness, slightness.

v vanish, evaporate, fade, dissolve, melt away, disappear.

adj unsubstantial, baseless, groundless, ungrounded, without foundation, fallacious, erroneous, untenable; insignificant, slight, thin, trifling, frivolous; imaginary, visionary, dreamy, shadowy, ethereal, airy, immaterial, spectral, illusory, incorporeal, intangible, bodiless, abstract; vacant, vacuous, empty, blank, hollow.

5 intrinsicality n ego, essence, quintessence, gist, pith, marrow, sap, lifeblood, backbone, heart, soul, core; principle, nature, constitution, construction, character, type, quality; habit, temper, temperament, personality, spirit, humor, grain, moods, features, peculiarities, aspects, idiosyncrasies, tendencies, bents; inbeing, inherence, essentiality.

v be intrinsic, be inherent.

adj intrinsic, inherent, implanted, innate, inborn, inbred, ingrained; essential, fundamental, basic, normal; inherited, congenital, hereditary, indigenous, in the blood, in the genes; instinctive, instinctual, internal, personal, subjective; characteristic, peculiar, idiosyncratic; fixed, set in one's ways, invariable, unchangeable, incurable, ineradicable.

adv intrinsically, at bottom, in effect, practically, virtually, substantially.

6 extrinsicality n extraneousness, externals.

adj extrinsic, extraneous, external, adventitious; collateral, accidental, incidental, objective.

adv extrinsically.

7 state *n* condition, case, circumstances, situation, status, surroundings, pass, plight, pickle; mood, temper, frame; constitution, structure, form, phase, frame, fabric, stamp, set, fit, mold; mode, style, fashion, light, complexion, character; tone, tenor, turn.

v be in a state.

8 circumstance *n* situation, phase, position, condition, posture, attitude, place, point; footing, standing, status; occasion, happening, event, juncture, conjunction; predicament, exigency, emergency, crisis, pinch, plight, pass; climax, apex, turning point.

adj circumstantial, conditional, provisional; contingent, incidental, adventitious; critical, climactic.

adv under the circumstances, under the conditions; thus, in such wise; accordingly, that being the case, since, seeing that, as matters stand; conditionally, provided, if, in case; if so, if it so happen, in the event of, provisionally, unless.

II. Absolute Relation

9 relation *n* connection, concern, bearing, reference; correlation, analogy; similarity, affinity, homogeneity, alliance, association, nearness; approximation, relationship; comparison, ratio, proportion; link, tie, bond.

v relate to, refer to; bear upon, regard, concern, touch, affect, have to do with, pertain to, appertain to, belong to; bring into relation with, associate, connect, parallel; link, bind, tie.

adj relative, relative to, relating to, referable to, with reference to; belonging to; related, connected, associated, affiliated, allied; in the same category, relevant.

adv as regards, about, concerning, with relation to, with reference to, with regard to, with respect to, in

connection with, under the head of, in the matter of.

10 [absence of relation] **non-relation** *n* irrelation, dissociation, lack of connection; disconnection, disjunction; inconsequence, irreconcilability, disagreement, heterogeneity; independence.

v have no relation to, have no bearing upon, have nothing to do with, have no connection with.

adj unrelated, irrespective, unallied, unconnected, disconnected, heterogeneous, independent; adrift, insular, isolated; extraneous, strange, alien, foreign, outlandish, exotic; irrelevant, inapplicable, not pertinent, beside the mark, off base; remote, farfetched, out-of-the-way, forced, detached, distanced; incidental, parenthetical.

adv parenthetically, by the way, by the by; incidentally.

11 [relations of kindred] **consanguinity** *n* relationship, kindred, blood; parentage, paternity, maternity, lineage, heritage; filiation, affiliation, connection, alliance, tie; family, blood relation, ties of blood, kinsman, kinfolk, kith and kin, relation, relative, one's own, one's own flesh and blood; fraternity, sorority, brotherhood, sisterhood; race, stock, generation.

v be related to, claim relationship with.

adj related, akin, consanguineous, allied, affiliated, connected; kindred, familial.

12 [double or reciprocal relation] **correlation** *n* correspondence, reciprocity, reciprocation, interdependence, mutuality, interchange, exchange.

v reciprocate, alternate, interchange, interact, interdepend; interchange, exchange; correlate, correspond, relate.

adj reciprocal, mutual, correlative, corresponding, analogous, complementary; equivalent, interchangeable, alternate.

adv reciprocally.

13 identity *n* sameness, exactness, equality, correspondence, parallelism, unity, convertibility, resemblance, similarity; self, oneself, name, personality; facsimile, duplicate, replica, copy, reproduction.

v be identical, coincide, coalesce.

adj identical, self, the same, selfsame; coincident, coinciding, coalescent, indistinguishable; one, equal, equivalent.

adv identically.

14 contrariety *n* contrast, foil, antithesis, oppositeness, opposition, contradiction, antipathy, antagonism; the reverse, the inverse, the converse, inversion, subversion, reversal, the opposite, antipodes.

v be contrary, contrast with, differ from, oppose; invert, revert, turn upside down; contradict, contravene; antagonize.

adj contrary, opposite, counter, converse, reverse; opposed, antithetical, contrasted, antipodean, antagonistic, opposing; conflicting, inconsistent, contradictory; negative, hostile.

15 difference *n* discrepancy, disparity, dissimilarity, inconsistency, variance, variation, diversity, imbalance, disagreement, inequality, inequity, divergence, contrast, contrariety; discrimination, distinction, nice distinction, shade, nuance, subtlety.

v differ, vary; diversify, modify, change, alter; contrast, mismatch; discriminate, distinguish.

adj different, diverse, heterogeneous, unlike, divergent, altered, changed, deviant, deviating, variant, varied, modified; diversified, various, divers, miscellaneous, manifold; other, another, not the same, unequal, unmatched, wide apart; distinctive, characteristic, discriminative.

16 uniformity *n* homogeneity, permanence, continuity, consistency, stability, accordance, standardization, conformity, agreement; regularity, constancy, evenness, sameness; monotony, routine, invariability.

v be uniform, accord with; conform to, assimilate; level, smooth, even.

adj uniform, homogeneous, of a piece, consistent; consistent, regular, constant, even, level; invariable, unchanging, unvarying, unvaried, unchanged, constant, regular; undiversified, solid, plain, dreary, monotonous, routine.

adv uniformly; always, invariably, without exception; ever, forever.

16a lack of uniformity *n* diversity, irregularity, unevenness, inconsistency, nonconformity, heterogeneity.

adj diversified, varied, irregular, inconsistent, motley, patchwork, uneven, rough; multifarious, of various kinds.

17 similarity *n* resemblance, likeness, similitude, semblance, affinity, approximation, parallelism; agreement, correspondence, analogy; brotherhood, family likeness; repetition, sameness, uniformity, identity; the like, fellow, match, pair, mate, twin, double, counterpart; alter ego, chip off the old block, birds of a feather, like two peas in a pod; simile, parallel, type, image, representation.

v be similar, resemble, look like, bear a resemblance, take after, approximate, parallel, match, rhyme with.

adj similar, resembling, like, alike; twin; analogous, parallel, of a piece; allied to, akin to, corresponding; approximate, much the same, near, close, something like; imitative, mock, pseudo, simulating, representing, representative; exact, true, lifelike, faithful, true to life, identical.

adv as if, so to speak; as it were, as if it were; quasi, just as.

18 dissimilarity *n* dissimilitude, unlikeness, difference; diversity, disparity, divergence; novelty, originality, uniqueness.

v be unlike, differ from, bear no resemblance; vary, diversify, differentiate.

adj dissimilar, unlike, different, disparate; unique, new, novel, unprecedented, unmatched, unequaled; diversified.

19 imitation *n* copying; copy, duplication, reproduction, replica; mocking, mimicry, aping; simulation, impersonation, representation, semblance, approximation, paraphrase, parody; plagiarism, forgery.

v imitate, copy, mirror, reflect, impersonate, duplicate, reproduce, simulate, counterfeit; mock, take off, mimic, ape, personate, parody, caricature, travesty; follow, emulate, pattern after, model oneself on, parallel, follow, take after.

adj imitative, modeled after, modeled on, based on; fake, phony, counterfeit, false, imitation, mock; duplicate, second hand.

adv literally, word for word, to the letter.

20 nonimitation *n* originality, uniqueness.

adj unimitated, uncopied; unmatched, unparalleled; inimitable, original, unique, special, one of a kind, rare, exceptional.

20a variation *n* alteration, change, modification; divergency, deviation, aberration, innovation.

v vary, change; deviate, diverge, alternate, modify.

adj varied, modified, diversified, altered, changed.

21 [result of imitation] **copy** *n* facsimile, counterpart, effigy, form, likeness, similitude, semblance, cast, mold, model, representation, image, portrait; reflection, shadow, echo; transcript, transcription, reproduction, imitation, carbon, ditto, stencil, duplicate, reprint, transfer, replica; parody, caricature, burlesque, travesty, paraphrase; counterfeit, forgery, deception.

adj faithful, lifelike, exact, similar.

22 [thing copied] **prototype** *n* original, model, pattern, precedent, standard; type, archetype, exemplar, paradigm, module, example; text, copy, design; die, mold; matrix, mint, seal, punch, intaglio, negative, plate, stamp.

v be an example, set an example.

23 agreement *n* unanimity, harmony, accord, accordance, concord, union, unity, understanding, settlement, treaty, pact; uniformity, conformity, consistency, congruity, logic, correspondence, parallelism, apposition; consent, assent, concurrence, cooperation.

v agree, accord, harmonize; correspond, tally, *(informal)* jibe; meet, suit, fit, befit, square with; dovetail, match; adapt, fit, accommodate, adjust.

adj agreeing, accordant, correspondent, congenial, harmonious; reconcilable, comfortable, compatible, congruous, consistent, logical, consonant, commensurate; in accordance with, in harmony with, in keeping with; apt, apposite, pat, pertinent; agreeable, happy, felicitous.

24 disagreement *n* discord, dissonance, dissidence, disunion, discrepancy, nonconformity, incongruity, dissension, conflict, opposition, antagonism, difference; disparity, disproportion, mismatch, variance, divergence, inequity, inequality.

v disagree, clash, jar, argue, quarrel, dispute.

adj disagreeing, discordant, dissonant, inharmonious; at variance, hostile, conflicting; antagonistic, clashing, disputing, factious, dissenting, irreconcilable, incompatible, inconsistent with; incongruous, disproportionate, disparate, divergent; disagreeable, uncongenial, mismatched; out of joint, out of step, out of tune.

III. Simple Quantity

25 [absolute quantity] **quantity** *n* size, mass, volume, amount, measure, measurement, substance, strength; mouthful, spoonful, handful; stock, batch, lot, dose.

adj quantitative, some, any, more or less.

26 [relative quantity] **degree** *n* grade, extent, measure, amount, ratio, standard, height, pitch; reach, range, scope, rate, caliber; gradation, shade, tint; tenor, tone, compass; sphere, station, rank, standing; point, mark, stage, level; intensity, strength.

adj comparative, gradual, shading off.

adv by degrees, gradually, step by step, bit by bit, little by little, inch by inch, drop by drop; in some degree, to some extent; up to a point.

27 [sameness of quantity or degree] **equality** *n* parity, symmetry, balance, counterbalance, evenness, monotony, level; equivalence, equipose, equilibrium; par, even keel, quits; identity, similarity; tie, dead heat, draw, drawn game, neck and neck race; match, peer, equal, mate, fellow, brother; equivalent.

v equal, match, reach, keep pace with, run abreast; come up to; balance, even the score; equalize, level, trim, adjust; strike a balance; restore equilibrium.

adj equal, even, level, monotonous, coequal, symmetrical, balanced; on a par with, on a level with, on an equal footing with, up to the mark; equivalent, tantamount, synonymous, quits, even, much the same, all one, one and the same; drawn, half and half, six of one and half a dozen of another.

adv equally, to all intents and purposes.

28 [difference of quantity or degree] **inequality** *n* disparity, dissimilarity, difference, odds, unevenness, imbalance; inferiority, shortcoming, deficiency, imperfection, inadequacy; mediocrity; superiority.

v be unequal, have the advantage, turn the scale, turn the tide; topple, overmatch; not come up to, fall short of, not come up to snuff.

adj unequal, uneven, imbalanced; disparate, partial, inferior, insufficient, deficient, inadequate, mediocre, short.

29 mean *n* medium, average, balance, middle, mid-point, center, median, golden mean; compromise, neutrality.

v split the difference, take the average, move to the center.

adj mean, intermediate, middle, average, standard, normal, neutral; mediocre, middle class, bourgeois, commonplace, run of the mill, egalitarian.

adv on the average, in the long run.

30 compensation *n* equation; indemnification, requital; compromise, measure for measure, tit for tat, eye for an eye, retaliation, equalization; setoff, off-set, counterpoise, ballast; indemnity, equivalent, *quid pro quo*, amends, reparation.

v compensate, indemnify, recompense, remunerate; counterbalance, counterpoise, countervail, offset, counteract, balance, balance out, make up for, square, even out, equalize; cover, neutralize, nullify; redeem, atone; make amends.

adj compensatory, compensating, equivalent, equal.

adv but, however, yet, still, notwithstanding, nevertheless, although, though, nonetheless; howbeit, albeit; at all events, at any rate, be that as it may, even so, on the other hand, at the same time.

31 greatness *n* magnitude, size, bulk, dimensions, vastness; multitude; enormousness, immensity, might, strength, intensity, fullness; importance, distinction, eminence, renown; quantity, store, volume, mass, bulk, heap; abundance, sufficiency.

v be great, soar, tower, rise above, transcend; enlarge, increase, expand.

adj great, large, considerable, big, huge, mammoth, gigantic; ample, abundant, sufficient; full, intense, strong; widespread, extensive, wholesale; goodly, noble, precious, mighty; utter, uttermost, arch, profound, intense, consummate; extraordinary, important, unsurpassed, supreme; complete, total, vast, immense, enormous, extreme, inordinate, excessive, extravagant, exorbitant, outrageous, monstrous; towering, stupendous, prodigious, marvelous; unlimited, infinite; ab-

solute, positive, stark, decided, unequivocal, essential, perfect; remarkable, notable, noteworthy.

adv [in a positive degree] truly;
decidedly, unequivocally, absolutely,
essentially, fundamentally, downright; [in a complete degree] entirely, completely, totally, wholly,
abundantly, fully, amply, widely; [in
a great or high degree] greatly,
much, indeed, very, very much,
most, pretty, pretty well, enough, in
a great measure, to a large extent;
richly, on a large scale, ever so much;
mightily, powerfully, extremely, ex-
ceedingly, intensely, exquisitely, consummately, acutely, indefinitely,
immeasurably, beyond compare, beyond measure, beyond all bounds,
incalculably, infinitely; [in a supreme degree] pre-eminently, superlatively, supremely, incomparably;
[in a too great degree] immoderately,
inordinately, exorbitantly, exces-
sively, enormously, preposterously,
monstrously, out of all proportion,
with a vengeance; [in a marked
degree] particularly, remarkably,
singularly, curiously, uncommonly,
unusually, peculiarly, notably, sig-
nally, strikingly, pointedly, mainly,
chiefly; famously, egregiously,
prominently, glaringly, emphatically,
strangely, wonderfully, amazingly,
surprisingly, astonishingly, incred-
ibly, marvelously, stupendously; [in a
violent degree] violently, furiously,
severely, desperately, tremendously,
extravagantly; [in a painful degree]
painfully, sadly, sorely, bitterly, piteously, grievously, miserably, cruelly,
woefully, lamentably, shockingly,
frightfully, fearfully, dreadfully, terribly, horribly.

32 smallness *n* littleness, tininess, diminutiveness; slenderness, thinness,
paltriness, slightness, paucity, fewness, sparseness, scarcity; unimportance, triviality, inconsequentiality,
pettiness, insignificance; meanness,
sordidness, selfishness, narrow-
mindedness; small quantity, modicum, atom, particle, molecule,
point, speck, dot, dab, mote, jot,
iota; minutiae, details, *soupçon*,
scintilla, granule; drop, droplet,

drizzle, sprinkling, dash, smack,
tinge; dole, scrap, shred, splinter;
mite, bit, morsel, crumb, seed; snippet, snatch, slip; chip, sliver; nutshell thimbleful, spoonful, handful,
mouthful; fragment, fraction, drop
in the ocean; trifle.

v be small.

adj small, little, tiny, diminutive,
petite, miniature, minuscule, minute, microscopic, infinitesimal;
fine; unimportant, trivial, minor,
secondary, trifling, inconsequential,
petty, paltry, insignificant; slender,
thin, slight, scanty, scant, meager,
insufficient; few, sparse, scarce;
low, so-so, middling, tolerable, inconsiderable, inappreciable; mean,
sordid, selfish, narrow, narrow-
minded, illiberal, ungenerous; feeble, weak, faint.

adv [in a small degree] to a small
extent; a wee bit; slightly, imperceptibly, faintly; miserably, wretchedly,
insufficiently, imperfectly; passably,
pretty well, well enough; [in a certain or limited degree] partially, in
part, to a certain degree; some,
rather, to some degree; simply, only,
purely, merely, at the least; ever so
little; almost, nearly, well nigh,
short of, not quite, all but, near the
mark; scarcely, hardly, barely, only
just, no more than; [in an uncertain
degree] about, thereabouts, somewhere about; [in no degree] noway,
nowise, not at all, not in the least, not
a bit, not a jot, not a whit, in no respect, by no means, on no account.

33 superiority *n* supremacy, pre-eminence, ascendancy, transcendence;
excellence, greatness, nobility, eminence, worthiness, preponderance,
predominance, prevalence, advantage; majority; quality, high caliber.

v be superior, exceed, excel, transcend, outdo, outweigh, outrival,
outrank; pass, surpass; top, cap,
outstrip, eclipse, predominate, prevail; take precedence, come first.

adj superior, greater, major,
higher, exceeding; supreme, greatest, utmost, paramount, pre-eminent, foremost, crowning; first-rate,
important, excellent, unrivaled,
matchless, priceless, unparalleled,

unequaled, unsurpassed, inimitable, incomparable, superlative, beyond, compare, transcendent.

adv beyond, more, over, over and above, at its height; [in a superior or supreme degree] eminently, pre-eminently, prominently, surpassingly, superlatively, supremely, above all, to crown all, *par excellence*; principally, especially, particularly, peculiarly.

34 inferiority *n* low quality, deficiency, imperfection, shortcoming, inadequacy; mediocrity, commonalty, commonness, poorness, meanness; minority, subordination, subjection.

v be inferior, fall short of, come short of, not come up to, not pass muster; want, lack.

adj inferior, minor, less, lesser, deficient; poor, indifferent, mean, base, bad, shabby, paltry, humble, imperfect, mediocre, common, commonplace; second-rate; poorer; secondary, minor, subordinate, lower; diminished, reduced, unimportant.

adv less, subpar; short of, under

35 increase *n* growth, augmentation, enlargement, extension, expansion, addition, increment, accretion, aggrandizement; development, rise, ascent.

v increase, grow, dilate, enlarge, expand, multiply; augment, add to, enlarge, greaten; extend, spread out, prolong; advance, rise, sprout, ascend; raise, exalt, deepen, heighten, intensify, magnify, redouble; aggrandize.

adj increasing, growing; additional, incremental; developmental.

36 decrease *n* diminution, abatement, decline, reduction, wane, falling-off, contraction, dwindling, shrinking, lessening, ebb, ebbing; subtraction, abridgment, shortening; depreciation, deterioration.

v decrease, lessen, abate, fall off, decline, contract, shrink, dwindle, wane, ebb, subside; diminish, deteriorate, depreciate, languish, decay; abridge, shorten, subtract.

adj decreased, decreasing, on the wane.

37 addition *n* increment, increase, enlargement, aggrandizement, accession; supplement, adjunct, attachment, addendum; annexation, interposition, insertion; uniting, joining.

v add, annex, affix, subjoin, tack on, append, attach, join, supplement, increase, augment, make an addition to; accrue, accumulate, pile up; total, sum, add up; reinforce.

adj additional, supplemental, supplementary; extra, accessory, auxiliary.

adv in addition, more, plus; and, also, likewise, too, further, furthermore, besides, to boot, etc., and so on, and so forth; over and above, moreover; with, as well as, together with, along with, in conjunction with.

38 deduction *n* subtraction, retrenchment, withdrawal, removal; mutilation, amputation, curtailment; shortening, abbreviation; decrease; cutback.

v deduct, subtract, retrench, withdraw, remove; take from, take away; shorten, abbreviate, cut back, pare down, reduce, decrease, diminish, curtail, eliminate, deprive of; mutilate, amputate, cut off, cut away, excise; pare, thin, thin out, prune, scrape, file.

adj subtracted, subtracting; removable, reducible; deductible.

adv less, short of; minus, without, excepting, except, with the exception of, save, exclusive of.

39 [thing added] **adjunct** *n* addition, affix, suffix, appendage, annex, augmentation, increment, reinforcement, accessory, accompaniment, sequel; addendum, complement, supplement, appendix, attachment; rider, offshoot, episode, corollary. *adj* additional.

40 [thing remaining] **remainder** *n* residue, remains, remnant, leftover, excess, superfluity, balance, surplus, rest, relic; leavings, odds and ends, residuum, dregs, refuse, crumbs, stubble, ruins, skeleton, stump.

v remain, survive, be left; be left over.

adj remaining, left, left over, residual; over, odd, spare, unused; superfluous; surviving.

40a [thing deducted] **decrement** *n* discount, defect, loss, deduction.

41 mixture *n* admixture, mix, combination, mingling, amalgamation, junction; infusion, suffusion, transfusion; infiltration, interlarding, interpolation; adulteration; thing mixed; tinge, tincture, touch, dash, sprinkling, spice, seasoning, infusion, compounds: alloy, amalgam, mélange, pastiche, miscellany, medley, patchwork, hotchpotch, gallimaufry, conglomeration, jumble, potpourri, farrago; cross, hybrid, mongrel.

v mix, join; combine, blend, mingle, commingle, confuse, jumble, unite, compound, amalgamate, adulterate; interlard, interlace, intertwine, interweave, interpolate; conjoin, associate, consort; instill, imbue, infuse, suffuse, transfuse, infiltrate, dash, tinge, tincture, season, blend, cross.

adj mixed, composite, half-and-half, hybrid, cross, mongrel, heterogeneous; motley, variegated, miscellaneous, promiscuous, indiscriminate.

adv among, amongst, amid, amidst, with; in the midst of.

42 [freedom from mixture] **simpleness** *n* purity, homogeneity; elimination, sifting, purification.

v simplify; sift, winnow, eliminate, strain, clean, purify; disentangle.

adj simple, uniform, homogeneous, single, pure, clear; unmixed, unadulterated, elemental, elementary, basic.

43 junction *n* joining, union; connection, conjunction, annexation, attachment; coupling, marriage, wedlock; confluence, communication, concatenation; meeting, assemblage, assembly, reunion; joint, joining, juncture, pivot, hinge, articulation; seam, stitch, linkage, link.

v join, unite, connect, link up, link; associate; put together, piece together, bind together; attach, fix, affix, fasten, bind, secure, clinch, twist, tie, string, strap, sew, lace, stitch, hem, knit, button, buckle, hitch, lash, splice gird, tether, picket, moor, harness, leash; chain; fetter, lock, hook, couple, link, yoke, bracket; marry, wed, bridge over, span; pin, bolt, clasp, clamp, screw, rivet; solder, weld, fuse; entwine, interlace, intertwine, interweave; entangle.

adj joined, joint; corporate, compact; firm, fast, close, tight, taut, secure, set, inseparable, indissoluble.

adv jointly, in conjunction with; fast, firmly; intimately.

44 disjunction *n* disconnection, disunion, disengagement, dissociation, discontinuity; isolation, insularity, insulation, separateness; dispersion, separation, parting, detachment, segregation; divorce; division, subdivision, break, fracture, rupture; dismemberment, dislocation, severance; fissure, breach, rent, split, rift, crack, cut, slit, incision.

v disjoin, disconnect, disengage, disunite, dissociate, divorce, part, detach, separate, disentangle, cut off, rescind, discontinue; segregate, set apart, keep apart, isolate, insulate; cut adrift, loose, set free, liberate; divide, subdivide, sever, dissever, cut, saw, snip, chop, ax, cleave, rive, rend, slit, split, splinter, chip, crack, snap, break, tear, burst, rend; wrench, rupture, shatter; hack, hew, slash, slice, cut up, carve, dissect, tear to pieces; disband, disperse, dislocate, break up, apportion, divide; part, part company, separate, leave.

adj disjoined, discontinuous, disjunctive; isolated, insular; separate, apart, asunder, loose, adrift, free; unattached, unconnected.

adv separately, one by one, severally, apart, adrift, asunder.

45 link *n* connective, connection, vinculum, copula, tie, bond, bridge; junction, bracket.

v link, bond, join, connect, conjoin, fasten, pin, bind, tie; bridge, span.

46 coherence *n* cohesion, cohesiveness, adherence, adhesion, adhesiveness; connection, union, conglomeration, aggregation, consolidation; stickiness, inseparability.

v cohere, adhere, stick, cling, cleave, hold, take hold, clasp, hug; hang together, stay together; glue, cement, paste, solder, weld; consolidate, solidify, agglomerate.

adj cohesive, adhesive, adhering, sticky; tenacious, tough; united, unified, inseparable, inextricable, (*informal*) together, (*informal*) tight.

47 incoherence *n* looseness, laxity, relaxation, nonadhesion; loosening, disjunction, disconnection; disagreement, inconsistency, incongruity.

v loosen, make loose, slacken, relax; detach, disjoin.

adj nonadhesive, noncohesive, detached, loose, slack, lax, relaxed, segregated, unconsolidated; inconsistent, incongruous, illogical, absurd, rambling.

48 combination *n* mixture; junction; union, unification, synthesis, incorporation, amalgamation, coalescence, fusion, blend, blending, mix, centralization; compound, alloy, amalgam, composition, composite.

v combine, unite, incorporate, amalgamate, absorb, blend, mix, merge, fuse, marry, consolidate, coalesce, centralize, cement, harden, solidify.

adj combined, unified.

49 decomposition *n* analysis, dissection, dissolution, breaking down; disjunction; corruption, decay, rot, putrefaction.

v decompose, analyze, dissolve; resolve into its elements, dissect, disperse, crumble; decay, rot, turn.

adj decomposed.

50 [principal part] **whole** *n* totality, entirety, total, sum, aggregate;

unity, completeness, integrity, indivisibility; bulk, mass, lump; body, trunk.

v form a whole, integrate, embody, amass, aggregate, assemble; amount to, come to, add up to.

adj whole, total, full, entire, undiminished, undivided, integral, complete, unimpaired, unbroken, faultless, sound, intact; indivisible, indissoluble.

adv wholly, altogether; totally, completely, entirely, all, all in all, wholesale, in a body, collectively, in the main, on the whole.

51 part *n* division, portion, piece, fragment, fraction, lump, bit, component, constituent, ingredient, element, section, segment, subdivision; member, limb, branch, bough, off-shoot, ramification; compartment, department, class.

v part, divide, break, disjoin; partition, apportion, allot.

adj fractional, fragmentary, sectional; divided, split up.

adv partly, in part, partially; piecemeal, bit by bit, by installments, in dribs and drabs, in drips and snatches; in detail.

52 completeness *n* wholeness, entirety, totality, solidarity, fullness, intactness, unity, perfection; thoroughness.

v complete, accomplish, fulfill, finish; fill, charge, load, replenish; fill up, fill in; saturate.

adj complete, entire, whole, full, intact, undivided, one, perfect, fulfilled; full, good, absolute, thorough, solid; exhaustive, radical, sweeping, thoroughgoing; consummate, unmitigated, sheer, unqualified, unconditional; brimming, brimful, chock-full, saturated, crammed, replete, fraught.

adv completely, altogether, outright, wholly, totally quite, utterly, fully, thoroughly, in all aspects, in every respect, out and out, to all intents and purposes; throughout, from first to last, from beginning to end, from top to bottom, from head to foot, every whit, every inch.

53 incompleteness n deficiency, shortcoming, insufficiency, imperfection; immaturity; noncompletion.

[part wanting] defect, deficit, omission, interval, break; discontinuity, missing link.

v be incomplete, fall short of; lack; neglect.

adj incomplete, imperfect, unfinished, uncompleted; defective, deficient, wanting, lacking, failing, short, short of; meager, lame, limp, perfunctory, sketchy, crude, immature; in progress, in preparation, going on, ongoing, proceeding.

adv incompletely.

54 composition n constitution, make-up, form; combination, compilation, incorporation, inclusion, synthesis.

v be composed of, be made up of, consist of; include, contain, hold, comprehend, take in, admit, embrace, embody; compose, constitute, form, make.

adj constituting.

55 exclusion n omission, exception, rejection, repudiation; exile, seclusion, segregation, separation, elimination, prohibition; restraint, keeping out.

v exclude, bar, leave out, shut out, keep out; reject, repudiate, blackball, throw out; lay aside, put aside, set aside; relegate, segregate, separate, seclude, banish, exile; pass over, omit, eliminate, weed out, winnow.

adj exclusive, not included in; inadmissible.

56 component n component part, integral part, element, constituent, ingredient; contents, feature, member, part; personnel.

v enter into, be part of, form part of; merge in, share in, participate; belong to, appertain to; form, make, constitute.

adj inclusive, comprehensive.

57 extraneousness n extrinsicality, externality; superfluousness; foreign body, foreign substance; intrusion.

v be extraneous, be unnecessary.

adj extraneous, foreign, alien, extrinsic, external; not germane,

nonessential, superfluous; excluded.

IV. Order

58 order n regularity, uniformity, arrangement, harmony, symmetry; course, routine, method, methodology; disposition, array, arrangement, system, economy, discipline, orderliness; gradation, progression, series, sequence, continuity; rank, place, grade, class, degree.

v order, regulate, manage, adjust, arrange, systematize, standardize, rank.

adj orderly, regular, systematic, methodical; in order, neat, tidy, well-regulated, well-organized, organized, uniform, symmetrical, businesslike, shipshape.

adv in order, methodically, in turn, in its turn; step by step, at regular intervals, systematically.

59 disorder n derangement, disarray, untidiness, irregularity, anomaly; anarchy, anarchism, disunion, discord; confusion, jumble, mess, muddle, hash, hodgepodge, chaos; perplexity, labyrinth, wilderness, jungle; raveling, entanglement, complication, convolution; turmoil, ferment, agitation, trouble, row, disturbance, convulsion, tumult, uproar, riot, rumpus, ruckus, scramble, fracas, melee, pandemonium.

v disorder, put out of order, derange, ruffle, rumble; confuse, jumble, mess up.

adj disorderly, out of order, out of place, irregular, desultory; anomalous, disorganized, straggling, unsystematic, untidy, slovenly, messy; indiscriminate, chaotic, confused, deranged; anarchic, inverted, convoluted, topsy-turvy; complex, complicated, perplexed, involved, raveled, entangled, knotted, tangled; troublesome, problematical; riotous, violent, turbulent, tumultuous.

adv irregularly, helter skelter; at cross purposes, (informal), after the flood.

60 [reduction to order] **arrangement** n plan, method, organization; preparation, groundwork, planning;

sorting, disposal, disposition, distribution, assortment, allotment, apportionment, graduation, groupings; analysis, classification, division, ordering, systematization.

v arrange, dispose, place, form; set out, marshal, range, array, rank, group, parcel out, allot, apportion, assign, dole out, distribute; sort, sift, put into shape; plan, prepare, organize, lay the groundwork; classify, divide, file, register, catalog, record, tabulate, index, graduate, rank; regulate, systematize, coordinate, organize, settle, fix; unravel, disentangle, straighten out.

adj arranged, ordered; methodical, orderly, regular, systematic.

61 [subversion of order] **derangement** *n* disorder, mess, disarray, disorganization; discomposure, disturbance, dislocation, perturbation, interruption.

v derange, disarrange, discompose, displace, misplace; mislay, disorder, disorganize; embroil, disconcert, convulse, unsettle, disturb, confuse, trouble, perturb, jumble, muddle, fumble; unhinge, dislocate, throw out of gear, throw out of whack; invert, turn upside down, turn topsy-turvy; complicate, confound, tangle, entangle; litter, scatter, mix.

62 precedence *n* coming before, the lead, superiority; precursor, antecedence; importance, consequence; priority, preference.

v precede, come before, forerun, come first; head, lead the way, usher in, introduce; set the fashion, influence, establish; have precedence, take precedence; place before, prefix, preface.

adj preceding, precedent, antecedent, anterior, prior, before; former, foregoing; preliminary, prefatory, introductory; preparatory.

adv before; in advance.

63 sequence *n* coming after, following, succession, order, series; posteriority; continuation; order of succession; outcome, consequence, result, sequel.

v succeed, come after, follow, ensure; replace.

adj succeeding, following; consequent, subsequent; proximate, next; sequential, consecutive.

adv after, subsequently; behind.

64 precursor *n* antecedent, precedent, predecessor, forerunner, pioneer, leader, bellwether; herald, harbinger; prelude, preamble, preface, prolog, proem, prefix, foreword, introduction; heading, frontispiece, groundwork; preparation.

adj prefatory, introductory, preliminary, precursory.

65 sequel *n* continuation, extension, supplement, outgrowth, offshoot, result, consequence, inference, deduction; result, consequence, aftermath, outcome, effect; conclusion, end, culmination, dénouement, finale, finish; appendage, suffix, epilog, postscript, tag, train, trail, wake; afterthought, afterpiece, second thoughts.

66 beginning *n* commencement, opening outset, start, initiation, inauguration; introduction, prelude; outbreak, onset, brunt; initiative, first move; origin, cause, source, bud, germ, genesis, birth, nativity, cradle; starting point, first step, square one; title page, head, heading; rudiments, basics, elements.

v begin, commence, open, start, initiate, inaugurate; conceive; set out, embark, depart; usher in, lead the way, take the lead, take the initiative, head, stand at the head, launch, set in motion, get going, take the first step, break ground; burst forth, break out; begin at the beginning, start again, start over, make a fresh start; originate, conceive, think up.

adj initial, introductory, inaugural; incipient, embryonic, rudimental, primal, essential, natal, nascent; first, foremost, leading; maiden, virgin.

adv first, in the first place, first and foremost; in the bud, in its infancy; from the beginning.

67 end *n* close, termination, conclusion, finale, finish, last word; consummation, climax, apex, dénouement; goal, destination; expiration, death, finality; limit, extreme, extremity; breakup, last stage, final stage, turning point, death blow.

v end, close, finish, terminate, conclude; expire, die, come to a close, draw to a close, run its course, run out, pass away; bring to an end, put an end to, make an end of, wrap up; get through, complete, consummate; stop, desist, call it quits.

adj final, terminal, concluding; conclusive, crowning, definitive, last, ultimate, consummate; ended, settled, decided, over, concluded, played out.

adv finally, at last, once and for all, over and done with.

68 middle *n* center, midpoint, midst; mean, midcourse, middle ground, compromise; core, kernel, heart, nucleus, nub; equidistance, bisection; equator, diaphragm, midriff.

adj middle, medial, mean, mid, median, midmost; intermediate, equidistant, central, halfway.

adv midway, halfway, in the middle.

69 [uninterrupted sequence] **continuity** *n* continuousness, consecutiveness, progression, constant flow, succession, train, series, chain, string, scale, gradation; round, suite; procession, column, retinue; pedigree, genealogy, lineage; rank, file, line, row, range, tier.

v follow in a line; arrange in a series, string together, file, thread, graduate, tabulate.

adj continuous, progressive, successive, serial, consecutive, unbroken, uninterrupted, gradual; linear, in a line; perennial, constant.

adv continuously, in succession, consecutively; gradually, step by step, in a column.

70 [interrupted sequence] **discontinuity** *n* disjunction, disconnectedness; interruption, break, fracture, fault, flaw, crack, cut; gap, interval, caesura, pause, *(informal)* breather, rest, intermission, parenthesis, episode.

v alternate; discontinue, break,

interrupt, intervene; pause, rest, take a breather, stop; break in upon, interpose; disconnect.

adj discontinuous, disconnected, unconnected, broken, interrupted; fitful, spasmodic, desultory, intermittent, irregular, alternate, recurrent, periodic.

adv at intervals, in snatches, by fits and starts.

71 term *n* rank, station, stage, step, phase; scale, grade, degree, status, position, place, point, mark, period, limit; stand, standing, footing.

72 assemblage *n* collection, levee, gathering, ingathering, muster; concourse, conflux, congregation; meeting, reunion, assembly, congress, convention, conclave, council; miscellany, compilation, menagerie; crowd, throng, mob, flood, rush, rash, deluge, press, crush, horde, body, tribe, crew, gang, squad, band, party, swarm, flock, bevy; company, troop, regiment, squadron, army; host, multitude, populace, clan, brotherhood, sisterhood, association; group, cluster, clump, batch, pack, assortment; accumulation, heap, lump, pile, mass, conglomeration, conglomerate, aggregation, aggregate; quantity.

v assemble, come together, collect, gather, muster; meet, unite, join, rejoin; cluster, flock, swarm, surge, stream, herd, crowd, throng, associate; congregate, concentrate, huddle; bring together, draw together, place together, lump together; convene, invoke; compile, group, assemble, unite; amass, accumulate, store.

adj assembled; closely packed, dense, crowded, teeming, swarming, populous.

73 dispersion *n* divergence, spreading, radiation, dissemination, diffusion, dissipation, distribution, apportionment, division.

v disperse, scatter, sow, disseminate, diffuse, shed, spread, dispense, disband, distribute, apportion, divide; break up, dispel, cast forth, strew, cast, sprinkle; issue, deal out, dole out.

adj dispersed, spread, scattered, strewn, diffuse, diffusive; sparse, widespread, broadcast; adrift, stray, disheveled.

74 [place of meeting] **focus** *n* center, gathering place, haunt, rendezvous, rallying point, headquarters, club, retreat.

v focus, bring to a point, bring to a focus; center on, bring out, clarify, elucidate.

75 class *n* division, subdivision, category, heading, order, section; department, province, domain; type, kind, sort, genus, species, variety, family, race, tribe, cast, clan, breed, sect.

76 inclusion *n* admission, acceptance into, incorporation, comprehension, reception.

v include, comprise, comprehend, contain, admit, embrace, receive, accept; inclose, circumscribe, encircle, encompass, embody, incorporate; number among, count among, fall under.

adj inclusive, comprehensive, extensive, all-embracing, compendious, sweeping; including, incorporating.

77 exclusion *n* (see 55).

78 generality *n* universality, catholicity, miscellany, miscellaneousness; generalization, simplification, oversimplification; prevalence, common run.

v be general, be universal, prevail, be true for everyone; render general, generalize, universalize; make a generalization, abstract, simplify.

adj general, universal, catholic, common, ecumenical, egalitarian, worldwide; prevalent, prevailing, rife, current; generic, collective, all-encompassing, comprehensive, all-inclusive, broad, widespread.

79 specialty *n* speciality, skill, ability, talent; individuality, singularity, distinctive feature, particularity, personality, characteristic, mannerism, idiosyncrasy, nonconformity; particulars, details, items; special feature.

v specify, particularize, individualize, specialize; designate, determine, single out, isolate, differentiate; be specific, come to the point, detail, get down to particulars.

adj special, particular, especial, individual, specific, proper, personal, original, private, respective, definite, certain, endemic, peculiar, characteristic, marked, appropriate, exclusive, singular, exceptional, idiomatic, unique.

adv specially, especially, in particular; each, apiece, severally, respectively, each to each, each to his own; in detail.

80 regulation *n* regularity, uniformity, constancy, clockwork, precision, exactness; routine, custom, formula, rule, form, procedure; standard, model, precedent, prototype; conformity, convention; nature, law, principle; normal state, ordinary condition, normalcy; hard and fast law.

adj regular, uniform, constant, steady; customary, conventional, formal, formulaic, procedural.

81 multiformity *n* variety, diversity.

adj multifold, multifarious, manifold, many-sided; heterogeneous, motley, mosaic; indiscriminate, irregular, diversified, diverse; of every description, all manner of kinds.

82 conformity *n* observance, compliance, assent; conventionality, customariness, agreement; example, instance, specimen, sample, illustration, exemplification, case in point.

v conform to, accommodate oneself to, adapt to; be regular, conform, follow the rules, obey the rules, go by the rules, comply, assent, agree, yield, give in, accept, harmonize; illustrate, stand as an example, embody.

adj conformable to rule, adaptable, agreeable, compliant, malleable; conventional, customary, standard, ordinary, common, habitual, usual, natural, normal, typical; formal, orthodox, strict, rigid, uncompromising; exemplary, illustrative.

adv by rule, in conformity with, in accordance with, in keeping with, consistent with; for the sake of conformity, as a matter of course, for form's sake; invariably, uniformly.

83 unconformity *n* nonconformity, unconventionality, nonobservance, informality; anomaly, variation, inconsistency, irregularity, incongruity, oddity, eccentricity, peculiarity, aberration, abnormality, exception; violation of custom, infraction, infringement; individuality, originality, mannerism, idiosyncrasy, quirk.

v be unconformable.

adj unconformable, unconventional, unnatural, odd, eccentric, peculiar, aberrant, abnormal, exceptional; anomalous, inconsistent, irregular, incongruous, arbitrary, whimsical, wanton; unusual, uncustomary, uncommon, rare, singular, unique, extraordinary; queer, quaint, strange; original, fantastic, newfangled, bizarre, outlandish, exotic, esoteric.

adv unless, except, save, beside.

V. Number

84 number *n* numeral, symbol, figure, cipher, digit, integer, round number, whole number, fraction; sum, total, product.

adj numeral; prime, fractional, decimal; positive, negative.

85 numeration *n* numbering, tallying, enumeration, reckoning, computation, calculation; arithmetic, calculus, algebra; statistics, poll, census, roll call; arithmetic operations.

v number, count, tell, tally, enumerate, add up, sum, reckon, compute, calculate, take account; muster, poll, recite; add, subtract, multiply, divide.

adj numeral, numerical; arithmetical, analytic, algebraic, statistical, numerable, computable, calculable.

86 list *n* catalog, index, listing, inventory, schedule, register, record, ledger, tally, file, table, calendar; directory, gazette, atlas, dictionary, thesaurus; roll, checklist.

87 unity *n* oneness, singleness, singularity, individuality; unification, unison, uniformity.

v unite, join, combine; isolate, insulate, seclude.

adj one, sole, single, solitary, lone; individual, apart, alone; unaccompanied, unattended, singlehanded, solo; singular, odd, unique; isolated, insular.

adv singly.

88 accompaniment *n* association, partnership, company; accessory, adjunct, concomitant, attachment, complement, attendant, fellow, associate, coexistence.

v accompany, join, escort, convoy, wait on; coexist with, consort with; associate with, couple with.

adj accompanying, fellow, twin, joint; associated with, coupled with; accessory, concomitant, attendant.

adv with, together with, along with, in company with, hand in hand, side by side; therewith, herewith.

89 duality *n* dualism, doubleness, polarity, biformity, duplexity; two, deuce, couple, brace, pair, twins.

v pair, mate, couple, bracket, pair off, yoke.

adj two, twain; dual, twin, two-sided, binary, binomial, duplex; coupled, both.

90 duplication *n* doubling, reduplication; iteration, repetition; renewal, duplicate, double, copy, carbon, facsimile.

v double; redouble, reduplicate; repeat, renew; duplicate.

adj double; doubled, duplicated; twin, duplicate, second.

adv twice, once more, over again.

91 bisection *n* halving, bifurcation, twofold division, forking, dichotomy, *(informal)* fifty-fifty split.

v bisect, divide in two, halve, divide, split, cut in two, cleave, fork, bifurcate; split down the middle, *(informal)* go halves.

adj bisected, cloven, cleft,

halved; bipartite; bifurcated; semi-, demi-, hemi-.

92 triality n trinity; three, triad, triplet, trio.
adj three, threefold, triform, tertiary.

93 triplication n tripling; triplicity.
v triple, treble, cube.
adj triple, treble; threefold, triplicate; third.
adv three times, thrice; in the third place, thirdly; triply, trebly.

94 trisection n tripartition, threefold division; third, third part.
v trisect, divide into three parts.

95 quaternity n four, tetrad, quartet, quarter.
v square, reduce to a square.
adj four, fourfold, quadrilateral.

96 quadruplication n quadrupling, multiplying by four.
v multiply by four, quadruplicate; fourth.
adv four times, in the fourth place, fourthly.

97 quadrisection n quartering, quadripartition, fourfold division; fourth part, quarter.
v quarter, divide into four parts.
adj quartered, quadripartite.

98 five, etc. n five; six, half a dozen; seven; eight; nine; ten, decade; eleven; twelve, dozen; thirteen, baker's dozen, long dozen; twenty, score; twenty-five, quarter of a hundred; fifty, half a hundred; hundred, century, centenary; thousand.

99 quinquesection n fivefold division
adj quinquepartite.

100 [more than one] **plurality** n two or more, couple, few, several; majority, multitude.
adj plural, more than one, upwards of, some, several, many, numerous.

100a [less than one] **fraction** n fractional part, segment, subdivision, part, portion.

101 zero n nothing, naught, (informal) zip; none, shutout; nobody.

102 multitude n multitudinous, multiplicity, profusion, mass, quantity, volume, abundance, amplitude, enormity; numbers, array, scores, droves, host, throng, collection; mob, crowd, assemblage.
v be numerous, swarm with, teem with, crowd, swarm, outnumber, multiply; people, populate.
adj multitudinous, manifold, profuse, multiple, teeming, populous, crowded, thick; many, several, sundry, various, numerous; endless, infinite.

103 fewness n paucity, scarcity, sparseness, scantiness; small number, small quantity; infrequency.
diminution of number: reduction, weeding, elimination.
v render few, reduce, diminish, weed, thin, eliminate, eradicate.
adj few, not many, scanty, scarce, sparse, rare, few and far between, limited, meager; sporadic, occasional, infrequent; reduced, diminished, pared back.

104 repetition n iteration, reiteration, recapitulation, restatement; sameness, monotony, harping, recurrence, tautology; redundance; rhythm, beat, echo, reverberation; reappearance, reproduction, duplication.
v repeat, iterate, reiterate, recapitulate, restate, rehash, go over again, harp on, hammer; reproduce, duplicate, echo; recur, revert, return, reappear, resume, return to, go back to; rehearse, go over the same ground.
adj repeated, repetitious, recurrent, recurring, frequent, incessant, never-ending, unceasing; repetitive, redundant, tautological; rhythmic, reverberant, reverberating; monotonous, harping, iterative; habitual.
adv repeatedly, often, again, anew, afresh, over again, once more; over and over, again and again, year after year; ditto, encore.

105 infinity n infinitude, infiniteness, perpetuity, endlessness, boundlessness, inexhaustibility, immeasurability, limitlessness, vastness, expanse.

v be infinite, have no limits, know no bounds, go on forever.

adj infinite, countless, numberless, limitless, boundless, measureless, unlimited, interminable, inexhaustible, incalculable; immense, vast, endless, perpetual; incomprehensible; eternal, perfect, omnipotent, absolute.

adv infinitely, *ad infinitum*.

VI. Time

106 time *n* duration, extent; period, interval, spell, term, space, span, season, stage; course; interim, interlude; interregnum, intermission; respite, break, timeout; era, epoch, season, age, year, date.

v time, measure, pace; continue, last, endure, go on, remain, persist, stand; pass time, spend time, while away the time, waste time, kill time, fill up the time.

adj permanent, lasting, durable; timely.

adv while, whilst, during, in the course of, for the time being, in due time; meantime, meanwhile, in the meantime, in the interim; till, until, up to, yet; the whole time, all the time, throughout, for good *(informal)* for keeps.

107 absence of time *n* no time; outside time.

adv never, at no time; on no occasion, nevermore.

108 [definite duration or period of time] **period** *n* interval, age, era, eon, epoch, term, time; year, decade, century, millennium; lifetime, generation.

109 [indefinite duration] **course** *n* march of time, course of time, flux, passing time.

v elapse, lapse, flow, run, proceed, advance, pass, flit, fly, slip, slide, drag, creep, crawl; run its course; expire, go by, pass by.

adv in due time, in due course, in due season, in time.

110 [long duration] **durability** *n* permanence, persistence, continuance, lastingness, standing, stability; survival, longevity; protraction, prolongation.

v last, remain, stand, endure, abide, continue, persist; tarry, drag on, drag out, prolong, protract, eke out, draw out, lengthen; outlive, outlast, survive.

adj permanent, durable, lasting, longstanding, stable, immutable, invariable, constant; enduring, abiding, perpetual; lingering, protracted, prolonged, spun-out.

adv long, for a long time, ever so long; long ago; all day long, all the livelong day.

111 [short duration] **transience** *n* impermanence, evanescence, ephemerality, transitoriness, mortality; suddenness, swiftness, changeableness, vicissitude, uncertainty.

v be transient, flit, pass away, fly, gallop, vanish, fade, evaporate, melt.

adj transient, transitory, evanescent, ephemeral, fleeting, flitting, flying, passing; impermanent, temporal, temporary, provisional, short-lived; perishable, precarious, vulnerable, mortal; brief, quick, brisk; sudden, momentary, instantaneous.

adv transiently, for the moment, for a time; awhile, soon; briefly.

112 [endless duration] **perpetuity** *n* eternity, timelessness, everlastingness, endlessness, infinity; constancy, endurance, durability, ceaselessness.

v last forever, endure, go on forever; perpetuate, immortalize, eternalize.

adj perpetual, eternal, timeless, everlasting, endless; unceasing, ceaseless, interminable, neverending, continuous, incessant, uninterrupted; unfading, imperishable, unvulnerable, immortal.

adv perpetually, always, ever, evermore, forever; constantly, continuously.

113 [point of time] **instantaneousness** *n* suddenness, abruptness; moment, instant, second, twinkling, trice, flash, crack, burst.

v be instantaneous, twinkle, flash.

adj instantaneous, momentary, sudden, instant, abrupt.

adv instantaneously, in no time, *(informal)* in two shakes (of a lamb's tail), presto, suddenly, like a shot, in a moment, all of a sudden, in a jiffy; immediately, on the spur of the moment, on a moment's notice.

114 [estimation, measurement and record of time] **chronometry** *n* chronology, timetable; almanac, calendar, register, chronicle, log, annal(s), journal, diary; clock, watch, stopwatch, timepiece, chronometer.

v fix the time, mark the time; date, register, chronicle; measure time, mark time, beat time.

adj chronological.

115 [false estimate of time] **anachronism** *n* misdate, misplacement, chronological error; disregard of time.

v misdate, antedate, postdate, anticipate; take no note of time.

adj misdated; undated, overdue; anachronistic, out of place, misplaced.

116 antecedence *n* priority, anteriority, precedence, pre-existence; antecedent, predecessor, precursor, forerunner.

v precede, antedate, come before; go before, lead, forerun; dawn, presage, herald, break the ground.

adj antecedent, prior, previous, anterior, preceding, pre-existent; former, foregoing, aforementioned; precursory, introductory.

adv before, prior to; earlier, previously, ere, already, yet, beforehand.

117 posteriority *n* succession, sequence; subsequence, following, continuance; successor, sequel, follower; future, futurity.

v follow after, come after, go after, succeed, be subsequent to.

adj posterior, subsequent, following, after, later, succeeding, successive, ensuing, resulting; posthumous.

adv subsequently, after, afterwards, since, later; next, close upon, thereafter, thereupon; ultimately.

118 present time *n* the present juncture, the present day; the times, the time being, right now.

adj present, actual, instant, current, existing.

adv at this time, at this moment; at the present time, now, at present, nowadays.

119 different time *n* other time; another time.

adv at that time, at that instant; then, on that occasion; when, whenever, whensoever; at some other time, at a different time, at some time or other.

120 contemporaneousness *n* simultaneousness, synchronism, simultaneity, coincidence, concurrence, coexistence, concomitance.

v coexist, concur, accompany, go side by side, keep pace with; synchronize.

adj simultaneous, coincident, concurrent, concomitant, coexisting; contemporary, contemporaneous, coeval.

adv simultaneously, concurrently, together, at the same time.

121 the future *n* futurity, hereafter, time to come, tomorrow, morrow; millennium, doomsday, day of judgment, crack of doom, flood; advent, eventuality; destiny, fate; heritage, heirs, posterity; prospect, expectation, anticipation.

v look forward, anticipate, expect, foresee; approach, await, threaten, impend, come near, draw near, come on.

adj future, to come; coming, impending, near, close at hand, in prospect; eventual, ulterior.

adv prospectively, hereafter, in future, in course of time, tomorrow; eventually, ultimately, sooner or later; henceforth, from this time; soon, early, on the eve of, on the point of, on the brink of.

122 the past *n* past time, days of old, days of yore, days gone by, yesterday, yesteryear, former times, ancient times; retrospection, memory; antiquity, history, time immemorial, remote past; ancestry, lineage, forbears; heritage.

v run its course, pass away, pass, lapse, blow over.

adj past, gone, gone by, passed away, bygone, elapsed, lapsed, expired, extinct, forgotten, irrecoverable, obsolete; former, pristine, late; foregoing, last, latter, recent; looking back, retrospective; retroactive.

adv formerly, of old, of yore, ago, over; long ago, years ago, a long while back, some time ago; lately, of late; retrospectively, ere now, before now, hitherto, heretofore; already, yet, up to this time.

123 newness *n* novelty, recentness, freshness; immaturity, greenness, youth, juvenility, innovation, uniqueness, originality; renovation, restoration; modernity, modernism, stylishness, fashionableness, newfangledness, fashion, faddishness, the latest thing, futurism, trendiness.

v renew, renovate, restore; modernize.

adj new, novel, recent, fresh; green, immature, unripe, young, youthful, untried, untested, virgin, virginal; modern, late, new, newfangled, stylish, fashionable, faddish, trendy, brand-new, up-to-date; renovated restored, spick and span.

adv newly, afresh, anew, lately, just now, of late.

124 oldness *n* age, antiquity; maturity, ripeness; decline, decay, old age, senility, superannuation; archaism, antiquarianism, relic, thing of the past; tradition, custom, common law.

v be old, have had its day, have seen its day; become old, age, fade.

adj old, ancient, antique; time-honored, venerable, traditional, vintage, of long standing; elderly, aged, hoary, decayed, senile, decrepit; primeval, primitive, aboriginal, primordial, antediluvian, prehistoric, archaic; traditional, prescriptive, customary, immemorial, inveterate, rooted; antiquated, outdated, outmoded, of other times; out of date, obsolete, out-of-fashion, out-of-

style, gone by, stale, old-fashioned, timeworn, crumbling, ramshackle, run-down, wasted.

125 morning, noon *n* morning, morn, dawn, daybreak, sunrise, sunup, forenoon, break of day, peep of day, prime of day, morningtide, matins, cockcrow, first blush, antemeridian, A.M.

noon, midday, noonday, noontide, meridian, prime, height, noontime.

spring, springtime; summer, summertime, midsummer.

126 evening, midnight *n* evening, eve, eventide, dusk, vespers, nightfall, sundown, sunset, twilight, curfew, bedtime; afternoon, post meridian, P.M.

midnight, end of the day, close of the day, witching hour, dead of night.

autumn, fall, harvest time; winter.

127 youth *n* juvenility, infancy childhood, boyhood, girlhood, minority, tender years, young years, formative years, never generation, tender age; cradle, nursery; puberty.

adj young, youthful, juvenile, green, callow, budding, immature, developing, underage, formative; younger, junior.

128 age *n* old age, advanced age, senility, years, gray hairs, declining years, golden years, mature years, decrepitude, anility, superannuation, longevity, ripe age, ripe old age; maturity, seniority, eldership.

adj aged, old, advanced, gray, elderly; senile, decline, failing, waning, ripe, overripe, mellow, venerable, wrinkled, wizened; older, elder, eldest.

129 infant *n* baby, babe, babe in arms, nursling, little one, tot, toddler, chick, kid, lamb, cherub; youth, youngster, child, minor; girl, lass, maiden, miss, schoolgirl; boy, lad, stripling, master, schoolboy.

adj infant, infantlike, puerile, girlish, boyish, childish, babyish; newborn, young.

130 veteran *n* old man, old woman, patriarch, matriarch, grandmother, grandfather, grandsire, seer, graybeard, forefather, elder.

adj aged, old.

131 adolescence *n* majority, adulthood, manhood, womanhood, maturity, ripeness, fullness, puberty, pubescence; teenage years, prepubescence.

v come of age, grow up, attain majority.

adj adolescent, teenage, pubescent, of age, grown up, full grown, adult, womanly, manly, marriageable, nubile.

132 earliness *n* punctuality, promptitude, speediness, readiness, expedition, alacrity, quickness, haste; suddenness; prematurity, precocity, precipitation, anticipation.

v be early, be beforehand; anticipate, forestall, steal a march on, get a head start; bespeak, secure, engage, pre-engage; accelerate, expedite, quicken, hasten, make haste, make time, hurry.

adj early, timely, punctual, on time, prompt; premature, precipitate, precocious, anticipatory; sudden, instantaneous, immediate, expeditious; unexpected.

adv early, soon, anon, betimes, before long; punctually, to the minute, on time, on the dot; beforehand, prematurely, precipitately, too soon, hastily, in anticipation, unexpectedly; suddenly, instantaneously, at short notice, on the spur of the moment; at once, on the spot, on the instant, at sight, straight, offhand, straightway; forthwith, summarily, immediately, shortly, quickly, speedily; presently, by and by, directly.

133 lateness *n* tardiness, slowness, sloth, tarrying, dilly-dallying, loitering; delay, procrastination, postponement, adjournment, retardation, protraction, prolongation; respite, reprieve, suspension, moratorium, stop, stay.

v be late, tarry, wait, stay, bide, take time, linger, loiter, dawdle, shilly-shally, dilly-dally; put off, defer, delay, lay over, suspend; retard, postpone, adjourn; procrastinate,

prolong, protract, drag out, draw out, lengthen, table, shelve, stall.

adj late, tardy, slow, dilatory, backward, unpunctual; delayed, overdue, belated.

adv late; backward, at the eleventh hour, at length, at last; ultimately, behind time; too late; slowly, leisurely, deliberately, at one's leisure, on one's own time.

134 opportuneness *n* timeliness, opportunity, occasion, suitable time, proper time, suitability, high time; crisis, turn, juncture; turning point, given time; nick of time, golden opportunity; clear stage, open field.

v be opportune, be suitable; seize the opportunity, seize the time, seize the day, *carpe diem*, use the occasion; suit the occasion, be expeditious, strike while the iron is hot.

adj opportune, timely, well-timed, seasonable, suitable, appropriate; providential, lucky, fortunate, happy, favorable, fortuitous, propitious, auspicious.

adv opportunely, in due time, in the nick of time, just in time, now or never; by the way, by the by, speaking of, while on the subject; on the spot, on the spur of the moment, since the occasion presents itself.

135 inopportuneness *n* untimeliness, unseasonableness, improper time, unsuitable time; *(informal)* bad timing; intrusion; anachronism.

v be ill timed, mistime, intrude, break in upon, *(informal)* butt in; lose an opportunity, waste an occasion, *(informal)* blow one's chance, let the opportunity slip by; waste time.

adj inopportune, untimely, unpropitious, unseasonable, unsuitable, inauspicious, unfavorable, unfortunate, unsuited, untoward, unlucky; ill-timed, mistimed, poorly timed; unpunctual, premature.

136 frequency *n* repetition, recurrence, iteration, reiteration.

v recur, repeat, reiterate; keep on, continue; attend regularly, visit often, patronize.

adj frequent, oft-repeated, recurring, incessant, constant, continual, perpetual; habitual, customary.

adv often, oft, oftentimes, frequently, repeatedly, day after day; daily, hourly, every day; perpetually, continually, constantly, incessantly, at all times; commonly, habitually, customarily; sometimes, occasionally, at times, now and then; every once in a while, from time to time.

137 infrequency *n* rarity, rare occurrence; long shot, surprise, *(informal)* mindblower.

v be rare, be infrequent.

adj infrequent, occasional, sporadic, rare, uncommon, unusual, unheard of, unprecedented; few, scant, scarce.

adv infrequently, rarely, seldom, scarcely, hardly; not often, hardly ever.

138 regularity [of recurrence] *n* periodicity, intermittence; beat, pulse, pulsation, rhythm; alternation, oscillation, vibration; bout, round, turn, revolution, rotation, rpm; cycle, period, routine; punctuality, regularity, steadiness.

v recur, revolve, return, come in its turn, come round again; beat, pulsate, alternate.

adj regular, periodic, periodical; serial, recurrent, cyclical, cyclic, recurring, rhythmical, rhythmic; intermittent, alternate, every other; regular, steady, punctual, continual, constant, regular as clockwork.

adv regularly, periodically, serially, cyclically; intermittently, alternately; by turns, in turn, in rotation, off and on, round and round.

139 irregularity [of recurrence] *n* uncertainty, unpredictability, haphazardness, fitfulness, capriciousness.

v be irregular, be haphazard.

adj irregular, uncertain, unpredictable, haphazard, fitful, capricious, flickering; spasmodic, sporadic.

adv irregularly, fitfully, capriciously, by fits and starts.

VII. Change

140 change *n* alteration, modulation, modification, variation, mutation,

permutation, qualification, deviation, turn, shift, innovation; diversion, break; transformation, transfiguration, transmutation, metamorphosis; conversion, revolution, inversion, reversal; displacement, transference, transposition; changeableness.

v change, alter, vary, modulate, qualify, diversify, tamper with, play with, experiment with; turn, shift, veer, tack, swerve, warp, deviate, turn aside; turn, take a turn, *(informal)* hang a turn; modify, revamp, transform, transfigure, transmute, metamorphose, convert; innovate, restructure, give a new turn to, recast, redesign, remodel.

adj changed, newfangled; changeable, variable, transformable; innovative.

141 permanence *n* stability, invariability, unalterability, immutability, constancy; endurance, durability, persistence; maintenance, preservation, conservation; obstinacy, immovability, inflexibility, immobility, rigidity.

v endure, bide, abide, stay, remain, last, persist, stand, stand fast; maintain, keep, keep up, preserve; subsist, live, outlive, survive.

adj permanent, lasting, unchanged, unchanging, fixed, stable, invariable, constant; enduring, durable, abiding, everlasting; intact, inviolate; persistent.

adv permanently, for good, for good and all.

142 cessation *n* discontinuation, discontinuance, halt, stoppage, termination, suspension, interruption, stopping; pause, rest, lull, respite, truce, break; interregnum, abeyance; completion, end, finish; stop, death.

v cease, discontinue, terminate, desist, stay; break off, leave off, hold, stop, pull up, stop short, halt, pause, rest; suspend, interrupt, delay, cut short, arrest, bring to a standstill; complete, end, finish, close up shop; wear away, go out, die out, pass away, die.

143 continuance [in action] *n* continuation, continuity, protraction, prolongation, maintenance, perpetuation; persistence, perseverance, repetition.

v continue, persist, go on, keep on, hold on; abide, keep, pursue, stick to; maintain course, carry on, keep up; sustain, uphold, hold up, keep going, maintain, preserve, perpetuate, prolong.

adj continuing, uninterrupted, unvarying; continuous, persistent, perpetual.

144 conversion *n* transformation, transmutation, reduction, change, changeover, resolution, assimilation; passage, transit, transition, shifting, flux; growth, progress, development; chemistry, alchemy.

v be converted into, become, turn into, lapse, shift; pass into, grow into, ripen into, merge into; melt, grow, ripen, mature, mellow; convert into, resolve into; make, render, mold, form, model, remodel, remake, do over, reform, reorganize; assimilate, bring into, reduce to.

adj convertible, transmutable, changeable.

145 reversion *n* return, revulsion, reverting, returning; alternation, rotation; inversion, recoil, reaction, reflex, repercussion, rebound, boomerang, ricochet, backlash, repulse; retrospection, retrogression, retrogradation, falling back; restoration, going back; turning point, turn of the tide.

v revert, return, turn back, reverse; relapse, regress, fall back; recoil, rebound; retreat; restore; undo, unmake; turn the tide.

146 [sudden or violent change] **revolution** *n* revolt, rebellion, overthrow, overturn, coup, *coup d'état*, rising, uprising, mutiny, counterrevolution; breakup, destruction, subversion, clean sweep; spasm, convulsion, throe, revulsion.

v revolt, rebel, rise, rise up; revolutionize, remodel, recast, change.

adj revolutionary, rebellious; new.

147 substitution *n* replacement, supplanting, commutation, exchange, change, shift.

substitute, expedient, makeshift, stopgap, equivalent, double, alternative, representative.

v substitute, put in the place of, change, exchange, interchange; replace, supplant, supersede, take the place of, stand for, represent, pinch hit, substitute for, sub; redeem, commute, alternate.

adv instead, in place of, in lieu of.

148 [double or mutual change] **interchange** *n* exchange, commutation, permutation, transposition; reciprocation, reciprocity, intercourse; barter, swap, trade; interchangeability; retaliation, reprisal, requital, retort, crossfire.

v interchange, exchange, barter, trade, swap, bandy, transpose, commute, reciprocate; give and take, battle with words; retort, requite, retaliate.

adj interchangeable, all-purpose, multi-purpose; reciprocal; mutual.

adv in exchange, vice versa, turn and turn about.

149 changeableness *n* mutability, inconstancy, volatility, instability; malleability, adaptability, versatility, mobility; vacillation, irresolution, indecision, capriciousness; oscillation, alternation, fluctuation, vicissitude; restlessness, fidgetiness, disquiet, disquietude; unrest, agitation.

v fluctuate, oscillate, vary, waver, flounder, shuffle, hem and haw, vacillate, tremble, alternate.

adj changeable, mutable, variable, malleable, adaptable, adjustable, versatile, mobile, transformable, convertible; inconstant, unsteady, unstable, unreliable, vacillating, oscillating, fluctuating; volatile, fitful, fickle, capricious, mercurial, indecisive, irresolute, flighty, impulsive, fanciful, erratic, wayward, wanton; restless, fidgety, tremulous, agitated; unfixed, unsettled.

150 stability n immutability, unchangeableness, constancy; firmness, fixity, solidity, steadiness, soundness, balance, stabilization, equilibrium, quiescence; immobility, immovability, fixedness; steadfastness, reliability, resolution; determination, obstinacy, stubbornness, pertinacity, tenacity, doggedness, will, pluck, resoluteness; permanence, endurance, perseverance, durability; continuity, uniformity changelessness.

v be firm, stick fast, stand firm; settle, establish, fix, set, stabilize; retain, keep hold; make sure, fasten, make solid.

adj stable, fixed, rigid, firm, steady, established, strong, sturdy, immovable, invariable, unvarying, permanent, unchangeable, unchanging, unalterable, immutable; enduring, constant, durable, lasting, abiding, secure, fast, perpetual; unwavering, steadfast, staunch, reliable, steady, solid, sound, balanced; resolute, obstinate, dogged, willful, stubborn, pertinacious, tenacious.

151 present events n event, occurrence, incident, affair, eventuality, happening, proceeding, transaction, fact; phenomenon; circumstance, situation, particular; adventure, episode, thrill; crisis, pass, emergency, contingency, impasse; things, doings, affairs, matters, issues; the world, life, the times.

v happen, occur, take place, come to pass, take place, come about, come round; fall out, turn out, befall, chance, prove, eventuate; turn up, crop up, arise, arrive, issue, ensue, start, hold; take its course, pass off; experience, meet with, meet up with, fall to, be one's lot, be one's fortune, find, encounter, undergo, go through, live through, endure, put up with.

adj happening, going on, doing, current; eventful, stirring, bustling, busy, full of incident.

adv eventually, finally; as things go, in the course of things, as it happens.

152 future events n destiny, luck, lot, chance, fortune, karma, doom, end; future, futurity, next world, hereafter; prospects, expectations, tomorrow.

v impend, hang over, hover, threaten, loom, await, come on, approach; foreordain, preordain; destine, predestine, doom, have in store for.

adj impending, destined; coming, in store, to come, at hand, near, close by, imminent, brewing, forthcoming; in the wind, in the cards, in prospect, looming, on the horizon.

adv in time, in the long run, in good time, in its own sweet time, eventually.

VIII. Causation

153 cause n origin, source, principle, element; prime mover, first cause; author, producer, creator; mainspring, agent, catalyst; groundwork, foundation, support; spring, fountain, well, fount, font; genesis, descent, remote cause, influence; pivot, hinge, axis, turning point; egg, germ, embryo, root, nucleus, seed; causality, causation, origination, production.

v cause, originate, give rise to, occasion, sow the seeds of, kindle, bring to pass, bring about; produce, create, set up, develop; found, broach, institute; induce, evoke, elicit, draw, provoke; determine, decide; conduce to, contribute, have a hand in, influence, effect.

adj causal, generative, productive, formative, creative; primal, primary, original, embryonic.

adv because.

154 effect n consequence, issue, derivation, upshot, outgrowth, development, fruit, crop, harvest, product, outcome, end, conclusion; offspring, offshoot, complications, concomitants, side effects.

v be the effect of, be due to, be owing to; originate in, originate from, rise from, spring from, proceed from, emanate from, come from, grow from, issue from, flow from, result from; depend upon, hinge upon.

adj owing to, resulting from, due to, derivable from, caused by; derived from, evolved from; derivative, hereditary.

adv consequently, as a consequence, necessarily.

155 [assignment of cause] **attribution** *n* theory, ascription, assignment, rationale, reference to, accounting for; imputation, derivation; explanation, interpretation, reason why.

v attribute to, ascribe to, impute to, refer to, point to, trace to, assign to; account for, derive from; theorize, speculate.

adj attributed, attributable, referable, due to, owing to.

adv hence, thence, therefore, *ergo*, for, since, on account of, because; why? wherefore? whence? how come? how so?

156 [absence of assignable cause] **chance** *n* fortune, fate, accident, hap, hazard, luck, fluke, *(informal)* freak; gamble, lottery, tossup, fifty-fifty chance, throw of the dice, heads or tails; probability, possibility, contingency, odds; speculation, gaming, gambling.

v chance, hap, turn up; fall to one's lot; stumble on, light on; take one's chances.

adj chancy, causal, fortuitous, accidental, *(informal)* iffy, adventitious, haphazard, random, indeterminate, flukey, *(informal)* freaky.

adv by chance, by accident; at random; perchance; as chance will have it.

157 power *n* potency, strength, puissance, might, force, energy, vigor; control, command, dominion, authority, rule, sway, ascendancy, sovereignty, omnipotence; ability, capability, facility, competence, competency, efficacy; validity, cogency.

v be powerful, control, command, rule; confer power, empower, invest, endow; arm, strengthen, authorize; compel, force.

adj powerful, potent, strong, mighty, energetic; able, capable,

competent, efficacious, equal to, up to, effective, efficient, adequate; omnipotent, almighty; influential, forceful.

adv powerfully.

prep by virtue of, by dint of.

158 impotence *n* inability, incapability, incapacity, infirmity, debility, disability; inefficacy, inefficiency, incompetence, ineptitude, feebleness, weakness, frailty, powerlessness; helplessness, prostration, paralysis, collapse, exhaustion; decrepitude, senility; sexual failure, barrenness.

v be impotent; collapse, faint, swoon, drop; render powerless, disable, disarm, incapacitate, disqualify, invalidate; cramp, tie the hands, paralyze, muzzle, cripple, maim, lame, hamstring, throttle, strangle, tie up in knots; unman, unnerve, enervate; shatter, exhaust, weaken; emasculate.

adj impotent, powerless, incapable, unable, incompetent, ineffective, inefficient, ineffectual, inept, unfit, unfitted, unqualified; disabled, incapacitated, crippled, paralyzed, paralytic; decrepit, senile, exhausted, worn out, used up, limp, spent; weak, frail, infirm, feeble, helpless; harmless; sterile, barren, frigid; emasculated, inadequate, inoperative; futile, fruitless, bootless, vain.

159 strength *n* power, force, might, vigor, health, stoutness, hardiness, lustihood, stamina, energy, potency, capacity; spring, bounce, tone, elasticity, tension; virility, vitality, nerve, verve; strengthening, invigoration, refreshment.

v strengthen, invigorate, brace, nerve, fortify, sustain, harden, steel; vivify, revivify, refresh, reinforce, restore.

adj strong, mighty, vigorous, forceful, hard, stout, robust, sturdy, hardy, powerful, potent, puissant; irresistible, invincible, indomitable, unconquerable, impregnable, inextinguishable, incontestable; able-bodied, athletic, muscular, sinewy, strapping, gigantic, Herculean.

adv strongly, by force.

160 weakness *n* debility, relaxation, languor, enervation; impotence, infirmity, fragility, flaccidity; frailty, delicacy, softness; senility, decrepitude.

v be weak, drop, crumble, give way, teeter, totter, tremble, shake, halt, limp, fade, languish, decline, flag, fail; weaken, enfeeble, cramp, debilitate, shake, enervate, unnerve; relax; dilute, water down.

adj weak, feeble, infirm, sickly; languid, faint, dull, slack, spent; limp, flaccid, powerless, impotent; relaxed, unstrung, unnerved; frail, fragile, delicate, flimsy; rickety, drooping, teetering, tottering, withered, shaky, shattered; palsied, decrepit, lame; decayed, rotten, worn, seedy, wasted, laid low.

161 production *n* creation, formation, fabrication, construction, manufacture; building, architecture, erection; organization, establishment; workmanship, craftsmanship, performance; achievement, product, end result; flowering, fructification, fruition, fulfillment; gestation, evolution, development, growth; gensis, generation, procreation; authorship, publication, works, *oeuvre*

v produce, perform, operate, do, make, form, construct, fabricate, frame, contrive, manufacture; build, raise, rear, erect, put up; set up, establish, constitute, compose, organize, institute; achieve, accomplish, fulfill; bud, flower, blossom, bloom, bear fruit, bring forth; propagate, beget, generate, procreate, engender; breed, hatch, develop, bring up; induce, cause.

adj productive, constructive, formative, creative; generative; prolific, blooming.

162 [nonproduction] destruction *n* waste, dissolution, breaking up, disruption; consumption; fall, downfall; ruin, perdition; breakdown, wreck, wrack, havoc, mess, chaos, cataclysm; desolation, extinction, annihilation; demolition; overthrow, subversion, suppression; dilapidation, devastation, road to ruin.

v perish, fall, tumble, topple, fall to pieces, break up, crumble, go to the dogs, go to wrack and ruin; destroy, do away with, demolish, tear up, overturn, overthrow, wipe out, (*informal*) waste; upset, subvert, undo; waste, squander, dissipate, dispel, dissolve; smash, squash, squelch, shatter, crumble, batter, crush, pull to pieces; fell, sink, scuttle, wreck, swamp, ruin, raze, level, expunge, erase, sweep away; lay waste, ravage, gut; disorganize, dismantle, take apart; devour, devastate, desolate, sap, exterminate, extinguish, stamp out, trample out, crush out, eradicate.

adj destructive, subversive, ruinous, incendiary, deadly, lethal, fatal; destroyed, wiped out, extinct.

163 reproduction *n* renovation, restoration, renewal, revival, regeneration, revivification, resuscitation, reanimation; resurrection; reappearance; generation, childbirth.

v reproduce, renovate, restore, renew, revive, regenerate, revivify, resuscitate, breathe new life into, reanimate, refashion, resurrect, bring back to life; give birth to, multiply, people the world.

adj reproductive; regenerative; restorative; renascent, reappearing, resurgent.

164 producer *n* originator, inventor, author, founder, generator, mover, creator maker, architect; backer, angel.

165 destroyer *n* spoiler, waster, ravager, wrecker, killer, assassin, executioner; cankerworm, bane; iconoclast, rebel, pessimist, cynic, nihilist, misanthrope.

166 parentage *n* family, ancestry, lineage, genealogy; procreator, progenitor.

paternity: fatherhood, fathership; father, dad, pop, sire, papa, (*informal*) old man; grandfather, grandsire.

maternity: motherhood; mother, mom, ma, mamma, mummy, mum, (*informal*) old lady; grandmother.

adj parental, familial, ancestral,

lineal, paternal, maternal; patriarchal, matriarchal.

167 posterity n progeny, breed, issue, offspring, brood, litter, family, children, grandchildren, heirs; child, son, daughter; descendant, heir, scion, (informal) chip off the old block; heredity.

adj filial.

168 productiveness n fecundity, fertility, fruitfulness, productivity; multiplication, propagation, procreation; creativity, inventiveness, originality.

v make productive, fructify, fulfill; procreate, generate, conceive, impregnate, fertilize; teem, multiply, produce, reproduce.

adj productive, prolific, fruitful, copious; teeming, fertile, fecund; procreative, generative, life-giving.

169 unproductiveness n infertility, sterility, barrenness, unfruitfulness, impotence; unprofitableness, wastefulness.

v be unproductive, do nothing, produce nothing, come to nothing.

adj unproductive, unfruitful, infertile, barren, sterile, arid; unprofitable, useless.

170 agency n operation, force, working, function, office, maintenance, exercise, work, play; causation, instigation, instrumentality, influence.

v operate, work, do; act, perform, play, support, sustain, maintain, take effect, quicken, strike; come into play, have free play; bring to bear upon, influence.

adj operative, efficient, efficacious, effectual, practical; at work, on foot, in operation, in force, in play, in action.

adv through the agency of, by means of.

171 energy n force, power, strength, intensity, vigor, zeal, dynamism, pep, fire, spirit, ebullience; life, activity, agitation, exertion, effervescence, ferment, fermentation, ebullition, bustle.

v give energy, energize, stimulate, kindle, excite, inflame, exert,

strengthen, invigorate; sharpen, intensify.

adj energetic, strong, forcible, potent, forceful, active, powerful, intense, vigorous, zealous, dynamic, ebullient, spirited, animated, keen, vivid, sharp, acute, incisive trenchant, biting; invigorating, rousing, stimulating; energized.

172 inertness n inertia, inactivity, torpor, languor, dullness, immobility, passivity, passiveness, lifelessness; quiescence, latency; inexcitability, sloth, indolence, irresolution, indecisiveness, cowardice, spinelessness.

v be inert, be inactive.

adj inert, inactive, immobile, unmoving, motionless, lifeless, passive, dead; sluggish, dull, heavy, flat, slack, tame, slow, blunt, torpid, languid; latent, dormant, sleeping, smoldering, quiescent.

adv in suspense, in abeyance.

173 violence n vehemence, fury, ferocity, impetuosity, boisterousness, turbulence, ebullition, effervescence, intensity, severity, acuteness; energy, force, might; fit, paroxysm, orgasm, spasm, convulsion, throe; exacerbation, exasperation, hysterics, excitability, passion; outbreak, outburst, uproar, riot, explosion, blow-up, blast, eruption; turmoil, disorder, ferment, agitation, storm, tempest; destruction, brutality, fighting, combat, warfare, hostilities; injury, wrong, outrage, injustice.

v be violent, ferment, effervesce; romp, rampage, run wild, run riot, rush, tear, run headlong, run amuck, go wild, kick up a row, (informal) flip out, go beserk; bluster, rage, roar, riot, storm, boil, boil over, fume, foam; explode, go off, detonate, thunder, blow up, flare, burst; render violent, sharpen, stir up, quicken, excite, incite, urge, lash, whip up; stimulate; irritate, inflame, kindle, accelerate, aggravate, exasperate, exacerbate, convulse, infuriate, madden, fan the fire, whip into a frenzy.

adj violent, vehement, acute,

sharp; rough, rude, bluff, boisterous, brusque, abrupt, wild, impetuous, rampant; disorderly, turbulent, blustering, raging, riotous, tumultuous, obstreperous; raving, frenzied, *(informal)* freaked, mad, unhinged, insane; desperate, furious, frantic, hysterical; savage, fierce, ferocious, physical, brutal, combative; uncontrollable, ungovernable, irrepressible, excited; spasmodic, convulsive, orgasmic; explosive, volcanic, stormy.

adv violently; by storm, by force.

174 moderation *n* temperateness, temperance, reasonableness, judiciousness, deliberateness, fairness; gentleness, mildness, calmness, peacefulness; quiet, calm, composure; lenity, lenience; relaxation, assuagement, tranquilization; pacification, mitigation; measure, middle ground, middle of the road.

v moderate, ally, meliorate, calm, pacify, assuage, lull, smooth, compose, still, calm, quiet, hush, sober, mitigate, soften, mollify, temper, qualify, alleviate, appease, lessen, abate, diminish; slake, curb, tame; arbitrate, referee, umpire, regulate.

adj moderate, temperate, reasonable, judicious, deliberate, fair, gentle, mild, calm, cool, sober, measured, unruffled, quiet, tranquil, still, peaceful, pacific; unexciting, even, smooth, bland, palliative; lenient, relaxed, easy going.

adv moderately, in moderation, within reason.

175 influence *n* importance, weight, pressure, preponderance, prevalence, sway; predominance, ascendancy; dominance, reign, rule, authority, power, control, capability; input, *(informal)* say, persuasion, play, leverage, vantage ground; patronage, protection, auspices.

v be influential, have a say, have input, carry weight, affect, sway, impress, bias, direct, control; move, activate, incite, impel, rouse, arouse, induce, persuade; dominate, predominate, outweigh, override, prevail.

adj influential, important, weighty; prevalent, rife, rampant,

dominant, predominant; potent, powerful, effective, authoritative.

175a absence of influence *n* impotence, powerlessness; unimportance, irrelevancy.

adj uninfluential, unpersuasive, weak, impotent, *(informal)* wishy-washy.

176 tendency *n* aptness, aptitude, disposition, predisposition, proclivity, proneness, propensity, susceptibility, inclination, leaning, bias, drift, trend, bent, turn; quality, nature, temperament; idiosyncrasy, cast, vein, mood, humor.

v tend, contribute, conduce, lead, dispose, incline, verge, bend to, gravitate toward, lean, drift, tend, affect; promote, influence.

adj tending, leaning; conducive, working toward, in a fair way to; liable, likely, influential, instrumental, useful, subsidiary, subservient.

177 liability *n* susceptibility, penchant, vulnerability, predilection, propensity, tendency; drawback, hindrance, obstacle, difficulty, impediment; responsibility, obligation, debt, debit, indebtedness, pledge.

v be liable, incur, lay oneself open to, run the risk of, stand a chance, expose oneself to.

adj liable, subject, exposed, likely, open, in danger of; obliged, responsible, accountable, answerable; contingent, incidental, possible.

178 concurrence *n* accordance, accord, agreement, consent, assent; cooperation, collaboration, partnership, alliance, concert, union.

v concur, conduce, conspire, contribute; agree, unite, combine, hang together, pull together, cooperate, collaborate; keep pace with, run parallel, go hand in hand with.

adj concurrent, cooperative, collaborative, joint, allied with, of one mind, at one with, in concert with.

179 counteraction *n* opposition, antagonism, contrariety, polarity; clashing, collision, interference, resistance, friction; reaction, response, counterblast, counter maneuver; neutralization, check, curb, hindrance; repression, restraint.

v counteract, run counter to, clash, cross, interfere with, conflict with; jostle, run up against, oppose, antagonize, withstand, resist, hinder, impede, check, curb, repress, restrain; recoil, react; neutralize, nullify, cancel out, undercut, undermine, undo; counterpoise, offset, balance out, compensate.

adj counteracting, antagonistic, conflicting, contrary, reactionary.

adv although.

prep in spite of, against.

Class II

Words Relating to Space

I. Space in General

180 [indefinite space] **space** *n* extension, extent, expanse, span, stretch, scope, range, latitude, spread, proportions, sweep, capacity, play, swing, expansion; elbowroom, room, breathing space, leeway; open space(s), free space, waste, desert, wild, wilderness; unlimited space, wide world, heavens, universe, solar system, outer space, abyss, the void, infinity.

adj spacious, roomy, extensive, expansive, capacious, ample; widespread, vast, worldwide, boundless, limitless, unlimited, infinite.

adv extensively, far and wide, right and left, from the four corners of the world, all over, from pole to pole, under the sun, on the face of the earth, from all points of the compass, to the four winds.

180a i**nextension** *n* nonextension, point, atom.

181 [definite space] **region** *n* sphere, ground, soil, area, realm, quarter, orb, hemisphere, circuit, circle; domain, tract, territory, country, county, province; clime, climate, zone, meridian, latitude.

adj regional, provincial, territorial.

182 [limited space] **place** *n* spot, point; niche, nook, hole, pigeonhole; locality; locale, situation.

adv somewhere, in some place, here and there, in various places.

183 **situation** *n* position, locality, locale, latitude and longitude, location; footing, standing, standpoint; aspect, attitude, posture, perspective, pose; place, site, station, post, predicament, whereabouts; bearings, direction; topography, geography; map, chart.

v be situated, be located, lie, have its seat in; situate, locate.

adj situated, located; local, topical, topographical.

adv here and there, hereabouts, thereabouts, in such and such a place.

184 **location** *n* place, situation; establishment, settlement, installation; anchorage, mooring, encampment.

v locate, place, situate, put, lay, set, make a place for, seat; station, lodge, quarter, house, post, install; establish, fix, settle, root; graft, plant; inhabit, domesticate, colonize, take root, establish roots, come to rest, settle down, take up quarters, locate oneself, relocate; squat, perch, bivouac, burrow, get a footing, encamp.

adj located, placed, ensconced, rooted, settled, moored.

185 **displacement** *n* dislocation, misplacement, derangement, transposition; ejection, expulsion, banishment, removal, exile.

v displace, dislodge, disestablish; misplace, disturb, disorder, unsettle, derange, confuse; transpose, set aside, transfer, remove, unload, empty, eject, expel, banish, exile; vacate, depart, leave.

adj displaced; unplaced, unhoused, unsettled, unestablished; homeless, out of place, misplaced, out of its element.

186 **presence** *n* attendance, company; occupancy, occupation; ubiquity, omnipresence, permeation, pervasion, pervasiveness, diffusion, dispersion; nearness, vicinity, proximity, closeness.

v be present; look on, attend, stand by, remain, find oneself; occupy, inhabit, dwell, stay, sojourn, live, abide, lodge, nestle, roost, perch, tenant; fill, pervade, permeate, run through.

adj present, attending; occupying, inhabiting, resident, moored; ubiquitous, omnipresent, pervasive, diffused; near, close, in proximity.

adv here, there, and everywhere; in presence of.

187 absence *n* nonappearance, nonattendance, absenteeism, nonresidence; emptiness, void, vacuum, vacancy, vacuity.

v be absent; keep away, play truant, absent oneself, stay away.

adj absent, not present, away, out, not here, not in, not present, off; wanting, lacking, missing, nonexistent; vacant, empty, void, vacuous, devoid.

adv without, minus, nowhere, *sans*; elsewhere.

188 inhabitant *n* resident, dweller, occupant; tenant, inmate, boarder, lodger; native, townsman, villager, citizen; population, community, society, state, people, race, nation.

v inhabit, live, reside, dwell.

adj indigenous, native, domestic.

189 habitation *n* abode, residence, domicile, lodging, dwelling, address, habitation, housing, quarters; home, homestead, motherland, fatherland, country; nest, lair, den, cave, hole, hiding place, cell, hive, haunt, habitat, perch, roost, retreat, *(informal)* pad, *(informal)* crashpad.

v inhabit, take up one's abode.

190 [things contained] **contents** *n* stuffing, cargo, lading, freight, shipment, haul, load, bale, burden.

v load, lade, ship, haul, charge, fill, stuff.

191 receptacle *n* container, holder, repository, vessel, receiver, depository, reservoir; storage areas; bulk containers; liquid containers; wrapping.

II. Dimensions

192 size *n* proportions, dimensions, magnitude, bulk, volume; largeness, greatness; expanse, amplitude, mass; capacity, tonnage; corpulence, obesity, plumpness; hugeness, enormousness, immensity; monstrosity, enormity; giant, monster, mammoth, behemoth, leviathan, elephant; lump, bulk, block, mass, clod, thumper, whopper, strapper, *(informal)* mother, mountain, mound, heap.

v be large; become large, expand.

adj sizable, large, big, great, considerable, bulky, voluminous, ample, massive, massy; capacious, comprehensive, spacious; mighty, towering, magnificent; corpulent; stout, fat, plump, obese, portly; full-grown, stalwart, brawny; hulky, unwieldy, bulky, lumpish, whopping, thundering, thumping; overgrown; huge, immense, enormous, mighty, vast, amplitudinous, stupendous; monstrous, gigantic, colossal.

193 littleness *n* smallness, diminutiveness, tininess; epitome; microcosm; vanishing point.

v be little; become little, decrease.

adj little, small, minute, diminutive, microscopic, submicroscopic; tiny, puny, wee, miniature, pigmy, dwarf, undersized, underdeveloped, dwarfish, stunted, dumpy, squat; imperceptible, invisible, infinitesimal.

194 expansion *n* increase, enlargement, extension, growth, development; augmentation, aggrandizement, increment, amplification; spreading, swelling, distention, puffiness, dropsy.

v expand, wide, enlarge, extend, grow, increase, swell, fill out; dilate, stretch, spread; bud, sprout, shoot, germinate, open, burst forth; outgrow, overrun; spread, extend, aggrandize; distend, develop, amplify, spread out, magnify; inflate, puff up, blow up, stuff, pad, cram, fatten; exaggerate.

adj expanded, larger; swollen,

expansive, widespread, overgrown, exaggerated, bloated, fat, turgid, tumid, dropsical; pot-bellied, chubby, corpulent, obese, heavy; full-blown, full-grown.

195 contraction n reduction, diminution; decrease, lessening, shrinking; collapse, emancipation, attenuation, atrophy; condensation, compression, compactness, compendium, squeezing.

v contract, become small, lessen, decrease, dwindle, shrink, narrow, shrivel, collapse, wither, wizen, fall away, waste, wane, ebb, decay, deteriorate; diminish, contract, draw in, constrict, condense, compress, squeeze, crush, crumple up, pinch, squash, cramp; pare, reduce, attenuate, scrape, file, grind, chip, shave, shear, cut down; circumscribe, limit, restrain, confine.

adj contracting, astringent; shrunk, shrunken, contracted; wizened, stunted, waning; compact.

196 distance n remoteness, farness, background, offing, far cry to, horizon, elongation; interval, remove, gap, span, reach, range; outpost, outskirts, foreign parts.

v be distant; extend to, stretch to, reach to, spread to; range.

adj distant, far off, far away, remote, far, afar, outlying, removed, at a distance, away, younder, yon; inaccessible, out of the way, unapproachable.

adv far off, far away, afar, away, a long way off.

197 nearness n closeness, propinquity, proximity, proximation; vicinity, neighborhood, contiguity; short distance, earshot, close quarters, stone's throw, gunshot, hair's breadth; approach, access.

v be near, neighbor, border upon, touch, stand next to; approximate, come close to, resemble; converge, crowd.

adj near, high, close, neighboring, adjoining, adjacent, bordering; proximate, approximate; at hand, handy; intimate.

adv near, nigh, hard by, close to, close upon, within reach, at one's fingertips.

198 interval n separation, space, break, gap, caesura, interspace, interstice, distance, hiatus, skip, division, opening; pause, recess, interim, respite, interlude, interregnum, interruption, term, spell, period; cleft, crevice, chink, cranny, crack, slit, fissure, rift, flaw, breach, rent, gash, cut, leak; ditch, dike, gorge, ravine, abyss, gulf.

v gape, open; intervene, interrupt.

199 continuity n contact, contiguousness, proximity, apposition, juxtaposition, touching, abutment, meeting.

v be contiguous, join, adjoin, abut on, border, touch, meet, graze, adhere; coincide, coexist.

adj contiguous, touching, in contact, end to end; close, near.

200 length n distance, extent, longitude, span, reach, range; lengthiness, elongation, size; duration, continuance, term, period.

v be long, stretch out, sprawl; extend to, reach to, stretch to; lengthen, stretch, elongate, extend; prolong, protract, draw out, spin out.

adj long, lengthy, extended, outstretched; lengthened, interminable; linear, lineal, longitudinal; tall, stringy, protracted, lanky.

adv lengthwise, at length, longitudinally.

201 shortness n brevity, littleness, shortening, abridgment, abbreviation, conciseness, condensation; retrenchment, curtailment, reduction.

v be short; shorten, abridge, abbreviate, condense, compact, compress, epitomize; retrench, cut short, reduce, pare down, clip back, cut back, prune, shear, shave, crop, chop up, hack up, truncate.

adj short, brief, curt; compendious, compact, compressed, condensed; stubby, stunted, stumpy, squat, dumpy; concise, pointed; curtailed, cut back, reduced, shortened, abbreviated, abridged.

202 breadth. thickness n breadth, width, latitude, amplitude, extent, diameter.

thickness, density, denseness, heaviness, bulk, body.

v be broad; expand, widen, be thick; thicken.

adj broad, wide, ample, extended, expansive, large; outspread, outstretched.

thick, dense, heavy, bulky, solid, compact; dumpy, squat, thickset.

203 narrowness. thinness n narrowness, slenderness, exiguity, closeness, straitness, scantiness, slightness, slimness.

thinness, slenderness, slimness, leanness, lankness, meagerness, skinniness.

v be narrow; narrow, taper, be thin; thin, slenderize, slim; dilute, water down.

adj narrow, close, slender, thin, fine, threadlike, slim, delicate; restricted, confined, limited; thin, emaciated, lean, skinny, meager, gaunt, spindly, lanky, scrawny, haggard, pinched, skeletal, wasted; frail, unsound, fragile; weak, shrill, faint, feeble; watery, waterish, diluted, unsubstantial.

204 layer n stratum, substratum, bed, zone, floor, stage, story, tier, slab, tablet, board, sheet, platter; scale, coat, peel, membrane, film, leaf, slice.

v slice, shave, pare, peel; plate, coat, veneer; cover; layer

adj layered, stratified, tiered; scaly, filmy, membranous, flaky.

205 filament n thread, fiber, strand, hair, cilia, tendril, gossamer, wire, strand, vein.

adj fibrous, threadlike, wiry, stringy, ropy; capillary.

206 height n altitude, stature, elevation, tallness; prominence, eminence, pre-eminence, loftiness, sublimity; top, peak, pinnacle, acme, summit, zenith, culmination.

v tower, soar, hover, cap, command; mount, bestride, surmount, overhang; heighten, elevate, raise up, rise up.

adj high, tall, elevated, towering, skyscraping, gigantic, huge, colossal; distinguished, prominent, eminent, pre-eminent, exalted, lofty, sublime; overhanging, overlying.

207 lowness n depression, debasement, prostration; flatness, proneness; lowlands, flatlands.

v be low; lie low, lie flat, crouch, slouch, wallow, grovel; underlie; lower, depress.

adj low, flat, level, low-lying; crouched, squat, prone, supine, prostrate, depressed; groveling, abject, sordid, mean, base, lowly, degraded, debased, ignoble, vile.

adv under, beneath, underneath, below, down, downward; underfoot, underground; downstairs, belowstairs.

208 depth n deepness, profundity, obscurity; depression, bottom, unfathomable space; pit, hollow, shaft, well, crater, chasm, abyss, bottomless pit; central part, midst, middle, bosom, womb, base, heart, core; soundings, draft, submersion, dive.

v deepen, hollow, plunge, sink, dig, excavate; sound, have the lead, take soundings.

adj deep, deep-seated, profound, mysterious, obscure, unfathomable; sunk, buried, submerged; bottomless, soundless, fathomless, unfathomed, abysmal, yawning, gaping.

adv beyond one's depth, out of one's depth, over one's head.

209 shallowness n superficiality, banality, triviality, frivolity, flimsiness, emptiness, vacancy; shallow, shoal, sand bar.

adj shallow, superficial, slight, cursory, trivial, banal, trashy, flimsy, substanceless, empty, vacuous, vacant; skin-deep, ankle-deep, knee-deep.

210 summit n top, peak, apex, pinnacle, vertex, acme, culmination, zenith; height, pitch, maximum, climax; crowning point, turning point, watershed.

v culminate, climax, crown, top.

adj highest, top, topmost, uppermost, tiptop; capital, head, polar; supreme, supernal.

211 base *n* bottom, stand, rest, pedestal, dado, understructure, substructure, foot, basis, foundation, ground, groundwork; principle, touchstone, fundamental part, element, ingredient; bottom; nadir, foot, sole, heel.

adj bottom, undermost, nethermost; fundamental, basic, elemental; based on, founded on, grounded on, built on; base, vile, venal.

212 verticality *n* perpendicularity, erectness; wall, precipice, cliff.

v be vertical, stand up straight, stand upright, stand erect, stand straight and tall.

adj vertical, upright, erect, perpendicular, straight, bolt upright, plumb.

adv vertically, on end, endwise.

213 horizontality *n* flatness; level, plane, stratum; horizon; recumbency, lying down, reclination, proneness, supination, prostration.

v be horizontal, lie, recline, lie down, lie flat, sprawl; render horizontal, flatten, level, prostrate, knock down, floor, fell.

adj horizontal, level, even, plane, flat, smooth; prone, supine, prostrate.

adv horizontally, on one's back.

214 suspension *n* hanging down, free swinging; pendant, tail, train, flap, pendulum.

v suspend, hang, swing, dangle; flap, trail, flow; depend.

adj suspended, pendent, hanging, swinging, dangling, pendulous; dependent.

215 support *n* foundation, base, basis, ground, footing, hold; supporter, prop, brace, stay, rib, truss, stalk, stilts, splint; bar, rod, boom, outrigger; staff, stick, crutch; bracket, ledge, shelf, trestle, buttress.

v support, bear, carry, hold, sustain, shoulder, bolster; shore up, hold up, prop up, brace; help, aid, maintain, sustain; base, found, ground.

adj supporting, supported; fundamental.

216 parallelism *n* coextension; comparison, affinity, correspondence, semblance, likeness, resemblance, analogy, equation.

v parallel, compare, relate, associate, connect, correspond to, equate.

adj parallel, coextensive, collateral, aligned, equal; like, similar, allied, corresponding, correlative, analogous, equivalent.

217 obliquity *n* incline, inclination, slope, slant; leaning, tilt, list, bend, curve; acclivity, rise, ascent, grade, rising ground, hill, bank; declivity, decline, downhill, dip, fall; steepness.

v be oblique, slope, slant, lean, incline, stoop, decline, descend; bend, careen, slouch, sidle; render oblique, sway, bias, slat, warp, incline, bend, crook, tilt, distort.

adj oblique, inclined; sloping, tilted; askew, asquint, awry, crooked; uphill, rising, ascending; downhill, falling, descending; declining, declivitous; steep, abrupt, sharp, precipitous; diagonal, transverse.

adv obliquely, on one side; askew, askance, edgewise, at an angle; sidelong, sideways, slantwise.

218 inversion *n* subversion, reversion, contraposition, transposition, transposal, conversion; contrariety, contradiction, opposition, polarity, antithesis; reversal, overturn, somersault, turn of the tide, revulsion, revolution.

v be inverted, turn about, wheel about, go about, turn over, go over, tilt over; invert, subvert, reverse, overturn, upturn, upset, turn topsyturvy; transpose.

adj inverted, inside out, wrong side out, upside down, topsy-turvy; inverse, reverse, obverse, opposite.

adv inversely.

219 crossing *n* intersection, grade crossing, crossroad, interchange; network, reticulation; net, netting, network, web, mesh, wicker, lace; mat, matting, plait, trellis, lattice, grating, grille, gridiron, tracery, fretwork, filigree; knot, entanglement.

v cross, intersect, interlace, intertwine, interweave, interlink, crisscross, twine, intwine, weave, twist, wreathe; dovetail, splice, link, link up; mat, plait, plat, braid; tangle, entangle, ravel; net, knot, twist.

adj crossing; crossed, matted, transverse; weaved, woven, intertwined, interlaced.

220 exteriority *n* outside, exterior; surface, superficies; covering, skin, face, appearance, façade, aspect, facet.

v be exterior, lie around, encircle.

adj exterior, external, outer, outside, outward, superficial; outlying, extraneous, foreign, extrinsic.

adv externally, out, over, outwards.

221 interiority *n* interior, inside, inner part, center, interspace; subsoil, substratum, contents, substance, pith, marrow, backbone, heart, bowels, belly, guts, lap, womb; recesses, innermost recesses, hollows, nook, niche, cave.

v be interior, be inside; inclose, circumscribe; intern; embed, insert.

adj interior, internal, inside, inner, inward, inmost, innermost; deepseated, inlaid, embedded, ingrained, innate, inherent, intrinsic, inborn; private, secret, intimate, confidential; home, domestic.

adv internally; inward, within, indoors, withindoors.

222 centrality *n* center, middle, midst; core, kernel, nucleus, heart, pole, axis, pivot, navel, nub, hub; centralization; center of gravity.

v be central; centralize, concentrate; focus on, bring into focus, get to the heart of.

adj central, middle, pivotal, focal, concentric; middlemost.

adv centrally; middle, midst.

223 covering *n* cover, canopy, awning, tent, marquee, umbrella, parasol, sunshade; shade, screen, shield; roof, ceiling, thatch, shed; top, lid; bandage, wrappings; coverlet, blanket, sheet, quilt, tarpaulin; skin, fleece, fur, hide; clothing, mask; peel, crust, bark, rind; veneer, coating, facing, varnish.

v cover, superimpose, overlay, overspread; wrap, encase, face, case, veneer, paper; conceal, cover over.

adj covered, clothed, wrapped; protected.

224 lining *n* inner coating, coating; filling, stuffing, padding, wadding.

v line, stuff, wad, pad, fill; coat, incrust, face, cover.

adj lined.

225 dress *n* clothing, covering, raiment, drapery, costume, attire, garb, apparel, wardrobe, outfit, clothes; equipment, livery, gear, rigging, trappings, togs, accouterments; uniforms, regimentals, suit.

v dress, clothe, drape, robe, array, fit out, deck out, garb, rig out, apparel; equip, harness, outfit, uniform; cover, wrap, wrap up, sheathe, swathe, swaddle.

adj dressed, clothed, clad, invested.

226 undress *n* nudity, nakedness, bareness, dishabille.

v undress, uncover, divest, expose, disrobe, strip, bare, doff, peel, take off, put off, lay open.

adj undressed, nude, naked, bare, stark-naked, exposed, in the buff, *au naturel*, in the altogether, in one's birthday suit; undressed, unclad, undraped, disrobed.

227 environment *n* environs, surroundings, outskirts, suburbs, purlieus, precincts, neighborhood.

v environ, surround, encompass, compass, inclose, enclose, circle, encircle, gird, twine round, hem in.

adj surrounding, circumjacent.

adv around, about; without; on every side, on all sides, right and left, every which way.

228 interspersion *n* interjacence, interlocation, interpenetration, permeation; interjection, interpolation, interlineation, intercalation; intervention, interference, interposition, intrusion; insinuation; insertion.

v intervene, come between, get between, interpenetrate; intersperse, permeate, introduce, throw in, work in, interpose, interject, interpolate, insert; interfere, intrude, obtrude.

adj intervening, interjacent; parenthetical, episodic; intrusive.

adv between, betwixt, among, amid, amongst; in the thick of, betwixt and between; parenthetically.

229 circumscription *n* limitation, enclosure; confinement, restraint.

v circumscribe, limit, bound, confine, inclose; surround, hedge in, fence in, wall in; imprison, restrain; enfold, bury, incase.

adj circumscribed, confined, restrained, imprisoned; buried in, immersed in, embosomed, embedded.

230 outline *n* circumference, perimeter, periphery; circuit, lines, contour, profile, silhouette.

v outline, draw, sketch, trace, profile.

231 edge *n* frame, fringe, trimming, trim, edging, skirting, hem; verge, brink, brim, lip, margin, border, skirt, rim, mouth; threshold, door, porch, portal; coast, shore.

v edge, skirt, border; trim, hem.

232 enclosure *n* envelope, case, wrapper; girdle, pen, fence, fold, cote, corral, stockyard, paddock, yard, pound, compound; fence, pale, paling, balustrade, rail, railing; hedge; wall, barrier, barricade; gate, gateway, door, doorway; boundary, border.

v enclose, circumscribe.

233 limit *n* boundary, bounds, extent, confine, term, pale, verge; termination, terminus; frontier, marches, outer edges, unknown; boundary line, border, edge; turning point, flood gate.

v limit, restrain, restrict, confine, check, hinder, bound, circumscribe, define.

adj limited, definite; terminal.

adv thus far, only so far, thus far and no further.

234 front *n* forefront, foreground, lead; face, frontage, façade, frontispiece, proscenium; vanguard, front rank, first rank, head of the column, advanced guard.

v front, face, confront; be in front, stand in front; come to the front.

adj fore, foremost; front, frontal, anterior, forward.

adv before, in front, in advance; ahead, right ahead, in the foreground; in the lead.

235 rear *n* back, background, rearguard, rear rank; distance, hinterland; rump, buttocks, posterior, rear, backside, hindquarters; wake, train; reverse, other side of the coin, *(informal)* flipside.

v be behind, bring up the rear; rear, bring up, nurture, raise; elevate, lift, loft, lift up, hold up; build, put up, erect.

adj rear, back, hindmost; posterior.

adv behind, in the rear, in the background, at the heels; after, aft, rearward.

236 side *n* laterality, flank, quarter, lee, hand; cheek, jowl, shoulder; profile, lee side, broadside.

v be on the side; be side by side, be cheek to cheek; flank, skirt, outflank, sidle.

adj sidelong, lateral; flanking, skirting; flanked.

adv sideways, sidelong; broadside, on one side, abreast, alongside, beside, side by side, cheek by jowl; laterally.

237 opposition *n* opposite, contraposition, opposite side, opposite poles, polarity, antithesis, reverse, inverse; counterpart, companion piece, complement.

v be opposite; stand as opposites, oppose.

adj opposite, reverse, inverse, converse; antipodal, antithetical, countering, opposing; fronting, facing, diametrically opposite; complementary.

adv over, over the way, over against; poles apart; face to face.

238 right *n* right hand, right side; off-side, starboard.

   adj right-handed, dextral.

239 left *n* left hand, left side; near side, port.

   adj left-handed, sinistral.

III. Form

240 form *n* shape, outline, mold, appearance, cast, cut, configuration; make, formation, frame, construction, cut, set, build, trim; mold, model, pattern; posture, attitude, convention, rule, formality, formula, ceremony, conformity.

   v form, shape, figure, fashion, carve, cut, chisel, hew, cast; shape, model, mold, fashion, cast, construct, build; stamp, cast, type.

   adj formal, ceremonial, ceremonious, conventional; regular, set, fixed, stiff, rigid.

241 formlessness *n* shapelessness, amorphism, asymmetry; disorder, chaos; misproportion, deformity, disfigurement, defacement, mutilation, truncation.

   v deface, disfigure, deform, mutilate, truncate.

   adj formless, shapeless, amorphous, asymmetrical, unformed, unshaped, unfashioned, unshapely, misshapen, out of proportion, disordered, chaotic; rough, rude, coarse, barbarous, rugged.

242 [regularity of form] symmetry *n* shapeliness, finish, comeliness, gracefulness, grace, beauty; proportion, uniformity, parallelism; regularity, evenness, balance, order, harmony, agreement.

   adj symmetrical, shapely, well set, finished; beautiful, lovely; classic, classical, formal, chaste, severe; regular, uniform, balanced, harmonious, ordered; even, parallel, equal.

243 [irregularity of form] distortion *n* contortion, warp, buckle, screw, twist, crookedness, obliquity; deformity, malformation, misproportion, disfigurement, monstrosity, ugliness; asymmetry.

   v distort, contort, warp, buckle, screw, twist, wrest; writhe, grimace, make faces; deform, disfigure, misshape.

   adj distorted, out of shape, irregular, unsymmetrical, awry, askew, crooked; not true, not straight, uneven; misshapen, ill-made, ill-fashioned, ill-proportioned, malformed, deformed.

244 angularity *n* bifurcation, bend, fork, crook, notch, angle; elbow, knee, knuckle, crotch; right angle, acute angle, obtuse angle; corner, nook, niche, recess.

   v angle, tilt, bend, fork, bifurcate.

   adj angular, bent, crooked, jagged, serrated; forked, bifurcate, cornered, V-shaped, hooked; akimbo.

245 curvature *n* curve, incurvature, bend; flexure, bending, crook, hook; deflection, turn, deviation, detour, sweep, curl, winding; curve, arc, arch, arcade, vault, bow, crescent, half-moon, horse-shoe, loop; parabola, hyperbola.

   v be curved, sweep, sag; deviate, turn; render curved, bend, curve, deflect, inflect, crook; turn, round, arch, arch over, bow, curl, coil, recurve.

   adj curved, bowed, vaulted, hooked, arched, arced; circular, nonlinear, semi-circular, rounded, crescent, crescent-shaped, lunar, demi-lune.

246 straightness *n* directness; inflexibility, stiffness; straight line, direct line, bee line.

   v be straight, go straight; render straight, straighten, rectify, correct, right; put right, put straight, unbend, unfold, uncurl, unravel.

   adj straight, even true, unbent, direct, rectilinear, linear, not curved, uncurved; square, erect, perpendicular, vertical, upright; candid, forthright, definite, reliable, plain, blunt, frank, sure, positive, irrefutable, certain, unequivocal, inescapable; honest, honorable, fair, just, equitable, impartial, aboveboard, reputable, scrupulous, worthy, lawful, licit, conscientious, decent, ethical; correct, sound, sane, accurate, true; sober, conventional, provincial, (informal) unhip, (informal) square, (informal) not with it.

247 [simple circularity] **circularity** n roundness, rotundity; circle, ring, hoop, areola; bracelet, armlet; eye, loop, wheel, cycle, orb, orbit; zone, belt, cord, band, sash, girdle, circuit; wreath, garland, crown, corona, coronet; necklace, collar; ellipse, oval.

v round; go around, encircle, circle.

adj round, rounded, circular, oval, elliptic, elliptical, egg-shaped.

248 [complex circularity] **convolution** n involution, winding, wave, undulation, sinuosity, meandering, twist, twirl; coil, roll, curl, buckle, spiral, corkscrew, worm, tendril; serpent, snake, eel; maze, labyrinth.

v wind, twine, entwine, twirl, wave, undulate, meander, turn; twist, coil, roll; wrinkle, curl, frizz, frizzle; wring, contort.

adj convoluted, winding, twisted; wavy, undulating, circling, snaky, serpentine; involved, intricate, complex, complicated, labyrinthine, tortuous, mazy; spiral, coiled.

adv in and out, round and round.

249 rotundity n roundness, cylindricality, sphericity, globularity; cylinder, barrel, drum; roll, roller, rolling pin; sphere, globe, ball, spheroid, globule; bulb, pellet, pill, marble, pea, knob, pommel.

v sphere, form into a sphere, roll into a ball, round.

adj rotund, round, circular, ball-shaped; cylindrical, spherical, globular; egg-shaped, pear-shaped, ovoid.

250 convexity n prominence, projection, swelling, bulge, protuberance, protrusion; hump, hunch, bunch; knob, node, nodule, bump, clump; pimple, pustule, pock, growth, polyp, blister, boil; nipple, teat, pap, breast; nose, beak, snout, nozzle; peg, button, stud, ridge; cupola, dome, arch; relief, high relief, low relief; hill, mountain, cape, ness,

promontory, headland; jetty, ledge, spur.

v project, bulge, protrude, jut out, stand out, stick out, stick up, start up, shoot up, swell up; raise; emboss.

adj convex, prominent, protuberant; bossed, nodular, bunchy, hummocky, bulbous, swollen, swelling, bloated, bowed, arched, bellied; salient, in relief, raised.

251 flatness n smoothness, evenness; plane, level; plate, platter, table, tablet, slab.

v flatten, level, even off.

adj flat, plane, even, smooth; level, smooth, horizontal; flat as a pancake.

252 concavity n depression, dip, hollow, indentation, dent, cavity, dint, dimple; excavation, pit, trough; cup, basin, crater; valley, vale, dale, dell, glade, grove, glen, cave, cavern.

v render concave, depress, hollow, scoop, scoop out, gouge; dig, delve, excavate, mine, stave in, tunnel.

adj concave, hollow, hollowed out; indented, dented, sunken, cupped; cavernous, rounded inward, incurved.

253 sharpness n acuteness, pointedness; point, spike, spine, needle, pin, prick, prickle, spur, barb, thorn; knife edge, cutting edge, razor edge.

v be sharp, taper to a point; sharpen, point, whet, barb, strop, grind, whittle.

adj sharp, keen, acute, trenchant; pointed, peaked, conical, spiked, spiky, tapering; studded, prickly, barbed, spiny, thorny, bristling, thistly; craggy, snaggy; cutting, sharp edged, razor sharp.

254 bluntness n dullness, obtuseness, roughness.

v be blunt; render blunt, dull, take off the point, round the edge.

adj blunt, dull, obtuse, dimwitted; rough, gruff; rounded, round, unsharpened, unpointed.

255 smoothness n polish, gloss; lubrication, lubricity.

v smooth, plane, file, scrape, shave, sand, sandpaper; level, press, flatten, roll; iron, steam press; polish, burnish, rub, wax, sleek, buff, glaze; lubricate, oil, grease.

adj smooth, polished, glossy, shiny, sleek, silken, silky; even, level, sanded; soft, downy, velvety; slippery, glassy, oily.

256 roughness *n* asperity, irregularity, corrugation, nodulation; grain, texture, pile, nap.

v roughen, rough up, crinkle, ruffle, rumple, crumple.

adj rough, uneven, irregular, rugged, scabrous, knotted, craggy, gnarled; shaggy, coarse, hairy, bristly, hirsute; scraggly, prickly, bushy; unpolished, unsmooth, rough-hewn, textured; downy, velvety, fluffy, woolly.

adv against the grain.

257 notch *n* dent, nick, cut, scratch, indentation; saw, tooth, scallop.

v notch, nick, cut, scratch, indent, jag, scarify, scallop.

adj notched, toothed, serrated.

258 fold *n* plait, ply, crease, pleat, tuck; wrinkle, ripple, rimple, pucker, ruffle.

v fold, double, plait, crumple, crease, pleat, wrinkle, crinkle, ripple, curl, rumple, frizzle, rimple, ruffle, pucker, corrugate; tuck, hem, gather.

adj folded.

259 furrow *n* groove, rut, scratch, streak, cut, crack, score, incision, slit; channel, gutter, trench, gulley, ditch, dike, moat, trough; ravine, valley.

v furrow, dig, plow; channel, flute, groove, incise, cut, engrave, etch, seam, cleave, score; wrinkle, knit, pucker

adj furrowed, ribbed, striated, fluted.

260 opening *n* hole, gap, aperture, orifice, perforation, pinhole, peephole, keyhole; slot, slit, rift, breach, cleft, chasm, fissure, rent; outlet, inlet, vent; portal, porch, gate, hatch, door, doorway, gateway; way, path, channel, passage.

v open, ope, gape, yawn; perforate, pierce, tap, bore, drill; mine, tunnel, dig to daylight; impale, spike, spear, gore, spit, stab, puncture, lance, stick, prick, riddle; uncover, unclose, lay bare, expose, bare, reveal; lay open, cut open, rip open, throw open.

adj open, unclosed, uncovered, exposed; ajar, wide-open, gaping, yawning; perforated, porous, reticulated, permeable; accessible, available, public.

261 closure *n* blockade, shutting up, obstruction, stoppage, clogging, sealing, plugging; contraction; constipation; culmination; cessation, completion, termination, windup; lid, top, cap, stopper, plug, barrier.

v close, plug, block up, stop up, fill up, cork up, cork, button up, stuff up, shut up, dam up; blockade, obstruct, hinder; bar, bolt, stop, seal, choke, throttle, shut.

adj closed, shut, unopened; unpierced, impervious, impermeable; impenetrable, impassable, pathless; tight, snug, airtight, unventilated, watertight, hermetically sealed.

262 perforator *n* piercer, borer, auger, drill, awl, scoop, corkscrew, probe, lancet, scalpel, needle, pin, stiletto, puncher, hole puncher, gouge; knife, spear, bayonet.

263 stopper *n* lid, cap, cover; cork, spike, stopcock, pin, plug, tap, faucet, valve, spigot, rammer, ramrod; wadding, stuffing, padding, stopping, bandage, tourniquet.

IV. Motion

264 motion *n* movement, action, activity, move, going; progress, locomotion; mobilization, mobility, movableness, motive power; unrest, restlessness; stream, flow, flux, run, course, stir; rate, pace, step, tread, stride, gait; velocity, speed.

v move, go, hie, budge, stir, pass, flit; hover around, hover about; shift, slide, glide, roll, roll on, flow, drift, stream, run, sweep along; wander, meander, browse, stroll, walk, perambulate; dodge, keep on one's toes, keep moving, hit the road, *(informal)* truck; move, impel, propel; mobilize.

adj moving, in motion, traveling, on the road; transitional, shifting, mobile, movable; mercurial, restless, unquiet, nomadic, transient.

adv under way; on the move, on the go, on the march.

265 rest *n* quiescence, stillness, quietude, calm, calmness, tranquillity, repose, serenity, peace, silence; pause, lull, cessation; stagnation, immobility, fixity.

v rest, be still, stand still, lie still, stand immobile, keep quiet; repose; remain, stay, pause, wait, mark time, hold, halt, stop short, cease, desist, discontinue, stop; stagnate, be inactive, immobilize; dwell, settle, settle down, establish roots; alight, arrive; stand fast, stand firm, stick fast; quell, becalm, hush, stay, lull, lull to sleep, tranquilize.

adj restful, quiescent, still, calm, tranquil, peaceful, undisturbed, unruffled, serene, silent; motionless, fixed, stationary; unmoved, stable, at rest, at a standstill, stock-still, sleeping, dormant, inactive, stagnant.

266 [locomotion by land] **journey** *n* traveling, travel, excursion, tour, trip, expedition, jaunt, pilgrimage; wayfaring, roving, gadding about, *(informal)* bumming around, nomadism, vagabondism; migration, immigration, moving; walk, promenade, constitutional, stroll, peregrination, perambulation, march, stroll, saunter, jaunt outing, hike, airing; horsemanship, horseback riding; drive, driving, motoring, ride, spin; cycling, biking; procession, cavalcade, caravan, file, cortege, column.

v journey, travel, tour, take a trip; flit, take wing, *(informal)* hit the road, rove, ramble, roam, prowl, *(informal)* bum, *(informal)* bum around; range, traverse, scour the country, wander, meander, saunter, gad about; move, migrate, immigrate.

adj journeying, traveling, on the road; itinerant, peripatetic, rambling, roving, gadding, flitting, vagrant, nomadic, migratory, wayfaring.

267 [locomotion by water or air] **navigation** *n* voyage, sail, cruise, passage, boat ride; aquatics, boating, yachting, sailing, shipping.

flight, air travel, flying, gliding; aeronautics, aviation.

v navigate, sail, put to sea, embark, shove off, spread the sails, make sail, take oar; go boating, cruise, float, drift, coast; row, paddle, pull, scull, punt, steam; ride the waves.

fly, take off, take wing, take to the skies; aviate, soar, glide, fly over, plane, jet.

adj sailing, nautical, naval, maritime, seagoing, seafaring, oceangoing; afloat; navigable.

flying, jetting; aloft, in flight; aviational, aeronautical, aerial.

268 traveler *n* wayfarer, journeyer, rover, rambler, wanderer, free spirit, nomad, vagabond, bohemian, gypsy, itinerant, vagrant, tramp, hobo, straggler, waif; pilgrim, palmer, seeker, quester; voyager, passenger, tourist, sightseer, excursionist, vacationer, globe-trotter, jet-setter; immigrant, emigrant, refugee, fugitive; pedestrian, walker, cyclist, biker, rider, horsewoman, horseman, equestrian, driver.

269 mariner, flier *n* mariner, sailor, seaman, seafaring man, sea dog; pilot, skipper, captain, commander, helmsman, steersman; crew, hands, mates; navigator, flier, airman, aviator, aviatrix, pilot, skipper; astronaut, cosmonaut, spaceman.

270 transference *n* transfer, move, shift, transit, transition, passage, transmission, transport, transplantation, transposition; removal, relegation, deportation, extradition.

v transfer, transmit, transport, convey, carry, bear, pass; move, shift, conduct, convey, bring, fetch, reach; send, delegate, consign, turn over, hand over, deliver; transpose, transplant, displace, remove, relegate, deport, extradite; shovel, ladle.

adj transferable, transmittable, transmissible, transportable, movable, portable.

271 carrier *n* porter, bearer, messenger, runner, courier; postman, letter carrier; conductor, conveyor, transporter; freighter, ship, barge; train, locomotive; truck, vehicle, carriage; beast of burden.

272 vehicle *n* conveyance, carriage, transportation, rig, car, motorcar, automobile, (*informal*) wheels, truck; wagon, cart, coach, chaise, buggy; bicycle, bike, motorcycle, motorscooter; train, sleeping car, cattle car, boxcar.

273 ship *n* vessel, boat, liner, freighter, steamer, schooner, sailboat, motorboat, merchant ship, barge, tugboat, tanker, trawler, yacht, cruiser, yawl, ketch, brig, brigantine, squarerigger, sloop, cutter, launch; navy, fleet.

airplane, plane, jet, jumbo jet, aircraft, glider, helicopter, dirigible, blimp, balloon, spaceship, capsule, module, space station.

274 velocity *n* rapidity, quickness, swiftness, celerity, speed, alacrity; acceleration, pickup, spurt, rush, dash, race, flying, flight.

v move quickly, speed, hie, hasten, post, scamper, run, race, shoot, tear, whisk, sweep, rush, dash, dash off; bolt, bound, spring, dart, flit; hurry, hasten, haste, accelerate, (*informal*) turn on the juice, quicken, speed up, take off like a shot.

adj fast, speedy, swift, rapid, quick, brisk, fleet; nimble, agile, expeditious, light-footed, fast as a bullet, quick as lightning.

adv swiftly, apace, at full speed, at full gallop, posthaste.

275 slowness *n* languor, sluggishness, slackness, sloth, indolence; deliberateness, moderation, leisureliness; tardiness.

v move slowly, creep, crawl, lag, drawl, linger, loiter, saunter, trail, drag, dawdle; plod, trudge, lumber; grovel, sneak, steal, worm one's way, inch; waddle, wobble, shuffle,

hobble, limp, shamble, amble, traipse, slouch, mince, mince steps, halt; flag, totter, teeter, stagger; retard, hinder, impede, obstruct; slacken, check, relax, moderate; brake, curb, slow, put on the brakes.

adj slow, slack, late, tardy; gentle, easy, unhurried, deliberate, gradual, moderate, leisurely; languid, sluggish, indolent, lazy; tedious, humdrum, dull, boring; dense, stupid.

adv slowly, leisurely; at half speed, at a snail's pace; gradually, little by little, step by step, inch by inch, bit by bit, one step at a time.

276 impulse *n* impetus, implosion, push, thrust, shove; propulsion; sudden impulse, yearning, craving; reaction, response, reflex; collision, clash, encounter, shock, bump, crash; impact; blow, stroke, knock, rap, tap, slap, smack, pat, dab; hit, whack, thwack, slam, punch, belt, kick, thump, cut, thrust, lunge.

v impel, push, urge, thrust, shove, heave, prod, shoulder, jostle, hustle, hurtle, jog, jolt; start, give a start to, set going, get going, drive; run against, bump against, butt against; collide with, run into, bang into, butt; strike, knock, bang, hit, thump, beat, slam, dash, punch, thwack, whack; batter, pelt, buffet, butt; hit, rap, slap, tap, pat, dab.

277 recoil *n* reflex, rebound, ricochet, boomerang, backfire, backlash; snap, elasticity; reverberation, resonance; reaction, response, rebuff, repulse, revulsion.

v recoil, rebound, richochet, boomerang, snap back, spring back, fly back; react, respond; reverberate, echo, quiver.

adj reactionary; elastic, backfiring.

278 direction *n* bearing, course, set, drift, tenor, trend, tendency, inclination; tack, aim, determination, intention; points of the compass, cardinal points; line, path, road, range, line of march; alignment.

v direct, point, aim; tend toward, point toward, conduct to, go to; bend, tend, verge, incline, deter-

mine; steer for, make for, aim at,
level at, set one's sights on, take aim,
hold a course for, be bound for.

adj direct, straight; bound for;
undeviating, unswerving.

adv toward, on the road to;
hither, thither, whither; directly,
straight, straightforward, point-
blank, on a line with.

279 deviation *n* diversion, digression,
departure from, aberration; divergence, zigzag, detour, circuit; warp,
refraction; swerving.

v deviate, alter one's course, turn,
bend, curve, swerve, heel, bear off;
divert, deflect, shift, shunt, turn
aside, crook, warp; stray, straggle,
digress, ramble, rove, drift, go
astray, go adrift; wander, wind,
twist, meander; veer, turn aside,
change direction, steer clear of,
dodge.

adj deviating, errant, aberrant;
discursive, desultory, loose, rambling, digressive, stray, erratic, undirected; circuitous, indirect, zigzag,
round-about, crooked.

adv astray, roundabout, wide of
the mark; circuitously.

280 [going before] **precedence** *n* priority; leading, heading, the lead,
van, vanguard; precursor, coming
beforehand.

v precede, go before, forerun;
usher in, introduce, herald; head,
take the lead, lead the way; take precedence, have priority, come first,
come before.

adv in advance, before, ahead, in
the vanguard, in front.

281 [going after] **sequence** *n* coming
after, following, sequel; shadow,
dangler, train.

v follow, come in sequence, go after; attend, be attendant on, follow in
the steps of, follow in the wake of,
trail, shadow; pursue; lag, fall behind.

adj following; sequential.

adv behind, after; in the rear.

282 [motion forward] **progression** *n*
progress, improvement proceeding,
advance, advancement, headway;

growth, rise, increase, development.

v proceed, advance, progress, get
on, get along, gain ground, press onward, forge ahead, make headway,
make progress, make strides, stride
forward; grow, develop, increase,
improve.

adj advancing; progressive, advanced.

adv forward, onward; forth, on,
ahead.

283 [motion backward] **regression** *n*
retrogression, retreat, recession, retirement, withdrawal; reflux, back-
water, return, recoil; backsliding;
deterioration, decrease, fall.

v regress, recede, return, revert,
retreat, back out, back down, turn
back, fall back, drop out, retire,
withdraw; lose ground, drop off, fall
behind; ebb, shrink, shy.

adj retrograde, retrogressive; re-
gressive, refluent, reflex.

adv backwards; aboutface.

284 propulsion *n* propulsive force,
impulse, push, projection, thrust,
drive, impulsion, impetus; throw,
fling, toss, shot, discharge.

v propel, project, throw, fling,
cast, pitch, chuck, toss, heave, hurl;
drive, sling, push, shove; send off,
fire off, discharge, shoot, launch, let
fly; put in motion, set in motion,
start, get going, impel; expel.

adj propulsive.

285 traction *n* drawing, hauling, pulling, towing, towage; yank, tug, drag,
jerk.

v draw, pull, haul, lug, drag, tug,
tow, trail, train, take in tow; wrench,
jerk, yank.

adj tractile; in tow.

286 [motion towards] **approach** *n* access, advent, advance; nearness, approximation.

v approach, near, draw near,
move towards, get close to; gain on,
get closer to; pursue, trail.

adj approaching; approximate;
impending, imminent.

287 [motion from] **recession** *n* retirement, withdrawal; flight, removal,
retreat; regression, return, falling

back, regress; reaction, reversal, recoil; departure, leave-taking.

v recede, move back, go back, move away from, retire, withdraw; drift, abate, fade, wane, ebb, subside, drift away, fall back, shrink; react, revert, relapse, recoil, regress; run away, fly, avoid.

288 attraction *n* attractiveness, inclination, affinity; pull, magnetism, gravity.

v attract, draw, drag, pull, magnetize, exert force; interest, invite, engage, fascinate, lure, allure, charm, decoy, bait.

adj attractive, attracting, enticing, seductive, alluring; have pull, magnetic, gravitational.

289 repulsion *n* aversion, antipathy, dislike; repulse, rebuff.

v repel, push, back, drive away, chase away, rebuff, beat back; repulse, revolt, offend, sicken, disgust, displease, irritate.

adj repulsive, repellent, averse, repelling.

290 convergence *n* confluence, conflux, concurrence, concourse, congress, coming together, meeting, joining.

v converge, concur, come together, meet, join, unite; gather together, concentrate, center.

adj convergent, confluent, concurrent.

291 divergence *n* division, radiation, spread, severance, separation, refraction, deflection; ramification, furcation, branching, forking, detachment; deviation, aberration, disparity, difference, variance, heterogeneity.

v diverge, ramify, radiate, branch off, fork, spread, swerve, scatter, disperse; divide, separate, part, sever; vary, deviate, dissent, disagree.

adj divergent, radial, radiant, centrifugal.

292 arrival *n* advent, coming; reaching, attainment, landing, debarkation, disembarkation; reception, welcome, welcoming.

v arrive, get to, come to, reach a point, attain, complete; light, alight, dismount; land, disembark, debark, deplane, detrain.

293 departure *n* embarkation; outset, start, starting point, place of departure, point of departure; removal, exit; exodus, flight; leave-taking, valediction, *adieu*, farewell, goodbye.

v depart, go away, take one's leave, start, set out, leave, retire, quit, withdraw, absent, go, *(informal)* split, take off, *(informal)* cut out, move off, move out, ship out, pack it up; vacate, evacuate, abandon; sally, set forth, set forward, go forth; embark, set sail, put out to sea, shove off, get under way, enplane, entrain.

294 [motion into] **ingress** *n* entrance, entry; influx, intrusion, inroad, incursion, invasion, irruption, penetration, infiltration; insinuation, insertion.

v enter, come in, pour in, flow in; burst in, break in, invade, intrude; penetrate, infiltrate, insinuate oneself.

adj incoming, inbound.

295 [motion out of] **egress** *n* exit, issue; emergence, emanation; outbreak, outburst, eruption; evacuation, leakage, percolation, oozing, drainage, drain; outpouring, gush, effluence, effusion, discharge.

v emerge, emanate, issue; pass out of, come out of, pour out of, flow out of; exude, leak, ooze, drain, drip, trickle, dribble; gush, gush out, pour out, spout, flow out, discharge; escape, find vent.

adj outgoing, outward, outbound.

296 [motion into, actively] **reception** *n* admission, admittance, entry, entrée; importation, introduction, initiation, induction, absorption; ingestion, eating, drinking; suction, sucking; insertion, injection.

v give entrance to, admit, introduce, usher, initiate, induct; receive, import, bring in, ingest, absorb, imbibe.

297 [motion out of, actively] **ejection**

n rejection, expulsion, eviction, dislodgment, banishment, exile; emission, effusion, discharge, evacuation, regurgitation, elimination.

v reject, eject, expel, evict, dislodge, banish, exile; push aside, push away, turn away, brush aside; empty, drain, clear out, clean out, purge, void, evacuate; vomit, spew, regurgitate, throw up, *(informal)* puke, retch, *(informal)* barf, belch out, burp out; discharge, eliminate, discard, get rid of, do away with, cast off, cut adrift, turn out, throw out, oust.

298 eating *n* dining, supping, taking nourishment; ingestion, chewing, mastication; imbibition, drinking, food, nourishment, nutrition, nutriment, sustenance, subsistence, provender, provisions, rations, keep, board, fare; drink, beverage, potion, draught.

v eat, feed, breakfast, lunch, dine, sup, break bread; taste, devour, wolf, swallow, gulp, bolt, gulp down, fall to, dig in; chew, masticate, bite, bite into, chomp, munch, crunch, gnaw, nibble, peck at; live on, live off, fatten, feast on.

drink, drink up, drink one's fill, quaff, *(informal)* down, chug, empty, sip.

adj eatable, edible, digestible; drinkable, potable; nutritious, nutritive.

299 excretion *n* discharge, emanation, exhalation, secretion, effusion, perspiration, sweat; evacuation, elimination, urination; hemorrhage, bleeding.

v excrete; emanate, exhale; secrete, perspire, seat; eliminate, evacuate; urinate.

300 [forcible ingress] **insertion** *n* implantation, injection, inoculation, infusion, importation, insinuation; interpolation; immersion, submersion, dip, plunge.

v insert, introduce, put in; inject, infuse, instill, inoculate, impregnate, imbue; graft, ingraft, implant, plant, bud; thrust in, stick in, shove in, ram in, stuff in, tuck in, press

in, drive in; immerse, merge; dip, plunge.

301 [egress] **extraction** *n* removal, elimination, extrication, eradication, extirpation, extermination, ejection; wrench, squeezing, pulling.

v extract, draw, draw out, take out, pull out, tear out, rip out, pluck out; wring from, wrench, pull; root out, weed out, rake out, eradicate, uproot, pull up, extirpate; evolve, elicit, draw forth; extricate, remove, eliminate; squeeze out.

302 [motion through] **passage** *n* transmission; permeation, penetration, infiltration; ingress, egress, voyage, trip, tour, excursion, journey; way, route, channel, avenue, road, path, way, thoroughfare, conduit.

v pass, pass through; penetrate, permeate, thread, go through, cut across; ford, traverse, cross; go, move, proceed; leave, go away, depart.

303 [motion beyond] **infringement** *n* transgression, trespass, encroachment, infraction.

v infringe, transgress, trespass, encroach; surpass, go beyond, shoot ahead of, overrun; overstep, overreach, overshoot; outstrip, outrun, outride, outdo; exceed, surmount, transcend, soar.

adv beyond the mark, ahead.

304 [motion short of] **shortcoming** *n* failure, falling short; default, defalcation; incompleteness, imperfection, deficiency, insufficiency, noncompletion.

v fall short, come up short, come short of, not reach; want, lack; fail, break down, collapse, come to nothing; fall through, cave in.

adj deficient, lacking, insufficient; incomplete, imperfect.

305 ascent *n* ascension; rising, rise, upgrowth; leap, jump; acclivity, hill, grade.

v ascend, rise, mount, climb upward, climb, arise; clamber, mount, scale, go up, get up; tower, soar, hover, surmount, scale the heights.

adj ascendant; rising, acclivitous.

306 descent *n* declension, inclination, declination, slope, declivity, grade, decline, drop, cliff, precipice, dip, hill; fall, falling, descending, sinking; downfall, tumble, slip, tilt, trip, lurch.

v descend, go down, drop down, come down, drop, fall, gravitate, slip, slide, settle; decline, set, sink, droop, wilt, slump; dismount, alight, get down; swoop down, stoop; tumble, trip, stumble, lurch, pitch, topple, tilt, sprawl.

adj declivitous, sloping, precipitous, steep; descending.

307 elevation *n* raising; erection, lift; upheaval; sublimation, exaltation; prominence, height.

v elevate, heighten, raise, lift, lift up, erect; set up, tilt up, rear, hoist, heave; uplift, upraise, uprear; exalt, enhance, advance; take up, drag up, fish up, drag, dredge.

adj elevated, stilted, rampant.

308 depression *n* lowering; dip, concavity; upset, overturn, overthrow; prostration, abasement, debasement, degradation; bow, curtsy, genuflection, kowtow, obeisance.

v depress, lower, let down, take down, cast down, let drop, let fall; sink, debase, bring low, abase, degrade, reduce; overthrow, overturn, upset, prostrate, level, fell; bow, curtsy, genuflect, kowtow, kneel, bend over, make obeisance.

adj depressed; at a low ebb; prostrate, horizontal.

309 leap *n* jump, hop, spring, bound, vault; dance, caper, frisk, buck.

v leap, jump, hop, spring, bound, vault, hurtle, hurdle; dance, caper, trip, skip, frisk, bob, flounce, start; trip the light fantastic toe, dance all night.

adj leaping; frisky, lively, springy.

310 plunge *n* dip, dash, rush, dive, leap; ducking, dunking, submersion, immersion.

v plunge, immerse, submerge, douse, souse, dunk, dip; dash, rush, hasten, hurry; dive, leap, jump; descend, drop, fall, hurtle over.

311 circular motion *n* circulation, circularity; turn, excursion; circumvention, circumnavigation, circling; turning; coil, corkscrew, spiral; full circle, full turn, turn, circuit, lap.

v turn, bend, wheel, turn a circle, turn around, make a U-turn, put about, make a complete circle; circle, go around, circuit, circumnavigate; whisk, twirl, twist.

adj circuitous, roundabout; circular.

312 rotation *n* revolution, gyration, circulation, roll; spinning, pirouette, convolution; whir, whirl, eddy, vortex, whirlpool, maelstrom; cyclone, tornado.

v rotate, turn, spin, revolve, wheel, whirl, twirl, spin around; pivot, swivel, circle around.

adj rotating, rotary, gyratory, revolving.

313 evolution *n* evolvement, unfolding, development.

v evolve, unfold, unfurl, unroll, unwind, develop.

adj evolutionary, evolutional.

314 [motion to and fro] **oscillation** *n* vibration, pulsation, undulation; pulse, beat, *(informal)* vibes, ripple, wave; alternation, coming and going, ebb and flow, ups and downs, flux and reflux; fluctuation, vacillation, irresolution.

v oscillate, vibrate, vacillate, swing, fluctuate, vary; undulate, wave; pulsate, beat, throb, ripple; reel, quake, quiver, quaver, shake; roll, toss, pitch; flounder, stagger, totter.

adj oscillating; undulatory; pulsating.

adv to and fro, up and down, back and forth, seesaw, zigzag, in and out, from side to side.

315 [irregular motion] **agitation** *n* stir, ripple, tremor, shake, jog, jolt, jar, jerk, shock, quiver, quaver, twitter, flicker, flutter; disquiet, perturbation, commotion, turbulence, turmoil, tumult; hubbub, bustle, fuss, ado, racket, fits; spasm, throe,

throb, palpitation, convulsion, fit;
disturbance, disorder, restlessness,
hypertension; ferment, fermentation, ebullition, effervescence, hurly-
burly; tempest, storm, groundswell,
whirlpool, vortex; whirlwind, tornado, cyclone, twister.

v be agitated, shake, tremble,
quiver, quaver, quake, shiver, twitter, writhe, toss, shuffle, tumble,
stagger, bob, reel, sway; waggle,
wriggle, dance, prance, stumble,
shamble, flounder, totter, teeter,
flounce, flop; throb, pulsate, beat,
palpitate, go pit-a-pat; flutter,
flicker, bicker, bustle; ferment, effervesce, foam, boil, bubble, simmer; agitate, shake, convulse, toss,
tumble, bandy, flap, whisk, jerk,
hitch, jolt, joggle, jostle, buffet, hustle, disturb, stir, shake up, churn,
jounce, wallop, whip.

adj agitated, shaking, pulsating,
tremulous, convulsive, jerky, shaky,
throbbing.

adv by fits and starts; in convul-
sions, in fits.

Class III

Words Relating
to Matter

I. Matter in General

316 materiality *n* corporeality, substantiality, flesh and blood, physicality; matter, body, substance, brute
matter, physical elements, material;
object, article, thing, materials.

science of matter; physics, natural
philosophy, physical science, materialism.

materialist, physicist.

v materialize, embody, body in.

adj material, bodily, corporeal,
physical, somatic, sensible, tangible,
palpable, touchable, substantial, unspiritual, materialistic.

317 immateriality *n* incorporeality,
insubstantiality, spirituality, ineffa-
bility.

adj immaterial, incorporeal, unsubstantial, intangible, ineffable,
untouchable, bodiless, unreal, un-

earthly, spiritual, psychical, otherworldly.

318 world *n* creation, nature, universe, solar system, galaxy, globe,
earth, wide world, sphere, macrocosm; heavens, firmament, vault,
celestial spaces, space, sky; heavenly bodies, planets, asteroids, com-
ets, meteors, constellations.

adj worldly, mundane, terrestrial, earthly, sublunary; cosmic, celestial, heavenly, astral, solar, lunar.

adv in all creation, on the face of
the earth, under the sun, here below.

319 gravity *n* gravitation, weight,
heaviness, pull, pressure, load, burden.

v gravitate, weigh, pull, press,
encumber, load, be heavy.

adj weighty, heavy, heavy as
lead, ponderous, lumpish, cumbersome, burdensome, cumbrous, massive, unwieldy, like a ton of bricks.

320 levity *n* lightness, buoyancy, volatility; ferment, leaven, yeast.

v be light, float, swim, waft;
lighten, leaven.

adj light, subtle, airy, weightless,
ethereal, volatile, buoyant, feathery.

II. Inorganic Matter

321 density *n* solidity, solidness,
impenetrability, impermeability;
condensation, solidification, consolidation, concretion, coagulation,
petrification, hardening, crystallization, thickening; solid body, mass,
block, knot, lump, conglomerate.

v be dense; solidify, condense,
consolidate, coagulate, congeal, set,
cohere, crystallize, petrify, harden;
condense, compress, thicken.

adj dense, solid, compact, close,
thick, substantial, massive; impenetrable, impermeable, coherent, cohesive, indivisible, indissoluble,
insoluble.

322 thinness *n* rarity, tenuity; rarefac-
tion, expansion, dilation, inflation.

v thin, rarefy, expand, dilate, inflate.

adj thin, rare, fine, tenuous,

compressible, flimsy, slight, light; unsubstantial.

323 hardness *n* rigidity, firmness, inflexibility, temper; induration, petrification, ossification, crystallization.

v harden, stiffen, cement, petrify, temper, ossify.

adj hard, solid, firm, inflexible, rigid, resistant, adamantine, impenetrable, strong, hard as a rock, hard as nails, tough.

324 softness *n* pliability, flexibility, pliancy, malleability, ductility, tractility, plasticity, flaccidity, elasticity; mollification, softening.

v soften, mollify, mash, knead, temper, bend, yield, give, relent, relax.

adj soft, tender, supple, pliant, pliable, flexible, limber, plastic, ductile, tractile, tractable, plastic, malleable, moldable, impressible, elastic; flabby, limp, flimsy, flaccid, doughy, mushy, squishy, waxy, soft as butter.

325 elasticity *n* springiness, spring, resilience, resiliency, give.

v be elastic, spring, give, bend, stretch; spring back, recoil.

adj elastic, tensile, springy, resilient, buoyant, rubbery.

326 inelasticity *n* want of elasticity, flaccidity, limpness, softness, mushiness.

adj inelastic, flaccid, limp.

327 tenacity *n* toughness, strength, cohesiveness, cohesion; stubbornness, obstinacy, grit.

adj tenacious, cohesive, tough, strong, resistant, gristly, stringy, gummy, adhesive, sticky, viscous, glutinous; stubborn, obstinate.

328 brittleness *n* fragility, frailty, breakability.

v be brittle; break, crack, snap, split, shiver, splinter, crumble, burst, fly, fly to pieces, shatter, give way.

adj brittle, fragile, breakable, frangible, delicate, frail, splintery, crisp.

329 structure *n* organization, constitution, anatomy, frame, framework, mold, form, architecture, construction, texture; tissue, grain, web, surface; coarseness; fineness.

adj structural, organizational, anatomical, anatomic, architectural, textural; fine, delicate, subtle, gossamery, filmy; coarse, homespun, rough, woolly.

330 granularity *n* pulverulence, sandiness, graininess, friability; powder, dust, sand, grit, grain, particle, crumb, fine powder.

reduction to powder; pulverization, granulation, disintegration, abrasion, attenuation, filing.

tools for pulverization: mill, grater, rasp, file, mortar and pestle, grinder, grindstone.

v grind, pulverize, granulate, grate, scrape, file, abrade, rasp, pound, beat, crush, crumble, disintegrate.

adj granular, powdery, mealy, floury, branny, dusty, sandy, arenose, gritty, crumbly.

331 friction *n* attrition, rubbing, abrasion, elbow-grease.

v rub, scratch, scrape, scrub, fray, rasp, curry, scour, polish, rub out, erase, grind.

332 [absence or prevention of friction] **lubrication** *n* anointment, oiling, greasing, coating, lathering.

v lubricate, oil, grease, lather; anoint.

333 fluidity *n* liquidity, liquefaction, solubility, fluency.

v be fluid, flow, run, pour, stream; liquefy.

adj fluid, liquid, watery, serous, sappy, juicy, soluble; fluent, unstable.

334 gaseity *n* gaseousness, vaporousness, volatility.

adj gaseous, vaporous, airy, etheric, voluble, evaporable; flatulent, windy.

335 liquefaction *n* liquefying, deliquescence, melting, thawing, solubleness, dissolution.

v liquefy, melt, thaw, dissolve.

adj deliquescent, soluble, dissolvable, solvent.

336 vaporization *n* atomization, steaming, boiling, distillation, gasification, evaporation.

v vaporize, atomize, distill, evaporate, gasify, boil, steam.

adj vapory, vaporous, volatile, evaporable, gaseous.

337 water *n* liquid, serum, lymph, fluid, aqua.

v add water, water, wet, moisten, dip, immerse, submerge, plunge, douse, dunk, drown, soak, steep, wash, sprinkle, splash, souse, drench; dilute; deluge, inundate.

adj watery, aqueous, liquid, fluid, wet, moist, humid, soggy, sodden, rheumy, hydrous, juicy, lush, succulent; waterish, adulterated, transparent, thin, weak, tasteless, insipid, vapid, flat, feeble, dull.

338 air *n* atmosphere, stratosphere, the open air; blue sky, sky; weather, climate, clime; ventilation, current, breath of air, wind, breeze.

v air, ventilate, fan, aerate, freshen, refresh, cool.

adj airy, open, exposed, breezy, windy; flatulent; effervescent; atmospheric, aerial, ethereal, aeriform.

adv in the open air, out in the open, out of doors, in the wide open spaces, under the stars.

339 moisture *n* dampness, humidity, dankness, dew, wetness, condensation; perspiration.

v moisten, sponge, damp, bedew, wet, soak, saturate, sodden, sop, drench; perspire.

adj moist, damp, watery, humid, dank, dewy, muggy, juicy, wet; soggy, mushy, marshy, muddy.

340 dryness *n* drought, aridity; dessication, drainage, evaporation.

v dry, dry up, soak up, sponge, swab, wipe; drain, parch, evaporate.

adj dry, arid, parched, juiceless, sapless, dry as a bone.

341 ocean *n* sea, main, deep, brine, salt water, waters, high seas, waves, billows, great waters, tides.

adj oceanic, marine, maritime, seagoing, oceanographic.

342 land *n* earth, ground, dry land, mother earth, *terra firma*; continent, inlands, interior, shore, coast, terrain, dirt, soil, rock, chalk; real estate, lands, grounds, acres, acreage.

v land, alight, arrive, disembark, come ashore, go ashore, tie up, set foot on dry land.

adj earthy, terrestrial, earthly, alluvial, landed, territorial, continental.

adv ashore, on land, on dry land.

343 gulf, lake *n* bay, inlet, estuary, bayou, arm, fjord, firth, lagoon, cove, mouth, natural harbor, sound, straits.

lake, loch, lough, mere, tarn, basin, reservoir, lagoon, pond, pool.

344 plain *n* plateau, champaign, grassland, pasture, pasturage, meadow, flat, moor, heath, tundra, prairie, lowland, steppe, field, desert, basin, fields, grounds.

345 marsh *n* swamp, morass, moss, fen, bog, quagmire, slough, wash, mud.

adj marshy, swampy, boggy, quaggy, soft, muddy, sloppy, squashy.

346 island *n* isle, islet, atoll, reef, ait, key, bar, holm, ridge, eyot, archipelago.

adj insular, sea-girt.

347 [fluid in motion] stream *n* stream, etc. (of water) **348**; (of air) **249**. *v* flow, etc., **348**; blow, etc., **349**.

348 [water in motion] river *n* running water, jet, spurt, squirt, spout, splash, rush, gush, torrent; fall, cascade, inundation; deluge; rain, rainfall, storm; trickle, drizzle, shower; stream, course, flux, flow, flowing, current, tide, race; spring, rill, rivulet, stream, river, tributary; rapids, flood, whirlpool, maelstrom, vortex, eddy; wave, billow, surge, swell, ripple, surf, breaker, white caps, rough seas, rolling seas, choppy seas; irrigation, pump, hose.

v flow, run, gush, pour, spout, roll, jet, well issue; drop, drip, dribble, drizzle, trickle, stream, overflow, inundate, deluge, flow over, splash, swash; gurgle, murmur, babble, bubble, sputter, spurt, regurgitate; ooze, flow out, squeeze; rain, rain hard, rain cats and dogs, rain in torrents, rain in buckets; flow into, open into, drain into; pour, pour out, shower down, irrigate, drench, spill.

adj fluent, tidal, streamy, showery, rainy, trickly, drizzly, bubbly.

349 [air in motion] **wind** *n* draft, air, breath of air, puff, whiff, zephyr, drift, blow; fresh wind, stiff breeze, keen blast, trade wind, gust, blast, breeze, squall, gale, storm, tempest, hurricane, whirlwind, tornado, twister, cyclone, monsoon.

v blow, waft, blow hard, blow great guns, stream, gust, blast, storm; respire, breathe, pant, puff, gasp, wheeze, cough; fan, ventilate, inflate, pump, blow up.

adj windy, drafty, breezy, stormy, tempestuous, cyclonic.

350 [channel for the passage of water] **conduit** *n* channel, duct, aqueduct, canal, trough, gutter, dike, main, gully, moat, ditch, drain, sewer, culvert, sough, siphon, pipe, tube, hose, funnel, tunnel, artery, spout, floodgate, watergate, sluice, lock, valve.

351 [channel for the passage of air] **air-pipe** *n* tube, shaft, flue, chimney, funnel, vent, hole, windpipe, duct.

352 **semiliquidity** *n* viscosity, adhesiveness, stickiness, glutinosity, pastiness.

v thicken, mash, squash, churn, beat up, blend.

adj semiliquid, semifluid; milky, muddy, creamy, slushy, starchy, gummy, gluey, sticky, slimy, oozy, thick, succulent, viscous, viscid, glutinous, adhesive, clammy.

353 [mixture of air and water] **bubble, cloud** *n* bubble, foam, froth, head, lather, suds, spray, surf, yeast; effervescence, fermentation, bubbling, boiling, gurgling, foaming.

cloud, vapor, fog, mist, haze, steam; nebula, nebulosity, cloudiness, opacity, dimness.

v bubble, boil, foam, froth, gurgle, lather, effervesce, ferment, fizzle.

cloud, fog, mist, steam, shadow, darken, cast over, steam up.

adj bubbly, foamy, frothy; effervescent.

cloudy, foggy, misty, hazy, steamy.

354 **pulpiness** *n* pulp, paste, dough, curd; fleshiness, fattiness, sponginess.

v pulp, mash, squeeze, juice, squash.

adj pulpy, pasty, doughy, fleshy, meaty, fatty.

355 **unctuousness** *n* unctuosity, oiliness, greasiness, lubricity; lubrication, ointment, grease, oil, anointment.

v oil, grease, lubricate.

adj unctuous, oily, greasy, oleaginous, slippery, slimy, slick.

356 **oil** *n* fat, butter, cream, grease, tallow, suet, lard, dripping, blubber; soap, wax; petroleum, gasoline, kerosene, propane, naphtha; vegetable oil, salad oil, olive oil, linseed oil; ointment, unguent, liniment, salve, balm.

356a **resin** *n* rosin, gum, wax, amber, ambergris, bitumen, pitch, tar, asphalt; varnish, lacquer, shellac, mastic, sealing wax, putty.

v resin, rosin; varnish, shellac, lacquer, overlay.

adj resinous, gummy, waxy.

III. Organic Matter

357 **animate matter** *n* nature, natural world, animated nature, living beings, organisms, organic remains, animal life, plant life, fauna, flora; protoplasm, cell.

science of living beings: biology, natural history, zoology, botany, anatomy, physiology, organic chemistry.

naturalist, biologist, zoologist, botanist.

adj animate, organic.

358 **inanimate matter** *n* mineral world, mineral kingdom, inorganic matter, brute matter.

science of the mineral kingdom: mineralogy, geology, metallurgy.

adj inanimate, inorganic, mineral.

359 life *n* existence, being; animation, vigor, vivacity, vitality, energy, vital spark, vital flame, lifeblood, spirit, soul; respiration, breath, breath of life; nourishment, nutriment, staff of life.

v be alive, live, breathe, respire, exist, subsist; be born, come into the world, see the light; quicken, revive, come to life; give birth to, bring to life, vitalize; vivify, reanimate; keep alive, *(informal)* keep going, *(informal)* hang in there.

adj alive, live, vigorous, vivacious, vital, energetic, lively, alive and kicking, active.

360 death *n* decease, demise, expiration, passing, dissolution, departure, release, rest, quietus, fall; end, cessation, loss of life, extinction, dying, mortality, doom, finale, stop; last breath, final gasp, death rattle, death agonies, hand of death, dying day, *rigor mortis*; decay, fatality, natural causes, death blow.

v die, decease, pass away, pass on, perish, expire, depart, dissolve; cease, end, vanish, disappear; fail, subside, fade, sink, fall, decline, wither, decay; be taken, yield, give in, breathe one's last, end one's days, depart this life, be no more, drop off, pop off, drop dead, drop down dead, break one's neck, give up the ghost, shuffle off the mortal coil, go the way of all flesh, turn to dust, *(informal)* kick the bucket, *(informal)* go out like a light, *(informal)* croak.

adj dead, lifeless, extinct, defunct, late, gone, no more, dead and gone, dead as a door nail; deadly, fatal, lethal.

361 [destruction of life; violent death] **killing** *n* murder, homicide, assassination, slaughter, bloodshed, carnage, butchery, massacre, holocaust; suffocation, strangulation, garrote, hanging, electrocution, gassing, drawing and quartering; suicide, regicide, parricide, matricide, fratri-

cide, infanticide; death blow, finishing stroke, *coup de grace*, execution; suicide; slaughtering, hunting, coursing, shooting, fishing; butcher, slayer, murderer, executioner, assassin, cutthroat, thug, guerilla, saboteur, garroter.

v kill, put to death, murder, slaughter, butcher, massacre, execute, behead, decapitate, guillotine, dispatch, *(informal)* waste; *(informal)* wipe out, strangle, garrote, hang, throttle, choke, stifle, suffocate, smother, asphyxiate, drown, gas, electrocute, stab, bayonet, cut, cut to pieces, cut to ribbons, mutilate, run through, put to the sword, shoot, gun down, do away with, *(informal)* blow away; hunt, spear; cut off, nip in the bud, cut down, give no quarter, decimate; commit suicide, destroy oneself, blow one's brains out, put an end to oneself.

adj murderous, homicidal, bloodthirsty, bloody, gory; mortal, fatal, lethal, deadly, deathly; suicidal.

362 corpse *n* body, remains, carcass, corse, cadaver, empty vessel, bones, skeleton, relics, mortal remains, mortal coil, clay, dust, ashes, earth, carrion, fodder, food for worms, shade, ghost.

adj corpselike, cadaverous.

363 interment *n* burial, sepulture, entombment, inhumation; cremation; funeral, funeral rites, obsequies, wake; knell, death bell, dirge, elegy; shroud, winding sheet, grave clothes; coffin, shell, sarcophagous, urn, pall, bier, catafalque, hearse; grave, pit, sepulchre, tomb, vault, crypt, catacomb, mausoleum, cemetery, burial ground, mortuary, graveyard, charnel house, morgue; monument, gravestone, tombstone, headstone, *memento mori*; exhumation, disinterment, autopsy, post mortem examination.

v inter, bury, lay in the grave, lay to rest, lay in the ground, consign to the grave, entomb; lay out, mummify, embalm; cremate; exhume, disinter, unearth.

adj burial, funeral, funeral, mortuary, sepulchral, cinerary.

364 animality *n* corporality, animal life, living being, flesh, flesh and blood; physique, strength, vigor, vitality.

adj animalistic, bodily, corporeal, fleshly.

365 vegetation *n* vegetable life, growth, plant life.

adj vegetative; rank, dense, lush, fecund.

366 animal *n* animal kingdom, brute creation, fauna; beast, brute, creature, living thing, creeping thing, dumb animal; mammal, quadruped, bird, reptile, fish, crustacean, shellfish, mollusk, worm, insect; flocks and herds, wild animals, domestic animals, livestock, game, beasts of the field, fowls of the air.

adj animal, animalistic, zoological.

367 vegetable *n* vegetable kingdom, flora, plant life, flowerage, herbage, shrubbery, foliage, leafage, leaves, foliation, verdure, greens; tree, shrub, bush, creeper, herb, fruit, grass.

v vegetate, germinate, shoot, sprout, shoot up, grow, swell, spring up, develop, increase, flourish, blossom, bloom.

adj vegetable, vegetal, vegetative, leguminous, herbal, herbaceous, botanic, verdant.

368 [science of animals] **zoology** *n* morphology, zoography, embryology, anatomy; comparative anatomy, animal physiology, comparative physiology, anthropology, ornithology, icthyology, paleontology, entomology.

adj zoological.

369 [science of plants] **botany** *n* phytology, vegetable physiology, dendrology; flora, botanic garden.

adj botanical, herbal, horticultural.

370 [management of animals] **ranching** *n* breeding, raising; taming, domestication; veterinary science.

v ranch, raise, breed; tame, domesticate, train, housebreak; cage, bridle, restrain.

adj bred; tame, domestic, domesticated, housebroken.

371 [management of plants] **agriculture** *n* farming, cultivation, husbandry, tillage; agronomy, agrobiology, agrology, agronomics; gardening, horticulture, floriculture, landscaping, arboriculture; forestry.

v cultivate, till, till the soil, work the land, farm, garden, sow, seed, plant; reap, mow, cut; plow, plough, harrow, rake, weed, hoe, lop; garden, landscape.

adj agricultural, agrarian; arable, fertile.

372 mankind *n* human race, man, woman, humankind, human species, humanity, mortality, people, human being, person, personage, individual, creature, fellow creature, fellow man, mortal, body, soul, somebody, someone, one, party, head, hand, heart.

people, persons, folk, public, society, community, group, general public, society of men, civilization, commonwealth, commonweal, body politic, human community, population, millions, multitudes.

adj human, mortal, personal, individual; social, national, civic, public; cosmopolitan, humanitarian.

373 man *n* make, manhood, masculinity, he, him; gentleman, sir, mister, Mr., master, swain, fellow, chap, boy.

male animal: cock, drake, gander, dog, boar, stag, hart, buck, stallion, tomcat, billygoat, ram, bull, ox; gelding, steer.

adj male, masculine, manly.

374 woman *n* female; womanhood, femininity, she, her; lady, gentlewoman, madam, madame, miss, (informal) ma'am, Ms., Mrs., matron, girl.

female animal: hen, bitch, sow, doe, roe, mare, nannygoat, ewe, cow.

adj female, feminine, womanly.

375 sensibility *n* sensation, sensitiveness, feeling, responsiveness, impressibility; sensation, impression, touch; consciousness.

v be sensible, be sensitive to, feel, touch, perceive; render sensible, sharpen, cultivate, stir, excite, sensitize; cause sensation, impress, excite an impression, stir.

adj sensitive, sensible, sensuous; perceptive, sentient, responsive, susceptible, conscious, aware, alive, acute, sharp, keen, vivid, lively.

adv to the quick.

376 insensibility *n* lack of feeling, obtuseness, paralysis, numbness, anesthesia; insusceptibility, unresponsiveness, unconsciousness.

v be insensible; render insensible, blunt, pall, numb, benumb, paralyze, deaden, freeze, anesthetize; cloy, stuff, satiate, drown; stupefy, stun.

adj insensible, senseless, unsusceptible, unresponsive, insensitive, numb, hard, dead; dull, dense, thick, obtuse, unperceptive; anesthetic, paralytic.

377 pleasure *n* bodily pleasure, sensuality, sensuousness, physical gratification, sex, sexuality, sensual delight, ecstasy, orgasm, climax; titillation, teasing; comfort, ease, relish, delight, joy, luxury, luxuriousness, pleasure, lap of luxury.

v feel pleasure, receive pleasure, enjoy, relish, revel in, bask in, swim in, luxuriate, feast on, wallow in, gloat over, *(informal)* dig, *(informal)* get off on, *(informal)* be turned on, *(informal)* get into; give pleasure, *(informal)* turn on, thrill, excite.

adj pleasurable, sensual, sensuous, sexual, voluptuous, luxurious, ecstatic, orgasmic, climactic; agreeable, comfortable, cordial, delightful, joyful; palatable, sweet, tasty; fragrant; melodious, lovely.

adv in comfort, in ecstasy, on a bed of roses.

378 pain *n* suffering, dolor, ache, aching, smart, shoot, shooting, twinge, twitch, gripe, gnip, hurt, cut, sore, soreness, tenderness, discomfort, malaise, disease; spasm, cramp, crick, stitch, convulsion, throe,

throb, pang; torment, torture, rack, anguish, agony.

v feel pain, suffer, undergo pain, ache, smart, bleed, tingle, shoot, twinge, twitch, writhe, wince, hurt; inflict pain, hurt, chafe, sting, bite, gnaw, gripe, pinch, tweak, grate, gall, fret, prick, pierce, wring, convulse; torment, torture, wrack, agonize.

adj painful, dolorous, sore, tender, raw, uncomfortable; convulsive, torturous.

379 touch *n* contact, feeling, tactility, palpability, impact, feel, sensation; manipulation, handling, rubbing, massaging, fondling, fingering, kneading, stroking, brushing, grazing over.

v touch, feel, handle, finger, fondle, thumb, paw, grab, rub, massage, knead, stroke, brush, manipulate, run the fingers over, graze over.

adj tactual, tactile, palpable.

380 sensations of touch *n* itching, tickling, titillation, scratching, pricking, stinging.

v itch, tingle, creep, thrill, prick, scratch, sting.

adj itching; ticklish, scratchy, itchy.

381 numbness *n* physical insensibility, lack of feeling, deadness.

v benumb, anesthetize, deaden, dull, drug.

adj numb, dull, benumbed, insensible, unfeeling, frozen, drugged, dead, deadened, dulled.

382 heat *n* warmth, caloricity, caloric, temperature; glow, flush, warmth, intensity, ardor, passion, fever, fervor, zeal; fire, spark, flame, blaze.

v be hot, glow, flush, sweat, swelter, smoke, stew, simmer, seethe, boil, burn, broil, blaze, flame; smolder, parch, fume, pant; heat, warm, thaw, defrost; stimulate, stir, animate, arouse.

adj hot, warm, mild, genial, tepid, lukewarm, unfrozen; heated, torrid, sultry, burning, fiery; sunny, tropical, suffocating, stifling, sweltering, oppressive, reeking, baking; fiery, incandescent, ebullient, glowing, smoking, blazing, on fire, afire, in flames, aflame, ablaze; ardent, fervent, fervid, angry, furious, vehement, intense, excited, excitable, irascible, animated, violent, passionate.

383 cold *n* coldness, iciness, frigidity, chilliness, coolness.

v be cold, shiver, quake, shake, tremble, shudder, quiver; chill, freeze, refrigerate.

adj cold, chilly, chill, cool, frigid, gelid, frozen, freezing, bitter, bitter cold, numbing, nipping, cutting, shivering, bleak, raw, frostbitten, icy, glacial, frosty, wintry, hibernal, arctic, polar; impassionate, unemotional, apathetic, unresponsive, unsympathetic, stoical, unfeeling, indifferent, coldblooded, heartless, imperturbable; polite, formal, reserved, hostile; deliberate, depressing, dispiriting, disheartening.

adj coldly, bitterly.

384 calefaction *n* heating, melting, fusion, liquefaction, combustion; cauterization; calcination; incineration; cremation; carbonization.

v heat, warm, chafe; fire, set fire to, set on fire, kindle, light, ignite, rekindle; melt, thaw, fuse, liquefy; burn, inflame, roast, broil, toast, cook, fry, grill, singe, parch, bake, scorch; brand, cauterize, sear, burn in; boil, digest, stew, sauté, cook, scald, parboil, simmer; take fire, catch fire.

adj heated, warmed, fired, burnt, scorched; molten; flammable, combustible, volcanic.

385 refrigeration *n* cooling, congelation, glaciation, icing; solidification, hardening.

v refrigerate, keep cold, chill, ice, congeal, freeze; cool, fan, refresh; benumb, starve, pinch, nip, cut, pierce, bite; quench, put out, stamp out, extinguish.

adj cooled, frozen, chilled; incombustible, inflammable, fireproof.

386 furnace *n* oven, stove, range; hearth, heater, kiln, oil burner,

space heater, blast furnace, forge, fire place, fiery furnace.

387 refrigerator *n* ice box, fridge, ice chest, frigidaire, cold storage, freezer, ice house.

388 fuel *n* firing, combustible; coal, hard coal, anthracite, bituminous coal, soft coal, carbon, coke, charcoal; wood, firewood, kindling, brushwood, log, cinder, ember, ash; turf, peat, fuel, oil, fossil fuel, petroleum, gasoline, kerosene; gas, natural gas, propane; electricity; unclear power; solar energy; waterpower, windpower.

v fuel, feed, stoke, fire; power.

adj carbonaceous; combustible, flammable, burnable.

389 thermometer *n* thermometograph, thermoscope, thermostat, telethermometer, pyrometer, calorimeter, glass, mercury.

390 taste *n* flavor, savor, sensation, gusto, relish; smack, smatch, tang, aftertaste; morsel, bit, sip.

v taste, flavor, savor, smatch, smack; tickle the palate, tickle the tastebuds; smack the lips.

adj tasty, savory, flavory, flavorful, flavored; palatable, digestible, *(informal)* edible.

391 tastelessness *n* insipidity; blandness, flatness, unsavoriness.

v be tasteless.

adj tasteless, insipid, bland, flat, weak, mild, vapid, wishy-washy, *(informal)* plastic, pasty.

392 pungency *n* piquancy, poignancy, tang, bite, nip, sharpness, acridity, bitterness, hotness, sourness, unsavoriness.

v be pungent; make pungent, season, spice, salt, pepper, pickle, brine, devil, smoke, curry.

adj pungent, strong, full-flavored, seasoned, highly seasoned, spiced; sharp, biting, nippy, acrid, bitter, sour, stinging, spicy, salty, peppery, piquant, hot; unsavory.

393 condiment *n* seasoning, flavoring, sauce, spice, relish; salt, pepper.

v season.

394 savoriness n flavor, flavorfulness, taste, tastiness, relish, piquancy, zest, tang, delectability, palatability.

v be savory, tickle the palate, taste good, taste great; savor, enjoy, appreciate, relish, like, taste.

adj savory, good, tasty, palatable, nice, dainty, delectable, flavorful, appetizing, delicate, delicious, exquisite, rich, luscious, full-flavored, pungent, ambrosial.

395 unsavoriness n tastelessness, flavorlessness, blandness; acridness, sourness.

v be unsavory, be unpalatable, taste bad, sicken, disgust, pall, nauseate, turn the stomach, make one sick.

adj unsavory, tasteless, flavorless, bland, flat; bad tasting, illflavored, acrid, bitter, sour, unpalatable, inedible, offensive, repulsive, nasty, vile, sickening, nauseous, loathsome, unpleasant, awful.

396 sweetness n sugariness, saccharinity, syrupiness, stickiness.

v sweeten, sugar, candy.

adj sweet, sugary, syrupy, honeyed, saccharine, candied, sticky gooey, luscious, lush, cloying; sweetened.

397 sourness n acridity, tartness, sharpness, vinegariness, acerbity, acidity.

v sour, acidify, acerbate, curdle, acidulate, ferment, spoil.

adj sour, acid, bitter, tart, sharp, vinegary, acidulous, astringent, acerbic, acrid; fermented, rancid, bad, spoiled, turned, curdled, gone bad; styptic, hard, rough.

398 odor n smell, scent; effluvium, exhalation, emanation; fume, essence, redolence.

v have an odor, smell, smell of, give out a smell; smell, scent, sniff, snuff, inhale.

adj odorous, odoriferous, smelly, strong smelling, redolent, pungent.

399 inodorousness n absence of smell, odorlessness.

v be inodorous, not smell, have no odor, be odorless.

adj odorless, scentless, unsmelling.

400 fragrance n aroma, redolence, perfume, sweet smell, sweet scent, smell.

v be fragrant, smell sweet, have a perfume, scent, perfume.

adj fragrant, aromatic, redolent, spicy, scented, perfumed, sweet scented, sweet smelling, odoriferous, odorific.

401 fetor n bad smell, bad odor, foul smell, offensive smell, stink, stench, fume, foulness, fetidness, rancidity, rankness, fustiness, mustiness.

v have a bad smell, smell bad, smell rotten, smell, stink, reek.

adj fetid, strong smelling, bad, strong, fulsome, offensive, rank, rancid, noisome, mephitic, miasmic, musty, fusty, foul, rotten, putrid, reeking, stinking, stinky, suffocating, nauseating, nauseous, (informal) gross.

402 sound n noise, tone, pitch, sound vibrations, strain, sonority, sonorousness, twang, intonation, cadence; audibility, resonance, voice.

science of sound: acoustics, phonology, phonetics, electronic sound, reproduction.

v sound, make a noise; give out sound, emit sound; resound, echo.

adj sounding, sonorous, resonant, audible, distinct.

403 silence n stillness, quiet, peace, hush, lull, quiescence, dead silence; muteness, speechlessness, taciturnity.

v silence, still, hush, stifle, muffle, stop, muzzle, gag; be silent, hold one's tongue, shut up, keep quiet, be still.

adj silent, quiet, still calm, noiseless, soundless, hushed, quiescent; mute, speechless, taciturn; solemn, soft, deathlike, awful, silent as the grave.

adv silently.

404 loudness n loud noise, power, resonance, thunderousness, roaring, vociferousness, clamorousness; din, clang, clangor, clamor, noise, roar, uproar, hubbub, boom, racket, outcry; blast, peal, swell, flourish of trumpets; boom; thunder, explosion.

v be loud, peal, swell, clang, boom, thunder, fulminate, roar, resound, bellow, scream, holler, shout; ring in the ears, pierce the ears, split the eardrums, stun, deafen; shake, awake.

adj loud, noisy, vociferous, resounding, clamorous, deafening, stentorian, boisterous, tumultuous, sonorous, deep, full, powerful, thundering, ear-splitting, piercing, uproarious, obstreperous, shrill, sharp.

adv loudly, noisily, at the top of one's voice, at the top of one's lungs, aloud.

405 faintness *n* faint sound, whisper, breath, undertone, murmur, hum; inaudibility; hoarseness.

v whisper, breathe, murmur, hum, mutter, speak softly, speak in low tones.

adj faint, whispered, indistinct, dim, inaudible, barely audible, low, stifled, muffled, murmured, muted; gentle, soft, languid, floating, flowing; hoarse, husky.

406 [sudden and violent sounds] snap *n* rap, thud, burst, explosion, detonation, discharge, firing, salvo, pop, bang, blast.

v rap, snap, tap, knock, click, clash, crack, crackle, crash, beat.

407 [repeated and protracted sounds] roll *n* drumming, tapping, rumbling, grumbling; dingdong, whirring, droning; ratatat, rubadub, pitapat; quaver, quiver, clutter, racket; peal of bells; reverberation.

v roll, drum, rumble, grumble, rattle, clatter, patter, clack; hum, trill, shake; chime, peal, toll; tick, beat.

408 resonance *n* ring, ringing, chime, clang, clangor, boom, roll, roar, rumble, thunder, vibrato, timbre, twang, vibration, reverberation, tintinnabulation, booming, quaver, ding-dong, echoing, sonorousness.

v resound, reverberate, re-echo; ring, jingle, chink, clink; gurgle, echo, ring in the ear.

adj resonant, resounding, reverberant, reverberating; deep-toned, deep-sounding.

408a nonresonance *n* dead sound, thud, thump, muffled, drums, cracked bell; damper, mute, muffler.

v sound dead, thud, thump; muffle, dampen, mute.

adj nonresonant, dampened, muted, muffled, deadened; dead.

409 [hissing sounds] sibilation *n* hissing, wheezing, buzzing, zipping, whooshing; high note.

v hiss, buzz, whiz, wheeze, whoosh, zip, rustle, whistle, fizzle; squash, sneeze.

adj sibilant; hissing, wheezy.

410 [harsh sounds] stridency *n* discord, dissonance, harshness, raucousness, atonality, clashing, grinding, grating, rasping, sharpness, creaking, shrillness.

v creak, grate, jar, jangle, clank, clink, grid, grate; scream, yelp.

adj strident, sharp, high, acute, shrill, atonal, unharmonious, unmusical, dissonant, discordant, cacophonous; piercing, ear-piercing, cracked; creaking, harsh, coarse, hoarse, rough, gruff, grating, jarring, guttural, squawking, acute, scratching, croaking, rasping, sour, clashing.

411 cry *n* shout, scream, yell, shriek, roar, howl, wail; exclamation, outcry, clamor, vociferation; hubbub, hullabaloo, chorus, hue and cry; entreaty, appeal, solicitation, plea, plaint, prayer, crying, weeping, wailing, sobbing, lament, whimper, whimpering, tears, moaning.

v cry, roar, shout, bawl, brawl, hoop, whoop, yell, bellow, howl, scream, screech, shriek, squeak, squeal, whine, whimper, wail, weep, sob, moan, lament; cheer, hoot; grumble, groan, complain; vociferate, raise one's voice, sing out, cry out, yell out, exclaim, holler, shout at the top of one's lungs.

adj crying, clamorous; vociferous; solicitous; stentorian.

412 [animal sounds] **ululation** n howling, crying, belling, screeching, singing, growling, purring.

v cry, roar, bellow, bark, yelp, yap, growl, snarl, howl, bay, grunt, snort, neigh, bray, mew, purr, caterwaul, bleat, low, moo, squeak, oink, baa, crow, croak, screech, caw, coo, gobble, quack, cackle, gaggle, chuck, cluck, clack, chirp, chirrup, twitter, cuckoo, hum, buzz, hiss, blatter.

413 **melody, concord** n melodiousness, tunefulness, sweet sounds, mellifluence, musicalness, euphony; timbre, tone color, pitch; tune song, aria, theme, measure, plainsong, canticle, strain, lay.

harmony, harmoniousness; rhythm, meter; symphony, euphony, consonance, attunement, modulation, syncopation; counterpoint, polyphony; concordance, pleasing combination.

v harmonize, chime, symphonize, blend; tune, accord.

adj melodious, musical, tuneful, melodic, lyrical, euphonious, singing, ringing, sweet-sounding, euphonic, mellifluous, dulcet, mellow, clear, sweet, rich, soft, silvery, agreeable, pleasing.

concordant, harmonious, agreeing, symphonious, suiting, congenial, blending, synchronized, consistent, in rapport, in unison, confluent, conjoined, symmetrical, proportionate, consonant, compatible.

414 **discord** n dissonance, atonality; harshness; racket, noise, inharmoniousness.

v be discordant; jar, grate.

adj discordant, dissonant, atonal, harsh; out of tune, tuneless, unmelodious, inharmonious, unmusical; jarring, grating, cacophonous, screeching.

415 **music** n sweet sounds, pleasing sounds, harmonious sounds, melody, song, tune, strain, air, harmony; classical music, popular music, folk music, jazz, electronic music; orchestral music, instrumental music, symphonic music, chamber music; ragtime, reggae, swing, bebop, bop,

barrelhouse, rock; pop music, vocal music, choral music, solo, duet, duo, sonata, trio, quartet, quintet, sextet, septet, octet.

v make music, perform; compose.

adj musical, lyrical; instrumental, orchestral, symphonic, vocal, choral, operatic.

416 **musician** [performance of music] n artist, performer, concert artist, player, soloist, instrumentalist, vocalist, accompanist, singer, minstrel; symphony orchestra, orchestra, chamber orchestra, band, rock and roll band, group, combo, ensemble, chamber group, quartet, trio; chorus, choir, vocal group.

v make music, play, perform, strike up, concertize, execute, accompany, present the music, solo, improvise, play the notes; sing, croon, warble, vocalize, spin a melody.

adj musical, instrumental, vocal, choral, operatic; lyrical, harmonious, brilliant, sharp, incisive.

417 **musical instruments** n orchestra, band, brass band, marching band, military band, ensemble, group; strings, plucked instruments, bowed instruments, hammered instruments; woodwinds, winds, tubed instruments, reed instruments, brass instruments; percussion; synthesizer.

418 **hearing** n audition, auscultation, listening, perception, audibility, ear; regarding, attending, heeding.

hearer, auditor, listener; eavesdropper.

v hear, listen, attend, lend an ear, bend an ear, (informal) tune in, give a hearing to, give audience to, prick up one's ears, be all ears; overhear, eavesdrop; heed, regard.

adj hearing, auditory, auricular.

419 **deafness** n hardness of hearing, inaudibility.

v be deaf, not hear; turn a deaf ear to, plug up one's ears; deafen, stun, split the eardrums.

adj deaf, stone-deaf, hard of

hearing; deafened, stunned; unheeding, inattentive.

420 light n ray, beam, stream, gleam, streak; sunbeam, moonbeam, aurora, dawn, sunrise, day-break, day, daylight, light of day, sunshine, broad daylight, glow, glint, glimmering; sun, moon; flush, halo, glory, aureole; spark, scintilla, scintillation, flash, blaze, coruscation; flame, lightening, flare; luster, sheen, shimmer, reflection, refraction; brightness, brilliancy, splendor, effulgence, radiance, illumination, radiation, luminosity, lucidity.

　　science of light: optics, photography, radioactivity.

　　v shine, glow, glitter, glisten, gleam, beam, flare, flare up, glare, flash, glimmer, shimmer, flicker, sparkle, scintillate, coruscate, flash, blaze; light, reflect, dazzle, bedazzle, daze, radiate; lighten, enlighten, light, irradiate, shed light upon, cast light upon, illuminate, illumine, kindle, fire.

　　adj luminous, lucent; light, bright, vivid, splendid, resplendent, lustrous, shiny, radiant; sheeny, glossy, glassy, sunny, burnished; cloudless, clear, unclouded; effulgent, blazing, ablaze, phosphorescent, aglow; iridescent.

421 darkness n blackness; obscurity, doom, murkiness, murk; duskiness, dusk, dimness; night, midnight, dead of night; shade, shadow, umbra, penumbra; obscuration, adumbration, extinction, eclipse, total eclipse.

　　v be dark; darken, obscure, shade, dim, shadow, overcast, cloud, becloud; extinguish, put out, blow out, snuff out.

　　adj dark, obscure, black, pitch black, nocturnal, overcast, cloudy, darkened; dingy, lurid, murky, gloomy, oppressive; shadowy, shady, umbrageous.

422 dimness n duskiness, shadowiness, gloominess, cloudiness, mist, mistiness, haze, haziness, fogginess, paleness, shade, nebulosity, gray, grayness.

　　v be dim, grow dim, darken, obscure, adumbrate, becloud, cloud, shadow, shade, eclipse, cloud over; blur, dull, fade, pale; glimmer, twinkle, flutter, flicker, waver.

　　adj dim, dull, dingy, lackluster, darkish, darkened, gray, dark, faint, pale, cloudy, misty, murky, overcast, nebulous, shadowy, umbrageous, blurry, hazy, opaque, foggy, bleary, gloomy, lurid, leaden.

423 [source of light] **luminary** n natural light, sun, moon, stars, flame, fire, spark, phosphorescence; artificial light, lamp, gas lamp, oil lamp, kerosene lamp, electric light, lantern, torch, candle, taper, light bulb.

　　v light, illuminate.

　　adj self-luminous; phosphorescent, radiant.

424 shade n cover, awning, umbrella, parasol, sunshade; screen, curtain, shutter, blind, gauze, veil, mantle, mask, sunglasses, (informal) shades; cloud, mist, fog, shadow.

　　v shade, veil, cover, screen, curtain, veil, draw a curtain, pull the shade, cast a shadow.

　　adj shady, shadowy, cloudy.

425 transparency n transparence, translucence, diaphanousness, clearness, lucidity, limpidity, thinness, sheerness, gauziness, flimsiness.

　　v be transparent, transmit light.

　　adj transparent, pellucid, lucid, diaphanous, translucent limpid, clear, crystalline, see-through, sheer, gauzy, flimsy.

426 opacity n opaqueness, darkness, cloudiness, filminess, haziness, mistiness, nontransparency.

　　v be opaque, obstruct the passage of light.

　　adj opaque, impervious to light, impenetrable to light, dim, filmy, thick, smoky, misty, smoggy, shady, murky, cloudy, hazy, obscure, clouded, foggy, unclear, frosted, nontransparent, nontranslucent.

427 semitransparency n opalescence, milkiness, pearliness; film, mist.

　　v let in partial light.

　　adj semitransparent, semipellucid, semiopaque, opalescent, pearly, nacreous, milky.

428 color *n* hue, tint, tinge, dye, complexion, shade, tincture, cast, coloration, tone, key; primary color, secondary color, complementary color; coloring; spectrum, prism, spectroscope; pigment, paint, dye, wash, stain.

v color, dye, tinge, stain, tint, paint, wash; illuminate, emblazon.

adj colored, dyed, tinted; prismatic, chromatic; bright, vivid, intense, deep, rich, gorgeous; fresh, unfaded; gaudy, florid, garish, showy, flashy, glaring; mellow, harmonious, pearly, sweet, delicate, tender, refined; dull, gray.

429 [absence of color] **colorlessness** *n* neutral tint, black and white, chiaroscuro, monochrome, etiolation, pallor, paleness, discoloration.

v lose color, fade, turn pale, become colorless, pale; deprive of color, bleach, wash out, blanch, tarnish, etiolate, tone down, whiten.

adj uncolored, colorless, hueless, pale, pallid, faint, dull, dun, wan, sallow, dingy, ashy, gray, ashen, lackluster; discolored; light-colored; fair, blond, white.

430 whiteness *n* milkiness, frostiness, silveriness, pearliness, etiolation, albification, decoloration, colorlessness; albinism.

v whiten, bleach, blanch, etiolate, whitewash.

adj white, snowy, frosted, snow-white, milk-white, milky, chalky, pearly, ivory, silver, silvery, opaline, whitish, albinistic, etiolated; bleached, blanched, fair, light, wan, pallid, pale, lackluster, colorless, anemic, sallow, faint.

431 blackness *n* darkness, swarthiness, lividness; ink, ebony, coal, charcoal, pitch; obscurity.

v black, blacken, darken; blot, smutch, smut, smirch.

adj black, sable, somber, livid, dark, inky, ebony, pitchy, swarthy, sooty, dingy, dusky, murky; jet-black, pitch-black, black as coal,

coal-black, kohl-black, black as night.

432 gray *n* grayness, neutral tint, silver, salt and pepper, dove color.

adj gray, iron-gray, silver, silvery, silverish, grayish, dun, drab, ashy, ashen, dove-colored, dapple-gray, grizzly, grizzled, hoary.

433 brown *n* brownness, beige, khaki.

adj brown, bay, dapple, auburn, nutbrown, chocolate, chestnut, cinnamon, russet, tawny, tan, brunette, mahogany, khaki, beige, ochre, sepia, hazel, brownish, coffee, cocoa, rust, roan, sorrel.

434 red *n* redness; blush, color.

v redden, blush, flush, get red in the face, turn color.

adj red, reddish, scarlet, crimson, blood red, bloody, cherry-colored, vermilion, carmine, maroon, pink, hotpink, rosy, ruby, salmon, wine-colored; red-faced, blushing, embarrassed; red as beet, red as a lobster, flushed, burning, fuming, flaming, inflamed; ruddy, glowing, blooming, warm, hot.

435 green *n* greenness, verdure, blue and yellow.

adj green, greenish, verdant, olive, pea-green, emerald, apple, Kelly green, blue-green, aquamarine, sea-green; grassy, verdurous; fresh, new, recent, young, innocent, naive, raw, unseasoned, immature, inexperienced, ignorant; sickly, wan, pale, livid; jealous, envious.

436 yellow *n* yellowness, jaundice.

v yellow, age, turn color, dry up.

adj yellow, yellowish, gold, golden, ocher, lemon, citrine, saffron, aureate, creamy, straw-colored, flaxen, blond, tawny, sallow; sordid, cheap; cowardly, *(informal)* chicken, craven, lily-livered, contemptible, despicable, mean, cringing, groveling; jaundiced.

437 purple *n* blue and red.

adj purple, purplish, lavender, lilac, magenta, orchid, violet, plum-colored, mauve.

438 blue *n* blueness.

adj blue, bluish, azure, marine

blue, navy, aquamarine, greenish blue; sapphire, turquoise, cobalt, baby blue; depressed, down in the dumps, *(informal)* in the pits. *(informal)* down, low.

439 orange *n* red and yellow; flame.

adj orange, orangy, orangish, brass, copper, apricot, tangerine, gold, flame-colored.

440 variegation *n* striation, spottiness, streakiness, iridescence, play of colors.

v variegate, diversify, streak, stripe, checker, speckle, bespeckle, fleck, dapple; dot, striate, tattoo, inlay; embroider, quilt.

adj variegated, multi-colored, many-colored, kaleidoscopic; iridescent, prismatic, opaline, nacreous, pearly; pied, piebald, mottled; dappled, salt ad pepper, marbled, flecked, speckled, spotty, studded, freckled, flecky, spotted, diversified; striped, veined, lined, striated, streaked, brindled, banded, checked, checkered, plaid, mosaic, inlaid.

441 vision *n* sight, optics, eyesight; view, look, glance, ken, glimpse, peep, peek, gaze, stare, leer; contemplation, regard, survey; point of view, outlook, viewpoint, perspective, standpoint; perspicacity, discernment, perception, penetration.

v see, behold, discern, perceive, have in sight, descry, sight, make out, discover, distinguish, recognize spy, espy, catch a glimpse of, command a view of, witness, envision, contemplate; look, view, eye, survey, scan, inspect, run the eye over, glance around; observe, watch, watch for, peep, peer, peek, pry, take a peep, leer, ogle, glare.

adj visual, ocular, optic; clearsighted, eagle-eyed, discerning; visionary, farsighted.

adv on sight, at first sight, at a glance.

442 blindness *n* sightlessness; cataract; ignorance.

v be blind, not see; grope in the dark; blind, hoodwink, dazzle; screen, hide, mask.

adj blind, eyeless, sightless, un-

seeing, dark, purblind, stone-blind; dimsighted, undiscerning, ignorant.

adv blindly, blindfold, darkly.

443 [imperfect vision] **dimsightedness** *n* nearsightedness, farsightedness, purblindness, prebyopia, myopia, astigmatism, color blindness, cataract, ophthalmia; squint, cross-eye, strabismus, lazy eye, cockeye, swivel eye, goggle eyes.

fallacies of vision: refraction, distortion, illusion, mirage, phantasm, vision, specter, apparition, ghost; mirror, lens.

v be dimsighted, see double, wink, blink, squint, look askance, screw up the eyes.

adj dimsighted, purblind, myopic, astigmatic, nearsighted, farsighted, colorblind; blear-eyed, goggle-eyed, cockeyed, crosseyed.

444 spectator *n* beholder, observer, looker-on, onlooker, witness, eyewitness, bystander, passerby; sightseer, audience, crowd; spy, sentinel.

v witness, behold, look on.

445 optical instruments *n* lens, magnifying glass, microscope; spectacles, monocle, eyeglasses, glasses, contact lens, goggles, pince-nez; telescope, lorgnette, binoculars, spyglass, opera glasses; mirror, looking glass, reflector; prism, kaleidoscope, stereoscope.

446 visibility *n* perceptibility, discernibleness, distinctness, clearness, clarity, perceivability, conspicuousness, definition, sharp outline; appearance, manifestation.

v be visible, appear, open to the view, present itself, show itself, reveal itself, peep up, show up, turn up, start up, pop up, crop up; glimmer, loom; burst forth, burst upon the view, come into sight, come into view, come forth, come forward, attract attention.

adj visible, perceptible, discernible, perceivable, apparent, obvious, manifest, plain, clear, distinct, definite, well-defined, outlined, well-marked; recognizable, palpable, glaring, conspicuous, in full view, in full sight, in front of one's nose, under one's nose, before one's eyes.

447 invisibility n indistinctness, imperceptibility, invisibleness, indefiniteness; mystery, obscurity, delitescence, haziness, cloudiness; concealment; latency.

v be invisible; be hidden; escape notice; render invisible, conceal, hide.

adj invisible, imperceptible; not in sight, out of sight, out of view, unseen; inconspicuous, covert; dim, faint, mysterious, dark, obscure, confused, indistinct, indistinguishable, shadowy, indefinite, undefined, unmarked, blurry, blurred, unfocused, out of focus, misty, veiled; concealed, hidden.

448 appearance n phenomenon, sight, show, scene, view; prospect, vista, perspective, lookout, outlook, bird's-eye view, scenery, landscape, picture, tableau; display, exposure; pageant, spectacle; aspect, phase, seeming, shape, form, manifestation, guise, look, complexion, color, image, mien, air, cast, carriage, comportment, demeanor; presence; feature, trait, lines, outline, contour, face, countenance, physiognomy, visage, profile, outsides.

v appear, be visible, seem, look, show, present; figure, cut a figure; present to the view.

adj apparent, seeming, ostensible.

adv apparently, to all appearance, ostensibly, seemingly, on the face of it, at first sight, to the eye.

449 disappearance n evanescence, eclipse; departure, exit; loss.

v disappear, vanish, dissolve, melt, melt away, fade, pass, pass out, go, depart, leave no trace, be gone.

adj disappearing, evanescent; departed, left; missing, lost, vanished.

Class IV
Intellectual Faculties
I. Formation of Ideas

450 intellect n rationality, mind, understanding, reason, faculties, judgment, sense, common sense, wits, brains, (informal) smarts; brain, head, pate, (informal) noodle, skull, (informal) upstairs.

v intellectualize, reason, understand, realize, ruminate; note, notice, mark, be aware of, take cognizance of.

adj intellectual, mental, cerebral, rational, sensical, commonsensical.

450a absence of intellect n want of intellect; inanity, imbecility, brutishness, brute instinct.

adj unintellectual, unintelligent, unrational, nonrational, emptyheaded.

451 thought n abstraction, concept, conception, opinion, judgment, belief, idea, notion, tenet, conviction, speculation, consideration, contemplation; meditation, pondering, reflection, musing, cogitation, thinking; intention, design, purpose, intent; anticipation, expectation; consideration, attention, care, regard; trifle, mote.

v think, cogitate, meditate, reflect, muse, ponder, ruminate, contemplate; consider, regard, suppose, look upon, judge, esteem, deem, count, account; bear in mind, recollect, recall, remember; intend, mean, design, purpose; believe, suppose; anticipate, expect.

adj thoughtful, contemplative, meditative, reflective, pensive, deliberate; lost in thought, absorbed, engrossed in; careful, heedful, mindful, regardful, considerate, attentive; discreet, prudent, wary, cautious, circumspect.

452 absence of thought n incogitancy, vacancy of mind, thoughtlessness, fatuity, vacuity, emptiness; inattention.

v not think, make the mind a blank, *(informal)* turn off the brain, *(informal)* tune out.

adj vacant, unoccupied, empty; unthinking; inattentive, absent, *(informal)* turned off, *(informal)* tuned out; thoughtless, inconsiderate, unmindful, unheedful, imprudent; unreflective.

453 idea *n* thought, conception, theory, notion; observation, impression, apprehension, perception, brainstorm, brainchild, fancy, *(informal)* flash; opinion, view, belief, sentiment, judgment, supposition; plan, object, objective, aim.

adj ideational.

454 topic *n* subject, theme, thesis, subject-matter, food for thought; business, affair, argument.

adj topical, thematic.

adv under consideration, in question.

455 curiosity *n* interest, inquisitiveness, inquiring mind, thirst for knowledge; spying, prying, meddlesomeness.

spy, eavesdropper, gossip.

v be curious, take an interest in, stare, gape, spy, pry.

adj curious, inquisitive, inquiring, prying, spying, peeping, meddlesome, interested.

456 incuriosity *n* lack of interest, incuriousness, indifference, unconcern.

v have no curiosity, take no interest in.

adj incurious, uninquisitive, uninquiring, uninterested, indifferent, impassive, bored, apathetic.

457 attention *n* attending to, attentiveness, intentiveness, care, consideration, observation, heed, regard, mindfulness, notice, watchfulness, alertness; study, scrutiny; civility, courtesy, respect, politeness.

v be attentive, attend, observe, look, see, notice, remark, regard, pay attention, heed; examine, study, scrutinize.

adj attentive, observant, mindful, heedful, thoughtful, alive, alert, awake, on the watch, wary, circum-

spectful, watchful, careful; polite, courteous, respectful, deferential.

458 inattention *n* inattentiveness, inconsideration, heedlessness, unmindfulness, disregard, unconcern.

v be inattentive, overlook, disregard, pay no attention to, gloss over.

adj inattentive, unobservant, unmindful, unheeding, thoughtless, blind to, deaf to, napping, asleep, lost.

459 care *n* heed, caution, prudence, pains, anxiety, regard, attention, vigilance, carefulness, solicitude, circumspection, alertness, watchfulness, wakefulness; accuracy, exactness.

v be careful, take care.

adj careful, cautious, circumspect, watchful, vigilant, guarded, wary, prudent, tactful; painstaking, meticulous, discerning, exact, thorough, concerned, scrupulous, particular, finical, conscientious, attentive, heedful, thoughtful.

460 neglect *n* disregard, dereliction, negligence, remissness, carelessness, failure, omission, default, inattention, heedlessness, recklessness.

v neglect, disregard, ignore, slight, overlook, omit, be remiss, be negligent.

adj neglectful, disregardful, remiss, careless, negligent, unmindful, inattentive, indifferent, heedless, inconsiderate, thoughtless, imprudent; unwary, unguarded; neglecting, neglected, unheeded, uncared for, unobserved, unnoticed, unattended to.

461 inquiry *n* investigation, examination, study, scrutiny, exploration, research, search, pursuit; inquiring, questioning, interrogation; query, question.

inquirer, investigator, inquisitor, inspector.

v inquire, ask, question, interrogate, query, investigate, examine, seek, search, look for, study, consider.

adj inquiring, inquisitive, curious, scrutinizing, questioning, exploring; inquisitorial, exploratory, interrogative.

462 answer n reply, response, retort, rejoinder; discovery, solution; rationale.

v answer, reply, respond, rebut, retort, rejoin; explain, interpret, discover, solve; satisfy, set at rest, atone for.

adj responsive; answerable, discoverable, soluble.

463 experiment n test, trial, examination, proof, assay, procedure; experimentation, research, investigation, analysis.

experimenter, analyzer, adventurer.

v experiment, try, test, examine, analyze, prove, assay, essay.

adj experimental, probative, analytic.

464 comparison n collation, association, relating, likening, correlation, comparative relation, setting side by side, juxtaposition.

v compare, collate, confront, place side by side, pit one against another, juxtapose, relate, correlate.

adj comparative, metaphorical, compared with; comparable.

465 discrimination n distinction, differentiation, diagnosis; appreciation, estimation, discernment, critique, judgment; nicety, refinement, taste.

v discriminate, distinguish, set apart, differentiate.

adj discriminating, critical, distinguishing, discriminative, discriminatory, choosy, picky; discerning, perceptive; tasteful, refined.

465a indiscrimination n indistinction, indistinctness, lack of discernment.

v be indiscriminate, not discriminate, confound, confuse.

adj indiscriminate, miscellaneous, undiscriminating.

466 measurement n survey, valuation, appraisement, assessment, estimate, estimation, reckoning, gauging; measure, standard, rule, gauge, scale.

v measure, survey, assess, rate, value, appraise, estimate.

adj measurable.

467 [on one side] **evidence** n facts, indication, sign, signal; ground, grounds, proof, testimony; information, deposition, affidavit, exhibit, citation, reference, confirmation, corroboration.

v be evident, evince, show, tell, cite, signal, indicate, imply, argue, bespeak; give evidence, testify, depose, witness.

adj evident, evidential, indicative, inferential, referential, corroborative, confirmatory.

468 counter-evidence n disproof, refutation, rebuttal, conflicting evidence, negation.

v rebut, refute, check, weaken, contravene, contradict, deny.

adj countervailing, contradictory, conflicting, unsupportive, uncorroborative.

469 qualification n modification, limitation, mitigation, narrowing, restriction, coloring, allowance, consideration, extenuation, extenuating, circumstances, condition, proviso, exception.

v qualify, modify, limit, mitigate, restrain, narrow, restrict, color, allow, allow for, make allowance for, consider, extenuate, except, make an exception, take into account, take into consideration.

adj qualified, qualifying, provided, conditional, extenuating, mitigating, admitting, supposing, with the proviso, provided that.

470 possibility n feasibility, practicality, likelihood, potentiality; contingency, chance.

v be possible, stand a chance, admit of, (informal) could be.

adj possible, imaginable, conceivable, credible, feasible, practical, performable, achievable, within reach, within the bounds of possibility, potential.

adv possibly, perhaps, perchance, peradventure, maybe.

471 impossibility n impracticality, unfeasibility, hopelessness.

v be impossible, have no chance.

adj impossible, not possible, inconceivable, incredible, unimaginable, unreasonable, unfeasible, impractical, unobtainable, unperformable, unachievable, beyond the bounds of reason, absurd, (informal) fat chance, (informal) no way.

472 probability n likelihood, likeliness, plausibility, tendency, prospect, good chance, reasonable, chance, expectation.

v be probable, point to, tend, imply, bid fair.

adj probable, likely, plausible, reasonable, presumable, well-founded, hopeful.

adv probably, in all probability, in all likelihood, most likely, presumably.

473 improbability n unlikelihood, bare possibility, implausibility, doubtfulness, questionableness.

v be improbable, not have much of a chance.

adj improbable, unlikely, implausible, doubtful, questionable, beyond all reasonable expectation.

474 certainty n fact, truth; infallibility, reliability, unquestionableness, inevitability, certitude, assurance, confidence, conviction.

v be certain, stand to reason, render certain, clinch, make sure; know.

adj certain, confident, sure, assured, convinced, satisfied, indubitable, indisputable, unquestionable, undeniable, incontestable, unimpeachable, irrefutable, unquestioned, incontrovertible, absolute, positive, plain, patent, obvious, clear; sure, inevitable, infallible, unfailing; fixed, agreed upon, settled, prescribed, determined, determinate, constant, stated, given; definite, particular, special, especial; reliable, trustworthy, dependable, trusty.

adv certainly, for certain, no doubt, doubtless, undoubtedly, (informal) sure enough.

475 uncertainty n insecurity, instability, unreliability, fallibility, danger; incertitude, doubt, doubtfulness, ambiguity, vagueness, questionableness, dubiousness; haziness, fogginess, obscurity; undependability, changeableness, variability, capriciousness, irregularity, fitfulness, chanciness.

v be uncertain, hesitate, flounder, waver; render uncertain, pose, puzzle, perplex, confuse, confound, bewilder; doubt, question.

adj uncertain, insecure, precarious, unsure, doubtful, unpredictable, problematical, unstable, unreliable, unsafe, fallible, perilous, dangerous; unassured, undecided, indeterminate, undetermined, unfixed, unsettled, indefinite, ambiguous, questionable, dubious; doubtful, vague, indistinct; undependable, changeable, variable, capricious, unsteady, irregular, fitful, desultory, chance, (informal) chancy.

476 reasoning n ratiocination, rationalism, dialectics; discussion, comment, argumentation, debate, disputation.

logic, induction, deduction, chain of thought, analysis, synthesis, syllogistic reasoning.

argument, case, proposition, terms, premises, postulate, data; inference, argumentum ad hominem, paralipsis, a priori, a posteriori, reductio ad absurdum, enthymeme, dilemma, on the horns of a dilemma.

reasoner, logician, dialectician, disputant, wrangler, arguer, debater, polemicist, casuist, rationalist.

arguments, reasons, pros and cons.

v to reason, discuss, argue, debate, dispute, wrangle; deduce, induce, infer, analyze, synthesize, postulate, propose, contend, demonstrate.

adj reasoning, rationalistic, dialectical, dialectic, argumentative, disputatious; logical, inductive, deductive, analytical, synthetic, syllogistic, inferential; demonstrable.

477 [the absence of reasoning] **intuition.** [false reasoning] **sophistry** n intuition, instinct, hunch, presentiment; insight, discernment, inspiration.

casuistry, jesuitry, perversion, equivocation, evasion, chicanery, quiddity, speciousness, *(informal)* bull, *(informal)* malarkey; bunk; false statement; fallacy, sophism.

sophist.

v intuit; reason falsely, pervert, quibble, equivocate, evade, mislead, gloss over, cavil, refine, subtilize, misrepresent, fence, beg the question.

adj intuitive, instinctive, instinctual, sophistical, equivocal, evasive, specious, fallacious, illogical, unsound, false, incorrect, untenable; inconsequential, weak, feeble, poor, flimsy, vague, nonsensical, absurd, foolish; frivolous, pettifogging, trifling, quibbling, nit-picking, subtle, over-refined.

adv intuitively, by intuition; illogically.

478 demonstration *n* proof, conclusiveness, example, verification, explanation.

v demonstrate, prove, establish, verify; evince, show, explain.

adj demonstrative, demonstrable, probative, conclusive, convincing; demonstrated, proven, proved, shown.

479 confutation *n* refutation, answer, disproof, invalidation, exposure.

v confute, refute, disprove, expose the error, overturn, invalidate.

adj confutable, refutable.

480 judgment *n* verdict, decree, decision, determination, conclusion, result, upshot, deduction, inference, assessment, opinion, estimate, criticism, critique; understanding, discrimination, discernment, perspicacity, sagacity, wisdom, intelligence, prudence, brains, taste, penetration, discretion, common sense.

judge, assessor, reviewer, critic, commentator; connoisseur.

v judge, estimate, consider, regard, esteem, appreciate, appraise, reckon, value; decide, determine, conclude, form an opinion, pass judgment; criticize, rate, rank; try, pass sentence upon, rule.

adj judicious, judicial, judgmental, determinate, conclusive; critical, discriminating, penetrating, perspicacious.

480a discovery *n* detection, determination, disclosure, trove, find.

v discover, learn of, ascertain, unearth, uncover, determine, ferret out, flush out, dig up; find out, detect, espy, descry, discern, see, notice, hit upon, stumble onto.

481 misjudgment *n* miscalculation, miscomputation, misconception, misinterpretation, misapprehension.

v misjudge, misconjecture, misconceive, misunderstand, misconstrue, misinterpret; overestimate, underestimate.

adj misjudging, ill-judging, wrongheaded, *(informal)* off base, wrong, in error.

482 overestimation *n* exaggeration, overvaluation, optimism; miscalculation.

v overestimate, overrate, overprize, overpraise, exaggerate, magnify, attach too much importance to, set too high a value on; miscalculate.

adj overestimated, overrated, inflated, pompous, pretentious.

483 underestimation *n* undervaluation, depreciation, detraction; modesty, self-depreciation; pessimism.

v underestimate, undervalue, underrate, depreciate, disparage, detract, slight, minimize, make light of, make little of, disregard.

adj underestimating, depreciating, depreciative, deprecatory; underestimated, depreciated, unvalued, unprized; modest, pessimistic.

484 belief *n* opinion, view, tenet, doctrine, dogma, creed; certainty, conviction, assurance, confidence, persuasion, believing, trust, reliance; credence, credit, acceptance, faith, assent.

v believe, credit, give credence to, accept, have faith in, give assent, accept; know, see, realize, assume, presume; thick, opine, hold, conceive, consider; rely on, put one's trust on, have confidence in.

adj certain, sure, assured, positive, cocksure, satisfied, confident, convinced, secure; believing, trusting, confiding, credulous; believed, accredited, trusted, accepted; believable, credible, trustworthy.

485 disbelief, doubt *n* disbelief, incredulity; dissent, change of mind, retraction.

uncertainty, irresolution, hesitation, hesitancy, vacillation, misgiving, suspense; scruple, qualm, mistrust, distrust, suspicion, skepticism.

unbeliever, nonbeliever; skeptic.

v disbelieve, discredit, dissent, doubt, distrust, mistrust, suspect, have qualms; hesitate, waver, demur.

adj unbelieving, incredulous, doubtful, disputable, questionable, suspicious; uncertain, unsure; doubting, hesitating, hesitant, wavering, irresolute, dubious, skeptical.

486 credulity *n* credulousness, gullibility, infatuation, superstition, self-deception, self-delusion.

gull, dupe, *(informal)* sucker.

v be credulous, swallow.

adj credulous, believing, trusting, unsuspecting, gullible; simple, silly, childish, stupid; infatuated, superstitious.

487 incredulity *n* incredulousness, caution, wariness, suspicion, doubt, skepticism, disbelief.

nonbeliever, skeptic, heretic.

v be incredulous, distrust, doubt, suspect.

adj incredulous, cautious, wary; suspicious, dubious, doubtful, skeptical, unbelieving.

488 assent *n* acknowledgment, agreement, concurrence, acquiescence, consent, allowance, approval, concord, accord, approbation.

v assent, acquiesce, accede, concur, agree, fall in, acknowledge, admit, yield, allow; own, avow, confess.

adj assenting, agreeing, concurring, consenting, of one accord, of the same mind; agreed, acquiescent.

489 dissent *n* difference, discordance, dissension, disagreement, dissatisfaction; opposition, protest; nonconformity, separation.

dissenter, protester, rebel, radical, dissident, nonconformist.

v dissent, differ, disagree, protest, contradict; repudiate.

adj dissenting, negative; dissident, contradictory, disagreeing, opposing; nonconformist.

490 knowledge *n* enlightenment, erudition, wisdom, science, letters, information, learning, scholarship, lore; understanding, discernment, perception, apprehension, comprehension, judgment.

v know, be aware of; understand, discern, perceive, realize, fathom, apprehend, comprehend, *(informal)* dig; *(informal)* be hip; learn, discover.

adj knowing, aware of, cognizant of, acquainted with, privy to; discerning, perceptive, *(informal)* sharp, shrewd; knowledgeable, educated, enlightened, erudite, wise, instructed, learned, well-educated, bookish, well-read; known, recognized, received.

491 ignorance *n* illiteracy, unenlightenment, unawareness, unlearnedness, unacquaintance, unconsciousness, inexperience, darkness, blindness, incomprehension, simplicity, stupidity.

v be ignorant, know nothing, have no idea, be blind to.

adj ignorant, illiterate, unlettered, uneducated, uninstructed, untaught, untutored, uninformed, unenlightened, nescient; shallow, superficial; stupid, dumb, thick, dull.

492 scholar *n* savant, wise man, sage, academician, thinker, intellectual, bibliomaniac, bookworm, pedant; student, pupil, disciple, learner.

493 ignoramus *n* illiterate, know-nothing, blockhead, numskull, dullard, simpleton, dunce, ass, fool, bonehead, duffer, dolt, turkey, twerp, idiot, imbecile, cretin, moron, dimwit, *(informal)* jerk.

494 truth *n* fact, reality, verity, veracity; accuracy, precision, exactness.

v be true, be the case, have a true ring.

adj true, factual, actual, real, authentic, genuine, veracious, truthful, veritable; pure, natural; accurate, exact, faithful, correct, precise; agreeing; right, proper; legitimate, rightful; to the point, *(informal)* right on, *(informal)* where it's at, *(informal)* on target.

495 error *n* fallacy, misconception, misapprehension, misunderstanding, misinterpretation, misjudgment; aberration, inexactness, laxity; mistake, fault, blunder, slip, oversight, flaw, stumble, bungle; delusion, false, impression.

v err, be in error, mistake, blunder, slip, go astray, trip up; misconceive, misapprehend, misunderstand, misinterpret, miscalculate, misjudge.

adj erroneous, in error, fallacious, mistaken, incorrect, inaccurate, false, wrong, untrue, *(informal)* off base, *(informal)* off the mark.

496 maxim *n* proverb, aphorism, dictum, saying, adage, apothegm, motto, epigram, *mot juste*, truism, words of wisdom, axiom.

adj proverbial, aphoristic, axiomatic, truistic, *(informal)* corny, trite.

adv as they say, as the saying goes.

'497 absurdity *n* nonsense, imbecility, foolishness, silliness, inanity, stupidity; farce, rhapsody, farrago, blunder, bathos; inconsistency, paradox, *non sequitur*, jargon, extravagance, exaggeration.

v be absurd, talk nonsense, play the fool.

adj absurd, nonsensical, ridiculous, silly, preposterous, foolish, inane, asinine, stupid, senseless, unreasonable, irrational, incongruous, self-contradictory, paradoxical, farcical, rhapsodic, bathetic, extravagant, exaggerated, bombastic, fantastic, meaningless.

498 intelligence, wisdom *n* intelligence, intellect, mind, capacity, understanding, discernment, reason, acumen, aptitude, penetration, brains, *(informal)*, smarts; knowledge, news, information, tidings.

discretion, reasonableness, judgment, discernment, insight, sense, common sense, sagacity, insight, understanding, prudence; knowledge, information, learning, sapience, erudition, enlightenment.

v be intelligent; understand, discern, reason; be wise, discriminate.

adj intelligent, understanding, intellectual, quick, bright; astute, clever, sharp, alert, bright, apt, discerning, canny, shrewd, nimble, penetrating; piercing, on the ball.

wise, discerning, judicious, sage, sapient, sensible, sound, penetrating, sagacious, intelligent, perspicacious, profound, rational, prudent, cautious, politic, reasonable, thoughtful, reflective; learned, educated, erudite, schooled.

499 imbecility, folly *n* imbecility, want of intelligence, incompetence, incapacity, vacancy, dull understanding, meanness, simplicity, shallowness, stolidity, hebetude, puerility, fatuity, silliness, foolishness, driveling, stupidity, idiocy.

frivolity, irrationality, trifling, ineptitude, silliness, eccentricity, extravagance; rashness.

v be imbecilic.

be foolish, trifle, drivel, dote, ramble.

adj imbecile, imbecilic, idiotic, fatuous, driveling; vacant, mindless, witless, brainless, weak-headed, addle-brained, muddle-headed, dull-witted, feeble-minded, half-witted, dull, shallow, stolid, dim-witted, thick-skulled; shallow, weak, wanting, soft, sappy, stupid, obtuse, blunt, stolid, doltish, thick as a brick, asinine; childish, childlike, infantile, puerile, simple.

foolish, silly, senseless, irrational, insensate, nonsensical, inept, frivolous, trifling; eccentric, crazed, rash, thoughtless, giddy, obstinate, bigoted, narrow-minded; foolish, unwise, injudicious, improper, unreasonable, ridiculous, stupid, asinine; ill-conceived, ill-advised, ill-judged, inexpedient, extravagant, frivolous, trivial, useless.

500 sage n wise man, master mind, thinker, philosopher, oracle, luminary, man of learning, expert, authority.

501 fool n simpleton, dolt, dunce, blockhead, nincompoop, ninny, numskull, ignoramus, booby, sap, dunderhead, dunderpate, idiot, natural, oaf, lout, loon, dullard; jester, buffoon, droll, zany, harlequin, clown; imbecile, moron, idiot, cretin.

502 sanity n soundness, mental balance, rationality, reason, sense, clearheadedness, lucidity, coherence, normality, sobriety, (informal) good head.

v be sane, (informal) have one's act together.

adj sane, rational, reasonable, sensible, clearheaded, level-headed, logical, sober, lucid, self-possessed, (informal) together.

503 insanity n disorder, imbalance, derangement, dementia, lunacy, madness, craziness, aberration, frenzy, raving, incoherence, delirium, delusion; (informal) oddity, eccentricity, twist, mania.

v be insane, become insane, lose one's senses, go mad, rave, rant, (informal) lose it.

adj insane, deranged, demented, lunatic, crazed, crazy, maniacal, mad, touched, cracked, unhinged, unsettled, daft, frenzied, possessed, delirious, far gone, wild, flighty, distracted, frantic, mad as a hatter, (informal) crackers, (informal) zonkers, (informal) nuts, (informal) zonko, (informal) weird, (informal) bananas, (informal) kaput.

504 madman n lunatic, maniac, bedlamite, raver, (informal) nut, (informal) weirdo, (informal) crazy; dreamer, romantic, rhapsodist, enthusiast, visionary, seer, fanatic.

505 memory n retention, retentiveness, remembrance, recollection,

reminiscence, retrospect; recognition; reminder, hint, suggestion, keepsake, souvenir, memento, token, memorial.

v remember, recall, recollect, call up, call to mind, bring to mind, think back upon, haunt one's thoughts, (informal) flash on; remind, suggest, hint, prompt, summon up, reminisce; retain, keep in mind, bear in mind, memorize, engrave in the mind, learn by heart; keep the memory alive.

adj reminiscent (of), mindful (of); fresh, alive, vivid; unforgotten, enduring, indelible, memorable, never to be forgotten, unforgettable, stirring, eventful.

506 oblivion n forgetfulness, short memory, slippery memory, untrustworthy memory, obliteration of the past, amnesia.

v forget, be forgetful, have a short memory, lose sight of, sink into oblivion; unlearn, efface from the memory, think no more of, consign into oblivion, banish from one's thoughts.

adj oblivious, forgetful, heedless, deaf to the past, insensible; out of mind, unremembered, forgotten, past recollection, buried, sunk into oblivion.

507 expectation n expectancy, anticipation, prospect, reckoning, calculation; suspense, waiting; hope, trust, assurance, confidence, reliance, presumption.

v expect, look for, look out for, look forward to, anticipate, await, hope for, wait for, foresee, prepare for, count on, rely on; predict, prognosticate, forecast.

adj expectant, watchful, vigilant, open-eyed, on tenterhooks, on one's toes, ready, in readiness, prepared, (informal) all set for; foreseen, long expected, prospective, in view, in sight, on the horizon, impending.

adv expectantly, on the watch, on edge, with bated breath.

508 nonexpectation n unforeseen occurrence, surprise, shock, blow, wonder, bolt out of the blue, astonishment; miscalculation, false expectation.

v not expect, be taken by surprise, catch unawares; burst upon, come out of nowhere, drop from the clouds; surprise, startle, stun, stagger, throw off one's guard, astonish.

adj nonexpectant, surprised, unwarned, unaware, off one's guard; unanticipated, unexpected, unlooked for, unforeseen; unheard of, startling; sudden.

adv unexpectedly, abruptly, suddenly, without warning.

509 [failure of expectation] **disappointment** *n* failure, defeat, frustration, unfulfillment, blighted hope, vain expectation, disillusion. (*informal*) come-down.

v be disappointed; disappoint, dash one's hopes, dash one's expectations, balk, jilt, tantalize; dumfound, disillusion, let down.

adj disappointed; disgruntled, disconcerted, aghast.

510 foresight *n* prudence, forethought, prevision, anticipation, precaution; forecast; prescience, fore-knowledge, prospect.

v foresee; look forward to, look ahead, look beyond; look into the future; see one's future, catch the lay of the land; anticipate, expect, assume, surmise, predict, forewarn.

adj anticipatory, prescient; far-sighted, prudent, provident; prospective, expectant.

511 prediction *n* prophecy, forecast, augury, prognostication, foretoken, portent, divination, soothsaying, presage.

v predict, foretell, prophesy, foresee, forecast, presage, augur, prognosticate, foretoken, portend, divine.

adj prophetic, oracular, portentous, premonitory.

512 omen *n* portent, foreboding, augury, sign, harbinger; sign of the times, symbol, warning.

513 oracle *n* prophet, prophetess, seer, soothsayer, augur, fortune-teller, witch, sibyl, necromancer, sorcerer, clairvoyant, interpreter.

514 supposition *n* assumption, presumption, condition, hypothesis, theory, postulate, proposition, thesis, theorem; conjecture, suggestion, guess, guesswork, suspicion, inkling, speculation.

v suppose, conjecture, surmise, suspect, guess, divine; theorize, speculate, presume, presuppose, assume, predicate; believe, take for granted; propound, put forth, propose, advance, hazard a suggestion, suggest.

adj assumed, given; conjectural, hypothetical, presumptive, theoretical, speculative, suggestive.

515 imagination *n* imaginativeness, fancy, invention, inspiration, creativity, originality, fiction, vision, fantasy, illusion, ideality, castles in the air, dreaming, dream, golden dreams; mental image, conception, idea, notion, thought, conceit, fancy, whim, figment, romance, vision, dream, chimera, shadow, illusion, phantasm, supposition, delusion; verve, vivacity, liveliness, animation.

v imagine, fancy, conceive, dream, idealize; create, originate, think up, devise, invent, coin, fabricate.

adj imaginative, fanciful, original, inventive, creative, visionary, ideal, unreal, illusory, unsubstantial, dreamy, dreamlike, romantic, fantastic, fabulous, chimerical, fantastical; vivacious, lively, animated; imaginable, conceivable, possible, believable; imagined.

II. Communication of Ideas

516 [idea to be conveyed] **meaning** *n* tenor, spirit, gist, trend, idea, purport, significance, signification, sense, import, denotation, connotation, interpretation; intent, intention, aim, object, purpose, design.

thing signified: matter, subject-matter, substance, gist, argument.

v mean, signify, denote, conote, express, import, purport; convey, imply, indicate; point to, allude to, touch on, drive at, involve; declare, affirm, state; intend, aim, design, purpose.

adj meaning; meaningful, pointed, poignant, significant, expressive.

517 meaninglessness *n* unmeaningness, absence of meaning, senselessness, emptiness, empty words, rhetoric, platitude, nonsense, jargon, gibberish, jabber, rant, bombast, *(informal)* hot air; inanity, rigmarole, absurdity, ambiguity.

v mean nothing, jabber, rant, say nothing.

adj meaningless, senseless, nonsensical, inexpressive, vague, trivial, insignificant.

518 intelligibility *n* comprehensibility, clearness, lucidity, coherence, explicitness, persicuity, precision, plain-speaking.

v be intelligible; render, intelligible, clear up, simplify, elucidate, explain; understand, comprehend, take in, catch on, grasp, follow, master.

adj intelligible, understandable, comprehensible, clear, clear as day, lucid, luminous, transparent; plain, distinct, pointed, clear-cut, obvious, explicit, precise; graphic, illustrative, expressive.

519 unintelligibility *n* incomprehensibility, vagueness, obscurity, ambiguity, uncertainty, confusion.

v be unintelligible; render, unintelligible, conceal, darken, confuse, perplex, mystify, bewilder.

adj unintelligible, incomprehensible, indecipherable, unfathomable, inexplicable, inscrutable, insoluble, impenetrable; puzzling, enigmatic, obscure, muddy, dim, nebulous, mysterious, *(informal)* strange, *(informal)* weird; inexpressible, incommunicable, ineffable, unutterable.

520 equivocalness *n* ambiguity, uncertainty, questionableness, dubiousness, indeterminateness; double-meaning, word-play, double entendre, pun, play on words, conundrum, riddle, quibble; equivocation, duplicity, prevarication, white lie.

v be equivocal; have two meanings; equivocate, prevaricate.

adj equivocal, ambiguous, uncertain, doubtful, questionable, dubious, indeterminate; duplicitous, enigmatic, double-edged, deceptive, misleading.

521 figure of speech *n* phrase, expression, euphemism, manner of speaking, colloquialism, idiom, image; metaphor, simile, imagery, poetic device, poetics, figures of beauty.

v employ figures of speech; image, speak prettily.

adj figurative, idiomatic, colloquial, colorful, imagistic, poetic, expressive, allusive.

522 interpretation *n* definition, explanation, explication, elucidation, translation; exegesis, exposition, comment, commentary, gloss; solution, answer, meaning.

v interpret, define, explain, explicate, elucidate, translate, shed light on, cast light on, decipher, decode, unravel, disentangle, gloss, annotate, expound, comment upon; construe, understand.

adj explanatory, expository, exegetical, interpretative, interpretive; interpretable, explicable, intelligible.

adv in explanation, that is to say, namely.

523 misinterpretation *n* misapprehension, misconception, misunderstanding, misreading, misconstruction, mistake; misrepresentation, perversion, exaggeration, false coloration, falsification, travesty.

v misinterpret, misapprehend, misconceive, misunderstand, misread, misconstrue, misapply, mistake; misrepresent, pervert, misstate, garble, falsify, distort, travesty, stretch the meaning, twist the meaning.

524 interpreter *n* translator, explainer, expounder, expositor, commentator, annotator, guide, critic; spokesman, speaker, representative.

525 manifestation *n* indication, expression, exposition, demonstration, showing, display, exhibition, declaration; materialization; openness, candor.

v make manifest, show, display, reveal, disclose, open, exhibit, evince, evidence, demonstrate, declare, express, make known; appear, be plain, come to light, materialize; indicate, point out.

adj manifest, evident, obvious, apparent, plain, clear, distinct, patent, open, palpable, visible, unmistakable, conspicuous, explicit; unreserved, downright, frank, plain spoken; barefaced, bold; manifested.

adv manifestly, openly, plainly, above board, in broad daylight, in plain sight.

526 latency *n* dormancy, latentness, quiescence, obscurity, darkness, hidden meaning, obscure meaning, undercurrent, suggestion, concealment; potentiality.

v be latent, lurk, smolder, underlie.

adj latent, dormant; lurking, secret, cryptic, veiled, hidden; potential; implied, implicit; allusive.

527 information *n* enlightenment, knowledge, news, data, facts, circumstances, situations, intelligence, advice; communication, notification, announcement, record; hint, suggestion, innuendo, inkling, whisper, insinuation.

informant, authority, intelligencer, reporter; informer, eavesdropper, detective, newsmonger; messenger.

guide, guidebook, handbook, manual, map, chart.

v inform, tell, acquaint with, impart to, make acquainted with, apprize, advise, enlighten; communicate, make known, express, mention, let fall, intimate, hint, insinuate, allude to, suggest; announce, report, give an account, disclose; know, learn, find out, get the scent of.

adj informed, communicated, reported, advised, apprized of, acquainted with, enlightened, published, (informal) filled in; declarative, expository, communicative.

528 concealment *n* hiding, secretion, ensconcing, sheltering, covering,

burying, screening; keeping secret, secrecy, hiding, disguising, veiling, camouflaging, obscuring, dissembling, obfuscation, evasiveness; reticence, reserve, reservation, suppression, silence, secretiveness.

v conceal, hide, secrete, cover, put away, ensconce, bury, screen, shelter, keep out of sight, stow away; keep secret, hide, disguise, veil, cloak, mask, camouflage, obscure, obfuscate, dissemble, be evasive.

adj concealed, hidden, secret, private, privy, confidential, in secret, close, undercover, in hiding, in disguise, covert, mysterious; furtive, stealthy, surreptitious, secretive, evasive, clandestine; reserved, reticent, suppressed, uncommunicative.

adv secretly, in secret, in private, behind closed doors, on the sly; confidentially; stealthily.

529 disclosure *n* revelation, divulgence, exposition, exposure; exposé, uncovering, muckraking; acknowledgment, avowal, confession.

v disclose, discover, uncover, lay open, expose, bring to light, unmask; reveal, make known, divulge, show, tell, unveil, unmask, communicate; let slip, let drop, betray, blurt out; acknowledge, allow, concede, grant, admit, own up, confess.

adj disclosed, revealed.

530 [means of concealment] **ambush** *n* ambuscade, lurking place, trap, snare, pitfall; hiding place, secret place, recess, hole, cubbyhole; screen, cover, shade, blinker, veil, curtain, cloak, cloud; mask, visor, disguise, masquerade.

v ambush, lie in wait for, set a trap for.

531 publication *n* issuance, distribution; announcement, proclamation, promulgation, propagation, pronouncement, declaration, disclosure, divulgence, advertisement, publicity; edition.

v publish, issue, distribute, print; make public, make known, announce, proclaim, promulgate, propagate, circulate, spread, disseminate, declare, disclose, divulge, advertise, publicize, get into print.

adj published; current, public, in circulation, in print, in black and white.

532 news *n* information, intelligence, tidings, report, rumor, scuttlebutt, hearsay, gossip, *(informal)* the word; newsstory, headlines, copy.

reporter, newsmonger, talebearer, gossip, tattler, informer.

v transpire, make news, make headlines; be rumored.

adj in the news, in the headlines, current, in circulation, in print.

533 secret *n* mystery; problem, question, difficulty, a confidence; unintelligibility.

adj secret, hidden, concealed, unrevealed, unknown, mysterious; reticent, secretive; private.

534 messenger *n* envoy, emissary, representative, intermediary, go-between, delegate, courier, runner, errand boy; intelligencer, reporter, newsmonger, spokesman, informant; forerunner, harbinger, herald, precursor.

535 affirmation *n* statement, profession, pronouncement, deposition, assertion, declaration; confirmation, ratification, endorsement; swearing, oath, affidavit; emphasis, dogmatism.

v affirm, state, assert, aver, avow, maintain, declare, swear, asseverate, depose, testify, say, pronounce; establish, confirm, ratify, approve, endorse, assent, acknowledge; swear, emphasize.

adj affirmative, declaratory, declarative, positive, assertive, emphatic, dogmatic; confirmative, corroborative, affirming, acquiescent.

536 negation. denial *n* nullification, invalidation.

disputation, confutation, contradiction, qualification; repudiation, rejection, abjuration, disavowal, disclaimer, recantation, retraction, rebuttal.

v negate, nullify, cancel, invalidate.

deny, dispute, controvert, contravene, oppose, gainsay, contradict, rebut; reject, renounce, abjure, disclaim, disavow; recant, revoke; refuse, repudiate, disown.

adj contradictory, negative.

537 teaching *n* instruction, education, pedagogy, pedagogics, edification, tutelage, tutorship; guidance, direction, preparation, schooling, learning, discipline; lesson, lecture, disquisition, discourse, explanation, harangue, homily, sermon, lore; doctrine, dogma, tenet, principle, rule, maxim, article of faith, creed, credo, belief, opinion.

v teach, instruct, edify, educate, inform, enlighten, prepare, discipline, train, drill, tutor, prime, coach, guide, direct, school, indoctrinate, inculcate, infuse, instill, imbue; expound, interpret, lecture, discourse, hold forth, sermonize, moralize.

adj educational, scholastic, academic, pedagogic, pedagogical, didactic; edifying, instructive.

538 misteaching *n* misinformation, misdirection, misguidance, perversion, sophistry, error.

v misteach, misinform, misinstruct, misdirect, misguide, pervert, mislead, misrepresent, confuse, bewilder, lie.

539 learning *n* acquisition of knowledge, acquirements, attainment, mental cultivation, scholarship, erudition, study, inquiry, questioning, search, pursuit of knowledge.

apprenticeship, tutelage, matriculation.

v learn, acquire, gain knowledge, memorize, master, study, grind, cram, *(informal)* book, read, peruse, pore over, wade through, ingest, burn the midnight oil, *(informal)* pull an all-nighter.

adj studious, industrious; scholarly, scholastic, well-read, learned, erudite.

540 teacher *n* instructor, tutor, lecturer, professor, don, master, schoolmaster, guide, counselor, adviser, mentor; preacher, missionary, propagandist.

541 learner n scholar, student, pupil, apprentice, novice, neophyte, beginner; disciple, acolyte, follower.

542 school n academy, educational institution, college, university, institute, seminary, place of learning.

schoolbook, textbook, text, primer, grammar, reader, workbook.

adj scholastic, academic, collegiate.

543 veracity n truthfulness, frankness, truth, sincerity, candor, honesty, probity, fidelity, accuracy.

v speak the truth, *(informal)* level with, *(informal)* be straight with.

adj veracious, true, truthful, sincere, honest, honorable, candid, frank, open, straightforward, honest, scrupulous, punctilious, trustworthy.

544 falsehood n falsification, lie, fib, untruth, distortion, deception, misrepresentation, fabrication, fiction, sham; untruthfulness, lying, prevarication, duplicity, double dealing, deceitfulness, equivocation, dissembling, cunning, guile, insincerity, dishonesty, inaccuracy.

v lie, fib, falsify, prevaricate, misrepresent, deceive, *(informal)* come on to, doctor, feign, pretend, play false, dissemble, counterfeit, fabricate.

adj false, untrue, wrong, mistaken, incorrect, erroneous; untruthful, lying, mendacious, dishonest, deceitful, treacherous, faithless, insincere, hypocritical, disingenuous, unfaithful, cunning, perfidious, two-faced, recreant; deceptive, misleading, fallacious, spurious, fraudulent, bogus, phony, sham, counterfeit.

545 deception n deceiving, guiling, falseness, untruthfulness; artifice, sham, cheat, imposture, deceit, treachery, subterfuge, stratagem, ruse, hoax, fraud, trick, wile, snare, trap, illusion, delusion.

v deceive, mislead, lead astray, take in, delude, cheat, cozen, dupe, gull, fool, bamboozle, hoodwink,

(informal) con, trick, double-cross, defraud, outwit; entrap, ensnare, betray.

adj deceptive, misleading, delusive, illusory, fallacious, specious, untrue, false, deceitful; tricky, cunning, insidious.

546 untruth n falsehood, fib, lie, fiction, story, tale, tall tale, fabrication, fable, forgery, invention.

v make believe, pretend, feign, sham, fib, lie.

adj untrue, false, trumped up, unfounded, invented, fictitious, fabulous.

547 dupe n gull, pigeon, laughingstock, greenhorn, fool, sucker, puppet, *(informal)* nebbish.

v be deceived, be the dupe of, fall into a trap, go for the bait, bite, swallow.

adj credulous, gullible, unsuspecting, trusting.

548 deceiver n dissembler, hypocrite, sophist, liar, *(informal)* fast talker, storyteller, *(informal)* faker, *(informal)* phony, fraud, *(informal)* four-flusher, *(informal)* shyster, confidence man, con man, cheat, swindler, imposter, pretender, humbug, adventurer, adventuress, serpent, snake in the grass.

549 exaggeration n overstatement, hyperbole, extravagance, coloring, coloration, embroidery, yarn, tale, *(informal)* shaggy dog story, *(informal)* fish story; tempest in a teacup, much ado about nothing, puffery, rant.

v exaggerate, magnify, amplify, expand, overestimate, overstate; heighten, color, embroider, puff up, fill out.

adj exaggerated, overwrought, bombastic, magniloquent, hyperbolic fabulous, extravagant, preposterous.

550 [means of communication] **indication** n symbolism, semiology; sign, symbol, index, indicator, pointer, note, token, symptom; type, mark, figure, emblem, insigne, cipher, device, representation; signal, beacon, alarm; feature, trait, characteristic, peculiarity, quality, earmark, cast; gesture, gesticulation, motion, cue, hint, clue, scent.

v indicate, denote, betoken, designate, signify, represent, stand for, typify, symbolize; note, mark, stamp; label, ticket; make a sign, signalize, signal, gesture, gesticulate; sign, seal, attest, underline, underscore, call attention to.

adj indicative, indicatory; connotative, denotative, typical, representative, symbolic, symbolical, characteristic, significant, emblematic.

551 record *n* trace, vestige, relic, remains; monument, achievement; account, chronicles, annals, history, note, register, memorandum, document, diary, log, journal, ledger.

v record, set down, place in the record, chronicle, enter, register, enter, list, enroll; commemorate, celebrate.

552 [suppression of sign] obliteration *n* erasure, cancelation, deletion, blot, effacement, extinction.

v obliterate, efface, expunge, erase, cancel, delete, blot out, rub out, strike out, wipe out, leave no trace.

adj obliterated, erased, blotted out; unrecorded.

553 recorder *n* notary, clerk, registrar, register, secretary, scribe, bookkeeper; annalist, historian, historiographer, chronicler, biographer, journalist, antiquarian, memorialist.

554 representation *n* depiction, imitation, illustration, delineation, expression, imagery, portraiture, figuration.

v represent, delineate, depict, portray, picture, figure, describe, trace, copy, illustrate, symbolize; personate, personify, play, mimic.

adj representative, imitative, illustrative, figurative, symbolic, descriptive.

555 misrepresentation *n* distortion, exaggeration, misfiguration, falsification, bad likeness, caricature.

v misrepresent, distort, overdraw,

exaggerate, falsify, caricature, daub.

556 painting *n* fine art, picture, depiction, representation, pictorialization, delineation, design, drawing, likeness, copy, imitation, fake, image.

art gallery, picture gallery, studio.

v paint, design, limn, draw, sketch, pencil, color; depict, represent.

adj pictorial, picturesque.

557 sculpture *n* carving, modeling, statuary; ceramics, potting.

statue, statuette, bust; cast, mold.

v sculpt, fashion, cast, mold, model, chisel, carve, cut, shape, form, figure, hew.

558 engraving *n* etching, chiseling, incising, plate engraving, photoengraving.

v engrave, grave, carve, incise, chisel, hatch, etch, stipple, print.

559 artist *n* painter, drawer, sketcher, designer, draftsman, cartoonist, caricaturist, sculptor, engraver.

560 language *n* speech, phraseology, style, expression, diction, jargon, dialect, terminology, vernacular, lingo, tongue.

literature, letters, belles, lettres humanities, classics, dead language; linguist.

v express, say, express by words.

adj lingual, linguistic; dialect, vernacular, current, colloquial, slangy, polyglot, literary.

561 letter *n* character, hieroglyph, symbol, alphabet, consonant, vowel, syllable, monosyllable, dissyllable, polysyllable.

spelling, orthography; phonetics; cipher, code; monogram, anagram.

v spell.

adj literal; alphabetical; syllabic; phonetic.

562 word *n* term, symbol, name, part of speech.

dictionary, vocabulary, lexicon, index, thesaurus, glossary.

etymology, derivation, philology, terminology, lexicography.

adj literal, verbal.

563 neology *n* neologism, new-fangled expression, *(informal)* hip expression, barbarism, corruption.
neologist, word coiner.
v coin words.
adj neologic, neological; colloquial, slang, *(informal)* hip, cant, barbarous.

564 nomenclature *n* naming; name, appellation, designation, epithet, nickname, *(informal)* moniker, *(informal)* handle, label, title, head, heading; style, proper name, surname, namesake.
v name, call, term, designate, denominate, style, entitle, dub, christen, baptize, nickname, characterize, specify, label.
adj titular, nominal.

565 misnomer *n* misnaming, malapropism; sobriquet, nickname, assumed name, alias, pen name, stage name, pseudonym, nom de plume, nom de guerre.
v misname, miscall, misterm; take an assumed name.
adj misnamed; soi-disant, self-styled; so-called.

566 phrase *n* expression, set phrase, turn of speech, idiom, tag phrase, figure of speech, euphemism, motto; phraseology.
v phrase, express, put into words, find the right words, arrange in words, voice, vocalize.

567 grammar *n* rules of language, usage, forms, style, formal features, constructions, parts of speech; accidence, syntax, inflection, case, declension, conjugation; grammar book, primer, rulebook.
grammarian.
adj grammatical, syntactic, syntactical.

568 solecism *n* ungrammatical, usage, bad grammar, faulty grammar, error, slip, inconsistency, impropriety.
v solecize.
adj ungrammatical, incorrect, inaccurate, faulty, inconsistent, improper.

569 style *n* diction, phraseology, wording; composition, mode of expression, choice of words, command of language, mode, manner, method, approach; kind, form, appearance, character, touch, characteristic, mark, signature, imprint, *(informal)* name.
v style, compose, express by words; write.
adj stylistic; characteristic; expressive.

570 perspicuity *n* clearness, clarity, lucidity, plainness, plain-speaking, distinctness, explicitness, exactness, intelligibility.
adj perspicuous, pellucid, clear, lucid, intelligible, plain, distinct, explicit, exact, definite, unequivocal.

571 obscurity *n* unintelligibility, involution, confusion, indistinctness, indefiniteness, ambiguity, vagueness, inexactness, impenetrability.
adf obscure, involved, confused, unintelligible, impenetrable, indefinite, vague, inexact, hidden, dark.

572 conciseness *n* brevity, summary, abridgment, terseness, pithiness, compression, tightness.
v be concise, condense, abridge, abstract, compress, tighten; come to the point.
adj concise, brief, compendious, short, terse, laconic, pithy, trenchant, succinct, compact, tight.
adv concisely, briefly, summarily, in short.

573 diffuseness *n* long-windedness, verbosity, wordiness, verbiage, looseness, exuberance, redundancy, profuseness, richness.
v be diffuse, enlarge, amplify, expand, inflate, meander, digress, ramble, run on and on.
adj diffuse, profuse, wordy, verbose, copious, exuberant, lengthy, long-winded, protracted, prolix, diffusive, roundabout; digressive, discursive, loose.

574 vigor *n* power, force, boldness, spirit, verve, heart, ardor, enthusiasm, raciness, glow, fire, warmth; loftiness, elevation, gravity, sublimity; eloquence, strong language.
adj vigorous, nervous, powerful, forcible, forceful, trenchant, biting,

incisive, impressive; spirited, lively, glowing, sparkling, racy, bold, pungent, pithy; lofty, elevated, sublime, grand, weighty; eloquent, vehement, impassioned, passionate.

575 feebleness *n* weakness, enervation, frailty, faintness.

adj feeble, tame, weak, meager, vapid, insipid; trashy, poor, dull, dry, languid; prosy, prosaic, slight; careless, loose, slip-shod, wishy-washy, sloppy, slovenly; puerile, childish.

576 plainness *n* simplicity, homeliness, restraint, severity.

v speak plainly, speak directly, come straight to the point, be straightforward, not beat around the bush.

adj plain, simple, homely, homey, unadorned, unvarnished, neat, homespun; severe, chaste, pure.

adv in plain terms, in plain English; point-blank.

577 ornament *n* floridness, ornateness, elegance, grandiloquence, magniloquence, rhetorical flourish, declamation, rhetoric, flourish, fancy talk, (*informal*) big words; pretention, inflation, bombast, fustian, rant, fine writing, fine speaking.

v ornament, overcharge, talk big, talk fancy.

adj ornate, ornamented, beautified, florid, rich, flowery, fancy; euphuistic, euphemistic; sonorous, high sounding, inflated, swelling, turgid, pompous, pedantic, stilted, high-flown, sententious, rhetorical, declamatory, grandiose, grandiloquent, magniloquent, bombastic, flashy.

578 elegance *n* taste, good taste, propriety, correctness; lucidity, purity, grace, ease; gracefulness, euphony, gentility, cultivation, polish, refinement.

purist, classicist.

adj elegant, polished, classic, classical, fine, tasteful, proper, correct; chaste, pure, graceful, easy, readable, fluent, flowing, unaffected, natural, mellifluous, euphonious, felicitous, neat, well put.

579 inelegance *n*. tastelessness, vulgarity, impropriety; bad diction, awkwardness, stiffness, turgidity, abruptness; barbarism, solecism, slang, mannerism, affectation, formality.

adj inelegant, graceless, ungraceful, harsh, abrupt, dry, stiff, cramped, formal, forced, labored, awkward, ponderous, turgid; artificial, mannered, affected, euphuistic; tasteless, barbarous, uncouth, rude, crude, vulgar.

580 voice *n* vocality, intonation, articulation, enunciation, distinctness, clearness, delivery; accent, accentuation, emphasis, stress; utterance, vocalization.

v voice, speak, utter; articulate, enunciate, vocalize, intone, pronounce, accent, accentuate, deliver.

adj vocal, oral; articulate, distinct, euphonious, melodious.

581 muteness *n* dumbness, silence, speechlessness; aphasia.

v be mute, be silent, be dumb; silence, muzzle, muffle, suppress, smother, gag, strike dumb, dumfound.

adj mute, silent, dumb, mum, tongue-tied; voiceless, speechless.

582 speech *n* talk, parlance, locution, conversation, parley, communication, prattle; talk, oration, address, discourse, lecture; recitation, sermon, harangue, tirade; oratory, eloquence, rhetoric, declamation.

speaker, spokesman, mouthpiece, orator, rhetorician.

v speak, utter, talk, voice, converse, communicate, pronounce, say, articulate; declaim, harangue, stump, spout, rant, lecture, sermonize, discourse, expatiate, soliloquize, address.

adj oral; talkative, conversational; declamatory.

583 [imperfect speech] inarticulateness *n* stammering, hesitation, muttering, mumbling, stuttering; reticence, taciturnity; speech impediment, aphasia.

v be inarticulate, stammer, hesitate, mutter, mumble, slur one's words, garble, sputter, hem and haw, whisper, croak, crack.

adj inarticulate, tongue-tied, speechless, voiceless, hesitant, reticent, taciturn.

584 loquacity *n* loquaciousness, volubility, talkativeness, verbosity, garrulity, volubility; chatter, jabber, prattle, twaddle.

talker, chatterer, chatterbox, babbler, ranter.

v be loquacious, talk a mile a minute, pour forth, prate, chatter, babble, gab, run off at the mouth, jabber, jaw, gush.

adj loquacious, voluble, talkative, verbose, wordy, garrulous, chatty, chattering, glib, fluent, effusive.

585 taciturnity *n* silence, muteness, reserve, reticence, uncommunicativeness.

v be silent, keep silence, keep quiet, hold one's tongue, say nothing.

adj taciturn, silent, mute, mum, reserved, reticent, guarded, uncommunicative, close-mouthed, quiet.

586 public address *n* allocution, speech, formal speech, address, invocation.

v speak to, address; invoke, hail, salute; lecture, pronounce.

587 response *n*. See **answer 462.**

588 conversation *n* interlocution, colloquy, confabulation, talk, *(informal)* rap, discourse, verbal interchange, dialog, oral communication; chat, chit, chit-chat, small talk, table talk, idle talk, prattle, gossip; conference, parley, interview, audience, *tête-à-tête*, council, congress; palaver, debate, discussion.

v converse, confabulate, talk together, hold a conversation, carry on a conversation, engage in a discussion; bandy words, chat, chit-chat, gossip, tattle, prate; discourse with, confer with; talk it over, *(informal)* rap, *(informal)* chew the fat.

adj conversational, conversable; chatty, gossipy.

589 soliloquy *n* monolog, apostrophe, aside.

v soliloquize, talk to oneself, think out loud, apostrophize.

590 writing *n* chirography, penmanship, calligraphy, hand; script, longhand, shorthand, stenography; handwriting, signature, mark, hand; manuscript, MS., document, script, writ, author's copy, copy, original; composition, authorship, work, opus, book, volume, tome, publication, article, poetry, verse, literature.

writer, author, scribe, scrivener, clerk, copyist, secretary.

v write, pen, copy, transcribe; print, scribble, scrawl, scratch; compose, draw out, write down, set down, put pen to paper, take up the pen, take pen in hand.

adj written, in writing, in black and white.

591 printing *n* lettering, typography; type; composition, print, letterpress, text, matter; copy, impression, proof.

printer, compositor, reader, proofreader, copyeditor.

v print, compose; go to press, publish, bring out, issue.

adj typographical, printed.

592 correspondence *n* letter, epistle, missive, note, post card; communication, dispatch, bulletin, circular.

v correspond, communicate, write to, send a letter.

adj epistolary; in touch with, in communication with.

593 book *n* booklet, writing, work, volume, tome, opus, tract, treatise, brochure, handbook; novel, story; script, libretto; publication.

writer, author, essayist, editor; bookseller, publisher; librarian, bibliophile, bookworm.

594 description *n* narration, account, recounting, telling, recital, relation, statement, report, record; delineation, portrayal, characterization, representation, depiction, sketch, vignette.

v describe, set forth, narrate, account, recount, recite, rehearse, tell, relate, detail; picture, delineate, portray, characterize, limn, represent, depict.

595 dissertation n treatise, essay, thesis, theme, tract, discourse, disquisition, investigation, study, discussion, exposition; commentary, critique, criticism, review, article, commentator, critic, essayist, reviewer.

v discuss a subject, treat, examine, comment, criticize, explain.

596 compendium n abstract, précis, epitome, analysis, digest, compendium, brief, abridgment, abbreviation, condensation, summary; draft, note, synopsis, outline, syllabus, contents, prospectus; compilation, collection, album, anthology; extracts, cuttings, fragments, pieces; list, inventory, survey.

v abridge, abstract, précis, epitomize, summarize; abbreviate, shorten, condense, compress; compile, collect, note; list, inventory, survey.

adj compendious, synoptic, analytic, analytical.

597 poetry n poetics; verse, poesy, versification, rhyming, rhymes, making verses, metrics; doggerel.

poet, laureate, bard, troubadour, minstrel, versifier, rhymer, sonneteer, rhapsodist, poetaster.

v poeticize, sing, versify, rhyme, make verses, compose.

adj poetic, poetical, rhythmic, metrical, lyrical, tuneful, musical; beautiful, lovely, tender, sensitive.

598 prose n writing, fiction, imaginative writing, narrative prose.

v write prose.

adj prosy, unpoetic, rhymeless, prosaic, dull, flat, matter-of-fact, unimaginative, commonplace, humdrum, pedestrian, trite, hackneyed, mediocre, stock, ordinary; fictional.

599 the drama n the stage, the theater; theatricals, dramaturgy, playwriting; play, drama, stage-play, opera.

performance, acting, representation, impersonation, stage business, actor, actress, player, performer, thespian.

theater, playhouse, operahouse, amphitheater.

dramatist, playwriter, playwright.

v dramatize, act, play, perform, personate, act a part, put on the stage, enact.

adj dramatic, theatrical, histrionic, stagy.

Class V

Voluntary Powers

I. Individual Volition

600 will n volition, free will, freedom; choice, wish, desire, pleasure, disposition, inclination; intent, purpose, option; determination, resolution, resoluteness, decision, forcefulness; force of will, will power, self-control.

v will, see fit, think fit, decide, decree, determine, direct, command, bid.

adj willful, voluntary, volitional, intentional; free, optional, discretionary; autocratic, obdurate, adamant.

adv willfully, voluntarily, at will; of one's own accord, intentionally, deliberately.

601 necessity n obligation, compulsion, subjection; fate, destiny, fatality; inevitability, inevitableness, unavoidability, unavoidableness, irresistibility; requirement, requisite, demand; instinct, impulse.

v be obligated, be obliged, be fated; necessitate, compel, subject; require.

adj necessary, essential, requisite, needful; inevitable, unavoidable, ineluctable, irresistible, inexorable; compulsory; involuntary, instinctive, automatic, blind, mechanical.

adv necessarily, of necessity, willy nilly.

602 willingness n disposition, inclination, leaning, propensity, frame of mind, liking, humor, mood, vein, bent, penchant, aptitude; geniality, cordiality, good will; alacrity, readiness, eagerness, enthusiasm; assent, compliance, agreement.

v be willing, incline, lean to, mind, hold to, to cling to; desire, acquiesce, assent, comply; find one's way to, give it a shot, *(informal)* take a swing at, *(informal)* lay into.

adj willing, fain, favorable, content, well disposed; ready, earnest, eager, desirous; genial, cordial.

adv willingly, freely, with pleasure, with all one's heart, graciously.

603 unwillingness *n* indisposition, disinclination, reluctance, dislike; aversion, indifference, slowness, lack of readiness, obstinacy; scrupulousness, hesitation, qualm, shrinking, holding back, recoil; averseness, dissent, refusal.

v be unwilling, dislike; demur, hesitate, shrink from, swerve, recoil; dissent, refuse.

adj unwilling, loath, reluctant, averse; laggard, backward, slow, slack, indifferent; scrupulous, hesitant.

adv unwillingly, grudgingly, against one's will, under protest.

604 resolution *n* determination, will, decision, strength of mind, resolve, firmness, energy, manliness, vigor, resoluteness; pluck, zeal, devotion; self-control, self-command, self-possession, self-reliance, self-restraint, self-denial; tenacity, perseverance, obstinacy, *(informal)* gumption.

v be resolute, resolve, will, determine, decide, make a resolution, conclude, fix, bring to a crisis, take a decisive step; stand firm, insist upon, make a point of, not give an inch.

adj resolute, firm, steadfast, resolved, purposeful, fixed, inflexible, bold, game, indomitable, relentless, tenacious, gritty, stern, irrevocable, obstinate.

adv resolutely, in earnest, earnestly, manfully.

604a perseverance *n* persistence, tenacity, resolution, doggedness, determination, steadfastness, indefatigability, pluck, stamina, backbone.

v persevere, persist, continue, keep on, last, stick it out, hang in there.

adj persevering, constant, steady, steadfast, persistent, tenacious, resolute, dogged, indefatigable, indomitable, staunch, true, game, *(informal)* tough.

605 irresolution *n* indecision, indetermination, instability, uncertainty; hesitation, hesitancy, vacillation, oscillation, changeableness, fluctuation, fickleness, weakness, frailty, timidity, cowardice.

v be irresolute, dawdle, dillydally, shilly-shally, hesitate, falter, waver, vacillate, change, fluctuate, blow hot and cold.

adj irresolute, indecisive, indeterminate, unstable, uncertain; hesitant, changeable, capricious, fickle, frail, feeble, weak, timid, *(informal)* soft, cowardly.

606 obstinacy *n* doggedness, persistence, pertinacity, resolution, intractability, firmness, immovability, inflexibility, obduracy, willfulness, perversity, stubbornness, mulishness; uncontrollability, wildness.

fixed idea, *idée fixe*, fanaticism, zealotry, infatuation, monomania; bigotry, intolerance, dogmatism.

bigot, dogmatist, zealot, fanatic.

v be obstinate, persist, die hard, fight, stick to an idea.

adj obstinate, dogged, persistent, pertinacious, resolute, intractable, firm, refractory, headstrong, willful, inflexible, immovable, perverse, stubborn, mulish, pigheaded; wayward, unruly, incorrigible, uncontrollable, wild; fanatic, zealous, monomaniacal; intolerant, dogmatic, arbitrary.

607 recantation *n* tergiversation, renunciation, abjuration, retraction, defection, apostasy, disavowal, revocation, reversal.

turncoat, apostate, renegade, deserter.

v recant, change one's mind, abjure, retract, renounce, disavow, revoke, defect, change sides.

adj changeful, irresolute, slippery, timeserving.

608 caprice n fancy, humor, whim, quirk, freak, fad, vagary, prank.

v be capricious.

adj capricious, erratic, eccentric, fitful, inconsistent, fanciful, whimsical, crotchety, freakish, wayward, wanton; contrary, captious, unreasonable, arbitrary, fickle; frivolous.

609 choice n selection, decision, pick, choosing, election, option, alternative, preference, predilection, desire.

v choose, select, elect, make a choice, prefer, pick cull, decide.

adj optional, discretional, preferential.

609a neutrality, absence of choice n neutrality, indifference; indecision, irresolution.

no choice, first come first served.

v be neutral, have no preference, waive, abstain.

take what's offered.

adj neutral, indifferent; indecisive, irresolute.

610 rejection n refusal, repudiation, renunciation; exclusion, elimination.

v reject, refuse, repudiate, decline, deny, rebuff, repel, renounce; discard, throw away, exclude, eliminate; jettison.

611 predetermination n premeditation, predeliberation, foregone conclusion; resolve, intention; fate, predestination, destiny.

v predetermine, predestine, premeditate, resolve beforehand, calculate.

adj aforethought; foregone.

adv advisedly, deliberately, intentionally.

612 impulse n sudden thought, flash, spurt, inspiration; improvisation.

v improvise, extemporize, flash on, hit on, come up with, pull out of a hat, pull out of the air; say what comes to mind.

adj impulsive, impromptu, spontaneous; extemporaneous.

adv extempore, extemporaneously; impromptu, offhand, impulsively.

613 habit n addiction, disposition, tendency, bent, wont; custom, prescription, practice, way, usage, wont, manner; prevalence; observance; conventionalism, conventionality, mode, fashion, vogue, conformity; rule, precedent, routine, rut, groove.

v habituate, inure, harden, season; accustom, familiarize; acclimate, accommodate; cling to, adhere to, acquire a habit, fall into a rut; be habitual, come into use, become a habit, take root.

adj habitual, customary, prescriptive, usual, general, ordinary, common, frequent, everyday, familiar, trite, commonplace, conventional, regular, set, stock, fixed, permanent; prevalent, current, fashionable; addictive.

adv habitually, as usual, as things go, as the world goes; as a rule, for the most part, generally.

614 disuse n desuetude, disusage, lack of practice.

v be unaccustomed, break a habit; disuse.

adj unaccustomed; unusual, original.

615 motive n reason, ground, principle, mainspring, purpose, cause, occasion, influence, impulse, instigation, spur, stimulus, incitement, incentive, inducement, consideration, temptation, motivation; intention, ulterior motive.

v motivate, induce, move, inspire, put up to, prompt, stimulate, spur, excite, arouse, rouse, incite, instigate; influence, sway, incline, dispose, lead, persuade, prevail upon, enlist, engage, invite, court, tempt, charm.

adj suasive, persuasive, seductive, attractive, provocative.

615a absence of motive n caprice, chance, absence of design.

v have no motive.

adj capricious, without rhyme or reason.

adv capriciously.

616 dissuasion n expostulation, remonstrance, deprecation, discouragement, damper, restraint, curb, check.

v dissuade, cry out against, remonstrate, expostulate, warn, disincline, indispose, shake, discourage, dishearten, disenchant; deter, hold back, restrain, repel, turn aside, wean from, damp, cool, chill, blunt.

adj dissuasive.

617 [ostensible motive, ground, or reason] **plea** *n* pretext, allegation, excuse; pretense, shallow excuse, lame excuse, makeshift.

v plead, allege, excuse, make a pretext of, pretend.

adj ostensible, alleged.

adv ostensibly, under the pretense of.

618 good *n* benefit, interest, service, behalf, advantage, improvement, gain, boot, profit, harvest; boon, blessing, good luck, prize, good fortune, windfall, godsend; prosperity, happiness, goodness.

v benefit, serve, profit, advantage.

adj commendable; useful, good, beneficial, advantageous.

619 evil *n* ill, harm, hurt, mischief, nuisance; damage, loss; disadvantage, drawback; disaster, accident, casualty, mishap, misfortune; calamity, catastrophe, tragedy, ruin, destruction, adversity; mental suffering, pain, anguish; outrage, wrong, injury, foul, play.

v be in trouble; harm, hurt, injure, ruin, destroy, torture.

adj evil, hurtful, injurious, harmful; disastrous, catastrophic, cataclysmic, tragic, ruinous.

620 intention *n* intent, purpose, project, undertaking, design, ambition, contemplation, view, proposal, meaning; object, aim, end, destination, mark, point, goal, target, prey, quarry, game; decision, determination, resolve, resolution, settled purpose.

v intend, mean, design, purpose, propose, contemplate, plan, expect, mediate, calculate, project, aim for, aim at, aspire at.

adj intentional, advised, express,

determinate, bound for, bent upon, in view, in prospect.

adv intentionally, advisedly, wittingly, knowingly, purposely, on purpose, by design, pointedly; deliberately.

621 [absence of design] **chance** *n* destiny, lot, fate, luck, good luck, turn, (*informal*) break, (*informal*) jinx, fortune; speculation, venture, stake, shot in the dark, fluke; wager, gambling, betting.

gambler, gamester, adventurer.

v chance, chance it, tempt fate, speculate, risk, venture, hazard, stake, wager, bet, place a bet, gamble, play for.

adj unintentional, accidental, random; fortuitous, lucky; speculative, venturesome.

adv unintentionally, unwittingly.

622 pursuit *n* pursuance, enterprise, undertaking, business, adventure, essay, quest, search.

v pursue, prosecute, follow, do, engage in, undertake, endeavor, seek, aim at, fish for, press on, go after, chase.

adj in quest of, in pursuit of.

623 avoidance *n* evasion, flight, escape, retreat, recoil, departure; abstention, abstinence, forbearance, inaction.

avoider, shirker, quitter, truant; fugitive, refugee, runaway, deserter.

v avoid, shun, steer clear of, keep clear of, evade, elude, shirk, fly from, turn away from; abstain, refrain, eschew, leave alone, not get involved; shrink, hold back, retire, recoil, flinch, blink, shy, dodge, beat a retreat, turn tail, run for one's life, head for the hills, take flight, beat it out; desert, sneak off, shuffle off, slink away, steal away, slip, sneak, bolt, abscond.

adj elusive, evasive, escapist, fugitive.

624 relinquishment *n* surrender, resignation, yielding, waiver, waiving, abdication, leaving, desertion, withdrawal, secession, abandonment, renunciation.

v relinquish, surrender, give up,

resign, yield, cede, waive, forswear, forgo, abdicate, leave, forsake, desert, renounce, quit, abandon, let go, resign, *(informal)* throw in the towel, call it quits, *(informal)* hang it up.

625 business *n* occupation, trade, craft, profession, calling, employment, vocation, pursuit; affair, matter, concern, transaction, undertaking; function, duty, office, position, part, role, capacity.

v employ oneself, undertake, turn one's hand to; be at work on, be engaged in, be occupied with.

adj businesslike; workaday, professional, official, functional; busy.

626 plan *n* scheme, plot, stratagem, policy, procedure, project, formula, method, system, organization, design, contrivance, device; drawing, sketch, draft, map, chart, diagram, representation; intrigue, cabal, conspiracy.

planner, designer, organizer, schemer, strategist, intriguer.

v plan, arrange, frame, scheme, plot, design, devise, contrive, invent, concoct, hatch; project, forecast; systematize, organize, cast, recast, lay groundwork.

adj procedural, formulaic, methodological, systematic, organizational; conspiratorial; strategic.

627 [path] method *n* road, procedure, way, means, manner, fashion, technique, process, course, route, track, beat, tack; door, gateway, channel, passage, avenue, means of access, approach.

adv how, in what way, in what manner; by what mode; one way or another, after this fashion.

628 mid-course *n* middle way, middle course, mean, golden mean; compromise, *(informal)* six of one and half a dozen of another, half measures, neutrality.

v steer a middle course, go straight; compromise, go half way, make a compromise.

adj moderate, midway; neutral, impartial.

629 circuit *n* roundabout way, digression, detour, loop, winding.

v go round about, make a circuit, detour, wind around, circle around; deviate, digress.

adj circuitous, indirect, roundabout; zigzag.

adv in a roundabout way, by an indirect course, indirectly.

630 requirement *n* requisite, requisition, need, necessity, wants, claim, demand, prerequisite; mandate, order, command, directive, injunction, charge, claim, precept.

v require, need, call for, have occasion for, necessitate, obligate; demand, request, need, order, enjoin, direct, ask.

adj requisite, necessary, essential, indispensable, needful; urgent, exigent, instant, crying.

adv of necessity.

631 instrumentality *n* mediation, intervention, medium, intermedium, vehicle, hand; aid; subservience. go-between, intermediary, minister.

v mediate, minister, intervene; be instrumental, aid.

adj instrumental, useful, serviceable; intermediary, intermediate.

adv through, by, whereby, thereby, by the agency of, by dint of, by means of.

632 means *n* resources, wherewithal, way, ways and means, know how, ability; agency, method, approach; capital, provisions.

v have the means, find the means, possess the means.

adj instrumental.

adv by means of; herewith, therewith; wherewithal.

633 instrument *n* tool, implement, utensil, machinery, equipment.

adj instrumental; mechanical.

634 substitute *n* deputy, alternate, understudy, stand-in, proxy, *(informal)* sub, replacement.

v to substitute for, sub.

635 materials *n* raw materials, resources, stuff, stock, staples, supplies.

636 store n stock, fund, mine, supply, reserve, reservoir, *(informal)* stash; accumulation, hoard, storing, storage.

v store, put aside, lay away; store up, put up, hoard away, accumulate, amass, garner; reserve, husband, *(informal)* stash, hold back.

adj in store, in reserve, spare.

637 provision n supply, grist, resources, store, provender, stock, food; catering, providing, purveying, purveyance, supplying.

v make provision, provide, lay in, lay in a stock, lay in a store; supply, furnish, purvey, provision, cater, stock, store, replenish.

638 waste n consumption, expenditure, dissipation, diminution, decline, emaciation, exhaustion, loss, destruction, decay, impairment; misuse, prodigality, wasting; ruin, devastation, spoilation, desolation.

v waste, consume, spend, throw out, expend, squander, misuse, misspend, dissipate; destroy, wear away, erode, eat away, reduce, wear down, exhaust, enfeeble, wear out.

adj wasteful, prodigal, spendthrift; destructive; wasted, gone to waste.

639 sufficiency n adequacy, enough, competence.

v be sufficient, suffice, do, just do, satisfy; have enough.

adj sufficient, enough, adequate, ample, up to the mark, competent, commensurate, satisfactory.

adv sufficiently, amply.

640 insufficiency n inadequacy, incompetence, incompleteness, deficiency, imperfection, shortcoming; paucity, scarcity, dearth, dole, pittance; emptiness, poorness, depletion, flaccidity.

v be insufficient, not suffice, not do, fall short of, *(informal)* not cut it; want, lack, need, require, be in want.

adj insufficient, inadequate, too little, not enough, incomplete, deficient, imperfect, wanting, short, scarce, meager, poor, thin, sparse, scant; incompetent, perfunctory.

641 redundance n superfluity, superabundance, too much, too many, exuberance, profuseness, profusion, plenty, repletion, plethora, congestion, surfeit, overdose, overflow; excess, surplus; repetition, verbosity.

v superabound, overabound, swarm, overflow, run over, run riot, overrun, overdose, overload, overdo, overwhelm; supersaturate, gorge, glut, load, drench, inundate, deluge, flood; choke, cloy, suffocate, pile on, lay on thick, lavish.

adj redundant, exuberant, inordinate, superabundant, excessive, overmuch, replete, profuse, lavish; exorbitant, extravagant, overweening, *(informal)* much; superfluous, unnecessary, needless, over and above, spare, duplicate; repetitious, verbose.

adv over and above, over much, out of proportion, beyond bounds, over one's head.

642 importance n consequence, substance, weight, moment, prominence, consideration, significance, import, concern, emphasis, interest, momentousness, weightiness; gravity, seriousness, solemnity; pressure, urgency, stress.

v be important, deserve consideration, be worthy of notice, merit attention; attach importance, ascribe importance, value, care for, set store by; import, signify, matter, boot, carry weight; accentuate, emphasize, lay stress on; mark, underline, underscore.

adj important, consequential, weighty, momentous, prominent, considerable, significant, notable, salient; grave, serious, earnest, grand, solemn, impressive, commanding, imposing; urgent, pressing, critical, crucial, paramount, essential, vital, prime, primary, principal, all-important, capital, foremost, of vital importance; superior, considerable; significant, telling, trenchant, emphatic.

643 unimportance n insignificance, immateriality, triviality, paltriness, indifference, nothing, trifling;

trumpery, trash, rubbish, frippery, chaff, bauble, trifle.

v be unimportant, not matter, matter little, signify little; make light of.

adj unimportant, of little account, of small importance, immaterial, unessential, nonessential, inconsequential, insignificant, inconsiderable, so-so; commonplace, ordinary, uneventful, mere, common; trifling, trivial, slight, slender, light, flimsy, shallow; frivolous, petty, niggling, piddling; poor, paltry, pitiful, sorry, mean, meager, shabby, beggarly, worthless, cheap, tawdry, trashy, gimmicky; unworthy of consideration, unworthy of notice; useless, of no account.

644 utility *n* usefulness, efficacy, helpfulness, service, use, stead, avail, help, aid; applicability, value, worth, productiveness.

v be useful, avail, serve, perform, help, aid, benefit; act a part, discharge a function, stand one in good stead.

adj useful, serviceable, functional, advantageous, valuable, productive, profitable, helpful, effectual, effective, efficacious, beneficial, salutary; applicable, available, practical, practicable, workable.

645 inutility *n* uselessness, inefficacy, ineptitude, inaptitude, inadequacy, inefficiency, unfruitfulness, futility, worthlessness, hopelessness.

v be useless, be of no help.

adj useless, unavailing, futile, inutile, fruitless, vain, ineffectual, profitless, bootless, valueless, worthless, hopeless; unserviceable, unusable, inoperative.

646 expedience *n* expediency, fitness, utility, suitability, profitability, advisability, propriety, appropriateness, desirability; opportunism, pragmatism, realism.

v be expedient, suit, befit, suit the occasion.

adj expedient, advantageous, opportune, fit, suitable, convenient, profitable, worthwhile, advisable,

meet, proper, becoming, appropriate, desirable.

647 inexpedience *n* inexpediency, impropriety, unfitness, unsuitability, inappropriateness, undesirability; inconvenience, impracticality.

v be inexpedient, be inconvenient, hinder.

adj inexpedient, inopportune, unfit, unsuitable, disadvantageous, discommodious, unadvisable, unseemly, improper, unworkable, impractical, inconvenient, unprofitable, useless, worthless.

648 [good qualities] **goodness** *n* virtue, excellence, merit, value, worth; perfection, eminence, superiority, masterpiece, *chef d'oeuvre*, prime, flower, cream, elite, pick, pick of the litter, salt of the earth, *(informal)* A-1, *(informal)* tops, second to none; gem, jewel, treasure, one in a million; beneficence.

v be good, excel, transcend, stand the test, pass muster, challenge comparison, vie, emulate, rival, *(informal)* dwarf the competition; be beneficial, do good, profit, benefit, improve, be the making of, do a world of good, produce a good effect, do a good turn.

adj good, excellent, better, superior, above par, fine, genuine, true; best, choice, select, rare, invaluable, priceless, inestimable, superlative, perfect, inimitable, first-rate, first-class, very best, crack, prime, tip-top, capital, *(informal)* tops; beneficial, valuable, advantageous, profitable, edifying, salutary, serviceable; favorable, propitious.

649 [bad qualities] **badness** *n* harmfulness, hurtfulness, virulence, painfulness, abomination, pestilence, guilt, depravity, vice, evil, malignity, malevolence; bane, plague, evil star, ill wind, bad omen, *(informal)* jinx, *(informal)* whammy; snake in the grass, skeleton in the closet, *(informal)* ghosts, *(informal)* demons; ill-treatment, annoyance, molestation, abuse, oppression, persecution, outrage, misusage, injury, damage.

v hurt, harm, injure, damage,

pain; wrong, aggrieve, oppress, persecute, trample upon, tread upon, walk over, overburden; weigh down, run down; victimize, maltreat, molest, abuse, ill-use, bruise, scratch, maul, smite, do violence, do harm, stab, pierce.

adj hurtful, harmful, baleful, injurious, deleterious, detrimental, noxious, pernicious, mischievous; oppressive, burdensome, onerous, malign, malevolent; virulent, venomous, corrosive, poisonous, deadly, destructive; bad, ill, dreadful, horrid, horrible, dire, rank, foul, rotten, as low as one can go, *(informal)* the pits; evil, wrong, reprehensible, hateful, abominable, detestable, execrable, damnable, infernal, diabolical; vile, base, villainous, cruel, mean, low; deplorable, wretched, sad, grievous, lamentable, pitiable, pitiful, woeful, painful.

650 perfection *n* ideal, summit, paragon, model, standard, pattern, mirror; impeccability, faultlessness, excellence; masterpiece, master stroke; transcendence, superiority.

v perfect, bring to perfection, ripen, mature, complete, finish; be perfect, transcend.

adj perfect, faultless, immaculate, spotless, unblemished, impeccable, exquisite, consummate; in perfect condition, sound, intact; best, model, standard, inimitable, beyond all praise.

651 imperfection *n* deficiency, inadequacy, insufficiency, immaturity; fault, defect, weak point, weak spot, flaw, taint, blemish, weakness, shortcoming, drawback.

v be imperfect, have a defect, not pass muster, fall short.

adj imperfect, deficient, inadequate, insufficient, immature, defective, faulty, unsound, out of order, out of tune, warped, lame, frail, weak, crude, incomplete, below par, found wanting; indifferent, middling, ordinary, mediocre, average, so-so, tolerable, fair, passable, decent, not bad, bearable, better than nothing; inferior, secondary, second-rate, poor substitute.

652 cleanness *n* purity, purification, purgation, cleanliness; ablution, lavation; neatness, tidiness, orderliness; cathartic, purgative, laxative; detergent, disinfectant.

v clean, cleanse, purify, purge, expurgate, clarify, refine; wash, launder, scour, scrub, disinfect, fumigate, deodorize, ventilate; rout out, clear out, sweep out, make a clean sweep of, start fresh; neaten, tidy up, order, put things in order.

adj clean, pure, immaculate, spotless, stainless, unsullied, sweet; neat, spruce, tidy, trim, kempt.

653 uncleanness *n* impurity, defilement, contamination, taint; decay, putrefaction, corruption, mold, mildew, rot, dry rot; squalor, slovenliness, filth, dirt, smut, grime, mud, mire, muck, quagmire, slime.

v be unclean, rot, putrefy, fester, rankle, reek, stink, mold, go bad; dirty, soil, tarnish, spot, smear, blot, blur, smudge, smirch; besmear, befoul, splash, stain, sully, pollute, defile, debase, contaminate, taint, corrupt.

adj unclean, dirty, filthy, grimy, soiled; dusty, smutty, sooty, slimy; slovenly, untidy, sluttish, dowdy, unkempt, unscoured, squalid; nasty, coarse, foul, impure, offensive, abominable, beastly, reeky, fetid; moldy, musty, moth-eaten, bad, gone bad, rancid, rotten, corrupt, putrid, carious, fecal; gory, bloody; gross.

654 health *n* soundness, well-being, vigor, good health, bloom, color, vitality, robust health.

v be in health, be healthy, bloom, flourish, feel fine, feel good.

adj healthy, healthful, in health, well, sound, hearty, hale, strong, hardy, robust, vigorous, fit as a fiddle, in top shape, chipper, *(informal)* all together.

655 disease *n* illness, sickness, ill health, ailment, infirmity, indisposition, complaint, disorder, malady; delicacy, delicate, condition, decline, deterioration, decay.

v ail, suffer, be affected with, droop, flag, languish, sicken, pine, gasp, waste away, fail; take sick, take ill, come down with; contract a disease, catch a bug.

adj ill, sick, indisposed, not well, unwell, in poor health, in bad health, ailing, poorly, laid up, bedridden, out of sorts, under the weather, *(informal)* in bad shape; sickly, infirm, unsound, unhealthy, *(informal)* falling apart, weak, lame, decrepit; diseased, morbid, mangy, corrupt, contaminated, leprous.

656 salubrity *n* healthiness, healthfulness, wholesomeness.

v be salubrious, be good for, agree with.

adj salubrious, healthy, healthful, salutary, wholesome, sanitary, bracing, invigorating, benign, nutritious, tonic, hygienic.

657 insalubrity *n* unhealthiness, unsoundness.

v be unhealthy, not be good for, disagree with.

adj insalubrious, unhealthy, unwholesome, noxious, noisome, deleterious, pestilential, bad, harmful, virulent, venomous, poisonous, septic, toxic, deadly.

658 improvement *n* amelioration, amendment, emendation, correction, revision, reformation, restoration, repair, betterment, gain, advancement, elevation, increase, refinement, elaboration; acculturation, cultivation, civilization.

reformer, radical.

v improve, mend, amend, get better; ameliorate, better, amend, emend, correct, right, rectify, revise, reform, restore, repair; advance, progress, ascend, increase, fructify, ripen, mature; refine, enrich, elaborate; promote, cultivate, foster, enhance.

adj better, better off, all for the better; emendatory, corrective, reformative, restorative, improving, progressive, improved.

659 deterioration *n* debasement, recession, retrogradation, degeneracy, degeneration, degradation, deprivation, depravity, retrogression;

detriment, damage, loss, injury, impairment, contamination, spoilage, corruption, adulteration; decline, declension, senility, decrepitude; decadence, decay, dilapidation, falling off, wear and tear, erosion, corrosion, rottenness, blight, atrophy, collapse.

v deteriorate, degenerate, fall off, wane, ebb, decline, droop, go down, go downhill, sink, go to seed, go to waste, lapse, break down, crack, shrivel, fade, wither, molder, rot, rankle, decay, go bad, rust, crumble, shake, totter, perish, die; taint, infect, contaminate, poison, canker, corrupt, pollute, vitiate, debase, degrade, adulterate; injure, impair, damage, harm, hurt, spoil, mar, despoil, dilapidate, waste, ravage; wound, maim, cripple, scotch, mangle, mutilate, disfigure, blemish, deface, warp; blight, rot, corrode, erode, wear away, wear out, sap, mine, undermine, shake the foundations of, break up, destroy, decimate.

adj deteriorated, unimproved, injured, degenerate, imperfect; battered, weathered, weather-beaten, all the worse for wear, stale, dilapidated, faded, shabby, threadbare, worn, far gone, *(informal)* had it; decayed, moth-eaten, worm-eaten, mildewed, rusty, moldy, seedy, timeworn, wasted, crumbling, moldering, rotten, blighted, tainted; decrepit, broken down, wornout, used up, out of commission, in a bad way, past cure, past hope, *(informal)* long gone.

660 restoration *n* reestablishment, replacement, reinstatement, renewal, rehabilitation, reconstruction, reproduction, rebuilding, renovation, revival, refreshment, resuscitation, revivification; renaissance, renascence, new birth, regeneration, reconversion, redress, retrieval, reclamation, recovery, resumption; repair, reparation, restitution, relief, deliverance, rectification, cure, healing; redemption.

v restore, recover, rally, revive, come round, pull through, get well, get over; reestablish, replace, rehabilitate, reinstate; reconstruct, rebuild, reproduce, reorganize, reconstitute, renew, renovate; redeem, reclaim, recover, retrieve, rescue, deliver; redress, recure; cure, heal, remedy, doctor, bring round; resuscitate, revive, reanimate, revivify, reinvigorate, refresh; recoup, make good, square; set to rights, correct, put in order; repair, retouch, patch up, fix.

adj restorative, recuperative, curative, remedial; restorable, remediable, retrievable, curable; restored, convalescent, renascent, reborn.

661 relapse *n* lapse, falling back, retrogradation, deterioration, backsliding.

v relapse, lapse, fall back, slip back, sink back, suffer a relapse, fall again.

adj retrograde.

662 remedy *n* help, redress, solution, answer, panacea; cure, relief, medicine, treatment, restorative, specific, medication, ointment, balm; antidote, corrective, antitoxin, counteractive.

doctor, physician, surgeon.

v remedy, cure, heal, set right, put right, doctor, nurse, restore, recondition, repair, redress; counteract, remove, correct, right, solve.

adj remedial, restorative, corrective, palliative; medicinal, therapeutic, curative; soluble.

663 bane *n* curse, evil, plague, scourge, pain, nuisance, thorn in the side, pain in the neck; poison, virus, venom; fungus, mildew, dry rot, canker, cancer; sting, fang, thorn, bramble, briar, nettle.

adj baneful, bad, sinister, pernicious, evil, baleful, poisonous, venomous, ruinous, unwholesome, harmful, deadly.

664 safety *n* security, surety, impregnability, invulnerability; safeguard, safety valve, precaution, custody, safe keeping, preservation, protection.

protector, guardian, warden, preserver, custodian, watchdog, sentinel, scout.

v be safe; protect, take care of, care for, preserve, cover, screen, shelter, shroud, guard, defend, secure, house, garrison; watch, patrol, look out, take precautions.

adj safe, secure, snug, warm, sure, sound, on the safe side, out of danger; dependable, trustworthy, sure, reliable; cautious, wary, careful; defensible, tenable, invulnerable, impregnable, unassailable, safe and sound.

665 danger *n* hazard, insecurity, instability, precariousness, slipperiness, risk, peril, jeopardy, liability, exposure; injury, evil; warning, alarm, apprehension.

v be in danger, run into trouble, lay oneself open to, hang by a thread, totter; endanger, expose to danger, imperil, jeopardize, adventure, venture, risk, hazard, threaten.

adj dangerous, hazardous, risky, perilous, precarious, unsafe, insecure, unstable, untrustworthy, unsteady, shaky, slippery, ominous, fearful, explosive, fraught with danger; defenseless, vulnerable, open, liable.

666 refuge *n* sanctuary, retreat, asylum, hiding place, stronghold, fortress, shelter, cover; anchor, mainstay, support, check, last resort, safeguard.

v seek refuge, take refuge, find refuge, take shelter, find safety.

667 pitfall *n* snare, trap, noose, ambush, snake in the grass, wolf in sheep's clothing, menace, complication, danger; slippery ground, weak foundation, rocks, reefs, sunken rocks, sand, quicksand, breakers, shoals, shallows, precipice, maelstrom.

668 warning *n* caution, notice, premonition, prediction, admonition, advice, lesson; alarm, omen, sign, signal, augury, portent, presage.

sentinel, sentry, watch, watchman, watchdog, patrol, scout, spy.

v warn, caution, admonish, forewarn; give notice, notify, appraise, inform; menace, threaten, portend.

adj premonitory, cautionary, advisory; ominous, portentous.

669 [indication of danger] **alarm** *n* alarum, alarm bell, tocsin, distress signal, siren, danger signal, hue and cry, SOS, cry, scream.

v alarm, sound the alarm, warn, cry out.

670 preservation *n* safekeeping, conservation; guarding, safeguard, shelter, protection, defense; maintenance, support, sustenance, continuance, retention, salvation.

v preserve, keep, conserve; guard, safeguard, shelter, shield, protect, defend, rescue; keep up, maintain, continue, support, uphold, sustain; retain; store, husband; cure, pickle, bottle, can.

adj preserved, unimpaired, uninjured, unhurt, safe, sound, intact; conservative, preservative.

671 escape *n* flight, evasion, loophole, retreat; reprieve, release, liberation; narrow escape, close call, near miss.

v escape, flee, abscond, fly, steal away, run away, *(informal)* take off, *(informal)* split; shun, fly, elude, evade, avoid.

adj stolen away, fled, *(informal)* cut out.

672 deliverance *n* extrication, disentanglement, rescue, reprieve, respite; liberation, release, emancipation, freedom; redemption, salvation.

v deliver, extricate, disentangle, rescue, reprieve, save, redeem; set free, liberate, release, emancipate, free; come to the rescue.

673 preparation *n* provision, plan, arrangement, anticipation, precaution, forecast, rehearsal; groundwork, homework, foundation, scaffolding; training, education, dissemination; readiness, ripeness, maturity.

v prepare, get ready, make ready, prime, arrange, make preparations, plan, devise, anticipate; lay the foundations, provide, order; mature, ripen, mellow, season, nurture; equip, arm, fit out, furnish; train, teach, prepare for, rehearse, make

provision for, take steps, provide against.

adj prepatory, precautionary, provident, preparative, preparatory; provisional, preliminary; prepared, ready, available, all ready, handy; ripe, mature, mellow.

674 nonpreparation *n* unpreparedness, unreadiness; improvidence.

v be unprepared; extemporize, improvise.

adj unprepared, incomplete, premature, rudimental, embryonic, immature, unripe, raw, green, coarse, crude, rough, unhewn, untaught, fallow, unready; out of order, nonfunctional, *(informal)* on the fritz, in disrepair, *(informal)* out of whack; shiftless, improvident, thoughtless, careless, slack, remiss, happy-go-lucky.

675 essay *n* trial, endeavor, effort, attempt, struggle, venture, adventure, speculation, experiment.

v essay, try, experiment; endeavor, strive, tempt, attempt, venture, adventure, speculate, tempt fortune, *(informal)* give it a go, *(informal)* take a shot at.

adj experimental, tentative, probationary; venturesome, adventurous, speculative.

adv experimentally, on trial.

676 undertaking *n* task, job, venture, engagement, compact, contract, enterprise; pilgrimage, quest.

v undertake, engage in, embark on, launch into, plunge into, volunteer; engage, promise, contract, take upon oneself, devote oneself to, determine, take up, take in hand; tackle, set about, fall to, begin, broach.

677 use *n* employ, exercise, application, appliance; disposal; consumption; agency, usefulness; benefit, recourse, resort, avail; utilization, utility, service, wear; usage.

v use, make use of, employ, put to use, put into operation, apply, set in motion, set to work; ply, work, wield, handle, manipulate; exert, exercise, practice, avail oneself of, profit by; resort to, have recourse to, recur to, take up, try; utilize, bring into play, press into service; use up, consume, expend, tax, task, wear.

adj useful, instrumental, utilitarian, subservient, employable, applicable, beneficial.

678 disuse *n* forbearance, abstinence; relinquishment, abandonment; desuetude.

v not use, do without, dispense with, let alone, forebear, abstain, spare, waive, neglect; keep back, reserve; disuse, lay up, shelve, set aside, put aside, leave off, have done with; supersede, discard, throw aside, relinquish, dismantle.

adj not in use, unemployed, unapplied; disused, unused, done with.

679 misuse *n* misusage, misemployment, misapplication, misappropriation; abuse, profanation, prostitution, desecration; waste.

v misuse, misemploy, misapply, misappropriate; abuse, profane, prostitute, desecrate; waste, squander, destroy; overwork, overtask, overtax.

680 action *n* movement, work, labor, performance, moving, working, performing, operation; deed, act, feat, exploit; conduct, behavior, procedure, execution; energetic activity, exercise, exertion, energy, effort; affair, encounter, meeting, engagement, conflict, combat, fight, battle.

actor, doer, worker.

v act, do, perform, execute, achieve, transact, enact; commit, perpetrate, inflict; exercise, prosecute, carry on, work, function, labor, operate, exert energy, be active; behave, conduct, feign, fake, imitate.

adj in action, in operation, operative.

681 inaction *n* passivity, inactivity, idleness, solthfulness; waiting, mulling around, killing time; rest, repose,

v not act, not do, be inactive, abstain from doing, do nothing, let alone, let things take their course; stand aloof, refrain, pause, wait,

bide one's time, cool one's heels, waste time, lie idle.

adj inactive, passive, idle, slothful; out of work.

682 activity *n* movement, hustle, bustle, stir, fuss, flurry, action, business; industry, assiduity, assiduousness, laboriousness, drudgery, diligence, perseverance, vigilance, wakefulness, restlessness, fidgetiness; briskness, liveliness, animation, life, vivacity, spirit, dash, energy; eagerness, zeal, ardor, vigor, abandon, exertion; earnestness, intentness, devotion.

v be active, busy oneself in, stir about, rouse oneself, speed, hasten, bustle, fuss, *(informal)* raise a ruckus; push, push ahead, *(informal)* step on it, *(informal)* move it, make progress; toil, plod, persist, persevere, hustle, *(informal)* hustle it, *(informal)* push; look sharp, keep moving, seize the opportunity, *carpe diem*, lose no time, dash off, make haste; have a hand in, trouble oneself about.

adj active, brisk, lively, busy as a bee, vivacious, alive, frisky; quick, prompt, ready, alert, spry, sharp, smart, awake, wide awake, eager, zealous; industrious, assiduous, diligent, vigilant; businesslike; restless, fussy, fidgety, busy.

683 inactivity *n* inaction, inertness, lull, quiescence; idleness, remissness, sloth, indolence, dawdling, laziness; dullness, languor, sluggishness, torpor, stupor, lethargy, procrastination.

idler, drone, dawdler, moper, lounger, loafer, sluggard, laggard, slumberer.

v be inactive, do nothing, dawdle, lag, hang back, slouch, loll, lounge, loaf, loiter, take it easy; fritter away time, idle, piddle, putter, dabble, dally, dilly-dally; languish, flag, relax; kill time, waste time.

adj inactive, motionless; indolent, lazy, slothful, idle, remiss, slack, inert, torpid, sluggish, languid, supine, heavy, dull, listless; laggard, slow, rusty, lackadaisical, irresolute; drowsy, lethargic, soporific, dreamy, dreamy-eyed.

684 haste n urgency, need, hurry, flurry, bustle, spurt, rush, dash, scramble, bustle, ado, precipitancy, precipitation; swiftness, celerity, alacrity, quickness, rapidity, dispatch, speed, expedition, promptitude, timeliness, promptness.

v haste, hasten, make haste, hurry, dash, push on, press on, press forward, scurry, bustle, scramble, rush, accelerate, urge, expedite, quicken, speed, precipitate, dispatch.

adj hasty, speedy, quick, hurried, swift, rapid, fast, fleet, brisk; precipitate, rash, foolhardy, reckless, indiscreet, thoughtless, headlong, testy, touchy, irascible, petulant, waspish, fretful, fiery, excitable, irritable, peevish.

685 leisure n spare time, free time, convenience, liberty, pause, stay, halt, lull, breather, (informal) letup, breathing spell, break, (informal) time out; interlude, vacation, holiday.

v have leisure, take one's time; rest, relax, repose.

adj leisure, spare, free; leisurely, slow, deliberate, quiet, calm, restful, peaceful, languid, easy, gradual.

686 exertion n effort, action, activity, endeavor, struggle, attempt, strain, trial, stress; labor, work, toil, travail; trouble, pain; energy.

v exert, exert oneself, labor, work, toil, sweat, drudge, strive, strain; work hard, rough it, buckle to, take pains, concentrate, spare no effort.

adj laborious, wearisome, burdensome, (informal) tough, (informal) rough, strenuous, herculean, Sisyphean.

687 repose n rest, sleep, slumber; relaxation, breathing spell; halt, pause, respite, cessation; day of rest, Sabbath; holiday, vacation, recess.

v repose, rest; relax, unbend, slacken, catch one's breath, get one's wind, take a breather, pause; recline, lie down, go to bed, take a

nap, go to sleep; take a holiday, go on vacation, shut up shop.

adj reposing, resting.

adv at rest.

688 fatigue n weariness, lassitude, tiredness, exhaustion, faintness; ennui, boredom, tedium, languor, yawning, drowsiness.

v be fatigued, yawn, droop, sink, flag, (informal) give out; gasp, pant, puff, blow, drop, swoon, faint; fatigue, tire, weary, exhaust, wear out; tax, task, strain; bore, tire, irritate, annoy.

adj fatigued, weary, drowsy, haggard, faint, exhausted, spent, tired, tired to death, worn out, (informal) gone; breathless.

689 refreshment n recovery of strength, restoration, revival, repair, relief.

v refresh, brace, strengthen, reinvigorate, revive, stimulate, freshen, cheer, enliven, reanimate; restore, repair, renew.

adj refreshing, restoring.

690 agent n doer, actor, performer, perpetrator, operator; practitioner, executioner, executor, executrix, minister, representative, deputy, servant, worker; participant, party to.

691 workshop n laboratory, factory, mill, mint, forge, studio; hive, beehive, seat of activity.

692 conduct n behavior, demeanor, action, actions, deportment, bearing, carriage, mien, manners; process, ways, practice, procedure, method; policy, tactics, strategy, plan; direction, management, execution, guidance, leadership, administration.

v conduct, behave, deport, act, bear; transact, execute, dispatch, discharge, proceed with, enact; direct, manage, carry on, supervise, regulate, administer, guide, lead.

adj procedural, practical, methodical, tactical, strategical, businesslike; directive, managerial, administrative, executive.

693 direction n guidance, advice, regulation, conduct, management, disposition, supervision, auspices, steerage, stewardship, ministration, administration, control, leadership, government, rule, command; order, command, instruction.

v direct, guide, advise, regulate, conduct, manage, control, dispose, supervise, overlook, steer, steward, pilot, minister, administer, legislate, lead, rule, govern, have charge of, command; order, instruct, prescribe.

adj directing, guiding, supervisory, managing, administering.

694 director *n* manager, governor, controller, superintendent, supervisor, overseer, inspector, foreman, surveyor, taskmaster, master, leader, boss; adviser, guide, pilot, captain, helmsman, driver; head, chief, principal, president, minister, official, functionary.

695 advice *n* counsel, opinion, recommendation, guidance, suggestion, persuasion, urging, exhortation; instruction, charge, injunction; admonition, warning, caution.

adviser, council, counselor, mentor.

v advise, give counsel to, suggest, recommend, prescribe, advocate, exhort, persuade; enjoin, enforce, charge, instruct; admonish, caution, warn; take counsel, confer, deliberate, discuss, consult, refer to; give counsel, offer counsel.

adj advisory, suggestive, persuasive, suasive; admonitory.

696 council *n* committee, court, chamber, cabinet, board, board of directors, advisory board, staff, syndicate, chapter; assembly, caucus, conclave, meeting, conference, session.

697 precept *n* direction, instruction, charge, prescript, prescription; golden rule, maxim, canon, law, code, act, statute, regulation, formula, form, technicality, rubric; order, command.

698 skill *n* skillfulness, dexterity, adroitness, expertness, proficiency, competence, facility, knack, mastery; accomplishment, acquirement,

attainment, ability, craft; knowledge, wisdom, *savoir faire*, tact, wit, sagacity, discretion, finesse, craftiness, cunning, management; cleverness, ingenuity, capacity, talent, talents, faculty, endowment, *forte*, turn, gift, genius; intelligence, sharpness, readiness, invention, inventiveness, aptness, aptitude, proclivity, capacity for, genius for, felicity, capability, qualification.

v be skillful, excel in, be master of, have a knack for; take advantage of.

adj skillful, dextrous, adroit, adept, expert, apt, handy, quick, deft, proficient, masterly, crack, first-rate, conversant; skilled, experienced, practiced, competent, efficient, qualified, capable, fit, fit for, trained, prepared, finished; clever, able, ingenious, felicitous, inventive; shrewd, sharp, smart, intelligent, cunning, tactful, discreet, wise, knowledgeable.

adv skillfully, artistically, with consummate skill.

699 unskillfulness *n* want of skill, incompetence, inability, inexpertness, maladroitness, ineptitude, clumsiness, awkwardness, carelessness, bumbling, bungling; indiscretion.

v be unskillful, blunder, bungle, boggle, fumble, botch, stumble.

adj unskillful, unskilled, inexpert, incompetent, unable, inapt, bungling, inept, maladroit, awkward, clumsy, gawky; unfit, illqualified, unhandy, not conversant; raw, rusty, out of practice.

700 expert *n* specialist, authority, master, professional, connoisseur, veteran, old hand, old soldier; genius, mastermind, wizard, prodigy, *(informal)* pro.

701 bungler *n* blunderer, blunderhead, fumbler, duffer, clown, *(informal)* turkey, butter-fingers, greenhorn, amateur, rookie, novice, *(informal)* Sunday driver, *(informal)* armchair quarterback.

702 cunning *n* craftiness, skillfulness, shrewdness, artfulness, wiliness, subtlety, finesse, artifice, device, stratagem, intrigue, craft, guile, chicanery, duplicity, subterfuge, deceit, deceitfulness, slyness, deception; ability, skill, adroitness, expertness.

v be cunning, maneuver, contrive, manipulate, intrigue, finesse, surprise.

adj crafty, shrewd, artful, wily, subtle, tricky, foxy, politic, insidious, stealthy, Machiavellian, deceitful, duplicitous, sly, deceptive; canny, astute; ingenious, clever, skillful, sharp.

703 artlessness *n* simplicity, innocence, naivete, unworldliness, inexperience, inexposure, plainness, plain speaking, sincerity, honesty, openness, candor, matter of factness, bluntness.

v be artless, speak one's mind, come to the point, pull no punches.

adj artless, natural, simple, innocent, naive, childlike, unsuspicious, unworldly, unartificial, plain; sincere, frank, open, candid, honest, ingenuous, guileless, straightforward, aboveboard, point-blank, plain spoken, outspoken, blunt, direct, matter of fact.

adv in plain English, in simple words, without mincing words.

704 difficulty *n* dilemma, predicament, quandary, fix, exigency, emergency, crisis, trouble, problem, scrape, entanglement, strait, pass, pinch; reluctance, unwillingness, obstinacy, stubbornness; demur, objection, obstacle; labor, task, hard task, herculean task.

v be difficult, pose, perplex, bother, nonplus, hinder; encumber, embarrass, entangle.

adj difficult, hard, arduous, troublesome, irksome, laborious, formidable; awkward, unwieldy, unmanageable; fastidious, particular, stubborn, intractable, perverse; obscure, complex, intricate, delicate, uncertain, ticklish, critical; unfeasible, impractical, impossible, hopeless; austere, rigid.

705 facility *n* ease, easiness, capability, feasibility, practicability; flexibility, pliancy, smoothness, child's play.

v be easy, run smoothly, work well; facilitate, smooth, ease, lighten, free, clear, disencumber, disentangle, extricate, unravel.

adj easy, facile; feasible, practicable, within reach, accessible; manageable, tractable, pliant, smooth.

adv easily, readily, smoothly.

706 hindrance *n* impediment, deterrent, hitch, encumbrance, obstruction, check, stricture, restraint, hobble, obstacle, stumbling block; interruption, interference; impeding, stopping, stoppage, preventing.

v hinder, interrupt, check, impede, retard, encumber, delay, hamper, obstruct, trammel, cramp, handicap; block, thwart, frustrate, disconcert, prevent.

adj obstructive, intrusive; onerous, burdensome, cumbersome, obtrusive.

707 aid *n* help, support, succor, assistance, service, furtherance; relief, rescue, charity; assistant, helper, supporter, servant; patronage, championship, advocacy, favor, interest.

v aid, support, help, succor, assist, serve, abet, back, second; spell, relieve, rescue; sustain, uphold, prop, hold up, bolster; promote, facilitate, ease, advocate; be of help, give help, give assistance, oblige, accommodate, humor, encourage.

adj aiding, auxiliary, helpful, supportive; charitable, friendly, amicable, well-disposed, neighborly.

708 opposition *n* antagonism, hostility, resistance, counteraction; competition, enemy, foe, adversary, antagonist; opposing, resisting, combating.

v oppose, resist, combat, withstand, thwart, confront, contravene, interfere; hinder, obstruct, prevent, check; contradict, gainsay, deny, refuse, dissent.

adj adverse, antagonistic, contrary, at variance, at odds, anti, at issue, in opposition; unfavorable, unfriendly, hostile, inimical, resistant.

adv against, versus, counter to,

in conflict with, at cross purposes; in spite, in defiance.

709 cooperation *n* concert, concurrence, agreement, concord, togetherness, harmony, unanimity; complicity, collusion, participation, combination, union, team-work; association, partnership, alliance, pool, coalition, confederation, fusion, fellowship, fraternity; unanimity, partisanship, spirit, party spirit, *esprit de corps.*

v cooperate, concur, combine, unite, pool, share, band together, pull together; act in concert, join forces, fraternize; conspire, be in league with; side with, go along with, join hands with, throw in one's lot with, rally round; participate, have a hand in.

adj cooperating, cooperative, participatory; in league, party to.

adv cooperatively, unanimously, shoulder to shoulder.

710 opponent *n* adversary, antagonist, competitor, rival, opposition; enemy, foe.

711 auxiliary *n* helper, aid, ally, assistant, confederate, collaborator, colleague, associate, partner, mate, friend.

712 party *n* group, gathering, assembly, assemblage, company, crew, band; clan, family, fellowship, community; body, faction, side, circle, clique, set, gang, claque, coterie, combination, ring, league, alliance, association.

v unite, join, band together, cooperate, assemble.

adj clannish, cliquish, communal, familial, fraternal.

713 discord *n* dissidence, dissonance, disagreement, clash, shock; variance, difference, dissension, misunderstanding, cross-purposes, odds, division, split, rupture, disruption, breach, schism, feud, conflict, struggle, argument, contention, quarrel, dispute, tiff, squabble, altercation, words; strife, outbreak.

v be discordant, disagree, clash, jar, conflict, differ, dissent, fall out,

quarrel, dispute, squabble, wrangle, bicker, have words with; split, break, disunite, feud.

adj discordant, dissident, dissonant; divisive, disruptive; contentious, argumentative, quarrelsome, disputatious, fractious; at variance, at cross purposes.

714 concord *n* accord, harmony, sympathy, agreement, union, unison, unity, peace; amity, friendship, alliance, *detente,* understanding, togetherness, conciliation.

v agree, accord, harmonize with, fraternize, understand one another, concur, pull together; side with, sympathize with.

adj concordant, congenial, in accord; harmonious, sympathetic, friendly, fraternal, conciliatory.

adv with one voice, unanimously, in concert with.

715 defiance *n* daring, courage, courageousness, bravery, boldness; assertiveness, aggressiveness; antagonism, insubordination, recalcitrance, rebelliousness, insolence, resistance.

v defy, challenge, resist, dare, brave, flout, scorn, despise.

adj defiant, daring, courageous, brave, bold; resistant, insolent, rebellious, recalcitrant, contumacious, insubordinate, antagonistic.

adv in the face of, under one's very nose.

716 attack *n* onslaught, assault, offense, battery, onset, charge, encounter, aggression, incursion, invasion, sally, sortie, raid, foray; criticism, blame, censure, abuse; assailant, aggressor, invader, attacker.

v assail, assault, molest, threaten, storm, charge, set upon, invade, bombard, beset, besiege, lay siege, storm; criticize, impugn, blame, censure, abuse; declare war, begin hostilities.

adj aggressive, offensive; critical, abusive.

adv on the offensive.

717 defense *n* guard, garrison, fortification, shield, shelter, screen, preservation, protection, guardianship, safeguard, security; justification, pleading, vindication.

v defend, guard, fortify, shield, shelter, screen, preserve, protect, keep safe, guard against, watch over, safeguard, secure; parry, repel, put to flight; uphold, maintain, justify, vindicate.

adj defensive, protective.

718 retaliation *n* reprisal, requital, retort, counterstroke, counterattack, retribution, reciprocation, reciprocity, recrimination, revenge, vengeance, reaction.

v retaliate, requite, retort, counterattack, revenge, repay, return, avenge.

adj retaliatory, vengeful, retributive, reciprocal, reactive.

adv in retaliation.

719 resistance *n* opposition, withstanding, front, stand, oppugnance, reluctance, repulsion; interference, friction; insurrection, insurgence, rebellion.

v resist, withstand, stand up, stand; confront, oppose, grapple with, rise up, revolt, rebel, repel, repulse.

adj resistant, refractory, recalcitrant, repulsive, repellent; stubborn, indomitable, obstinate.

720 contention *n* struggling, struggle, strife, discord, dissention, quarrel, disagreement, squabble, feud; rupture, break, falling out; opposition, belligerency, combat, conflict, competition, rivalry, contest; disagreement, dissension, debate, wrangle, altercation, dispute, argument, controversy.

v contend, struggle, strive, fight, battle, combat, vie, compete, rival; debate, dispute, argue, wrangle; assert, maintain, claim.

adj contentious, combative, belligerent, combative, warlike, quarrelsome, pugnacious; competitive.

721 peace *n* treaty, truce, accord, amity, harmony, concord; calm, quiet, tranquillity, peacefulness, calmness; order, security.

v be at peace; keep the peace; make peace.

adj peaceful, tranquil, placid, serene, calm, complacent; mellow, halcyon, pacific; peaceable; amicable, friendly, amiable, mild, gentle.

722 warfare *n* fighting, hostilities, war, combat, battle, ordeal; tactics, strategy, generalship.

v war, make war, wage war, fight, give fight, battle, do battle, combat, contend, cross swords.

adj warlike, contentious, belligerent, combative, bellicose, martial, military, militant.

adv to arms.

723 pacification *n* conciliation, reconciliation, accommodation, arrangement, adjustment, compromise; amnesty, peace offering, truce, armistice, suspension of hostilities.

v pacify, reconcile, propitiate, placate, conciliate, accommodate, appease, make peace; quiet, calm, tranquilize, assuage, still, smooth, moderate, ameliorate, mollify, meliorate, soothe, bury the hatchet.

adj pacific, conciliatory.

724 mediation *n* negotiation, arbitration, parley; intervention, intercession, interposition.

mediator, arbiter, arbitrator, peacemaker, go-between, negotiator, moderator, diplomat.

v mediate, intercede, intervene, interpose, interfere; step in, negotiate, arbitrate.

adj mediatory.

725 submission *n* nonresistance, obedience, compliance, acquiescence, yielding, submissiveness, pliancy; surrender, cessation, capitulation; resignation, passivity, docility.

v succumb, submit, yield, bend, acquiesce, resign, agree, obey, comply, bow, surrender, capitulate.

adj submissive, obedient, compliant, acquiescent, passive, docile, tame, humble.

726 combatant *n* fighter, contestant, disputant, battler, litigant, contender, competitor, militarist, soldier, warrior, polemic, candidate; antagonist, foe, enemy, opponent, rival, adversary, assailant, opposition, assailer, assailant, assaulter, opposer, opponent.

727 arms n weapons, weaponry, armaments, armor, ammunition, munitions, deadly weapons.

v arm, outfit, ready for battle, prepare for battle.

728 arena n battleground, battlefield, field of battle, theater, ring, lists; playhouse, amphitheater, stage, boards; Colosseum, gymnasium, playing field.

729 completion n culmination, finish, conclusion, close, termination, end, finale; upshot, result; final touch, crowning touch; consummation, accomplishment, achievement, fulfillment; performance, execution; perfection, thoroughness.

v complete, finish, end, conclude, close, terminate, finalize; consummate, perfect, accomplish, do, fulfill, achieve, effect, execute, enact, dispatch, discharge.

adj whole, entire, full, intact, unbroken, one, perfect; done, consummate, perfect, thorough, through-and-through.

adv completely, thoroughly; perfectly.

730 noncompletion n incompleteness, nonfulfilment, nonperformance; neglect, shortcoming.

v not complete, leave unfinished, leave undone; neglect, leg alone, let slip; fall short of.

adj incomplete, unfinished, sketchy.

731 success n progress, advance; hit, stroke, trump card; good fortune, good luck, luck, break; prosperity, achievement, fulfillment, accomplishment; ascendancy, mastery, conquest, victory, triumph; proficiency, skill, mastery.

v succeed, attain an end, secure an objective; progress, advance; accomplish, achieve, effect, complete; prosper, find fulfillment, fulfill oneself; master, conquer, triumph, surmount, overcome.

adj successful, prosperous, well-

to-do; victorious, triumphant; masterful, proficient.

adv successfully, with flying colors, in triumph.

732 failure n unsuccessfulness, miscarriage, abortion, failing; neglect, omission, dereliction, non-performance; deficiency, insufficiency, defectiveness; blunder, mistake, fault, slip, mishap, scrape, mess, fiasco, breakdown; decline, decay, deterioration, loss; bankruptcy, insolvency, bust, dud.

v fail, come short, fall short, disappoint, miss the mark, miscarry, abort, blunder, botch, make a mess of, (*informal*) blow it, founder, flounder, sink, go amiss, go wrong, go hard with; fall off, dwindle, decline, fade, weaken, wane, give out, cease; desert, forsake.

adj unsuccessful, abortive, stillborn, fruitless, bootless, ineffectual, inefficient, insufficient, useless; lost, undone, bankrupt; wide of the mark, erroneous; frustrated, thwarted, foiled, defeated; defective, faulty.

adv unsuccessfully, in vain, to little purpose.

733 trophy n medal, prize, palm, laurel, honor, accolade, decoration, reward, recognition, triumph, celebration.

734 prosperity n well-being, success, fortune, wealth, affluence.

v prosper, thrive, flourish, rise, make one's way, flower, grow, blossom, bloom, fructify, succeed, (*informal*) make it.

adj prosperous, successful, wealthy, rich, well-to-do, well-off; favorable, propitious, fortunate, lucky, auspicious, golden, bright.

735 adversity n calamity, distress, catastrophe, crisis, disaster, failure; bad luck, hard times, misfortune, (*informal*) downers, (*informal*) bummers, trouble, hardship, pressure, affliction, wretchedness.

v go downhill, go to the dogs, decay, sink, decline, come to grief, (*informal*) hit the pits, fall on evil days.

adj adverse, unfavorable, unlucky, unfortunate; calamitous, disastrous, critical, dire, catastrophic; unprosperous, hapless, in a bad way, under a cloud, in adverse circumstances, down in the mouth.

adv adversely; if worst comes to worst.

736 mediocrity *n* average capacity, ordinariness, commonplaceness, insignificance, passableness, tolerableness, indifference, inferiority, paltriness, triviality; moderation, golden mean.

v jog on, get along.

adj mediocre, average, normal, ordinary, commonplace, run-of-the-mill, insignificant, tolerable, unimportant, indifferent, inferior, poor, slight, paltry; moderate, reasonable, temperate, respectable.

II. Intersocial Volition

737 authority *n* control, influence, jurisdiction, command, rule, sway, power, dominion, supremacy; expert, adjudicator, arbiter, judge, sovereign, ruler; warrant, justification, permit, permission, sanction, liberty, authorization.

v authorize, empower, commission, allow, permit, sanction, approve; warrant, justify, legalize, support, back; rule, sway, control, administer, govern.

adj authoritative, peremptory, magisterial, imperative, dogmatic, masterful; executive, administrative, sovereign, regnant, supreme, dominant, paramount, predominant, preponderant, influential, official, decisive, valid, absolute.

738 [absence of authority] **laxity** *n* laxness, looseness, slackness, lenience, toleration, relaxation, loosening, licence, freedom.

v be lax, tolerate, relax, give a free rein.

adj lax, loose, slack, remiss, lenient, negligent, careless, weak.

739 severity *n* seriousness, gravity, sternness, harshness, austerity, rigidity, rigorousness, strictness, stringency, relentlessness, abruptness, curtness; arbitrariness, absolutism, despotism, dictatorship, autocracy, tyranny, oppression; strength, force, brute force, coercion.

tyrant, disciplinarian, despot, taskmaster, oppressor, inquisitor.

v be severe, tyrannize, domineer, dominate, bully, inflict, wreak, be hard on, ill-treat, maltreat, oppress, trample on, crush, coerce.

adj severe, serious, grave, stern, harsh, austere, rigid, stiff, dour, rigorous, strict, strait-laced, stringent, relentless, hard, inexorable, abrupt, peremptory, curt, short; arbitrary, absolute, despotic, dictatorial, autocratic, tyrannical, oppressive, coercive, inquisitorial, ruthless, cruel, malevolent, arrogant.

adv severely, with a high hand, with a heavy hand.

740 lenience *n* leniency, tolerance, toleration, moderation, mildness, gentleness, favor, indulgence, forbearance, quarter, compassion, clemency, mercy.

v be lenient, tolerate, bear with, favor, indulge, allow.

adj lenient, tolerant, mild, easy, easy-going, gentle, tender, indulgent, compassionate, sympathetic, merciful.

741 command *n* order, ordinance, direction, bidding, injunction, charge, mandate, behest, ukase, commandment, requisition, requirement, instruction, dictum, act, fiat; demand, exaction, claim, request; control, mastery, disposal, rule, sway, power, domination.

v command, order, direct, bid, demand, charge, instruct, enjoin, require, impose; degree, enact, ordain, dictate, prescribe; appoint; claim, lay claim to.

adj commanding, authoritative.

742 disobedience *n* noncompliance, nonobservance, insubordination, contumacy, infraction, infringement, defiance, unruliness, rebelliousness, obstinacy, stubbornness, resistance, mutinousness, mutiny, rebellion.

insurgent, mutineer, rebel, revolutionary, rioter, traitor, *(informal)* radical.

v disobey, transgress, violate, disregard, defy, infringe, shirk, resist, mutiny, rebel, revolt.

adj disobedient, insubordinate, contumacious, defiant, refractory, unruly, fractious, rebellious, mutinous, obstinate, stubborn, unsubmissive, uncompliant, recalcitrant, insurgent, riotous.

743 obedience *n* observance, compliance, docility, tractability, deference, respect, duty, subservience, submissiveness, obsequiousness; allegiance, loyalty, fealty, homage, devotion.

v obey, comply, submit, follow, attend to, serve.

adj obedient, submissive, compliant, tractable, docile, deferential, respectful, dutiful, loyal, subservient.

adv obediently, in compliance with, in obedience to.

744 compulsion *n* coercion, constraint, duress, enforcement, conscription, force; impulse, necessity.

v compel, force, make, drive, coerce, constrain, enforce, impel, require, necessitate, oblige, motivate; subdue, subject, bend, bow, overpower.

adj compelling, compulsory, coercive, forcible, constraining; obligatory, necessary, unavoidable, inescapable, ineluctable, irresistible, inexorable.

adv by force, forcibly, on compulsion.

745 master *n* lord, commander, commandant, chief, head, leader, director, ruler, boss, authority.

746 servant *n* subject, retainer, follower, henchman, domestic, menial, help, helper, employee, worker, laborer.

v serve, function, answer, assist, help, aid, provide, cater, satisfy; wait on, attend.

747 [insignia of authority] **scepter** *n* regalia, staff, symbol, emblem, flag, badge; title.

748 freedom *n* liberty, independence, autonomy, noninterference; immunity, franchisement, franchise, privilege, latitude, scope; ease, facility; frankness, openness; familiarity, license, looseness, laxity.

v be free, have scope, do as one likes, do what one wants; free, liberate, permit, allow, set free.

adj free, independent, at large, loose, scot free; unconstrained, unconfined, unchecked, unhindered, unobstructed, unbound, uncontrolled, ungoverned, unchained, unfettered, unshackled, uncurbed, unbridled, unmuzzled; unrestricted, unlimited, unconditional; absolute; discretionary; wanton, rampant, irrepressible, unvanquished; immune, exempt, freed; autonomous.

adv freely.

749 subjection *n* dependence, subordination, thrall, thralldom, subjugation, bondage, serfdom, slavery, servitude, enslavement; service, employ, tutelage, constraint, yoke, submission, obedience.

v be subject, be at the mercy of, depend upon, fall prey to, play second fiddle to, serve, submit; subject, subjugate, master, tame, tread down, weigh down, enslave, enthral, rule.

adj subject, dependent, subordinate; under control, in harness.

750 liberation *n* disengagement, release, enlargement, emancipation, enfranchisement, deliverance, extrication, discharge, dismissal, acquittal, absolution.

v liberate, set free, free, disengage, release, emancipate, enfranchise, deliver, extricate, discharge, dismiss, unfetter, disenthrall, set loose, loose, let out, acquit, absolve.

adj liberated, freed.

751 restraint *n* restriction, circumscription, limitation, control, confinement, curb, check, suppression, constraint, repression.

v restrain, check, keep down, repress, curb, bridle, suppress, compel, hold, keep, constrain; restrict, circumscribe, confine, hinder.

adj restrained, constrained, restrictive, suppressive, repressive; imprisoned, pent up, under restraint.

752 prison *n* jail, gaol, cage, coop, pen, penitentiary, jailhouse, cell, block, dungeon, lock-up, stir, irons, *(informal)* calaboose; *(informal)* hoosegow, *(informal)* the joint, *(informal)* the big house.

753 keeper *n* custodian, guard *(informal)* screw, jailer, gaoler, warder, escort, body-guard; protector, guardian, governor, governess, teacher, tutor, nurse.

754 prisoner *n* captive, convict, con, jailbird.
    v be imprisoned, stand convicted.
    adj in prison, in custody, in chains, under wraps, in stir.

755 [vicarious authority] **commission** *n* delegation, consignment, assignment, deputation, legation, mission, embassy, agency, special committee; errand, charge, permit; appointment, nomination, charter.
    v commission, delegate, consign, assign, charge, entrust, authorize; appoint, name, nominate, ordain; install, induct, invest, employ, empower.

756 abrogation *n* abolition, cancelation, annulment, repeal, retraction, revocation, remission, recision, nullification, invalidation.
    v abrogate, abolish, cancel, annul, repeal, retract, revoke, rescind, nullify, void, invalidate.
    adj null and void.

757 resignation *n* abjuration, renunciation, abdication, abandonment, desertion, relinquishment, retirement.
    v resign, quit, give up, abjure, renounce, forgo, disclaim, abrogate, abandon, desert, relinquish, retire.

758 consignee *n* trustee, nominee, committee, delegation, delegate, commission; functionary, agent, representative, messenger.

759 deputy *n* substitute, proxy, delegate, representative, surrogate, alternate, second, assistant.

v stand for, represent, answer for.

760 permission *n* authorization, warrant, sanction, liberty, license, enfranchisement, franchise, leave, permit, liberty, permission, allowance, consent, concession, tolerance, sufferance, indulgence, favor.
    v permit, allow, let, tolerate, bear with, agree to, suffer, concede, accord, favor, humor, indulge; grant, empower, franchise, charter, confer, license, authorize, warrant, sanction.
    adj permitted, permissive, indulgent, libertarian, tolerant; permissible, allowable, legal, legalized, lawful, legitimate.

761 prohibition *n* interdiction, injunction, prevention, embargo, ban, restriction, disallowance.
    v prohibit, forbid, interdict, veto, disallow, bar, restrict, limit; prevent, hinder, preclude, obstruct.
    adv prohibitive, proscriptive, restrictive; preventive.

762 consent *n* assent, acquiescence, acceptance, acknowledgment, permission, compliance, concurrence, agreement, approval; accord, concord, consensus, settlement, ratification, confirmation.
    v consent, assent, agree, concur, permit, allow, let, yield, grant, comply, accede, acquiescence.
    adj compliant, agreeable, amendable.

763 offer *n* proposal, proposition, overture, tender, bid; offering, gift.
    v offer, present, proffer, tender; propose, give, move, put forward advance, hold out, make a motion; hawk, merchandise, offer for sale.
    adj for sale, in the open market.

764 refusal *n* rejection, spurning, denial, rebuff, repulse, repudiation; abnegation, protest, renunciation; disclaimer.
    v refuse, decline, reject, spurn, turn down, deny, rebuff, repulse, repudiate; resist, repel, repudiate, renounce, disclaim, rescind, revoke.
    adj noncompliant, dissident, recalcitrant, reluctant.

765 request n claim, demand, application, appeal, solicitation, petition, suit, entreaty, supplication, prayer.

v request, ask, ask for, beg, sue, petition, entreat, supplicate, solicit, beseech, plead, implore, require, demand, importune, clamor for.

adj importunate, clamorous, solicitous.

766 [negative request] deprecation n expostulation, intercession, mediation, protest, disapproval, remonstrance.

v deprecate, protest, expostulate, enter a protest, disapprove, remonstrate.

adj deprecatory, expostulatory; remonstrative; unsought.

767 petitioner n claimant, aspirant, postulant, seeker, solicitor, suitor, applicant, suppliant, supplicant; competitor, bidder; beggar, mendicant, (informal) bum, (informal) streetwalker.

768 promise n undertaking, word, covenant, commitment, pledge, assurance, profession, vow, oath, guarantee, warranty, obligation, contract.

v promise, undertake, engage, enter into, bind oneself, commit oneself, pledge, agree, assure, warrant, guarantee, covenant, swear, give one's word; secure, give security, underwrite.

adj promissory, upon one's oath, on one's honor; promised, pledged, committed, bound, sworn.

769 compact n contract, treaty, contract, pact, bargain, arrangement, (informal) deal.

v contract, negotiate, bargain, stipulate, make terms; agree, engage, promise; complete, settle, confirm, subscribe, endorse.

adj compactual, contractual, promissory.

770 conditions n terms, articles, clauses, provisions, provisos, stipulations, promises, obligations, covenants.

v condition, stipulate, insist upon, contract, provide, bind, tie, oblige.

adj conditional, provisional.

adv conditionally, provisionally, on condition.

771 security n guarantee, warranty, bond, tie, pledge, promise, contract; mortgage, lien, pawn; stake, deposit, collateral, (informal) IOU, (informal) mark, promissory note; deed, bill of sale, receipt, certificate, title; sponsorship, surety, bail.

v give security, post bail, pawn, mortgage; guarantee, warrant, assure, promise; accept, endorse, underwrite, sponsor, stand for.

772 observance n performance, compliance, obedience, execution, discharge, acquittance, fulfillment, satisfaction, adhesion, acknowledgment, fidelity, faithfulness.

v observe, comply with, respect, abide by, acknowledge, adhere to, be faithful to, obey, act up to; meet, fulfill; carry out, execute, perform, satisfy, discharge.

adj observant, compliant, faithful, obedient, true, honorable; punctilious, scrupulous, as good as one's word.

adv faithfully.

773 nonobservance n evasion, failure, omission, noncompliance, neglect, negligence, laxity, laxness, carelessness, irresponsibility, disobedience; infringement, infraction, violation, transgression.

v fail, neglect, evade, omit, elude, ignore, disregard, discard, set at naught; infringe, transgress, violate, break.

adj nonobservant, lax, loose, disdainful, evasive, elusive, negligent, irresponsible, disobedient.

774 compromise n adjustment, negotiation, concession; compensation.

v compromise, bend, give and take, split the differences, come to an agreement, opt for the mean, adjust, arrange, settle.

775 acquisition n procurement, appropriation, gain, attainment, purchase, gift, find; profit, earnings, wages, winnings, income, proceeds, produce, crop, harvest, benefit.

v acquire, appropriate, gain, win,

earn, attain, gather, collect; take over, take possession of, procure, secure, obtain, get, come into, receive, get hold of; profit, turn to profit.

adj profitable, advantageous, gainful, remunerative.

776 loss *n* damage, injury, privation, lapse, forfeiture, deprivation.

v lose, incur a loss, miss, mislay, let slip, forfeit; waste, get rid of.

adj lost, bereft, minus, deprived of, cut off, rid of; long lost, irretrievable.

777 possession *n* ownership, occupancy, holding, proprietorship, tenure, tenancy, control, custody; belonging.

v possess, own, have, hold, occupy, control, command, have to oneself, have in hand, belong to.

adj possessing, possessed of, in possession of, master of, in hand, at one's disposal; possessive, custodial.

777a exemption *n* exception, immunity, impunity, release.

v exempt, excuse, release; not have, be without.

adj exempt from, immune from, devoid of, without.

778 [joint possession] participation *n* partnership, co-ownership, joint tenancy, common holding, communion, community of possessions; communism, socialism, collectivism; cooperation.

participant, sharer, partner, copartner, shareholder; communist, socialist.

v participate, partake, share, share in, go halves, split up, divide, have in common, own in common.

adj participatory, joint, common, collective, communal, communist, communistic, socialist, socialistic.

779 possessor *n* holder, occupant, tenant, lessee; proprietor, proprietress, master, mistress, owner.

780 property *n* possession, possessions, goods, effects, chattels, estate, belongings, assets, means, resources land, real estate, acreage;

ownership, right; attribute, quality, characteristic, feature.

781 retention *n* keeping, holding, detention, custody, preservation, maintenance.

v retain, keep, hold, hold fast, secure, withhold, preserve, detain, reserve, maintain.

adj retentive.

782 relinquishment *n* renunciation, surrender, resignation, yielding, waiver, abdication, desertion, abandonment, quitting.

v relinquish, renounce, surrender, give up, resign, yield, cede, waive, forswear, forgo, abdicate, leave, forsake, desert, quit, abandon, let go, discard, cast off, dismiss, divest oneself.

adj cast off, done away with, left, forsworn, given up, left behind.

783 transfer *n* sale, lease, release, exchange, interchange; transference, transmission, changing hands.

v transfer, convey, assign, grant, consign, make over, hand over, pass, transmit, change, exchange, interchange, change hands; devolve, succeed.

adj transferable, conveyable, transmissive, exchangeable.

784 giving *n* bestowal, presentation, concession, delivery, consignment, dispensation, endowment, investiture, award; charity, almsgiving, liberality, generosity, philanthropy; gift, donation, present, boon, favor, grant, offering; allowance, contribution, donation, bequest, legacy; alms, largesse, bounty, help, gratuity; bribe, bait.

giver, granter, donor.

v give, bestow, confer, grant, accord, award, assign, entrust, consign; invest, allow, settle upon, donate, bequeath, leave; furnish, supply, help; afford, spare, favor with, lavish; deliver, hand, pass, turn over, present, give away, dispense, dispose of, give out, deal out, dole out, mete out, fork out; pay, render, impart.

adj charitable, beneficent, tributary, liberal, generous, philanthropic.

785 receiving n acquisition, reception, acceptance, admission, recipient, receiver, legatee, grantee, donee, beneficiary, pensioner.

v receive, acquire, admit, take in, accept; come into, fall to one, accrue.

adj receiving; received.

786 apportionment n allotment, consignment, assignment, allocation, distribution, dispensation, division, partition; portion, lot, share, measure, dose, dole, ration, ratio, proportion, quota, allowance.

v apportion, divide, distribute, dispense, allot, share, mete, portion out, parcel out, dole out, deal, carve, administer; partition, assign, appropriate, appoint.

adj distributive; respective.

787 lending n loan, advance, accommodation, mortgage, investment.

v lend, loan, advance, accommodate, lend on security, pawn; let, lease.

788 borrowing n pledging, pawning; appropriating, stealing, theft.

v borrow, pledge, pawn, borrow money; hire, rent, lease; appropriate, use, steal from, imitate.

789 taking n appropriation, capture, apprehension, seizure, abduction, dispossession, deprivation, expropriation, divestment, confiscation, eviction; extortion, theft; reprisal, recovery.

v take, catch, hook, nab, bag, pocket, receive, accept; reap, cull, pluck, gather; appropriate, assume, possess oneself of, help oneself to, commandeer, make free with; take away, abduct, steal, seize, snatch, snap up, capture, get hold of, take from, take away from, dispossess, expropriate, oust, eject, divest, confiscate, usurp, strip, fleece; retake, resume, recover.

adj predatory, rapacious, parasitic, greedy, ravenous.

790 restitution n return, restoration, reinvestment, rehabilitation, repara-

tion, atonement, compensation, recovery.

v return, restore, give back, render, give up, let go; recoup, reimburse, compensate, reinvest, remit, rehabilitate, repair, make good, settle up; recover, get back, redeem, take back again.

adj compensatory, redemptive, recouperative.

791 stealing n theft, thievery, robbery, swindling, fraud, appropriation.

v steal, take, thieve, rob, pilfer, purloin, (informal) swipe, filch, embezzle, swindle, appropriate, fleece, defraud, (informal) rip off, (informal) screw.

adj thievish, light-fingered, piratical, predatory.

792 thief n robber, pilferer, filcher, rifler, crook, (informal) rip-off artist, cheat; burglar, house-breaker, second-story man, safecracker.

793 booty n spoils, plunder; prize, loot, catch, pickings, stolen goods, (informal) haul.

794 barter n exchange, trade, traffic, commerce, business, bargain; dealing, transaction, negotiation.

v barter, trade, exchange, traffic, bargain, swap, buy and sell, give and take, haggle, negotiate, drive a bargain, transact.

adj commercial, mercantile; interchangeable, in trade, for sale, marketable.

795 purchase n buying, purchasing, acquisition; bargain, buy.

buyer, purchaser, shopper, customer, client, patron, clientele.

v purchase, buy, acquire, get, obtain, procure; shop, market, go shopping.

796 sale n selling, vendition, commerce, mercantilism, transaction, exchange, auction, trade.

seller, vendor, merchant.

v sell, trade, barter, vend, exchange, deal in, dispose, merchandise, hawk.

adj salable, marketable, vendible, for sale.

797 merchant *n* trader, dealer, seller, salesman, saleswoman, tradesman, shopkeeper, retailer, hawker, huckster, peddler, broker.

798 merchandise *n* goods, wares, commodity, articles, stock, produce, product, staple commodity, store, cargo.

v merchandise, sell.

799 market *n* mart, marketplace, fair, bazaar, business district, mall, shopping center, store, department store, establishment, place of business, office.

800 money *n* finance, accounts, funds, assets, wealth, supplies, ways and means, wherewithal, capital, almighty dollar, cash, currency, hard cash, *(informal)* bucks, change, small change, *(informal)* green, greenbacks; sum, amount, balance.

adj monetary, pecuniary, financial, fiscal.

801 treasurer *n* bursar, banker, purser, receiver, steward, trustee, accountant, paymaster, cashier, teller, financier.

802 treasury *n* bank, exchequer, strongbox, stronghold, coffer, chest, depository, purse, moneybag, safe, vault, cash box, cash register, till; securities, stocks, bonds, notes.

803 wealth *n* riches, fortune, opulence, affluence, easy circumstance, *(informal)* silver spoon, independence, competence, sufficiency, solvency; provision, livelihood, maintenance, means, resources, substance; income, capital, money.

v be wealthy, be rich.

adj wealthy, rich, affluent, well-off, well-to-do, comfortable.

804 poverty *n* indigence, penury, pauperism, destitution, want, need, neediness, lack, privation, distress, difficulties, straits, bad straits.

v be poor, want, lack, starve, live from hand to mouth, go to the dogs.

adj poor, indigent, destitute, poverty-stricken, needy, penniless, broke, *(informal)* bust, hard up, insolvent, seedy, beggarly.

805 credit *n* trust, score, tally, account, *(informal)* tab, bill.
creditor, lender, usurer.

v credit, accredit, entrust, keep an account with.

806 debt *n* obligation, liability, debit, score, duty, due.
debtor, borrower.

adj liable, answerable for, in debt; unpaid, in arrear.

807 payment *n* discharge, settlement, clearance, liquidation, satisfaction, reckoning, arrangement; acknowledgment, release, receipt, voucher; installment, remittance.

v pay, settle, liquidate, discharge, quit, acquit oneself of, reckon up, satisfy, compensate, reimburse, remunerate, recompense, make payment, square accounts, balance accounts, pay in full.

adj out of debt, solvent; straight, clear.

808 nonpayment *n* default, protest, repudiation; insolvency, bankruptcy, failure.

v not pay, default, fail, stop payment; run up bills.

adj in debt.

809 expenditure *n* outlay, expenses, disbursement, payment, costs, fees.

v expend, spend, pay out, disburse, *(informal)* fork out, lay out.

810 receipt *n* value received, acknowledgment of payment.

v receive, take, get, bring in.

adj profitable, remunerative.

811 accounts *n* money matters, finance, budget, bill, score, reckoning, account; statement, ledger, inventory, register, book, books, sheet; balance.
accountant, auditor, bookkeeper, financier.

v keep accounts, enter, post, book, credit, debit, balance.

812 price *n* amount, cost, expense, charge, figure, demand, damage, fare, hire, wages; worth, rate, value, valuation, appraisal; market price, quotation; bill, invoice.

v price, set a price, fix a price, appraise, assess, charge, demand, ask, require, exact; fetch, sell for, bring in, yield, accord.

813 discount n abatement, reduction, depreciation, allowance, qualification, rebate, sale.

v discount, put on sale, reduce, take off, allow, deduct, abate, rebate.

814 dearness n expensiveness, costliness, high price; overcharge, extravagance, exorbitance.

v be expensive, cost a lot; overcharge, bleed, fleece, extort.

adj dear, expensive, costly, precious; extravagant, exorbitant, unreasonable; priceless.

815 cheapness n low price, depreciation, bargain, value, *(informal)* steal, *(informal)* great buy.

v be cheap, cost little.

adj cheap, moderate, reasonable, inexpensive, dirt cheap.

816 liberality n generosity, munificence, bounty, bounteousness, hospitality, charity.

v be liberal, spend freely, give, spare no expense.

adj liberal, free, generous, bountiful, hospitable, munificent, beneficient, princely, charitable.

817 economy n frugality, thrift, thriftiness, saving, care, husbandry, retrenchment, parsimony.

v economize, save, retrench, husband.

adj economical, frugal, careful, thrifty, chary, parsimonious.

818 prodigality n unthriftiness, waste, wastefulness, profusion, profuseness, extravagance, profligacy, lavishness, squandering.

prodigal, spendthrift, squanderer.

v be prodigal, squander, lavish, misspend, waste, dissipate, fritter one's money.

adj prodigal, profuse, unthrifty, improvident, wasteful, profligate, extravagant, lavish.

819 parsimony n stinginess, illiberality, avarice, rapidity, rapacity, venality, cupidity, selfishness.

miser, niggard, churl, skinflint, codger, scrimp, *(informal)* tightwad, usurer, Scrooge.

v be parsimonious, grudge, begrudge, stint, pinch, hold back, withhold, starve, famish.

adj parsimonious, penurious, stingy, cheap, miserly, mean, pennywise, niggardly, tight, ungenerous, churlish, mercenary, venal, covetous, usurious, avaricious, greedy, rapacious, selfish.

Class VI

Words Relating to the Sentient and Moral Powers

I. Affections in General

820 affections n character, qualities, disposition, nature, spirit, temper, temperament, idiosyncrasy, habit, bent, bias, predisposition, proclivity, propensity, humor, mood, sympathy; soul, heart, inner man, essence; passion, driving spirit, ruling passion.

adj affected, characterized, formed, cast, molded, tempered, predisposed, prone, inclined, imbued; inborn, ingrained, deeprooted.

adv at heart.

821 feeling n consciousness, impression; emotion, passion, sentiment, sensibility; sympathy, empathy; fervor, ardor, zeal, warmth, tenderness, sensitivity, sentimentality, susceptibility, pity; sentiment, opinion.

v feel, receive an impression, respond to.

adj feeling, emotional, sensitive, tender; sympathetic; emotional, impassioned, passionate, fervent, tender, sensitive; heart-felt, thrilling, rapturous, soul-stirring; moved, touched, affected.

adj heart and soul, from the bottom of one's heart.

822 sensibility n responsiveness, sensitiveness, awareness, susceptibility, impressibility, tenderness, sentimentality, sentimentalism; excitability; appreciation, understanding, moral sensibility.

v be sensitive, have a soft spot in one's heart.

adj sensitive, impressionable, susceptible, tender, warm-hearted, sentimental; excitable; aware, understanding, appreciative.

823 insensibility *n* insensitiveness, impassivity, apathy, coldness, callousness; imperturbable; dullness, boorishness.

v be insensible, not care, be unaffected, have no interest in.

adj insensitive, unconscious, unaware; inattentive, indifferent, lukewarm; apathetic, impassive, unimpressionable; cold-blooded, cold-hearted, unmoved, unaffected, callous, thick-skinned, uncaring.

adv in cold blood.

824 excitation *n* excitation of feeling; mental excitation; galvanism, stimulation, provocation, inspiration, infection; animation, agitation, perturbation; fascination, intoxication, ravishment; irritation, anger, passion, thrill.

v excite, affect, touch, move, impress, interest, animate, inspire, infect, awake; evoke, provoke; stir up, wake up, light up; rouse, arouse, stir, fire, kindle, inflame; stimulate, quicken, sharpen, whet, wet the appetite, fan the fire, raise to a fervor; absorb, rivet, intoxicate, fascinate, enrapture; agitate, perturb, ruffle, fluster, disturb, startle, shock, stagger, astound, electrify, galvanize; irritate.

adj excited, excitable, wrought up, overwrought, upset, hysterical, hot, red-hot, flushed, feverish, boiling, ebullient, seething, fuming, raging, raving, frantic, mad, distracted, beside oneself; exciting, warm, glowing, fervid, soul-stirring, thrilling, overwhelming, overpowering, sensational.

825 [excess of sensitiveness] **excitability** *n* impetuosity, vehemence, boisterousness, impatience, intolerance, irritability, restlessness, agitation; passion, excitement, fever, tumult, ebullition, tempest, fit, paroxysm,

explosion, outburst, agony; violence, rage, fury, furor, desperation, madness, distraction, delirium, frenzy, hysterics.

v be impatient, lose patience, fuss, fidget; lose one's temper, flare up, burn, boil over, foam, fume, rage, rant, run wild, go mad, go into hysterics.

adj excitable, high-strung, nervous, irritable, impatient, intolerant; feverish, hysterical, delirious, mad; hurried, restless, fidgety, fussy; vehement, violent, wild, furious, fierce, fiery, hotheaded; overzealous, enthusiastic, impassioned, fanatical; rabid, clamorous, turbulent, tumultuous, boisterous; impulsive, impetuous, passionate, uncontrolled, uncontrollable, ungovernable, irrepressible, volcanic.

826 inexcitability *n* imperturbability, even temper, dispassion, patience, impassivity; coolness, calmness, composure, placidity, serenity, quietude; self-possession, self-restraint, stoicism; resignation, submission, sufferance, endurance, forbearance, fortitude, moderation, restraint.

v bear, endure, tolerate, suffer, put up with, reconcile oneself to, resign oneself to, brook, swallow, make the best of; stomach; compose, appease, propitiate, repress, calm down, cool down.

adj inexcitable, imperturbable, unsusceptible, dispassionate, enduring, stoical, staid, sober, sedate; easygoing, peaceful, placid, calm, cool; composed, collected, unruffled, content, resigned, subdued.

II. Personal Affections

827 pleasure *n* happiness, gladness, delectation, enjoyment, delight, joy, glee, cheer, cheerfulness, well-being, satisfaction, gratification, comfort, ease; felicity, bliss, enchantment, transport, rapture, ravishment, ecstasy, luxury, sensuality, voluptuousness.

v be pleased, joy, enjoy oneself, have one's head in the clouds, fall into raptures; be pleased with, derive pleasure from, take pleasure in, *(informal)* get into, delight in, rejoice in, indulge in, luxuriate in, relish, love, enjoy, like, *(informal)* dig, take a fancy to, take a shine to.

adj happy, blissful, joyful, gladsome, cheerful; comfortable, at ease, content; ecstatic.

adv happily, with pleasure.

828 pain *n* suffering, distress, torture, misery, dolor, anguish, agony, torment, throe, pang, ache, smart, twinge, stitch; displeasure, dissatisfaction, discomfort, discomposure, disquiet, malaise, inquietude, uneasiness, vexation, discontent, dejection, weariness; annoyance, irritation, worry, affliction, bore, bother, mortification, plague; care, solicitude, trouble, trial, ordeal, burden, load, fret; prostration, desolation, despair.

v suffer, afflict, torture, torment, distress, despair; hurt, harm, injure, trouble, grieve, disquiet, discomfort, discompose, worry, irritate, vex, mortify, plague.

adj uncomfortable, uneasy, weary; unhappy, infelicitous, poor, wretched, miserable, woebegone, careworn, cheerless, sorry, sorrowful, stricken, in tears, in despair.

829 pleasurableness *n* pleasantness, agreeableness, delectability, delight, congeniality; sprightliness, cheer, cheerfulness, liveliness; attraction, attractiveness, charm, fascination enchantment, witchery, seduction, winning ways, amenity, amiability; loveliness, beauty, brightness; goodness.

v be pleasurable, afford pleasure, offer pleasure, please, charm, delight, gladden, cheer; attract, invite, allure, stimulate, interest, captivate, fascinate, enchant, entrance, enrapture, bewitch, ravish, enravish, transport; agree with, satisfy, gratify; slake, satiate, quence; regale, refresh, treat, amuse.

adj pleasurable, pleasant, agreeable, enjoyable, delightful, congenial, amiable; comfortable, cordial, genial, gladsome, sweet, delectable, nice, dainty, delicate, delicious, luscious, luxurious, voluptuous, sensual; attractive, lovely, beautiful, seductive, rapturous, ecstatic, beatific, heavenly; fair, sunny, bright; gay, sprightly, merry, cheery, cheerful, lively, vivacious.

830 painfulness *n* trouble, care, trial, affliction, blow, burden, curse, mishap, misfortune, adversity; annoyance, nuisance, grievance, bore, bother, vexation, mortification; wound, sore, sore subject, thorn in the side, skeleton in the closet; sorry sight, heavy news, bad news; affront, insult, offense.

v pain, hurt, wound, sadden, displease, annoy, trouble, disturb, cross, perplex, irk, vex, mortify, worry, plague, bother, pester, harass, badger, bait, heckle, irritate, anger, persecute, provoke; harrow, torment, torture; affront, insult, give offense, offend, maltreat, mistreat; sicken, disgust, revolt, nauseate, repel, shock, horrify, appal.

adj painful, hurtful, dolorous; unpleasant, disagreeable, unpalatable, bitter, distasteful; unwelcome, undesirable, obnoxious; dismal, dreary, melancholy, grievous, piteous, woeful, rueful, mournful, deplorable, pitiable, lamentable, pathetic; invidious, vexatious, troublesome, irksome, wearisome, worrisome; intolerable, insufferable, unsupportable, unbearable, unendurable, grim, dreadful, fearful, frightful, dire, odious, hateful, repulsive, repellant, abhorrent, horrid, horrible, offensive, nauseous, loathsome, vile, hideous; sore, severe, grave, hard, harsh, cruel; ruinous, disastrous, calamitous, tragic; burdensome, onerous, oppressive, cumbersome.

adv painfully.

831 content *n* contentment, complacency, satisfaction, ease, serenity, comfort; conciliation, resignation.

v gratify, satisfy, set at ease, comfort, appease, conciliate, reconcile.

adj contented, complacent, satisfied, sanguine, comfortable; assenting, acceding, resigned, willing, agreeable.

adv to one's heart's content.

832 discontent n discontentment, dissatisfaction, uneasiness, disquietude, restlessness, displeasure.

v be discontented, repine, regret, fret, chafe, grumble; dissatisfy, disappoint, disconcert.

adj discontented, dissatisfied, displeased, uneasy, restless, dejected, malcontent, regretful, down in the dumps.

833 regret n sorrow, lamentation, grief, remorse, penitence, contrition, repentance.

v regret, deplore, lament, feel sorry about, grieve at, bemoan, bewail, rue, mourn for, repent.

adj regretful, sorry, lamentable, rueful; penitent, contrite.

834 relief n deliverance, alleviation, ease, assuagement, mitigation, comfort, solace, consolation; help, assistance, aid.

v relieve, ease, alleviate, assuage, mitigate, allay, comfort, soothe, lessen, abate, diminish; cheer, comfort, console; aid, help, assist, succor, refresh, remedy, support.

adj soothing, consoling, assuaging, comforting, palliative, curative.

835 aggravation n worsening, heightening, intensification, exaggeration; (informal) annoyance, irritation, vexation.

v aggravate, worsen, intensify, heighten, increase, make serious, make grave.

adj worse, intensified, irritated.

adv from bad to worse, out of the frying pan and into the fire.

836 cheerfulness n geniality, high spirits, liveliness, vivacity, joviality, jocularity, mirth, merriment, exhilaration.

v cheer, gladden, enliven, inspirit, delight, rejoice, exhilarate, animate, encourage; shout, applaud, acclaim, salute.

adj cheery, gay, blithe, happy, lively, spirited, sprightly, joyful, joyous, mirthful, buoyant, sparkling, vivacious, gleeful, sunny, jolly; pleasant, bright, gay, winsome, gladdening, cheery, cheering, inspiring, animating, hearty, robust.

adv cheerfully.

837 dejection n depression, heaviness, heavy heart, melancholy, sadness, dumps, doldrums, despondency, gloom, weariness, disgust, despair, hopelessness.

v be dejected, lose heart, frown, mope, droop, despond, brood over, sink, despair.

adj unhappy, depressed, dispirited, disheartened, discouraged, despondent, (informal) down, downhearted, sad, melancholy, lugubrious, heartsick, dismal, gloomy, miserable, desolate; pessimistic, cynical.

adv with a long face, with tears in one's eyes.

838 rejoicing n exaltation, triumph, jubilation, reveling, merrymaking, celebration, paean; smile, smirk, grin, giggle, titter, laughter, guffaw, shout, peal of laughter.

v rejoice, congratulate oneself, clap one's hands, dance, skip, sing, hurrah, cry for joy, leap with joy, exalt, triumph; smile, smirk, grin, giggle, titter, chuckle, cackle, laugh, crow, burst out, shout, split, roar, shake one's sides, split one's sides.

adj jubilant, exultant, triumphant, flushed, (informal) high, elated, laughing, convulsed with laughter.

839 lamentation n lament, howl, wail, wailing, complaint, moan, moaning, groan, sob, sigh; dirge, elegy, monody, threnody.

v lament, bewail, bemoan, deplore, grieve, scream, sob, cry, weep, mourn over, sorrow over.

adj lamenting, in mourning, sorrowful, mournful, lamentable, tearful, plaintive.

840 amusement n enjoyment, entertainment, recreation, diversion, relaxation, pastime, pleasure, playing, festivity.

v amuse, entertain, cheer, divert, enliven, interest; amuse oneself, play, sport, make merry.

adj amusing, entertaining, pleasant, witty, jovial, jolly, playful.

841 weariness n ennui, lassitude, fatigue, exhaustion, boredom; tedium, monotony, dullness.

v weary, tire, fatigue, bore, exhaust.

adj wearisome, tiresome, boring, tedious, irksome, monotonous, humdrum, dull, prosaic, trying; weary, drowsy, exhausted, tired, wearied, fatigued; uninterested, impatient, dissatisfied.

842 wit n drollery, facetiousness, pleasantry, repartee, cleverness, humor, fun; understanding, intelligence, sagacity, wisdom, intellect, mind, sense.

v joke, jest, banter, pun.

adj witty, quick, quick-witted, nimble, sharp, clever, facetious, whimsical, pleasant, humorous, playful, sparkling, scintillating; intelligent, sagacious, wise, perceptive, insightful.

843 dullness n heaviness, flatness, stupidity, obtuseness, lack of originality, banality.

v be dull, blunt, deaden, benumb.

adj dull, uninteresting, unimaginative, dry, prosaic, matter-of-fact, commonplace, boring, tedious, dreary, vapid; stupid, stolid, slow, flat.

844 humorist n wit, wag, comedian, comedienne, joker, jester, wisecracker, epigrammatist, punster, buffoon, clown, fool, satirist, lampooner, cutup, funnyman.

845 beauty n loveliness, pulchritude, elegance, grace, gracefulness, comeliness, seemliness, fairness, attractiveness, brilliance, radiance, splendor, gorgeousness, magnificence, sublimity.

v beautify.

adj beautiful, handsome, comely, seemly, attractive, lovely, pretty, fair, fine, elegant, beauteous, graceful, pulchritudinous, brilliant, radiant, gorgeous, magnificent; artistic, aesthetic, picturesque.

846 ugliness n homeliness, inelegance, unsightliness, distortion, disfigurement, deformity, frightfulness.

v deface, disfigure, distort.

adj ugly, displeasing, hard-featured, unlovely, unsightly, unseemly, homely; hideous, gruesome, repulsive, offensive, revolting, terrible, base, vile, squalid, gross, monstrous, heinous; disagreeable, unpleasant, objectionable.

847 ornament n ornamentation, adornment, decoration, embellishment, frills, finery.

v ornament, embellish, adorn, decorate, beautify.

adj ornamental, decorative; ornamented, ornate, embellished, beautified.

848 blemish n disfigurement, deformity, defect, flaw, fault, taint, blot, spot, speck.

v stain, sully, spot, taint, tarnish, injure, mar, damage, deface, impair.

adj disfigured, injured, imperfect, discolored, freckled, pitted.

849 simplicity n plainness, homeliness; clarity, chasteness, restraint, severity, lack of adornment, lack of affectation.

v simplify, uncomplicate, clarify, strip to essentials, get back to basics.

adj simple, plain, homely, natural, unadorned, unaffected, unembellished, neat, unassuming, unpretentious; chaste, severe; clear, straightforward, lucid.

850 [good taste] taste n good taste, delicacy, refinement, polish, elegance, grace, discrimination, culture, cultivation.

v show taste, appreciate, judge, criticize, discriminate.

adj tasteful, in good taste, decorous, attractive, cultivated, cultured, refined, discriminative, polished, felicitous, appropriate, suitable, apt, becoming, pleasing.

adj tastefully, elegantly.

851 [bad taste] vulgarity n bad taste, barbarism, coarseness, lack of decorum, ill-breeding, boorishness; gaudiness, tawdriness, finery, frippery, tinsel.

v be vulgar; vulgarize.

adj vulgar, in bad taste, unrefined, boorish, common, coarse, ill-bred, ill-mannered, ignoble, mean, plebeian, crude, rude, shabby; gaudy, tawdry, flashy, garish, crass, showy, (informal) tacky.

852 fashion n custom, style, vogue, mode, rage, craze; conventionality, conformity; society, polite society, beau monde; manners, breeding, air, demeanor, savoir-faire, gentility, decorum, propriety, etiquette.

v be fashionable, be the rage; fashion, adapt, suit, fit, adjust; make, shape, frame, form, mold.

adj fashionable, in vogue, à la mode, all the rage; modish, stylish, conventional, customary; well-bred, well-mannered, civil, polite, courteous, polished, refined, genteel, decorous.

853 ridiculousness n outrageousness, silliness, absurdity.

v be ridiculous, make a fool of oneself, play the fool.

adj absurd, preposterous, extravagant, asinine, laughable, nonsensical, silly, funny, ludicrous, droll, comical, farcical, outlandish, outrageous, fantastic.

854 fop n fine gentleman, dandy, (informal) dude, coxcomb, beau, man about town, prig, jackanapes.

855 affectation n affectedness, pretense, pretention, airs, mannerisms, unnaturalness, display, show, sham, feigning, simulation, foppery.

v affect, act a part, put on airs, pretend, assume, feign, counterfeit, simulate, pose, attitudinize.

adj affected, pretentious, ostentatious, feigned, artificial, stilted, mannered, stagey, theatrical, modish, unnatural.

856 ridicule n derision, scoffing, mockery, gibes, jeers, taunts, raillery; satire, burlesque, sneer, banter, wit, irony.

v ridicule, deride, banter, chaff, twit, mock, taunt, make fun of, sneer at, burlesque, satirize, rail at, lampoon jeer at, scoff at (informal) put down.

adj derisory, derisive, sarcastic, ironic, ironical, burlesque, mocking.

857 [object and cause of ridicule] **laughing-stock** n butt, game, fair game, fool, dupe, original, oddity, queer fish, square, straight, buffoon.

858 hope n confidence, trust, reliance, faith, assurance; expectation, expectancy, anticipation, longing, desire, dream, wish.

v hope, trust, rely on, lean on, have faith in; hope for, expect, presume, anticipate; long for, desire.

adj hopeful, expectant, sanguine, optimistic, confident; probable, promising, propitious, reassuring, encouraging, cheering, inspiriting.

859 hopelessness n despair, desperation, despondency, dejection, pessimism.

v despair, give up hope, despond.

adj hopeless, despairing, desperate, despondent, forlorn, disconsolate; irremediable, remediless, unremedial, incurable.

860 fear n apprehension, consternation, dismay, alarm, trepidation, dread, terror, fright, horror, panic; anxiety, solicitude, suspicion, misgiving, concern; awe, reverence, veneration.

v fear, be afraid of, apprehend, distrust, dread; revere, venerate, reverence.

adj fearful, afraid, apprehensive, dismayed, alarmed, frightened, terrified, horrified, aghast, terror-stricken, horror-stricken, panic-stricken; anxious, concerned, solicitous, suspicious; fearful, awesome, awe-inspiring; awful, dreadful, terrible.

861 courage n fearlessness, dauntlessness, intrepidity, guts, fortitude, pluck, spirit, nerve, heroism, daring, audacity, bravery, mettle, valor, hardihood, bravado, gallantry.

v dare, venture, look danger in the face, take heart, take the bull by the horns.

adj courageous, fearless, dauntless, intrepid, (informal) gutsy, spirited, stout-hearted, resolute, bold, heroic, daring, audacious, brave, valorous, enterprising, adventurous, gallant.

862 cowardice n fear, poltroonery, dastardliness, faint-heartedness, yellow streak, dread, timidity, baseness, abject fear.

coward, poltroon, craven, sneak, lily-liver, (informal) chicken.

v be cowardly, cower, skulk, quail, hide.

adj cowardly, fearful, craven, dastardly, pusillanimous, recreant, timid, timorous, faint-hearted, lily-livered, chicken-hearted, fearful, afraid, scared, spineless, (informal) chicken.

863 rashness n haste, impetuosity, recklessness, impulsiveness, heedlessness, thoughtlessness, imprudence, indiscretion, audacity, carelessness, foolhardiness.

v be rash, plunge.

adj rash, hasty, impetuous, reckless, headlong, precipitate, impulsive, thoughtless, heedless, imprudent, indiscreet, careless, unwary, foolhardy, presumptuous, audacious.

864 caution n prudence, discretion, circumspection, heed, care, wariness, heedfulness, vigilance, forethought; warning, admonition, advice, injunction, counsel.

v be cautious, take care; warn, admonish, advise, counsel.

adj cautious, prudent, heedful, careful, watchful, discreet, wary, vigilant, alert, provident chary, circumspect, guarded.

865 desire n longing, fancy, craving, yearning, wish, want, need, hunger, appetite, thirst; request, wish, ambition, aspiration; love, passion, lust.

v desire, wish for, long for, crave, want, wish, covet, fancy; ask, request, solicit; lust for.

adj desirous, desiring, craving, wishful, hungry, thirsty, covetous, fervent, ardent, lustful.

866 indifference n unconcern, listlessness, apathy, insensibility, coolness, insensitiveness, inattention.

v be indifferent, take no interest in, have no heart for, spurn, disdain.

adj indifferent, unconcerned, listless, apathetic, cool, cold, lukewarm, insensitive, inattentive.

867 dislike n disinclination, disrelish, distaste, disgust, repugnance, antipathy, antagonism, aversion, hatred, horror, loathing.

v dislike, disrelish, be averse to, be disinclined, be reluctant, have no taste for; disgust, repel, nauseate, hate, loathe.

adj disliking, disinclined, averse, loath, dislikable, distasteful, disagreeable, offensive, repulsive, repugnant, repellent, abhorrent, nauseating, disgusting, loathsome.

868 fastidiousness n nicety; hypercriticism; discernment, discrimination, judiciousness, keenness, perspicacity.

v be fastidious, split hairs.

adj fastidious, nice, dainty, delicate; hard to please, finicky, hypercritical, fussy, querulous, meticulous, exacting, scrupulous, proper, priggish, prim; discerning, discriminative, judicious, keen, sharp, perspicacious, sagacious.

869 satiety n repletion, saturation, glut, surfeit; disgust, weariness.

v sate, satiate, saturate, cloy, glut, stuff, gorge, surfeit; gall, disgust, bore, tire, weary.

adj satiated, glutted, stuffed, gorged, surfeited; disgusted, bored, tired, weary.

870 wonder n surprise, marvel, astonishment, stupefaction, amazement, awe, admiration, bewilderment, puzzlement.

v wonder, think, speculate, conjecture, meditate, ponder, question; marvel, admire, be surprised, start, stare, startle, astonish, amaze, astound, stagger, stupefy, bewilder, dumfound

adj marvelous, wonderful, extraordinary, remarkable, awesome, startling, wondrous, miraculous, astonishing, amazing, astounding, unique, curious, strange, odd, peculiar; astonished, surprised, aghast, agog, startled, breathless, awestruck, spell-bound, lost in wonder, amazed, fascinated, bewildered.

871 expectance *n* expectancy, expectation.

v expect, foresee, assume, not be surprised, make nothing of.

adj expecting, expectant, relied on, expected, figured on, foreseen.

872 prodigy *n* phenomenon, wonder, marvel, miracle; freak, monstrosity, spectacle, curiosity; genius, intellectual giant, wizard, mastermind, expert, sage, child genius, wunderkind.

873 repute *n* estimation, reputation, account, regard, report; name, standing, distinction, credit, respect, respectability, dignity, greatness, eminence, honor, renown.

v consider, esteem, account, hold, regard, deem, reckon; be held in high repute, be distinguished.

adj reputed, regarded, accounted; reputable, respected, respectable, esteemed, celebrated, distinguished, dignified, honored, renowned, eminent.

874 disrepute *n* disgrace, dishonor, disfavor, discredit, ill repute, low repute, bad name, shame, degradation, obloquy, debasement, ignominy, infamy, stain, spot, blot, tarnish, taint.

v disgrace oneself, have a bad name, shame, disgrace, dishonor, tarnish, stain, taint, blot.

adj disreputable, base, low, unsavory, shady, unworthy, disgraced, vile, ignominious, dishonorable, opprobrious, shameful, disgraceful, infamous, tainted, tarnished.

875 nobility *n* distinction, eminence, stateliness, majesty, grandeur, dignity, loftiness, profundity, highmindedness; rank, condition, high birth, gentility, quality, royalty, aristocracy, lord, lady.

v be noble; ennoble.

adj noble, exalted, honorable, dignified, imposing, stately; titled, aristocratic, patrician, high-born.

876 commonalty *n* the common people, the lower classes, commoners,

multitude, proletariat, populace, rank and file, bourgeoisie, general public, citizenry, peasantry, crowd, herd, rabble.

adj common, mean, low, base, ignoble, vulgar, homely, plebeian, proletarian, low-born, obscure, rustic, boorish, uncivilized.

877 title *n* honor, name, designation, decoration.

adj titled.

878 pride *n* self-respect, self-assurance, self-esteem, conceit, vanity, egotism, arrogance, vainglory, self-importance; insolence, haughtiness, superciliousness, presumption.

v be proud, presume, swagger, give oneself airs.

adj proud, high-minded, dignified, stately, noble, imposing, honorable, creditable; self-assured, self-satisfied, contented, egotistical, vain, conceited, arrogant, haughty, smug, overbearing, over-confident, snobbish, supercilious, presumptuous.

879 humility *n* modesty, humbleness, meekness, lowliness, submissiveness.

v lower, abase, debase, degrade, humiliate, mortify, shame, subdue, crush, break.

adj humble, low, lowly, unassuming, plain, common, poor, meek, modest, submissive, unpretentious; respectful, polite, courteous.

adj with downcast eyes, on bended knee.

880 vanity *n* pride, conceit, self-esteem, self-complacency, egotism, self-admiration, self-love, self-glorification; hollowness, emptiness, sham, triviality.

v be vain, have too high an opinion of oneself, inflate, puff up.

adj vain, conceited, egotistical, self-complacent, proud, vainglorious, arrogant, overweening, inflated; useless, hollow, trifling, trivial.

881 modesty *n* humility, diffidence, timidity, bashfulness; moderation, decency, propriety, simplicity, chastity, prudery, prudishness.

v be modest, retire, give way to, stay in the background.

adj modest, humble, diffident, timorous, bashful, sheepish, shy; moderate, humble, unpretentious, decent, becoming, proper, inextravagant, unostentatious, retiring, unassuming, unobtrusive; demure, prudish, chaste, pure, virtuous.

adv modestly, humbly, quietly, privately, without ceremony.

882 ostentation *n* pretention, pretentiousness, semblance, show, showiness, pretense, display, pageantry, pomp, pompousness, flourish, splendor.

v show off, parade, display, exhibit, blazon forth, emblazon, flaunt.

adj ostentatious, pretentious, showy, flashy, grand, pompous, garish, gaudy, flaunting, high-sounding, sumptuous, theatrical, dramatic, solemn, majestic, ceremonious, punctilious, over-blown.

adv with a flourish.

883 celebration *n* ceremony, ceremonial, commemoration, solemnization, observance, memorialization, festival, festivity.

v celebrate, commemorate, observe, keep; proclaim, announce; praise, extol, laud, glorify, honor, applaud, commend; solemnize, ritualize.

adj celebrational, commemorative, honorific, commendatory; celebrated, famous, renowned, illustrious, eminent, famed.

adv in honor of, in commemoration of, in celebration of.

884 boasting *n* bragging, swaggering, braggadocio, bravado.

 boaster, braggart, blusterer, *(informal)* windbag.

v exaggerate, brag, vaunt, swagger, crow, strut, talk big.

adj boasting, boastful, pretentious, vainglorious, elated, exultant, jubilant, triumphant.

885 [undue assumption of superiority] **insolence** *n* boldness, rudeness, disrespect, impertinence, impudence,

haughtiness, arrogance, audacity, abusiveness, contemptuousness.

v be insolent, swagger, assume, presume, take liberties, ride rough-shod over.

adj insolent, bold, rude, disrespectful, impertinent, impudent, brazen, brassy, haughty, arrogant, audacious, presumptuous, overbearing, abusive, contemptuous, insulting.

886 servility *n* submissiveness, obsequiousness, abasement, slavishness, cringing, fawning, meanness, baseness, groveling, sycophancy, slavery.

 toady, sycophant, boot-licker, *(informal)* apple-polisher, *(informal)* brown-noser.

v be servile, cringe, bow, stoop, kneel, toady, fawn, lick the boots of; sneak, crawl, crouch, cower.

adj servile, obsequious, slavish, cringing, fawning, sycophantic, groveling, sniveling, mealy-mouthed, abject, base, mean.

887 blusterer *n* swaggerer, braggart, boaster, windbag, bully, ruffian, rowdy, redneck.

III. Sympathetic Affections

888 friendship *n* amity, friendliness, harmony, concord, fellow-feeling, sympathy, good will, affection; companionship, comradeship, fellowship, fraternity, intimacy.

v be friendly, have an acquaintance with, keep company with, know, sympathize with, befriend, make friends with.

adj friendly, kind, kindly, amiable neighborly, brotherly, cordial, genial, well-disposed, benevolent, kind-hearted, affectionate; helpful, advantageous, propitious; acquainted, familiar, intimate.

adv amicably, with open arms.

889 enmity *n* unfriendliness, dislike, discord, ill will, antagonism, animosity, hostility, malevolence, hatred.

v be at odds with.

adj inimical; unfriendly, alienated, estranged, hostile.

890 friend *n* companion, acquaintance, crony, chum, pal, mate, fellow, bosom buddy, intimate, confidant; well-wisher, patron, supporter, backer, advocate, partisan, defender, sympathizer; ally, associate.

891 enemy *n* foe, adversary, opponent, antagonist, attacker.

892 sociality *n* sociableness, gregariousness, social interaction, social intercourse, comradeship, camaraderie, companionship, cordiality, good fellowship, conviviality.

    v be sociable, consort with, fraternize, welcome.

    adj sociable, gregarious, social, warm, genial, cordial, friendly, convivial, amicable, clubbish, chummy, neighborly, hospitable.

893 seclusion. exclusion *n* privacy, retirement, withdrawal, solitude, sequestration, retreat, isolation, hiding, secrecy. elimination, prohibition, exception, omission, preclusion, rejection, ejection, expulsion, banishment, ostracism, exile.

    recluse, hermit, cenobite, outcast, castaway, pariah, wastrel, foundling.

    v seclude oneself, retire, withdraw, retreat, sequester, isolate, hide. exclude, eliminate, prohibit, reject, eject, expel.

    adj secluded, retired, withdrawn, sequestered, private, isolated, solitary, excluded, eliminated, prohibited, omitted, precluded, rejected, ejected, repulsed, banished, ostracized, exiled.

894 courtesy *n* civility, sociability, politeness, good manners, good behavior, affability, gentility, graciousness, courtliness, respect.

    v be courteous, behave well.

    adj courteous, civil, polite, well-mannered, well-bred, gentlemanly, gallant, urbane, debonair, affable, gracious, courtly, respectful, obliging.

895 discourtesy *n* disrespect, ill-breeding, bad manners, tactlessness, rudeness, impudence, vulgarity.

    v be discourteous.

    adj discourteous, ill-bred, ill-mannered, uncivil, ill-behaved, ungentlemanly, impolite, ungracious, vulgar, crude, disrespectful, rude.

896 congratulations *n* felicitation, compliment, salute, salutation.

    v congratulate, offer congratulations, salute.

    adj congratulatory; complimentary.

897 love *n* affection, liking, regard, friendliness, kindness, kindliness, tenderness, fondness, devotion, warmth, attachment, yearning, passion, rapture, adoration, idolatry.

    lover, admirer, suitor, adorer, wooer; beau, sweetheart, flame, love, truelove, paramour, boyfriend, girlfriend, ladylove, idol, darling, angel, beloved.

    v love, like, be fond of, have affection for, be enamored of, be in love with, cherish, adore, revere, adulate, idolize.

    adj loving, smitten, affectionate, tender, fond, attached, enamored, devoted, amorous, passionate, adoring; lovable, adorable, winning, enchanting, bewitching.

898 hate *n* dislike, aversion, animosity, hatred, antipathy, detestation, loathing, abhorrence, odium, horror, repugnance.

    v hate, dislike, detest, abhor, loathe, despise, execrate, abominate.

    adj hateful, detestable, odious, abominable, loathsome, abhorrent, repugnant, invidious, obnoxious, offensive, disgusting, nauseating, revolting, vile, repulsive; hating, averse from, set against, bitter, spiteful, malicious.

899 favorite *n* pet, minion, idol, jewel, spoiled child, apple of one's eye, man after one's own heart; love, dear, darling, honey, sweetheart.

900 resentment *n* displeasure, pique, umbrage, animosity, bitterness, envy, jealousy, anger, wrath, indignation.

    v resent, take offense, bristle over, chafe, fume, frown, pout, snarl, gnash, growl, scowl, glower, grouch, bear a grudge.

adj resentful, offended, bitter, worked up, angry, wrathful, irate, indignant; envious, jealous.

901 irascibility *n* irritability, excitability, sensitivity.

v be irascible, quick to fly off the handle, have a temper.

adj irascible, testy, short-tempered, hot-tempered, quick-tempered, touchy, temperamental, irritable, snappish, petulant, overly sensitive, choleric.

901a sullenness *n* moodiness, moroseness, churlishness, sluggishness.

v be sullen, frown, scowl, sulk, pout.

adj silent, reserved, sulky, morose, moody, ill-humored, sour, vexatious, bad-tempered, surly, cross, grumpy, peevish, perverse; gloomy, dismal, cheerless, overcast, somber, mournful, dark; slow, sluggish, dull, stagnant.

902 [expression of affection or love] **endearment** *n* embrace, caress, hug, kiss, blandishment, dalliance, love token.

v endear, embrace, caress, blandish, flirt, dally.

adj endearing.

903 marriage *n* wedding, nuptials, matrimony, wedlock; union, alliance, association, confederation.

married man, married woman, husband, wife, spouse, mate, partner, consort, better half, *(informal)* old man, *(informal)* old lady.

v marry, tie the knot, take to the altar, wive, couple.

adj married, wed, united.

904 celibacy *n* sexual abstinence; bachelorhood.

celibate, unmarried man, bachelor, unmarried woman, spinster, old maid, virgin, maiden; priest.

adj celibate, unmarried.

905 divorce *n* marital separation, legal separation; separation, disunion, isolation.

v divorce, *(informal)* split up, separate, isolate.

adj divorced, separated, *(informal)* split up.

906 benevolence *n* kindness, kindliness, humanity, tenderness, kindheartedness, unselfishness, generosity, liberality, charity, philanthropy, altruism.

good Samaritan, sympathizer, altruist.

v wish well, take an interest in, treat well, comfort, benefit, assist, aid.

adj benevolent, kind, kindly, well-disposed, kind-hearted, humane, tender, tender-hearted, unselfish, generous,, liberal, benevolent, obliging, charitable, philanthropic, altruistic.

907 malevolence *n* ill will, enmity, rancor, resentment, malice, maliciousness, spite, spitefulness, grudge, hate, hatred, venom.

v bear ill will.

adj malevolent, malicious, resentful, spiteful, begrudging, hateful, venomous, vicious, hostile, ill-natured, evil-minded, rancorous.

908 malediction *n* curse, swear, imprecation, denunciation, cursing, damning, damnation, execration; slander.

v curse, swear, imprecate, denounce, damn, execrate; slander.

909 threat *n* menace, danger, indication, portent, foreboding, prognostication; intimidation.

v threaten, menace, endanger, indicate, presage, impend, portend, augur, forebode, foreshadow, prognosticate; frighten, denounce, intimidate, cow, badger.

adj threatening, menacing, endangering, impending, arguring, foreshadowing, foreboding, ominous, inauspicious, sinister, frightening, intimidating.

910 philanthropy *n* humaneness, compassion, humanitarianism, benevolence, helpfulness, munificence, public spirit, charity.

philanthropist, humanitarian, patriot.

adj philanthropic, humanitarian, benevolent, munificent, altruistic, public spirited, civic minded, charitable.

911 misanthropy *n* hatred of mankind, incivism.

misanthrope, man-hater; misogynist, woman-hater.

adj misanthropic, antisocial, uncivil.

912 benefactor *n* succorer, patron, supporter, contributor, friend.

913 evildoer *n* wrongdoer, troublemaker, subversive, oppressor, destroyer.

914 pity *n* sympathy, compassion, commiseration, condolence, mercy.

v pity, commiserate, feel sorry for, be sorry for, sympathize with, feel for.

adj pitying, compassionate, sympathetic, touched, moved, affected, feeling.

914a pitilessness *n* cruelty, meanness, ruthlessness, hard-heartedness.

v have no pity for.

adj pitiless, merciless, cruel, mean, unmerciful, ruthless, implacable, relentless, inexorable, hard-hearted, stony.

915 condolence *n* lamentation, sympathy, consolation.

v condole with, console, sympathize, lament.

916 gratitude *n* thanks, thankfulness, appreciation, indebtedness.

v be grateful, thank, appreciate.

adj grateful, appreciative, thankful, obliged, beholding, indebted, in one's debt.

917 ingratitude *n* thanklessness, unthankfulness.

ingrate.

v be ungrateful.

adj ungrateful, unthankful, unmindful, thankless.

918 forgiveness *n* pardon, excuse, indulgence, remission, reprieve, amnesty, grace, absolution.

v forgive, pardon, excuse, absolve, reprieve, acquit.

adj forgiving.

919 revenge *n* vengeance, retaliation, requital, reprisal, retribution, vindictiveness, vengefulness.

avenger, vindicator, nemesis.

v revenge, avenge, retaliate, requite, vindicate.

adj revengeful, vengeful, vindictive, spiteful, malevolent, resentful, malicious, malignant, unforgiving, implacable.

920 jealousy *n* envy, resentment; suspicion; watchfulness, vigilance.

v be jealous.

adj jealous, envious, resentful; suspicious; solicitous, watchful, vigilant.

921 envy *n* jealousy, enviousness, grudge, covetousness.

v envy, covet, begrudge, resent.

adj envious, covetous, jealous, begrudging.

IV. Moral Affections

922 right *n* virtue, justice, fairness, integrity, equity, equitableness, uprightness, rectitude, morality, morals, goodness, honor, lawfulness; accuracy, truth.

v be right; do right.

adj right, just, good, equitable, moral, fair, upright, honest, lawful; correct, proper, suitable, fit; correct, true, accurate; genuine, legitimate, rightful.

adv righteously, rightfully, lawfully, rightly, justly, fairly, equitably.

923 wrong *n* evil, wickedness, misdeed, sin, vice, immorality, iniquity, inequity, injustice, unlawfulness.

adj wrong, injure, harm, maltreat, abuse, oppress, cheat, defraud, dishonor.

adj wrong, bad, evil, wicked, sinful, immoral, iniquitous, reprehensible, unjust, crooked, dishonest; erroneous, inaccurate, incorrect, false, untrue, mistaken; improper, unappropriate, unfit; awry, amiss, out of order.

adv wrongly, wickedly, sinfully.

924 claim n due, right, privilege, prerogative, prescription, demand, sanction, warrant, license.

claimant, appellant.

v claim, deserve, have the right, be entitled.

adj claiming, having a right to, privileged, prescribed, sanctioned allowed, licensed, authorized, due.

925 [absence of right] unrightfulness n impropriety, illegitimacy, presumption.

usurper, pretender.

v be unentitled.

adj unrightful, having no right to unentitled, unauthorized, unwarranted, illegitimate, not licensed.

926 duty n obligation, function, responsibility, onus, burden, business; conscience, moral imperative, sense of duty; homage, respect, reverence.

v do one's duty, behoove, become, befit, beseem; observe, perform, fulfill, discharge.

adj obligatory, binding, imperative, incumbent, under obligation, obliged, bound, tied, duty bound; dutiful, respectful, docile, submissive, deferential, reverential, obedient.

927 dereliction of duty n nonobservance, nonperformance, neglect, failure, carelessness, fault, infraction, violation, transgression.

v neglect, slight, fail, violate.

adj undutiful, negligent, careless, at fault, failing, in violation.

927a exemption n immunity, impunity, privilege, freedom, exception, excuse, dispensation.

v exempt, excuse, release, acquit, discharge, free.

adj exempt, immune, privileged, freed, excepted, excused, unbound.

928 respect n esteem, deference, regard, consideration, estimation, veneration, reverence, homage, honor, admiration, approbation, approval, affection, feeling; respects, regards, duty; regard, consideration, attention, devotion.

v honor, revere, reverence, esteem, venerate, regard, consider, de-

fer to, admire; adulate, adore, love; regard, heed, attend, notice, consider.

adj respectful, courteous, polite, well-mannered, well-bred, civil, deferential; respected, estimable, venerable, admirable; respecting, heeding, considering, regarding, attending.

929 disrespect n discourtesy, impoliteness, rudeness, crudeness, incivility, impudence, impertinence, irreverence, derision.

v hold in disrespect, be disrespectful, insult, deride, scoff, mock, sneer, jeer, deride, ridicule, scorn.

adj disrespectful, discourteous, impolite, rude, crude, uncivil, impudent, impertinent, irreverent insulting, derisive, scornful.

930 contempt n scorn, disdain, derision, contumely; dishonor, disgrace, shame.

v feel contempt for, contemn, scorn, disdain, deride, despise.

adj contemptible, despicable, mean, low, miserable, abject, base, vile; contemptuous, scornful, disdainful, derisive; dishonorable, disgraceful, shameful.

931 approbation n approval, sanction, esteem, admiration, commendation.

v approbate, approve, esteem, value, honor, admire, appreciate, sanction, endorse, commend, praise.

adj commendatory, complimentary, laudatory; approved, praised, in high esteem, in favour; praiseworthy, commendable, good, meritorious, estimable, creditable.

932 disapprobation n disapproval, dislike, disesteem, odium, disparagement, deprecation, denunciation, censure.

v disapprove, dislike, object to, frown upon, censure, blame, reproach, reprove, admonish, berate.

adj disapproving, disparaging, reproachful, defamatory, denunciatory, condemnatory.

933 flattery n adulation, charming, lip-service, (informal) brown-nosing, fawning, flunkeyism, sycophancy.

v flatter, curry favor, slobber over, *(informal)* lay it on thick, wheedle, fawn, court, *(informal)* brown-nose, pander to, overpraise.

adj flattering, adulatory, honey-mouthed, smooth-tongued, servile, sycophantic.

934 detraction *n* detracting, disparagement, belittling, defamation, vilification, calumny, abuse, slander, aspersion, deprecation.

v detract, run down, criticize, decry, disparage, blacken, belittle, depreciate, cast aspersions, defame, malign, abuse, slander, vilify.

adj detracting, disparaging, belittling, derogatory, depreciating, calumnious, abusive, slanderous, vilifying, scurrilous.

935 flatterer *n* adulator, toady, flunkey, *(informal)* apple-polisher, fawner, sycophant, *(informal)* brown-noser, bootlicker, opportunist, courtier.

936 detractor *n* reprover, critic, carper, slanderer, *(informal)* hatchet man, backbiter, defamer, castigator, satirist, cynic, reviler.

937 vindication *n* exoneration, exculpation, acquittal; justification, warrant, support, defense.

apologist, vindicator, defender.

v vindicate, exonerate, acquit, clear; uphold, justify, maintain, defend, support.

adj vindicating, vindicated, exonerated, exonerating, exculpatory, acquitted; justified, warranted, supported.

938 accusation *n* arraignment, indictment, charge, incrimination, impeachment; accusal, blaming, inculpation, charging, imputation.

accuser, prosecutor, plaintiff; relator, informer; appellant.

v charge; arraign, indict, charge, incriminate, impeach; blame, inculpate, charge, involve, point to, impute.

adj accused, accusing, accusatory, accusative, incriminatory, imputative.

939 probity *n* honesty, uprightness, virtue, rectitude, integrity.

v be honorable.

adj honest, honorable, virtuous, upright, scrupulous, high-principled.

940 improbity *n* dishonesty, wickedness, immorality, evil.

v be dishonest, play false.

adj dishonest, dishonorable, unscrupulous, immoral, wicked, evil.

941 knave *n* rogue, rascal, blackguard, sneak, villain, scoundrel.

942 disinterestedness *n* impartiality, fairness, lack of bias, unselfishness, generosity, liberality.

v be disinterested.

adj disinterested, unbiased, unprejudiced, unselfish, impartial, fair, generous, liberal.

943 selfishness *n* self-interest, self-seeking, self-love, egoism, egotism, solipsism, illiberality, parsimony, stinginess, meanness.

v be selfish, cultivate one's own garden, look after oneself, feather one's own nest.

adj selfish, self-centered, self-indulgent, self-interested, self-seeking, egotistical, solipsistic, illiberal, parsimonious, stingy, cheap, mean.

944 virtue *n* virtuousness, goodness, uprightness, morality, ethics, probity, rectitude, integrity; excellence, merit, quality, asset; innocence, chastity, purity.

v be virtuous, have the virtue of.

adj virtuous, right, upright, moral, righteous, good, chaste, pure.

945 vice *n* fault, sin, depravity, iniquity, immorality, wickedness; blemish, blot, imperfection, defect.

v sin, err, transgress, trespass.

adj vicious, immoral, depraved, profligate, wicked, sinful, sinning, corrupt, bad, iniquitous, reprehensible, blameworthy, censurable, wrong, improper; spiteful, malignant, malicious, malevolent; faulty, defective; ill-tempered, bad-tempered, refractory.

946 innocence n purity, virtue, virtuousness, faultlessness, spotlessness; guiltlessness, blamelessness; uprightness, honesty; naïveté, simplicity, artlessness, guilelessness, ingenuousness.

v be innocent.

adj innocent, pure, untainted, sinless, virtuous, virginal, blameless, faultless, impeccable, spotless, immaculate; guiltless, blameless; upright, honest, forthright; naïve, simple, unsophisticated, artless, guileless, ingenuous.

947 guilt n guiltiness, culpability, criminality; sinfulness.

v be guilty.

adj guilty, culpable, to blame, in fault.

948 good man n model, paragon, hero, soldier, saint, salt of the earth, (informal) ace.

949 bad man n wrong-doer, evil-doer, sinner, scoundrel, miscreant, villain, wretch, monster, devil, demon, scum of the earth.

950 penitence n contrition, atonement, compunction, repentance, remorse, regret.

penitent, prodigal son.

v be penitent, repent, rue, regret.

adj penitent, sorry, contrite, repenting; repentant, atoning, amending, remorseful, regretful; penitential.

951 impenitence n irrepentance, obduracy, hardness of heart.

v be impenitent, show no remorse.

adj impenitent, uncontrite, not sorry, obdurate, unrepentant, remorseless; unrepenting, unrepented, unatoned; irreclaimable.

952 atonement n satisfaction, reparation, compensation, amends, quittance; redemption, expiation, reclamation, conciliation, propitiation.

v atone, atone for; give satisfaction, satisfy, make amends; expiate, propitiate, reclaim, redeem, repair, absolve, purge, shrive, do penance, repent.

adj atoning, propitiating, propiti-

atory, redemptive, expiating, expiatory.

953 temperance n moderation, self-restraint, self-control, continence; sobriety, even-temperedness, calmness, coolness, detachment, dispassion.

vegetarian; teetotaler; abstainer.

v be temperate, abstain, forbear, restrain.

adj temperate, moderate, self-controlled, self-restrained, frugal, sparing; sober, calm, cool, detached, dispassionate.

954 intemperance n excess, exorbitance, inordinateness, extravagance; indulgence, high living, self-indulgence, epicurism, epicureanism, sybaritism; inabstinence, alcoholism.

v be intemperate, indulge, wallow in.

adj intemperate, excessive, exorbitant, inordinate, extravagant; indulgent, self-indulgent, epicurean.

954a sensualist n sybarite, voluptuary, pleasure-seeker, epicure, epicurean, libertine, hedonist.

955 asceticism n puritanism, austerity, abstemiousness, self-abnegation, self-denial, total abstinence, self-motivation.

ascetic, anchorite, puritan, martyr; hermit, recluse.

v abstain, deny oneself, fast, starve.

adj ascetic, puritanical, austere, abstemious, rigorous, rigid, stern, severe, harsh, strict, self-denying, self-mortifying.

956 fasting n day of fasting; going hungry, starving oneself, starvation.

v fast, starve, famish.

adj fasting, starving, unfed; starved, half-starved, hungry.

957 gluttony n greed, greediness, voracity; epicurism, gormandizing, gulosity, crapulence, over-eating, (informal) piggishness.

glutton, epicure, cormorant, hog, (informal) pig.

v be gluttonous, hog; overeat, gorge, stuff oneself, make a pig of oneself, guzzle, bolt, devour, engorge, gobble up.

adj gluttonous, greedy, voracious; epicurean, gormandizing, crapulent, swinish, *(informal)* piggish.

958 sobriety *n* abstinence, teetotalism.

teetotaler, abstainer.

v be sober, abstain, take the pledge.

adj sober, unintoxicated, on the wagon, *(informal)* straight, *(informal)* dry, dry as a bone.

959 drunkenness *n* intemperance, drinking, inebriety, insobriety, intoxication, alcoholism.

drunkard, sot, tippler, drinker, inebriate, dipsomaniac, alcoholic, *(informal)* boozer, *(informal)* lush, *(informal)* juicer.

v be drunk, drink, imbibe, booze, guzzle, swill, soak, sot, lush, drink like a fish, hit the bottle.

adj drunk, drunken, sotted, intoxicated, inebriated, tipsy, tight, *(informal)* potted, *(informal)* stewed, *(informal)* stewed to the gills, dead drunk, *(informal)* plowed, *(informal)* plastered, *(informal)* tanked, *(informal)* wasted, *(informal)* juiced, *(informal)* blown away, *(informal)* high, *(informal)* flying, *(informal)* feeling no pain.

960 purity *n* cleanness; decency, decorum, delicacy; continence, chastity, innocence, modesty, virtue, virginity; simplicity, genuineness, faultlessness, perfection; guiltlessness, honesty, uprightness.

virgin, vestal virgin.

v be pure.

adj pure, decent, delicate; innocent, continent, chaste, virginal, modest, virtuous, undefiled, unsullied, unstained, untainted, uncorrupted, clean, spotless, immaculate; simple, genuine, faultless, perfect; honest, upright; unmixed, unadulterated, uncontaminated.

961 impurity *n* indecency, indelicacy; incontinence, immodesty, lewdness, concupiscence, prurience, lechery; grossness, obscenity, ribaldry, smut, bawdry; uncleanness, adulteration, contamination, defilement; fault, flaw, imperfection; guilt, sin, sinfulness.

v be impure.

adj impure, indecent, indelicate; incontinent, immodest, unchaste, concupiscent, lewd, prurient, lecherous; gross, obscene, ribald, dirty, smutty, bawdy; unclean, sullied, defiled, contaminated, adulterated; tainted, stained, corrupted, jaded; faulty, flawed, imperfect; guilty, sinning, sinful, wicked.

962 libertine *n* rake, roué, debauchee, lecher, sensualist, voluptuary, profligate, seducer, deceiver, courtesan, prostitute, strumpet, harlot, whore, street-walker, trollop, hussy, bitch, slut, minx.

963 legality *n* legitimacy, legitimateness, lawfulness; duty, obligation.

law, code, constitution, charter, statute, regulation, decree, order.

v legalize; legislate, enact, ordain, decree, codify, formulate, pass a law.

adj legal, legitimate, authorized, licit, lawful, legalized, legislated; constitutional.

964 illegality *n* illegitimacy, unlawfulness, illicitness, lawlessness.

v be illegal, offend against the law, violate the law.

adj illegal, unlawful, illegitimate, illicit, contraband, unconstitutional, unchartered, unwarranted, unauthorized, unlicensed, proscribed, prohibited, outlawed, criminal; lawless, arbitrary, despotic, unanswerable, unaccountable.

965 [executive] jurisdiction *n* judicature, authority, power, right, control; territory, range, magistracy.

v judge, sit in judgment; administer.

adj jurisdictive, judicial, administrative; inquisitorial.

966 tribunal *n* court, courtroom, board, bench, court of law, court of justice, bar of justice, judgment seat, dock, forum, witness-chair.

967 judge n justice, judiciary, magistrate, judicator, adjudicator, jurist, juror; moderator, arbiter, arbitrator, umpire; referee.

v judge, adjudge, determine, hear a cause, try a case, pass sentence.

adj judicial, judicious, juridical, legal, juristic, judicatory, jurisdictive.

968 lawyer n attorney, attorney-at-law, counselor, barrister, solicitor, pleader, counsel, advocate, counselor-at-law, legal adviser; prosecutor, prosecuting attorney, district attorney, public prosecutor, attorney general.

bar, legal profession.

v practice law, be called to the bar, plead, read the law.

adj learned in the law.

969 lawsuit n suit, action, cause, dispute, contention; case, debate, litigation, legal proceedings, legal action, legal process, trial, debate, pleadings, argument, argumentation, disputation, prosecution; writ, summons, subpoena, affidavit, suitor, party to a suit, litigant, verdict, decision; precedent.

v go to the law, sue, file a claim, bring to trial, put on trial, serve, serve with a writ, cite, arraign, prosecute, bring an action against, indict, impeach, attach, summon.

adj litigious.

970 acquittal n clearance, exculpation, exoneration, absolution, discharge, pardon; impunity, immunity.

v acquit, exculpate, exonerate, clear, absolve, pardon; discharge, release, liberate, set free.

adj acquitted, cleared, exculpated, exonerated; discharged, released, set free.

971 condemnation n conviction, guilty verdict, proscription.

v condemn, convict, find guilty, damn, doom, proscribe; stand condemned.

adj condemned, condemnatory, convicted.

972 punishment n sentence, judgment, penalty, retribution, discipline, chastisement, castigation, reproof, correction.

v punish, inflict punishment, correct, discipline, penalize, reprove, castigate, chasten, administer correction. scold, berate, jail, incarcerate, execute, torture, banish, flog, whip, lash, scourge.

adj punishing, punitive, castigatory, penalized, penalizing; punished, castigated.

973 reward n recompense, prizes, desert, compensation, pay, remuneration, requital, merit; bounty, premium, bonus; reparation, redress; retribution, reckoning, amends.

v reward, recompense, requite, compensate, pay, remunerate.

adj rewarding, remunerative, compensatory, retributive, reparatory; rewarded.

974 penalty n punishment, retribution, pain, pains, penance; fine, forfeit, damages, sequestration, incarceration, confiscation.

v penalize, punish; fine, confiscate, sequester; penalized, punished.

975 scourge n punishment, flogging; affliction, calamity, plague, bane, pest, nuisance; whip, lash, strap, throng, rod, cane, stick; prison, house of correction.

gaoler, jailer, executioner, hangman.

976 deity n divinity, god, godhead, omnipotence, providence, lord, the almighty, supreme being, first cause, prime mover, author, creator, the infinite, the eternal, the all-powerful, the all-merciful, omnipresence.

adj divine, godly, almighty, holy, hallowed, sacred, heavenly, celestial, sacrosanct; superhuman, supernatural, spiritual, ghostly, unearthly.

977 angel n glorified spirit, beneficent spirit, ministering spirit, heavenly spirit, winged being, seraph, cherub, archangel, helper, servant, guardian; (informal) friend, patron, protector, guardian angel, love.

adj angelic, seraphic, cherubic, spiritual, ethereal; pure, good righteous, ideal, beautiful; *(informal)* adorable, entrancing, transporting, rapturous, lovely, enrapturing.

978 devil *n* Satan, Lucifer, Beelzebub; tempter, evil one, evil spirit, serpent, evil incarnate.
    diabolism, satanism.
    adj devilish, satanic, diabolic, infernal, hellish.

979 fabulous spirit *n* god, goddess, fairy, fay, sylph, faun, nymph, nereid, dryad, sea-maid, oread, naiad, mermaid, kelpie, nixie, sprite, pixie, elf.
    adj fabulous, mythological, imaginary, sylphic.

980 demon *n* demonology; devil, fiend, evil spirit, incubus, monster, succubus, succuba, fury, harpy, ghoul, vampire, ogre, gnome, imp, kobold, dwarf, urchin, troll, sprite, bad fairy, leprechaun; ghost, specter, apparition, spirit, shade, shadow, vision, hobgoblin, wraith, spook, banshee, siren, satyr.
    adj demonic, supernatural, weird, uncanny, unearthly, spectral, ghostly, ghostlike, elfin, fiendish, impish, haunted.

981 heaven *n* kingdom of heaven, kingdom of god, heavenly kingdom, paradise, nirvana; celestial bliss, glory.
    adj heavenly, celestial, supernal, unearthly, paradisaic, paradisical, beatific, elysian, blissful, beautiful, divine, blessed, beautified, glorified.

982 hell *n* Gehenna, inferno, Hades, Erebus, pandemonium, abyss, limbo; *[informal]* torment, torture, pain, agony, suffering.
    adj hellish, infernal, stygian, satanic, diabolic, devilish; *[informal]* painful, agonizing, excruciating, horrifying, unendurable.

983 theology *n* theosophy, divinity, hagiography, theologics, theism, monotheism, religion, religious persuasion, dogma, creed, credo, doctrine, tenet, articles of faith.
    theologian, theologue, divine.

    adj theological, religious, theosophical, hagiological.

983a orthodoxy *n* soundness; strictness, faithfulness, adherence, observance; truth, true faith, religious truth.
    adj orthodox, sound, strict, faithful, catholic, doctrinal, authoritative, official, traditional; scriptural, divine, Christian; conventional, established, approved, prescriptive, prevailing, customary.

984 heterodoxy *n* unorthodoxy, nonconformity, iconoclasm, doubt, skepticism, recusancy, dissent, misbelief, error, heresy, schism, apostasy.
    pagan, heathen, dissenter, nonconformist, skeptic, heretic, atheist.
    adj heterodox, nonconformist, nonconforming, iconoclastic, doubting, skeptical, unscriptural, unorthodox, uncanonical, recusant, dissenting, misbelieving, heretical, schismatic.

985 revelation *n* disclosure, discovery, expression, declaration, expression, utterance, publication, admission, confession, acknowledgment; enlightenment, proclamation, announcement; Christian Revelation, Scriptures, Word of God.
    adj revelatory; instructive; confessional.

986 religious writings *n* Scriptures, *Bible*, Old Testament, New Testament, The Vedas, Upanishads, Bhagavad Gita, Koran, Alcoran, Avesta.

987 piety *n* godliness, devoutness, devotion, humility, veneration, sanctity, grace, holiness; reverence, regard, respect.
    believer, devotee, pietist, righteous man.
    v be pious, have faith; believe, revere, venerate, sanctify, consecrate.
    adj pious, devout, godly, reverent, religious, holy, sacred, pietistic, saintly; devoted, humble, reverential.

988 impiety *n* irreverence, irreligion, scoffing, profaneness, profanity, blasphemy, desecration, sacrilege, sin, sinfulness; hypocrisy, cant, sanctimony, sanctimoniousness.

sinner, scoffer, blasphemer, sacrilegist, hypocrite.

v be impious, scoff, swear, profane, blaspheme, desecrate, revile, commit sacrilege.

989 irreligion *n* ungodliness, laxity, impiety, indifference, apathy, skepticism, doubt, disbelief, incredulity, agnosticism, freethinking, atheism, infidelity.

skeptic, doubter, nonbeliever, agnostic, cynic, freethinker, atheist, infidel, heathen.

v be irreligious, doubt, disbelieve, lack faith, question.

adj irreligious, godless, ungodly, unholy, unhallowed, undevout; skeptical, doubting, unbelieving, indifferent, apathetic, incredulous, freethinking, agnostic, atheistic, faithless; worldly, earthly, unspiritual.

990 worship *n* reverence, homage, adoration, honor; regard, idolizing, idolatry, deification; prayer, supplication, petition; service, celebration, rites.

worshiper, congregation, suppliant, communicant, celebrant.

v worship, adore, adulate, idolize, deify, love, like; pray, kneel, bow, fall on one's knees; invoke, supplicate, offer prayers, petition; praise, bless, laud, glorify, magnify, sing praises.

adj worshiping, revering, adoring, honoring; worshipful, reverential, honorific, celebrational.

991 idolatry *n* idolism, idolatrousness, idolization, fetishism, idolworship, deification, demonology; blind adoration, extravagant love, fervor, ardency, enchantment, hero worship.

idol, image, icon, symbol, statue, false god, pagan deity.

v idolize, worship idols, idolatrize, worship, glorify, put on a pedestal, canonize, deify, apotheosize; dote upon, treasure, prize.

adj idolatrous, idol-worshiping,

pagan, fetishistic; adoring, impassioned, lovesick.

992 sorcery *n* occultism, magic, witchery, enchantment, witchcraft, spell, necromancy, divination, charm, conjuration, bewitchery, spiritualism.

v practice sorcery, conjure, charm, enchant, bewitch, divine, entrance, mesmerize, cast a spell, call up spirits, raise spirits.

adj magic, magical, bewitching, enchanting, charming, incantory, weird, cabalistic, talismanic; charmed, bewitched, enchanted.

993 spell *n* charm, incantation, exorcism, voodoo, trance, rapture, suggestion, jinx, hocus-pocus, mumbojumbo, abracadabra.

994 sorcerer *n* magician, conjuror, necromancer, wizard, witch, exorcist, charmer, medicine man, shaman, medium, clairvoyant, mesmerist, soothsayer, guru.

995 churchdom *n* church, ministry, priesthood, sisterhood, prelacy, hierarchy.

v call, ordain, consecrate, bestow, elect.

adj ecclesiastical, clerical, priestly, pastoral, ministerial, hierarchical.

996 clergy *n* clerical, ministry, priesthood, the cloth, clergyman, divine, ecclesiastic, churchman, pastor, shepherd, minister, preacher, parson, father, reverend, priest, rabbi.

v receive the call, take orders.

adj clerical; ordained.

997 laity *n* fold, flock, congregation, assembly, brethren, people; layman, parishioner.

v secularize.

adj lay, laical, secular, civil, temporal.

998 rite *n* ceremony, observance, function, service, procedure, form, usage.

v perform a rite.

adj ritualistic, ceremonial.

999 canonicals *n* religious garments, vestments, robe, gown, surplice.

1000 temple *n* place of worship, house of god, cathedral, church, chapel, meetinghouse, synagogue, tabernacle, mosque, shrine, pantheon; monastery, priory, abbey, friary, convent, nunnery, cloister; parsonage, rectory, vicarage.

   adj churchly, cloistered, monastic.

Index

accredit v 805
accredited adj 484
accretion n 35
accrue v 37, 785
acculturation n 658
accumulate v 37, 72, 636
accumulation n 72, 636
accuracy n 459, 494, 543, 922
accurate adj 246, 494, 922
accusal n 938
accusation n 938
accusative adj 938
accusatory adj 938
accused adj 938
accuser n 938
accusing adj 938
accustom v 613
ace n 948
acerbate v 397
acerbic adj 397
acerbity n 397
ache n 378, 828; v 378
achievable adj 470
achieve v 161, 680, 729, 731
achievement n 161, 551, 729, 731
aching n 378
acid adj 397
acidify v 397
acidity n 397
acidulate v 397
acidulous adj 397
acknowledge v 488, 529, 535, 772
acknowledgment n 488, 529, 762, 772, 807, 985
acknowledgment of payment n 810
acme n 206, 210
acolyte n 541
acoustics n 402
acquaintance n 890
acquainted adj 888
acquainted with adj 490, 527
acquaint with v 527
acquiesce v 488, 602, 725, 762
acquiescence n 488, 725, 762
acquiescent adj 488, 535, 725
acquire v 539, 775, 785, 795
acquire a habit v 613
acquirement n 698
acquirements n 539
acquisition n 775
acquisition n 785, 795
acquisition of knowledge n 539
acquit v 750, 918, 927a, 937, 970
acquit oneself of v 807
acquittal n 970

acquittal n 750, 937
acquittance n 772
acquitted adj 937, 970
acreage n 342, 780
acres n 342
acrid adj 392, 395, 397
acridity n 392, 397
acridness n 395
act n 680, 697, 741; v 170, 599, 680, 692
act a part v 599, 644, 855
act in concert v 709
acting n 599
action n 680
action n 264, 682, 686, 692, 969
actions n 692
activate v 175
active adj 171, 359, 682
activity n 682
activity n 171, 264, 686
actor n 599, 680, 690
actress n 599
actual adj 1, 118, 494
actuality n 1
actually adv 1
act up to v 772
acumen n 498
acute adj 171, 173, 253, 375, 410, 410
acute angle n 244
acutely adv 31
acuteness n 173, 253
adage n 496
adamant adj 600
adamantine adj 323
adapt v 23, 852
adaptability n 149
adaptable adj 82, 149
adapt to v 82
add v 37, 85
addendum n 37, 39
addiction n 613
addictive adj 613
addition n 37
addition n 35, 39
additional adj 35, 37, 39
addle-brained adj 499
address n 189, 582, 586;
  v 582, 586
add to v 35
add up v 37, 85
add up to v 50
add water v 337
adept adj 698
adequacy n 639
adequate adj 157, 639
adhere v 46, 199
adherence n 46, 983a
adhere to v 613, 772
adhering adj 46
adhesion n 46, 772
adhesive adj 46, 327, 352
adhesiveness n 46, 352
adieu n 293
ad infinitum adv 104
adjacent adj 197

adjoin v 197, 199
adjoining adj 197
adjourn v 133
adjournment n 133
adjudge v 967
adjudicator n 737, 967
adjunct n 39
adjunct n 37, 88
adjust v 23, 27, 58, 774, 852
adjustable adj 149
adjustment n 723, 774
administer n 965; v 692, 693, 737, 788, 965
administer correction v 972
administering adj 693
administration n 692, 693
administrative adj 692, 737, 965
admirable adj 648
admiration n 870, 928, 931
admire v 870, 928, 931
admirer n 897
admission n 76, 296, 785, 985
admit v 54, 76, 296, 488, 529, 785
admit of v 470
admittance n 296
admitting adj 469
admixture n 41
admonish v 668, 695, 864, 932
admonition n 668, 695, 864
admonitory adj 695
ado n 315, 684
adolescence n 131
adolescent adj 131
adorable adj 897, 977
adoration n 897, 990
adore v 897, 928, 990
adorer n 897
adoring adj 897, 990, 991
adorn n 847
adornment n 847
adrift adj 10, 44, 73;
  adv 44
adroit adj 698
adroitness n 698, 702
adulate v 897, 928, 990
adulation n 933
adulator n 935
adulatory adj 933
adult adj 131
adulterate v 41, 659
adulterated adj 337, 961
adulteration n 41, 659, 961
adulthood n 131
adumbrate v 422
adumbration n 421
advance n 282, 286, 731, 787; v 35, 109, 282, 307, 514, 658, 731, 763, 787

advanced *adj* 128, 282
advanced age *n* 128
advanced guard *n* 234
advancement *n* 282, 658
advancing *adj* 282
advantage *n* 33, 618;
  v 618
advantageous *adj* 618,
  644, 646, 648, 775, 888
advent *n* 121, 286, 292
adventitious *adj* 6, 8, 156
adventure *n* 151, 622, 675;
  v 665, 675
adventurer *n* 463, 548,
  621
adventuress *n* 548
adventurous *adj* 675, 861
adversary *n* 708, 710, 726,
  855
adverse *adj* 708, 735
adversely *adv* 735
adversity *n* 735
adversity *n* 619, 830
advertise *v* 531
advertisement *n* 531
advice *n* 695
advice *n* 527, 668, 693,
  864
advisability *n* 646
advisable *adj* 646
advise *v* 527, 693, 695, 864
advised *adj* 527, 620
advisedly *adv* 611, 620
adviser *n* 540, 694, 695
advisory *adj* 668, 695
advisory board *n* 696
advocacy *n* 707
advocate *n* 890, 968;
  v 695, 707
aerate *v* 338
aerial *adj* 267, 338
aeriform *adj* 338
aeronautic *n* 267
aeronautical *n* 267
aeronautics *n* 267
aesthetic *adj* 845
afar *adj* 196; *adv* 196
affability *n* 894
affable *adj* 894
affair *n* 151, 454, 625, 680
affairs *n* 151
affect *v* 9, 175, 176, 824,
  855
affectation *n* 855
affectation *n* 579
affected *adj* 579, 820, 821,
  855, 914
affectedness *n* 855
affection *n* 888, 897, 928
affectionate *adj* 888, 897
affections *n* 820
affidavit *n* 467, 535, 969
affiliated *adj* 9, 11
affiliation *n* 11
affinity *n* 9, 17, 216, 288
affirm *v* 516, 535
affirmation *n* 535
affirmative *adj* 535

affirming *adj* 535
affix *n* 39; *v* 37, 43
afflict *v* 828
affliction *n* 735, 828, 830,
  975
affluence *n* 734, 803
affluent *adj* 803
afford *v* 784
afford pleasure *v* 829
affront *n* 830; *v* 830
afire *adj* 382
aflame *adj* 382
afloat *adj* 1, 267
aforementioned *adj* 116
aforethought *adj* 611
afraid *adj* 860, 862
afresh *adv* 104, 123
aft *adv* 235
after *adj* 117; *adv* 63, 117,
  235, 281
aftermath *n* 65
afternoon *n* 126
afterpiece *n* 65
aftertaste *n* 390
after the flood *adv* 59
after this fashion *adv* 627
afterthought *n* 65
afterwards *adv* 117
again *adv* 104
again and again *adv* 104
against *adv* 708; *prep* 179
against one's will
  adv 603
against the grain
  adv 256
age *n* 128
age *n* 106, 108, 124; *v* 124,
  435
aged *adj* 124, 128, 130
agency *n* 170
agency *n* 632, 677, 755
agent *n* 690
agent *n* 153, 758
agglomerate *n* 46
aggrandize *v* 35, 194
aggrandizement *n* 35, 37,
  194
aggravate *v* 173, 835
aggravation *n* 835
aggregate *n* 50, 72; *v* 50
aggregation *n* 46, 72
aggression *n* 716
aggressive *adj* 716
aggressiveness *n* 715
aggressor *n* 716
aggrieve *v* 649
aghast *adj* 509, 860, 870
agile *adj* 274
agitate *v* 315, 824
agitated *adj* 149, 315
agitation *n* 315
agitation *n* 59, 149, 171,
  173, 824, 825
aglow *adj* 420
agnostic *adj* 989
agnosticism *n* 989
ago *adv* 122

agog *adj* 870
agonize *v* 378
agonizing *adj* 982
agony *n* 378, 825, 828, 982
agrarian *adj* 371
agree *v* 23, 82, 178, 488,
  714, 725, 762, 768, 769
agreeable *adj* 23, 82, 377,
  413, 762, 829, 831
agreeableness *n* 829
agreed *adj* 488
agreed upon *adj* 74
agreeing *adj* 23, 413, 488,
  494
agreement *n* 23
agreement *n* 16, 17, 82,
  178, 242, 488, 602, 709,
  714, 762, 769
agree to *v* 760
agree with *v* 656, 829
agricultural *adj* 371
agriculture *n* 371
agrobiology *n* 371
agrology *n* 371
agronomics *n* 371
agronomy *n* 371
ahead *adv* 234, 280, 282,
  303
aid *n* 707
aid *n* 631, 644, 711, 834;
  v 215, 631, 644, 707, 746,
  834, 906
aiding *adj* 707
ail *v* 655
ailing *adj* 655
ailment *n* 655
aim *n* 278, 453, 516, 620;
  v 278, 516
aim at *v* 278, 620, 622
aim for *v* 620
air *n* 338
air *n* 349, 415, 448, 852;
  v 338
aircraft *n* 273
airing *n* 286
airman *n* 269
air-pipe *n* 351
airplane *n* 273
airs *n* 855
airtight *adj* 261
air travel *n* 267
airy *adj* 4, 320, 334, 338
ait *n* 346
ajar *adj* 260
akimbo *adj* 244
akin *adj* 11
akin to *adj* 17
alacrity *n* 132, 274, 602,
  684
à la mode *adj* 852
alarm *n* 669
alarm *n* 550, 665, 668,
  860; *v* 669
alarm bell *n* 669
alarmed *adj* 860
alarum *n* 669
albeit *adv* 30

albification n 430
albinism n 430
albinistic adj 430
album n 596
alchemy n 144
alcoholic n 959
alcoholism n 954, 959
Alcoran n 986
alert adj 457, 498, 682, 864
alertness n 457, 459
algebra n 85
algebraic adj 85
alias n 565
alien adj 10, 57
alienated adj 889
alight v 265, 292, 306, 342
aligned adj 216
alignment n 278
alike adj 17
alive adj 359, 375, 457, 505, 682
alive and kicking adj 359
all adv 50
allay v 834
all but adv 32
all day long adv 110
allegation n 617
allege v 617
alleged adj 617
allegiance n 743
all-embracing adj 76
all-encompassing adj 78
alleviate v 174, 834
alleviation n 834
all for the better adj 658
alliance n 9, 11, 178, 709, 712, 714, 903
allied adj 9, 11, 216
allied to adj 17
allied with adj 178
all-important adj 642
all in all adv 50
all-inclusive adj 78
all manner of kinds adv 81
allocation n 786
allocution n 586
all of a sudden adv 113
all one adj 27
allot v 51, 60, 786
allotment n 60, 786
all over adv 180
allow v 469, 488, 529, 737, 740, 748, 760, 762, 784, 813
allowable adj 760
allowance n 469, 488, 760, 784, 786, 813
allowed adj 924
allow for v 469
alloy n 41, 48
all-purpose adj 148
all ready adj 673
all set for adj 507
all the livelong day adv 110

all the rage adj 852
all the time adv 106
all the worse for wear adj 659
allude to v 516, 527
allure v 288, 829
alluring adj 288
allusive adj 521, 526
alluvial adj 342
ally n 711, 890; v 174
almanac n 114
almighty adj 157, 976
almighty dollar n 800
almost adv 32
alms n 784
almsgiving n 784
aloft n 267
alone adj 87
alongside adv 236
a long way off adv 196
a long while back adv 122
along with adv 37, 88
aloud adv 404
alphabet n 561
alphabetical adj 561
already adv 116, 122
also adv 37
alter v 15, 140
alteration n 20a, 140
altercation n 713, 720
altered adj 15, 20a
alter ego n 17
alternate v 534, 759; v 12, 20a, 70, 138, 147, 149
adj 12, 70, 138
alternately adv 138
alternation n 138, 145, 149, 314
alternative n 147, 609
alter one's course v 279
although adv 30, 179
altitude n 206
altogether adv 50, 52
altruism n 906
altruist n 906
altruistic adj 906, 910
always adv 16, 112
amalgam n 41, 48
amalgamate v 41, 48
amalgamation n 41, 48
amass v 50, 72, 636
amateur n 701
amaze v 870
amazed adj 870
amazement n 870
amazing adj 870
amazingly adv 31
amber n 356a
ambergris n 356a
ambiguity n 475, 517, 519, 520, 571
ambiguous adj 475, 520
ambition n 620, 865
amble v 275
ambrosial adj 394
ambuscade n 530

ambush n 530
ambush n 667; v 530
ameliorate v 658, 723
amelioration n 658
amenable adj 762
amend v 658
amending adj 950
amendment n 658
amends n 30, 952, 973
amenity n 829
amiability n 829
amiable adj 829, 888
amicable adj 707, 721, 892
amicably adv 888
amid adv 41, 228
amidst adv 41
amiss adj 923
amity n 714, 721, 888
ammunition n 727
amnesia n 506
amnesty n 723, 918
among adv 41, 228
amongst adv 41, 228
amorous adj 897
amorphism n 241
amorphous adj 241
amount n 25, 26, 800, 812
amount to v 50
amphitheater n 599, 728
ample adj 31, 180, 192, 202, 639
amplification n 194
amplify v 194, 549, 573
amplitude n 102, 192, 202
amplitudinous adj 192
amply adv 31, 639
amputate v 38
amputation n 38
amuse v 829, 840
amusement n 840
amuse oneself v 840
amusing adj 840
anachronism n 115
anachronism n 135
anachronistic adj 115
anagram n 561
analogous adj 12, 17, 216
analogy n 9, 17, 216
analysis n 49, 60, 463, 476, 596
analytic adj 85, 463, 596
analytical adj 476, 596
analyze v 49, 463, 476
analyzer n 463
anarchic adj 59
anarchism n 59
anarchy n 59
anatomic adj 329
anatomical adj 329
anatomy n 329, 357, 368
ancestral adj 166
ancestry n 122, 166
anchor n 666
anchorage n 184
anchorite n 955
ancient adj 124

ancient times n 122
and adv 37
and everywhere adv 186
and so forth adv 37
anemic adj 430
anesthesia n 376
anesthetic adj 376
anesthetize v 376, 381
anew adv 104, 123
angel n 977
angel n 164, 897
angelic adj 977
anger n 824, 900; v 830
angle n 244; v 244
angry adj 382, 900
anguish n 378, 619, 828
angular adj 244
angularity n 244
anility n 128
animal n 366
animal adj 366
animalistic adj 364, 366
animality n 364
animal kingdom n 366
animal life n 357, 364
animal physiology n 368
animate v 382, 824, 836;
  adj 357
animated adj 171, 382,
  515
animated nature n 357
animate matter n 357
animating adj 836
animation n 359, 515, 682,
  824
animosity n 889, 898, 900
ankle-deep adj 209
annalist n 553
annal(s) n 114
annals n 551
annex n 39; v 37
annexation n 37, 43
annihilate v 2
annihilation n 2, 162
annotate v 522
annotator n 524
announce v 527, 531, 883
announcement n 527,
  531, 985
annoy v 688, 830
annoyance n 649, 828,
  830, 835
annul v 756
annulment n 756
anoint v 332
anointment n 332, 355
anomalous adj 59, 83
anomaly n 59, 83
anon adv 132
another adj 15
another time n 119
answer n 462
answer n 479, 522, 662;
  v 462, 746
answerable adj 177, 462
answerable for adj 806
answer for v 759

antagonism n 14, 24, 179,
  708, 715, 867, 889
antagonist n 708, 710,
  726, 891
antagonistic adj 14, 24,
  179, 708, 715
antagonize v 14, 179
antecedence n 116
antecedence n 62
antecedent n 64, 116;
  adj 62, 116
antedate v 115, 116
antediluvian adj 124
antemeridian n 125
anterior adj 62, 116, 234
anteriority n 116
anthology n 596
anthracite n 388
anthropology n 368
anti n 708
anticipate v 115, 121, 132,
  451, 507, 510, 673, 858
anticipation n 121, 132,
  451, 507, 510, 673, 858
anticipatory adj 132, 510
antidote n 662
antipathy n 14, 289, 867,
  898
antipodal adj 237
antipodean adj 14
antipodes n 14
antiquarian n 553
antiquarianism n 124
antiquated adj 124
antique adj 124
antiquity n 122, 124
antisocial adj 911
antithesis n 14, 216, 237
antithetical adj 14, 237
antitoxin n 662
anxiety n 459, 860
anxious adj 860
any adj 25
apace adv 274
apart adj 44, 87; adv 44
apathetic adj 383, 456,
  823, 866, 989
apathy n 823, 866, 989
ape n 19
aperture n 260
apex n 8, 67, 210
aphasia n 581, 583
aphorism n 496
aphoristic adj 496
apiece adv 79
aping n 19
apologist n 937
apostasy n 607, 984
apostate n 607
a posteriori n 476
apostrophe n 589
apostrophize v 589
apothegm n 496
apotheosize v 991
appal v 830
apparel n 225; v 225

apparent adj 446, 448,
  525
apparently adv 448
apparition n 4, 443, 980
appeal n 411, 765
appear v 446, 448, 525
appearance n 448
appearance n 220, 240,
  446, 569
appease v 174, 723, 826,
  831
appellant n 924, 938
appellation n 564
append v 37
appendage n 39, 65
appendix n 39
appertain to v 9, 56
appetite n 865
appetizing adj 394
applaud v 836, 883
apple adj 435
apple of one's eye n 899
apple-polisher n 886, 935
appliance n 677
applicability n 644
applicable adj 644, 677
applicant n 767
application n 677, 765
apply v 677
appoint v 741, 755, 786
appointment n 755
apportion v 44, 51, 60, 73,
  786
apportionment n 786
apportionment n 60, 73
apposite adj 23
apposition n 23, 199
appraisal n 812
appraise v 466, 480, 668,
  812
appraisement n 466
appreciate v 394, 480,
  850, 916, 931
appreciation n 465, 822,
  916
appreciative adj 822, 916
apprehend v 490, 860
apprehension n 453, 490,
  665, 789, 860
apprehensive adj 860
apprentice n 541
apprenticeship n 539
apprize v 527
apprized of adj 527
approach n 286
approach n 197, 569, 627,
  632; v 121, 152, 286
approaching adj 286
approbate v 931
approbation n 931
approbation n 488, 928
appropriate v 775, 786,
  788, 789, 791; adj 23,
  134, 646, 850
appropriateness n 646
appropriating n 788

appropriation n 775, 789, 791

approval n 488, 762, 928, 931

approve v 535, 737, 931

approved adj 931, 983a

approximate v 17, 197; adj 17, 197, 286

approximation n 9, 17, 19, 266

apricot adj 439

a priori adj 476

apt adj 23, 498, 698, 850

aptitude n 176, 498, 602, 698

aptness n 176, 698

aqua n 337

aquamarine v 435, 438

aquatics n 267

aqueduct n 350

aqueous adj 337

arable adj 371

arbiter n 724, 737, 967

arbitrariness n 739

arbitrary adj 83, 606, 608, 739, 964

arbitrate v 174, 724

arbitration n 724

arbitrator n 724, 967

arc n 245

arcade n 245

arced adj 245

arch n 245, 250; v 245; adj 31

archaic adj 124

archaism n 124

archangel n 977

arched adj 245, 250

archetype n 22

archipelago n 346

architect n 164

architecture n 161, 329

arch over v 245

arctic adj 383

ardency n 991

ardent adj 382, 865

ardor n 382, 574, 682, 821

arduous adj 704

area n 181

arena n 728

arenose adj 330

areola n 247

argue v 24, 467, 476, 720

arguer n 476

argument n 454, 476, 516, 713, 720, 969

argumentation n 476, 969

argumentative adj 476, 713

arguments n 476

argumentum ad hominem n 476

aria n 413

arid adj 169, 340

aridity n 340

arise v 151, 305

aristocracy n 875

aristocratic adj 875

arithmetic n 85

arithmetical adj 85

arithmetic operations n 85

arm n 343; v 157, 673, 727

armaments n 727

armistice n 723

armlet n 247

armor n 727

arms n 727

army n 72

aroma n 400

aromatic adj 400

around adv 227

arouse v 175, 382, 615, 824

arraign v 938, 969

arraignment n 938

arrange v 58, 60, 626, 673, 774

arranged adj 60

arrange in a series v 69

arrange in work v 566

arrangement n 60

arrangement n 58, 673, 723, 799

arrangement n 807

array n 58, 102; v 60, 225

arrest v 142

arrival n 292

arrive v 151, 265, 292, 342

arrogance n 878, 885

arrogant adj 739, 878, 885, 860

artery n 350

artful adj 702

artfulness n 702

art gallery n 556

article n 3, 316, 590, 595

article of faith n 537

articles n 770, 798

articles of faith n 983

articulate v 580, 582; adj 580

articulation n 43, 580

artifice n 545, 702

artificial adj 579, 855

artificial light n 423

artist n 559

artist n 416

artistic adj 845

artistically adv 698

artless adj 703, 946

artlessness n 703

artlessness n 946

as a consequence adv 154

as a matter of course adv 82

as a rule adv 613

ascend v 35, 305, 658

ascendancy n 33, 157, 175, 731

ascendant adj 305

ascending adj 217

ascension n 305

ascent n 305

ascent n 35, 217

ascertain v 480a

ascetic n 955; adj 955

asceticism n 955

as chance will have it adv 156

ascribe importance v 642

ascribe to v 155

ascription n 155

as good as one's word adj 772

ash n 388

ashen adj 429, 432

ashes n 362

ashore adv 342

ashy adj 429, 432

aside n 589

as if adv 17

as if it were adv 17

asinine adj 497, 499, 853

as it happens adv 151

as it were adv 17

ask v 461, 630, 765, 812, 865

askance adv 217

askew adj 217, 243; adv 217

ask for v 765

asleep adj 458

as low as one can go adj 649

as matters stand adv 8

aspect n 183, 220, 448

aspects n 5

asperity n 256

aspersion n 934

asphalt n 356a

asphyxiate v 361

aspirant n 767

aspiration n 858, 865

aspire at v 620

asquint adj 217

as regards adv 9

ass n 493

assail v 716

assailant n 716, 726

assailer n 726

assassin n 165, 361

assassinate v 361

assassination n 361

assault v 416; v 716

assaulter n 726

assay n 463; v 463

assemblage n 72

assemblage n 43, 102, 712

assemble v 50, 72, 72, 712

assembled adj 72

assembly n 43, 72, 696, 712, 997

assent n 488

assent v 23, 82, 178, 484, 602, 762; v 82, 488, 535, 602, 762

assenting adj 488, 831

assert v 535, 720

assertion n 535

assertive adj 535

assertiveness n 715
assess v 466, 812
assessment n 466, 480
assessor n 480
asset n 944
assets n 780, 800
asseverate v 535
assiduity n 682
assiduous adj 682
assiduousness n 682
assign v 60, 755, 783, 784, 786
assignment n 155, 755, 786
assign to v 155
assimilate v 16, 144
assimilation n 144
assist v 707, 746, 834, 906
assistance n 707, 834
assistant n 707, 711, 759
associate n 88, 711, 890; v 9, 41, 43, 72, 216
associated adj 9
associated with adj 88
associate with v 88
association n 9, 72, 88, 464, 709, 712, 903
assortment n 60, 72
assuage v 174, 723, 834
assuagement n 174, 834
assuaging adj 834
assume v 484, 510, 514, 789, 855, 871, 885
assumed adj 514
assumed name n 565
assumption n 514
assurance n 474, 484, 507, 768, 858
assure v 768, 771
assured adj 474, 484
asteroids n 318
as the saying goes adv 496
as the world goes adv 613
as they say adv 496
as things go adv 151, 613
astigmatic adj 443
astigmatism n 443
astonish v 508, 870
astonished adj 870
astonishing adj 870
astonishingly adv 31
astonishment n 508, 870
astound v 824, 870
astounding adj 870
astral adj 318
astray adv 279
astringent adj 195, 397
astronaut n 269
astute adj 498, 702
asunder adj 44; adv 44
as usual adv 613
as well as adv 37
asylum n 666
asymmetrical adj 241
asymmetry n 241, 243

at a different time adv 119
at a distance adj 196
at a glance adv 441
at all events adv 30
at all times adv 136
at a low ebb adj 306
at an angle adv 217
at any rate adv 30
at a snail's pace adv 275
at a standstill adj 265
at bottom adv 5
at cross purposes adj 713; adv 59, 708
at ease adj 827
at fault adj 927
at first sight adv 441, 448
at full gallop adv 274
at full speed adv 274
at half speed adv 275
at hand adj 152, 197
at heart adv 82
atheism n 989
atheist n 984, 989
atheistic adj 989
athletic adj 159
at intervals adv 70
at issue adj 708
at its height adv 33
at large adj 748
atlas n 86
at last adv 67, 133
at length adv 133, 200
atmosphere n 338
atmospheric adj 338
at no time adv 107
at odds adj 708
atoll n 346
atom n 32, 180a
atomization n 336
atomize v 336
atonal adj 410, 414
atonality n 410, 414
at once adv 132
atone v 30, 952
atone for v 462, 952
atonement n 952
atonement n 790, 952
at one's disposal adj 777
at one's fingertips adv 197
at one's leisure adv 133
at one with adj 178
atoning adj 950, 952
at present adv 118
at random adv 156
at regular intervals adv 58
at rest adj 265; adv 687
atrophy n 195, 659
at short notice adv 132
at sight adv 132
at some other time adv 119
at some time or other adv 119
attach v 37, 43, 969

attached adj 897
attach importance v 642
attachment n 37, 39, 43, 88, 897
attach too much importance to v 482
attack n 716
attacker n 716, 891
attain v 292, 775
attain an end v 731
attain majority n 131
attainment n 292, 539, 698, 775
attempt n 675, 686; v 675
attend v 186, 281, 418, 457, 746, 928
attendance n 186
attendant n 88; adj 88
attending v 418; adj 186, 928
attending to n 457
attend regularly v 136
attend to v 743
attention n 457
attention n 451, 459, 928
attentive adj 451, 457, 459
attentiveness n 457
attenuate v 195
attenuation n 195, 330
attest v 550
at that instant adv 119
at that time adv 119
at the eleventh hour adv 133
at the heels adv 235
at the least adv 32
at the present time adv 118
at the same time adv 30, 120
at the top of one's lungs adv 404
at the top of one's voice adv 404
at this moment adv 118
at this time adv 118
at times adv 136
attire n 225
attitude n 8, 183, 240
attitudinize v 855
attorney n 968
attorney-at-law n 968
attorney general n 968
attract v 288, 829
attract attention v 446
attracting adj 288
attraction n 288
attraction n 829
attractive adj 288, 615, 829, 845, 850
attractiveness n 288, 829, 845
attributable adj 155
attribute n 780
attributed adj 155
attribute to v 155
attribution n 155

baneful *adj* 663
bang *n* 406; *v* 276
bang into *v* 276
banish *v* 55, 185, 297, 972
banished *adj* 893
banish from one's thoughts *v* 506
banishment *n* 185, 297, 893
bank *n* 217, 802
banker *n* 801
bankrupt *adj* 732
bankruptcy *v* 732, 808
banshee *n* 980
banter *n* 856; *v* 842, 856
baptize *v* 564
bar *n* 215, 346, 968; *v* 55, 261, 761
barb *n* 253; *v* 253
barbarism *n* 563, 579, 851
barbarous *adj* 241, 563, 579
barbed *adj* 253
bard *n* 597
bare *v* 226, 260; *adj* 226
barefaced *adj* 525
barely *adv* 32
barely audible *adj* 405
bareness *n* 226
bare possibility *n* 473
barf *v* 297
bargain *n* 769, 794, 795, 815; *v* 769, 794
barge *n* 271, 273
bark *n* 223; *v* 412
bar of justice *n* 966
barrel *n* 249
barrelhouse *n* 415
barren *adj* 158, 169
barrenness *n* 158, 169
barricade *n* 232
barrier *n* 232, 261
barrister *n* 968
barter *n* 794
barter *n* 148; *v* 148, 794, 796
base *n* 211
base *n* 208, 215; *v* 215; *adj* 34, 207, 211, 649, 846, 874, 876, 886, 930
based on *adj* 19, 211
baseless *adj* 2, 4
baseness *n* 862, 886
bashful *adj* 881
bashfulness *n* 881
basic *adj* 5, 42, 211
basics *n* 66
basin *n* 252, 343, 344
basis *n* 211, 215
bask in *v* 377
bass *n* 897, 854
bastard *n* 897, 854
baste *n* 25, 72
bathetic *adj* 497
bathos *n* 497
batter *v* 162, 276
battered *adj* 659
battery *n* 716

battle *n* 680, 722; *v* 720, 722
battlefield *n* 728
battleground *n* 728
battler *n* 726
battle with words *v* 148
bauble *n* 643
bawdry *n* 961
bawdy *adj* 961
bawl *v* 411
bay *n* 343; *v* 412; *adj* 433
bayonet *n* 262; *v* 361
bayou *n* 343
bazaar *n* 799
be *v* 1
be absent *v* 187
be absurd *v* 497
be active *v* 680, 682
be affected with *v* 655
be afraid of *v* 860
be agitated *v* 315
beak *n* 250
be alive *v* 359
be all ears *v* 418
beam *n* 420; *v* 420
be an example *v* 22
bear *v* 215, 270, 692, 826
bearable *adj* 651
bear a grudge *v* 900
bear a resemblance *v* 17
bearer *n* 271
bear fruit *v* 161
bear ill will *v* 907
bearing *n* 9, 278, 692
bearings *n* 183
bear in mind *v* 451, 505
bear no resemblance *v* 18
bear off *v* 279
be artless *v* 703
bear back *v* 703
bear upon *v* 9
bear with *v* 740, 760
beast *n* 366
beastly *adj* 653
beast of burden *n* 271
beasts of the field *n* 366
beat *n* 104, 138, 314, 627; *v* 138, 276, 314, 315, 330, 406, 407
beat a retreat *v* 623
beat back *v* 289
beat it out *v* 623
be at odds with *v* 889
be at peace *v* 721
be attendant on *v* 281
be attentive *v* 457
be at the mercy of *v* 749
beat time *v* 114
beat up *v* 352
be at work on *v* 625
beau *n* 897, 854
beau monde *n* 852
beauteous *adj* 845
beautified *adj* 577, 847

beautiful *adj* 242, 597, 829, 845, 977, 981
beautify *v* 845, 847
beauty *n* 845
beauty *n* 242, 829
be averse to *v* 867
be aware of *v* 450, 490
be beforehand *v* 132
be behind *v* 235
be beneficial *v* 648
be blind *v* 442
be blind to *v* 491
be blunt *v* 254
bebop *n* 415
be born *v* 359
be bound for *v* 278
be brittle *v* 328
be broad *v* 202
be called to the bar *v* 968
becalm *v* 265
be capricious *v* 608
be careful *v* 459
because *adv* 153, 155
be cautious *v* 864
be central *v* 222
be certain *v* 474
be cheap *v* 815
be cheek to cheek *v* 236
becloud *v* 421, 422
be cold *v* 383
become *v* 144, 926
become a habit *v* 613
become colorless *v* 429
become insane *v* 503
become large *v* 192
become little *v* 193
become old *v* 124
become small *v* 195
becoming *adj* 646, 850, 881
be composed of *v* 54
be concise *v* 572
be contiguous *v* 199
be contrary *v* 14
be converted into *v* 144
be courteous *v* 894
be cowardly *v* 862
be credulous *v* 486
be cunning *v* 702
be curious *v* 455
be curved *v* 245
bed *n* 204
be dark *v* 421
bedazzle *v* 420
be deaf *v* 419
be deceived *v* 547
be dejected *v* 837
be dense *v* 321
bedew *v* 339
be difficult *v* 704
be diffuse *v* 573
be dim *v* 422
be dimsighted *v* 443
be disappointed *v* 509
be discontented *v* 832
be discordant *v* 414, 713
be discourteous *v* 895

be dishonest v 940
be disinclined v 867
be disinterested v 942
be disrespectful v 929
be distant v 199
be distinguished v 873
bedlamite n 504
bed-ridden adj 655
be drunk v 959
bedtime n 126
be due to v 154
be dull v 843
be dumb v 581
be early v 132
be easy v 705
beehive n 691
be elastic v 325
bee line n 246
Beelzebub n 978
be enamored of v 897
be engaged in v 625
be entitled v 924
be equivocal v 520
be evasive v 528
be evident v 467
be expedient v 646
be expeditious v 134
be expensive v 814
be exterior v 220
be extraneous v 57
be faithful to v 772
befall v 151
be fashionable v 852
be fastidious v 868
be fated v 601
be fatigued v 688
befit v 23, 846, 926
be firm v 150
be fluid v 333
be fond of v 897
be foolish v 499
before adv 62; adj 62, 116, 234, 280
beforehand adv 116, 132
before long adv 132
before now adv 122
before one's eyes adj 446
be forgetful v 506
beful v 653
be fragrant v 400
be free v 748
befriend v 888
be friendly v 888
beg v 765
be general v 78
beget v 161
beggar n 767
beggarly adj 643, 804
begin v 66, 676
begin at the beginning v 66
beginner n 541
beginning n 66
be gluttonous v 957
be gone v 449
be good v 648

be good for v 656
be grateful v 916
be great v 31
begrudge v 819, 921
begrudging adj 907, 921
beg the question v 277, 477
be guilty v 947
be habitual v 613
behalf n 618
be haphazard v 139
be hard on v 739
behave v 680, 692
behave well v 894
behavior n 680, 692
behead v 361
be healthy v 654
be heavy v 319
be held in high repute v 873
behemoth n 192
behest n 741
be hidden v 447
behind adv 63, 235, 281
behind closed doors adv 528
behind time adv 133
be hip v 490
behold v 441, 444
beholder n 444
beholding adj 916
be honorable v 939
behoove v 926
be horizontal v 213
be hot v 382
be identical v 13
beige n 433; adj 433
be ignorant v 491
be illegal v 964
be ill timed v 135
be imbecilic v 499
be impatient v 825
be impenitent v 951
be imperfect v 651
be impious v 988
be important v 642
be impossible v 471
be impotent v 158
be imprisoned v 754
be improbable v 473
be impure v 961
be inactive v 172, 265, 681, 683
be inarticulate v 583
be in a state v 7
be inattentive v 458
be incomplete v 53
be inconvenient v 647
be incredulous v 487
be in danger v 665
be indifferent v 866
be indiscriminate v 465a
be in error v 495
be inert v 172
be inexpedient v 647
be inferior v 34
be infinite v 104

be influential v 175
be infrequent v 137
be in front v 234
being n 1, 3, 359
be in health v 654
be inherent v 5
be in league with v 709
be in love with v 897
be innocent v 946
be inodorous v 399
be insane v 503
be insensible v 376
be insensitive v 823
be inside v 221
be insolent v 885
be instantaneous v 113
be instrumental v 631
be insufficient v 640
be intelligent v 498
be intelligible v 518
be intemperate v 954
be interior v 221
be intrinsic v 5
be in trouble v 619
be inverted v 218
be invisible v 447
be in want v 640
be irascible v 901
be irregular v 139
be irreligious v 989
be irresolute v 605
be jealous v 920
be large v 192
be late v 133
belated adj 133
be latent v 526
be lax v 738
belch out v 297
be left v 40
be left over v 40
be lenient v 740
be liable v 177
be liberal v 816
belief n 484
belief n 451, 453, 537
believable adj 484, 515
believe v 451, 484, 514, 987
believed adj 484
believer n 987
believing n 484; adj 484, 486
be light v 320
be little v 193, 934
belittling n 934; adj 934
belles lettres n 560
bellicose adj 720, 722
bellied adj 250
belligerency n 720
belligerent adj 720, 722
belling n 412
bellow v 404, 411, 412
bellwether n 64
belly n 221
be located v 183
be long v 200
belonging n 777

belongings n 780
belonging to adj 9
belong to v 9, 56, 777
be loquacious v 584
be loud v 404
beloved n 897
be low v 207; adv 207
below par adj 651
belowstairs adv 207
belt n 247, 276
be made up of v 54
be master of v 698
bemoan v 833, 839
be modest v 881
be mute v 581
be narrow v 203
bench n 966
bend n 217, 244, 245;
v 217, 244, 245, 278,
311, 324, 325, 725, 744,
774
bend an ear v 418
bending n 245
bend over v 308
bend to v 176
be near v 197
beneath adv 207
benefactor n 912
beneficence n 648
beneficent adj 784
beneficent spirit n 977
beneficial adj 618, 644,
648, 677
beneficiary n 785
beneficient adj 816
benefit n 618, 677, 775;
v 618, 644, 648, 906
be negligent v 460
be neutral v 609a
benevolence n 906
benevolence n 910
benevolent adj 888, 906,
906, 910
benign adj 656
be noble v 875
be no more v 360
bent n 176, 602, 613, 820;
adj 244
bents n 5
bent upon adj 620
benumb v 376, 381, 385,
843
benumbed adj 381
be numerous v 102
be obligated v 601
be obliged v 601
be oblique v 217
be obstinate v 606
be occupied with v 625
be odorless v 399
be of help v 707
be of no help v 645
be old v 124
be one's fortune v 151
be one's lot v 151
be on the side v 236
be opaque v 426

be opportune v 134
be opposite v 237
be owing to v 154
be parsimonious v 819
be part of v 56
be penitent v 950
be perfect v 650
be pious v 987
be plain v 525
be pleased v 827
be pleased with v 827
be pleasurable v 829
be poor v 804
be possible v 470
be powerful v 157
be present v 186
be probable v 472
be prodigal v 818
be proud v 878
be pungent v 392
be pure v 960
bequeath v 784
bequest n 784
be rare v 137
be rash v 863
berate v 932, 972
bereft adj 776
be regular v 82
be related to v 11
be reluctant v 867
be remiss v 460
be resolute v 604
be rich v 803
be ridiculous v 853
be right v 922
be rumored v 532
be safe v 664
be salubrious v 656
be sane v 502
be savory v 394
beseech v 765
beseem v 926
be selfish v 943
be sensible v 375
be sensitive v 822
be sensitive to v 375
be servile v 886
beset v 716
be severe v 739
be sharp v 253
be short v 201
beside adj 83, 236
be side by side v 236
beside oneself adj 824
besides adv 37
beside the mark adj 10
besiege v 716
be silent v 403, 581, 585
be similar v 17
be situated v 183
be skillful v 698
be small v 32
besmear v 653
be sober v 958
be sociable v 892
be sorry for v 914
bespeak v 132, 467

be specific v 79
bespeckle v 440
best adj 648, 650
be still v 265, 403
bestow v 784, 995
bestowal n 784
be straight v 246
be straightforward v 576
be straight with v 543
bestride v 206
be subject v 749
be subsequent to v 117
be sufficient v 639
be suitable v 134
be sullen v 901a
be superior v 33
be surprised v 870
bet v 621
be taken v 360
be taken by surprise
v 508
be tasteless v 391
be temperate v 953
be that as it may adv 30
be the case v 494
be the dupe of v 547
be the effect of v 154
be the making of v 648
be the rage v 852
be thick v 202
be thin v 203
betimes adv 132
betoken v 550
be transient v 111
be transparent v 425
betray v 529, 545
be true v 494
be true for everyone v 78
better v 658; adj 648, 658
better half n 903
betterment n 658
better off adj 658
better than nothing
adj 651
betting n 621
between adv 228
betwixt adv 228
betwixt and between
adv 228
be unaccustomed v 614
be unaffected v 823
be uncertain v 475
be unclean v 653
be uncomfortable v 83
be unentitled v 925
be unequal v 28
be ungrateful v 917
be unhealthy v 657
be uniform v 16
be unimportant v 643
be unintelligible v 519
be universal v 78
be unlike v 18
be unnecessary v 57
be unpalatable v 395
be unprepared v 674
be unproductive v 169

be unsavory v 395
be unskillful v 699
be unwilling v 603
be useful v 644
be useless v 645
be vain v 880
beverage n 298
be vertical v 212
be violent v 173
be virtuous v 944
be visible v 446, 448
be vulgar v 851
bevy n 72
bewail v 833, 839
be weak v 160
be wealthy v 803
bewilder v 475, 519, 538, 870
bewildered adj 870
bewilderment n 870
be willing v 602
be wise v 498
bewitch v 829, 992
bewitched adj 992
bewitchery n 992
bewitching adj 897, 992
be without v 777a
be worthy of notice v 642
beyond adv 33
beyond all bounds adv 31
beyond all praise adj 650
beyond all reasonable expectation adj 473
beyond bounds adv 641
beyond compare adj 33; adv 31
beyond measure adv 31
beyond one's depth adv 208
beyond the bounds of reason adj 471
beyond the mark adv 303
Bhagavad Gita n 986
bias n 176, 820; v 175, 217
Bible n 986
bibliomaniac n 492
bibliophile n 593
bicker v 315, 713
bicycle n 272
bid n 763; v 600, 741
bidder n 767
bidding n 741
bide v 133, 141
bide one's time v 681
bid fair v 472
bier n 363
biformity n 89
bifurcate v 91, 244; adj 244
bifurcated adj 91
bifurcation n 91, 244
big adj 31, 192
bigot n 606
bigoted n 499
big words n 577
bike n 272

biker n 268
biking n 266
bill n 805, 811, 812
bill of sale n 771
billow n 348
billows n 341
billygoat n 373
binary adj 89
bind v 9, 43, 45, 770
binding adj 926
bind oneself v 768
bind together v 43
binoculars n 445
binomial adj 89
biographer n 553
biography n 553
biologist n 357
biology n 357
bipartite adj 91
bird n 366
bird's-eye view n 446
birds of a feather n 17
birth n 66
bisect v 91
bisected adj 91
bisection n 91
bisection n 68
bit n 32, 51, 390
bit by bit adv 26, 51, 275
bitch n 374, 962
bite n 392; v 298, 378, 385, 547
bite into v 298
biting adj 171, 392, 574
bitter adj 383, 392, 395, 397, 830, 898, 900
bitter cold adj 383
bitterly adv 31, 383
bitterness n 392, 900
bitumen n 356a
bituminous coal n 388
bivouac v 184
bizarre adj 83
bizarre adj 421; adj 421, 431
black and white n 429
black as coal adj 431
black as night adj 431
blackball v 55
blacken v 431, 934
blackguard n 941
blackness n 431
blackness n 421
blame n 716; v 716, 932, 938
blameless adj 946
blamelessness n 946
blameworthy adj 945
blaming n 938
blanch v 429, 430
blanched adj 430
bland adj 174, 391, 395
blandish v 902
blandishment n 902
blandness n 391, 395
blank n 2, 4; adj 2, 4
blanket n 223
blaspheme v 988
blasphemer n 988

blasphemy n 988
blast n 173, 349, 404, 406; v 349
blast furnace n 386
blatter v 412
blaze n 382, 420; v 382, 420
blazing adj 382, 420
blazon forth v 882
bleach v 429, 430
bleached adj 430
bleak adj 383
blear-eyed adj 443
bleary adj 422
bleat v 412
bleed v 378, 814
bleeding n 299
blemish n 848
blemish n 651, 945; v 659
blend n 48; v 41, 41, 48, 352, 413
blending n 48, 413
bless v 990
blessed adj 981
blessing n 618
blight n 659; v 659
blighted adj 659
blighted hope n 509
blimp n 273
blind n 424; v 442; adj 442, 601
blind adoration n 991
blindfold adv 442
blindly adv 442
blindness n 442
blindness n 491
blind to adj 458
blink v 443, 623
blinker n 530
bliss n 827
blissful adj 827, 981
blister n 250
blithe adj 836
bloated adj 194, 250
block n 192, 321, 752; v 706
blockade n 261; v 261
blockhead n 493, 501
block up v 261
blond adj 429, 435
blond n 11
blood red adj 434
blood relation n 11
bloodshed n 361
bloodthirsty adj 361
bloody adj 361, 434, 653
bloom n 654; v 161, 367, 654, 734
blooming adj 161, 434
blossom n 367, 734
blot n 552, 848, 874, 945; v 431, 653, 874
blot out v 552
blotted out adj 552
blow n 276, 349, 508, 830; v 347, 349, 688
blow great guns v 349

brassy adj 885
bravado n 861, 884
brave v 715; adj 715, 861
bravery n 715, 861
brawl v 411
brawny adj 192
bray v 412
brazen adj 885
breach n 44, 198, 260, 713
breadth n 202
breadth n 202
break n 44, 53, 70, 106,
   140, 142, 198, 621, 685,
   720, 731; v 44, 51, 70,
   328, 713, 773, 879
breakability n 328
breakable adj 328
break a habit v 614
break bread v 298
breakdown n 162, 732;
   v 304, 659
breaker n 348
breakers n 667
breakfast v 298
break ground v 66
break in v 294
breaking down n 49
breaking up n 162
break in upon v 70, 135
break of day n 125
break off v 142
break one's neck v 360
break out v 66
break the ground v 116
breakup n 67, 146; v 44,
   73, 162, 659
breast n 250
breath n 359, 405
breathe v 1, 349, 359, 405
breathe new life into
   v 163
breathing space n 188
breathing spell n 685, 687
breathless adj 688, 870
breath of air n 338, 349
breath of life n 359
breed adj 370
breed n 75, 167; v 161, 359
breeding n 370, 852
breeze n 338, 349
breezy adj 338, 349
brethren n 997
brevity n 201, 572
brewing adj 152
briar n 663
bribe n 784
bridge n 45; v 45
bridge over v 43
bridle v 370, 751
brief n 596; adj 111, 201,
   572
briefly adv 111, 572
brig n 273
brigantine n 273

bright adj 420, 428, 498,
   734, 829, 836
brightness n 420, 829
brilliance n 845
brilliancy n 420
brilliant adj 416, 845
brim n 231
brimful adj 52
brimming adj 52
brindled adj 440
brine n 341; v 392
brink v 270
bring about v 153
bring forth v 161
bring in v 296, 810, 812
bring into v 144
bring into focus v 222
bring into play v 677
bring into relation with
   v 9
bring low v 308
bring out v 74, 591
bring round v 660
bring to a crisis v 604
bring to a focus v 74
bring to an end v 67
bring to a point v 74
bring to a standstill v 142
bring to bear upon v 170
bring together v 72
bring to life v 359
bring to light v 529
bring to mind v 505
bring to pass v 153
bring to perfection v 52
bring to trial v 969
bring up v 161, 235
bring up the rear v 235
brink v 231
brisk adj 111, 274, 682,
   684
briskness n 682
bristle over v 900
bristling adj 253
bristly adj 256
brittle adj 328
brittleness n 328
broach v 153, 676
broach adj 78, 202
broadcast adj 73
broad daylight n 420
broadside n 236; adv 236
brochure n 593
broil v 382, 384
broke adj 804
broken adj 70
broken down adj 659
broker n 797
brood n 167
brood over v 837
brook v 826
brother n 27
brotherhood n 11, 17, 72
brotherly adj 888

brown n 433
brown adj 433
brownish adj 433
brownness n 433
brown-nose v 933
brown-noser n 886, 935
brown-nosing v 933
browse v 264
bruise v 649
brunette adj 433
brunt n 66
brush n 379
brush aside v 297
brushing n 379
brushwood n 388
brusque adj 173
brutal adj 173
brutality n 173
brute n 366
brute creation n 366
brute force n 739
brute instinct n 450a
brute matter n 316, 358
brutishness n 450a
bubble n 353
bubble n 353; v 315, 348,
   353
bubbling n 353
bubbly adj 348, 353
buck n 309, 373
buckle n 243, 248; v 43,
   243
buckle to v 686
bud n 66; v 161, 194, 300
budding adj 127
budge v 264
budget n 811
buff v 255
buffet v 276, 315
buffoon n 501, 844, 857
buggy n 272
built n 240; v 161, 235,
   240
building n 161
built on adj 211
bulb n 249
bulbous adj 250
bulge n 250; v 250
bulk n 31, 50, 202
bulk containers n 191
bulky adj 192, 202
bull n 373, 477
bulletin n 592
bully n 887; v 739
bum v 266
bum around v 266
bumbling adj 699
bumming around n 266
bump n 250, 276
bump against v 276
bunch n 250
bunchy adj 250
bungle n 495; v 699
bungler n 701
bungling n 699; adj 699
bunk n 477
buoyancy n 320

buoyant *adj* 320, 325, 836
burden *n* 190, 319, 828, 830, 826
burdensome *adj* 319, 649, 686, 706, 830
burglar *n* 792
burial *n* 363; *adj* 363
burial ground *n* 363
buried *n* 208, 506
buried in *adj* 229
burlesque *n* 21, 856; *v* 856; *adj* 856
burn *v* 382, 384, 825
burnable *adj* 388
burn in *v* 384
burning *adj* 382, 434
burnish *n* 255
burnished *adj* 420
burnt *adj* 384
burn the midnight oil *v* 539
burp out *v* 297
burrow *v* 184
bursar *n* 801
burst *n* 113, 406; *v* 44, 173, 328
burst in *v* 294
burst forth *v* 66, 194, 446
burst out *v* 838
burst upon *v* 508
burst upon the view *v* 446
bury *v* 229, 363, 528
burying *n* 528
bury the hatchet *v* 723
bush *n* 367
bushy *adj* 256
business *n* 625
business *n* 454, 622, 682, 794, 928
business district *n* 799
businesslike *adj* 58, 625, 682, 692
bust *n* 557, 732
bustle *n* 171, 315, 882, 684; *v* 315, 682, 684
bustling *adj* 151
busy *adj* 151, 625, 682
busy as a bee *adj* 682
busy oneself *v* 682
but *adv* 30
butcher *n* 361; *v* 361
butchery *n* 361
butt *n* 857; *v* 276
butt against *v* 276
butter *n* 356
butter-fingers *n* 701
butt in *v* 135
buttocks *n* 235
button *n* 250; *v* 43
button up *v* 261
buttress *n* 215
buy *n* 795; *v* 795
buy and sell *v* 794
buyer *n* 795
buying *n* 795
buzz *v* 409, 412
buzzing *n* 409

by *adv* 631
by accident *adv* 156
by and by *adv* 132
by an indirect course *adv* 629
by chance *adv* 156
by degrees *adv* 26
by design *adv* 620
by dint of *adv* 631; *prep* 157
by fits and starts *adv* 70, 139, 315
by force *adv* 159, 173, 744
bygone *adj* 122
by installments *adv* 51
by intuition *adv* 477
by means of *adv* 170, 631, 632
by no means *adv* 32
by rule *adv* 82
bystander *n* 444
by storm *adv* 173
by the agency of *adv* 631
by the by *adv* 10, 134
by the way *adv* 10, 134
by turns *adv* 138
by virtue of *prep* 157

C

cabal *n* 626
cabalistic *adj* 992
cabinet *n* 696
cackle *v* 412, 838
cacophonous *adj* 410, 414
cadaver *n* 362
cadaverous *adj* 362
cadence *n* 402
caesura *n* 70, 198
cage *n* 752; *v* 370
calamitous *adj* 735, 830
calamity *n* 619, 735, 975
calcination *n* 384
calculable *adj* 85
calculate *v* 85, 611, 620
calculation *n* 85, 507
calculus *n* 85
calefaction *n* 384
calendar *n* 86, 114
caliber *n* 28
call *v* 564, 995
call attention to *v* 550
call for *v* 630
calligraphy *n* 590
calling *n* 625
call it quits *v* 67, 624
callous *adj* 823
callousness *n* 823
callow *adj* 127
call to mind *v* 505
call up *v* 505
call up spirits *v* 992
calm *n* 174, 265, 721; *v* 174, 723; *adj* 174, 265, 403, 685, 721, 826, 953
calm down *v* 826
calmness *n* 174, 265, 721, 826, 953

caloric *n* 382
caloricity *n* 382
calorimeter *n* 389
calumnious *adj* 934
calumny *n* 934
camaraderie *n* 892
camouflage *v* 528
camouflaging *n* 528
can *v* 670
canal *n* 350
cancel *v* 536, 552, 756
cancelation *n* 552, 756
cancel out *v* 179
cancer *n* 663
candid *adj* 246, 543, 703
candidate *n* 726
candied *adj* 396
candle *n* 423
candor *n* 525, 543, 703
candy *v* 396
cane *n* 975
canker *n* 663; *v* 659
cankerworm *n* 165
canny *adj* 498, 702
canon *n* 697
canonicals *n* 999
canonize *v* 991
canopy *n* 223
cant *n* 988; *v* 217
canticle *n* 413
cap *n* 261, 263; *v* 33, 206
capability *n* 157, 175, 698, 705
capable *adj* 157, 698
capacious *adj* 180, 192
capacity *n* 157, 159, 180, 192, 498, 825, 698
capacity for *n* 698
cape *n* 250
caper *n* 309; *v* 309
capillary *adj* 205
capital *n* 632, 800, 803; *adj* 210, 642, 648
capitulate *v* 725
capitulation *n* 725
caprice *n* 608
caprice *n* 615a
capricious *adj* 139, 149, 475, 605, 608, 615a
capriciously *adv* 615a
capriciousness *n* 139, 149, 475
capsule *n* 273
captain *n* 269, 694
captious *adj* 608
captivate *v* 829
captive *n* 754
capture *n* 789; *v* 789
car *n* 272
caravan *n* 266
carbon *n* 21, 90, 388
carbonaceous *adj* 388
carbonization *n* 384
carcass *n* 362
cardinal points *n* 278
care *n* 459

changeable *adj* 140, 144,
149, 475, 605
changeableness *n* 149
changeableness *n* 111,
140, 475, 605
changed *adj* 15, 20a, 190
change direction *v* 279
changeful *adj* 607
change hands *v* 783
changelessness *n* 150
change of mind *v* 485
change one's mind *v* 485
changeover *n* 144
change sides *v* 607
changing hands *n* 783
channel *n* 260, 302, 350,
627; *v* 259
chaos *n* 59, 162, 241
chaotic *adj* 59, 241
chap *n* 373
chapel *n* 1000
chapter *n* 696
character *n* 5, 7, 561, 569,
820
characteristic *n* 79, 550,
569, 780; *adj* 5, 15, 79,
550, 569
characterization *n* 594
characterize *v* 564, 594
characterized *adj* 820
charcoal *n* 388, 431
charge *n* 630, 695, 697,
716, 741, 755, 812, 938;
v 52, 190, 695, 716, 741,
755, 812, 938, 938, 938
charging *n* 938
charitable *adj* 707, 784,
816, 906, 910
charity *n* 707, 784, 816,
906, 910
charm *n* 829, 992, 993;
v 288, 615, 829, 992
charmed *adj* 992
charmer *n* 994
charming *adj* 933; *adj* 992
charnel house *n* 363
chart *n* 183, 527, 626
charter *n* 755, 963; *v* 760
chary *adj* 817, 864
chase *v* 622
chase away *v* 289
chasm *n* 208, 260
chaste *adj* 242, 576, 578,
849, 881, 944, 960
chasten *v* 972
chasteness *n* 849
chastisement *n* 972
chastity *n* 881, 944, 960
chat *n* 588; *v* 588
chattels *n* 780
chatter *n* 584; *v* 584
chatterbox *n* 584
chatterer *n* 584
chattering *adj* 584
chatty *adj* 584, 588
cheap *adj* 435, 643, 815,
819, 943

cheapness *n* 815
cheat *n* 545, 548, 792;
v 545, 923
check *n* 179, 616, 666, 706,
751; *v* 179, 233, 275, 468,
706, 708, 751
checked *adj* 440
checker *v* 440
checkered *adj* 440
checklist *n* 86
cheek *n* 236
cheek by jowl *adv* 236
cheer *n* 827, 829; *v* 411,
689, 829, 834, 836, 840
cheerful *adj* 827, 829
cheerfully *adv* 836
cheerfulness *n* 836
cheerfulness *n* 827, 829
cheering *adj* 836, 858
cheerless *adj* 828, 901a
cheery *adj* 829, 836, 836
chemistry *n* 144
cherish *v* 897
cherry-colored *adj* 434
cherub *n* 129, 977
cherubic *adj* 977
chest *n* 802
chestnut *n* 433
chew *v* 298
chewing *n* 298
chew the fat *v* 588
chiaroscuro *n* 429
chicanery *n* 477, 702
chick *n* 129
chicken *n* 862; *adj* 862
chicken-hearted *adj* 862
chief *n* 694, 745
chiefly *adv* 31
child *n* 129, 167
childbirth *n* 163
child genius *n* 872
childhood *n* 127
childish *adj* 129, 486, 499,
575
childlike *adj* 499, 703
children *n* 167
child's play *n* 705
chill *v* 383, 385, 616;
adj 383
chilled *adj* 385
chilliness *n* 383
chilly *adj* 383
chime *n* 408; *v* 407, 413
chimera *n* 515
chimerical *adj* 515
chimney *n* 351
chink *n* 198; *v* 408
chip *n* 32; *v* 44, 195
chip off the old block
n 17, 167
chipper *adj* 654
chirography *n* 590
chirp *v* 412
chirrup *v* 412
chisel *v* 240, 557, 558
chiseling *n* 558
chit *n* 588

chit-chat *n* 588; *v* 588
chock-full *adj* 52
chocolate *adj* 433
choice *n* 609
choice *n* 800; *adj* 648
choice of words *n* 569
choir *n* 416
choke *v* 261, 361, 641
choleric *adj* 901
chomp *v* 298
choose *v* 609
choosing *n* 609
choosy *adj* 465
chop *v* 44
choppy seas *n* 348
chop up *v* 201
choral *adj* 415, 416
choral music *n* 415
chorus *n* 411, 416
christen *v* 564
Christian *adj* 983a
Christian Revelation
n 985
chromatic *adj* 428
chronicle *n* 114; *v* 114,
551
chronicler *n* 553
chronicles *n* 551
chronological *adj* 114
chronological error *n* 115
chronology *n* 114
chronometer *n* 114
chronometry *n* 114
chubby *adj* 194
chuck *v* 284, 412
chuckle *v* 838
chug *v* 298
chum *n* 890
chummy *adj* 892
church *n* 995, 1000
churchdom *n* 995
churchman *n* 996
churl *n* 819
churlish *adj* 819
churlishness *n* 901a
churn *n* 315, 352
cilia *n* 205
cinder *n* 388
cinerary *adj* 363
cinnamon *adj* 433
cipher *n* 84, 550, 561
circle *n* 181, 247, 712;
v 227, 247, 311
circle around *v* 312, 629
circling *n* 311; *adj* 248
circuit *n* 629
circuit *n* 181, 230, 247,
279, 311; *v* 311
circuitous *adj* 279, 311,
629
circuitously *adv* 279
circular *n* 592; *adj* 245,
247, 249, 311
circularity *n* 247
circularity *n* 311
circular motion *n* 311
circulate *v* 531

codify v 963
coequal adj 27
coerce v 739, 744
coercion 739, 744
coercive adj 739, 744
coeval adj 120
coexist v 120, 199
coexistence n 88, 120
coexisting adj 120
coexist with v 89
coextension n 216
coextensive adj 216
coffee adj 433
coffer n 802
coffin n 363
cogency n 157
cogitate v 451
cogitation n 451
cognizant of adj 490
cohere v 46, 321
coherence n 46
coherence n 502, 518
coherent adj 321
cohesion n 46, 327
cohesive adj 46, 321, 327
cohesiveness n 46, 327
coil n 248, 311; v 245, 248
coiled adj 248
coin n 515
coincide v 13, 199
coincidence n 120
coincident adj 13, 120
coinciding adj 13
coin words v 563
coke n 388
cold n 383
cold adj 383, 866
cold-blooded adj 383, 823
cold-hearted adj 823
coldly adv 383
coldness n 383, 823
cold storage n 387
collaborate v 178
collaboration n 178
collaborative adj 178
collaborator n 711
collapse n 158, 195, 659;
  v 158, 195, 304
collar n 247
collate v 464
collateral n 771; adj 6,
  216
collation n 464
colleague n 711
collect v 72, 596, 775
collected adj 826
collection n 72, 102, 596
collective adj 78, 778
collectively adv 50
collectivism n 778
college n 542
collegiate adj 542
collide with v 276
collision n 179, 276
colloquial adj 521, 560,
  563
colloquialism n 521

colloquy n 588
collusion n 709
colonize v 184
color n 428
color n 434, 448, 654;
  v 428, 469, 549, 556
coloration n 428, 549
colorblind adj 443
color blindness n 443
colored adj 428
colorful adj 521
coloring n 428, 469, 549
colorless adj 429, 430
colorlessness n 429
colorlessness n 430
colossal adj 192, 206
Colosseum n 728
column n 69, 266
combat n 173, 680, 720,
  722; v 708, 720, 722
combatant n 726
combating n 708
combative adj 173, 720,
  722
combination n 48
combination n 41, 54, 709,
  712
combine v 41, 48, 87, 178,
  709
combined adj 48
combo n 416
combustible n 388;
  adj 384, 388
combustion n 384
come about v 151
come after v 63, 117
come ashore v 342
come before v 62, 116, 280
come between v 228
come close to v 197
comedian n 844
comedienne n 844
come-down n 509; v 306
come down with v 655
come first v 33, 62, 280
come forth v 446
come forward v 446
come from v 154
come in v 294
come in its turn v 138
come in sequence v 138
come into v 775, 785
come into play v 170
come into sight v 446
come into the world v 359
come into use v 613
come into view v 446
comeliness n 242, 845
comely adj 845
come near v 121
come of age v 131
come on v 121, 152
come on to v 544
come out of v 295
come out of nowhere
  v 508
come round v 151, 660

come round again v 138
come short v 732
come short of v 34, 732
come straight to the
  point v 576
come to v 50, 292, 359
come to a close v 67
come to an agreement
  v 774
come together v 72, 290
come to grief v 735
come to light v 525
come to nothing v 169,
  304
come to pass v 151
come to rest v 184
come to the front v 234
come to the point v 79,
  572, 703
come to the rescue v 672
comet n 318
come up short v 304
come up to v 27
come up with v 612
comfort n 377, 827, 831,
  834; v 831, 834, 834, 906
comfortable adj 23, 377,
  803, 827, 829, 831
comforting adj 834
comical adj 853
coming n 292; adj 121,
  152
coming after n 63, 281
coming and going n 314
coming before n 62
coming beforehand n 280
coming beforehand n 290
command n 741
command n 157, 630, 693,
  697, 737; v 157, 206, 600,
  693, 741, 777
commandant n 745
command a view of v 441
commandeer n 789
commander n 269, 745
commanding adj 642, 741
commandment n 741
command of language
  n 569
commemorate v 551, 883
commemoration n 883
commemorative adj 883
commence v 66
commencement n 66
commend v 883, 931
commendable adj 618,
  931
commendation n 931
commendatory adj 883,
  931
commensurate adj 23,
  639
comment n 476, 522; v 595
commentary n 522, 595
commentator n 480, 524,
  595
comment upon v 522

conceive v 66, 168, 484, 515
concentrate v 72, 222, 290, 688
concentric adj 222
concept n 451
conception n 451, 453, 515
conceptual adj 7
concern n 9, 625, 642, 860; v 9
concerned adj 459, 860
concerning adv 9
concert n 178, 709
concert artist n 416
concertize v 416
concession n 780, 774, 784
conciliatory adj 723
conciliate v 723, 831
conciliation n 714, 723, 831, 952
conciliatory adj 714
concise adj 201, 572
concisely adv 572
conciseness n 572
conciseness n 201
conclave n 72, 696
conclude v 67, 480, 604, 729
concluded adj 67
concluding adj 67
conclusion n 65, 67, 154, 480, 729
conclusive adj 67, 478, 480
conclusiveness n 478
concoct v 626
concomitance n 120
concomitant adj 88; adj 88, 120
concomitants n 154
concord n 413, 714
concord n 23, 413, 488, 709, 721, 762, 888
concordance n 413
concordant adj 413, 714
concourse n 72, 290
concrete adj 3
concretion n 321
concupiscence n 961
concupiscent adj 961
concur v 120, 178, 290, 488, 709, 714, 762
concurrence n 178
concurrence n 23, 120, 290, 488, 709, 762
concurrent adj 120, 178, 290
concurrently adv 120
concurring adj 488
condemn v 971
condemnation n 971
condemnatory adj 932, 971
condemned adj 971
condensation n 195, 201, 321, 339, 596

condense v 195, 201, 321, 572, 596
condensed adj 201
condiment n 393
condition n 7, 8, 469, 514, 875; v 770
conditional adj 8, 469, 770
conditionally adv 8, 770
conditions n 770
condolence n 915
condolence n 914
condole with v 915
conduce v 176, 178
conduce to v 153
conducive adj 176
conduct n 692
conduct v 680, 693; v 270, 692, 693
conduct oneself v 680
conductor n 271
conduct to v 278
conduit n 350
conduit n 302
confabulate v 588
confabulation n 588
confederate n 711
confederation n 709, 903
confer v 695, 760, 784
conference n 588, 696
confer power v 157
confer with v 588
confess v 488, 529
confession n 529, 985
confessional adj 985
confidant n 890
confidence n 474, 484, 507, 533, 858
confidence man n 548
confident adj 474, 484, 858
confidential adj 221, 528
confidentially adv 528
confiding adj 484
configuration n 240
confine v 233; v 195, 229, 233, 751
confined adj 203, 229
confinement n 229, 751
confirm v 535, 769
confirmation n 467, 535, 762
confirmative adj 535
confirmatory adj 467
confiscate v 789, 974
confiscation n 789, 974
conflict n 24, 680, 713, 720; v 713
conflicting adj 14, 24, 179, 468
conflicting evidence n 468
conflict with v 179
confluence n 43, 290
confluent adj 290, 413
conflux n 72, 290
conform v 82

conformable to rule adj 82
conformity n 82
conformity n 16, 23, 80, 240, 613, 852
conform to v 16, 82
confound v 61, 465a, 475
confront v 234, 464, 708, 719
confuse v 41, 59, 61, 185, 465a, 475, 519, 538
confused adj 59, 447, 571
confusion n 59, 519, 571
confutable adj 479
confutation n 479
confutation n 538
confute v 479
congeal v 321, 385
congelation n 385
congenial adj 23, 413, 714, 829
congeniality n 829
congenital adj 5
congestion n 641
conglomerate n 72, 321
conglomeration n 41, 46, 72
congratulate v 896
congratulate oneself v 838
congratulations n 896
congratulatory adj 896
congregate v 72
congregation n 72, 990, 997
congress n 72, 290, 588
congruity n 23
congruous adj 23
conical adj 253
conjectural adj 514
conjecture n 514; v 514, 870
conjoin v 41, 45
conjoined adj 413
conjugation n 567
conjunction n 8, 43
conjuration n 992
conjure v 992
conjurer n 994
con man n 548
connect v 9, 43, 45, 216
connected adj 9, 11
connection n 9, 11, 43, 45, 46
connective n 45
connoisseur n 480, 700
connotation n 516
connotative n 550
connote v 516
conquer v 731
conquest n 731
consanguineous adj 11
consanguinity n 11
conscience n 926
conscientious adj 246, 459
conscious adj 375
consciousness v 375, 821

conscription n 744
consecrate v 987, 995
consecutive adj 63, 69
consecutively adv 69
consecutiveness n 69
consensus n 762
consent n 762
consent n 23, 178, 488, 760; v 762
consenting adj 488
consequence n 62, 63, 65, 154, 642
consequent adj 63
consequential adj 642
consequently adv 154
conservation n 141, 670
conservative adj 670
conserve v 670
consider v 451, 461, 469, 480, 484, 873, 928
considerable adj 31, 192, 642
considerate adj 451
consideration n 451, 457, 469, 615, 642, 928
considering adj 928
consign v 270, 755, 783, 784
consignee n 758
consignment n 755, 784, 786
consign to oblivion n 506
consign to the grave v 363
consistency n 16, 23
consistent adj 16, 23, 413
consistent with adv 82
consist in v 1
consist of v 54
consolation n 834, 915
console v 834, 915
consolidate n 46, 48, 321
consolidation n 46, 321
consoling adj 834
consonance n 413
consonant n 561; adj 23, 413
consort n 903; v 41
consort with v 88, 892
conspicuous adj 446, 525
conspicuousness n 446
conspiracy n 626
conspiratorial adj 626
conspire v 178, 709
constancy n 16, 80, 112, 141, 150
constant adj 16, 69, 80, 110, 138, 141, 150, 474, 604a
constant flow n 69
constantly adv 112, 138
constellations n 318
consternation n 860
constipation n 261
constituent n 51, 56
constitute v 54, 56, 161
constituting adj 54

constitution n 5, 7, 54, 329, 963
constitutional adj 266; adj 963
constrain v 744, 751
constrained adj 751
constraining adj 744
constraint n 744, 749, 751
constrict v 195
construct n 161, 240
construction n 5, 161, 240, 329
constructions n 567
constructive adj 161
construe v 522
consult v 695
consume v 638, 677
consummate v 67, 729; adj 31, 52, 67, 650, 729
consummately adv 31
consummation n 67, 729
consumption n 162, 638, 677
contact n 199, 379
contact lens n 445
contain v 54, 76
container n 191
contaminate v 653, 659
contaminated adj 655, 961
contamination n 653, 659, 961
contemn v 930
contemplate v 441, 451, 620
contemplation n 441, 451, 620
contemplative adj 451
contemporaneous adj 120
contemporaneousness n 120
contemporary adj 120
contempt n 930
contemptible adj 435, 930
contemptuous adj 885, 930
contemptuousness n 885
contend v 476, 720, 722
contender n 726
content n 831
content adj 602, 826, 827
contented adj 831, 878
contention n 720
contention n 713, 969
contentious adj 713, 720, 722
contentment n 831
contents n 190
contents n 56, 221, 596
contest n 720
contestant n 726
contiguity n 199
contiguity n 197
contiguous adj 199
contiguousness n 199
continence n 953, 960
continent n 342; adj 960

continental adj 342
contingency n 151, 156, 470
contingent adj 8, 177
continual adj 136, 138
continually adv 136
continuance n 143
continuance n 110, 117, 200, 670
continuation n 63, 65, 143
continue v 1, 106, 110, 136, 143, 604a, 670
continuing adj 143
continuity n 69
continuity n 16, 58, 143, 150
continuous adj 69, 112, 143
continuously adv 69, 112
continuousness n 69
contort v 243, 248
contortion n 243
contour n 230, 448
contraband adj 964
contract n 676, 768, 769, 771; v 36, 195, 676, 769, 770
contract a disease v 655
contracted adj 195
contracting adj 195
contraction n 195
contraction n 36, 261
contractual adj 769
contradict v 14, 468, 489, 708
contradiction n 14, 218, 536
contradictory adj 14, 468, 489, 536
contraposition n 218, 237
contrariety n 14
contrariety n 15, 179, 218
contrary adj 14, 179, 608, 708
contrast n 14, 15; v 15
contrasted adj 14
contrast with v 14
contravene v 14, 468, 536, 708
contribute v 153, 176, 178
contribution n 784
contributor n 912
contrite adj 833, 950
contrition n 833, 950
contrivance n 626
contrive v 161, 626, 702
control n 157, 175, 693, 737, 751, 777, 965; v 157, 175, 693, 737, 777
controller n 694
controversy n 720
controvert v 536
contumacious adj 715, 742
contumacy n 742
contumely n 930
conundrum n 520

daylight *n* 420
day of fasting *n* 956
day of judgment *n* 121
day of rest *n* 687
days gone by *n* 122
days of old *n* 122
days of yore *n* 122
daze *v* 420
dazzle *v* 420, 442
de *n* 220, 234
dead *adj* 172, 360, 376, 381, 408a
dead and gone *adj* 360
dead as a door nail *adj* 360
dead drunk *adj* 959
deaden *v* 376, 381, 843
deadened *adj* 381, 408a
dead heat *n* 27
dead language *n* 560
deadly *adj* 162, 360, 361, 649, 657, 663
deadly weapons *n* 727
deadness *n* 381
dead of night *n* 126, 421
dead silence *n* 403
dead sound *n* 408a
deaf *adj* 419
deafen *v* 404, 419
deafened *adj* 419
deafening *adj* 404
deafness *n* 419
deaf to *adj* 458
deaf to the past *adj* 506
deal *v* 786, 794
dealer *n* 797
dealing *n* 794
deal in *v* 796
deal out *v* 73, 784
dear *n* 899; *adj* 814
dearness *n* 814
dearth *n* 640
death *n* 360
death *n* 67, 142
death agonies *n* 360
death bell *n* 363
death blow *n* 67, 360, 361
deathlike *adj* 403
deathly *adj* 361
death rattle *n* 360
debark *n* 292
debarkation *n* 292
debase *v* 308, 653, 659, 879
debased *adj* 207
debasement *n* 207, 308, 659, 874
debate *n* 476, 588, 720, 969; *v* 476, 720
debater *n* 476
debauchee *n* 962
debilitate *v* 160
debility *n* 158, 160
debit *n* 177, 806; *v* 811
debonair *adj* 894
debt *n* 806
debt *n* 177

debtor *n* 806
decade *n* 98, 108
decadence *n* 659
decapitate *v* 361
decay *n* 49, 124, 360, 638, 653, 655, 659, 732; *v* 36, 49, 195, 360, 659, 735
decayed *adj* 124, 160, 659
decease *n* 360; *v* 360
deceit *n* 545, 702
deceitful *adj* 544, 545, 702
deceitfulness *n* 544, 702
deceive *v* 544, 545
deceiver *n* 548
deceiver *n* 962
deceiving *adj* 545
decency *n* 881, 960
decent *adj* 246, 651, 881, 960
deception *n* 545
deception *n* 21, 544, 702
deceptive *adj* 520, 544, 545, 702
decide *v* 153, 480, 600, 604, 609
decided *adj* 31, 87
decidedly *adv* 31
decimal *adj* 84
decimate *v* 361, 659
decipher *v* 522
decision *n* 480, 600, 604, 609, 620, 969
decisive *adj* 737
deck out *v* 225
declaim *v* 582
declamation *n* 577, 582
declamatory *adj* 577, 582
declaration *n* 525, 531, 535, 985
declarative *adj* 527, 535
declaratory *adj* 535
declare *v* 516, 525, 531, 535
declare war *v* 716
declension *n* 306, 567, 659
declination *n* 306
decline *n* 36, 124, 217, 306, 638, 655, 659, 732; *v* 36, 160, 217, 306, 360, 610, 659, 732, 735, 764; *adj* 128
declining *adj* 217
declining years *n* 128
declivitous *adj* 217, 306
declivity *n* 217, 306
decode *v* 522
decoloration *n* 430
decompose *v* 49
decomposed *adj* 49
decomposition *n* 49
decorate *v* 847
decoration *n* 733, 847, 877
decorative *adj* 847
decorous *adj* 850, 852
decorum *n* 852, 960
decoy *v* 288
decrease *n* 36

decrease *n* 38, 195, 283; *v* 36, 38, 193, 195
decreased *adj* 36
decreasing *adj* 36
decree *n* 480, 963; *v* 600, 741, 963
decrement *n* 40a
decrepit *adj* 124, 158, 160, 655, 659
decrepitude *n* 128, 158, 160, 659
decry *v* 934
deduce *v* 476
deduct *v* 38, 813
deductible *adj* 38
deduction *n* 38
deduction *n* 40a, 65, 476, 480
deductive *adj* 476
deed *n* 680, 771
deem *v* 451, 873
deep *n* 341; *adj* 208, 404, 428
deepen *v* 35, 208
deepness *n* 208
deep-rooted *adj* 820
deep-seated *adj* 208; 221
deep-sounding *adj* 408
deep-toned *adj* 408
deface *v* 241, 659, 846, 848
defacement *n* 241
defalcation *n* 304
defamation *n* 934
defamatory *adj* 932
defame *v* 936
defamer *n* 936
default *n* 304, 460, 808; *v* 808
defeat *n* 509
defeated *adj* 732
defect *n* 40a, 53, 651, 848, 945; *v* 607
defection *n* 607
defective *adj* 53, 651, 732, 945
defectiveness *n* 732
defend *v* 664, 670, 717, 937
defender *n* 890, 937
defense *n* 717
defense *n* 670, 937
defenseless *adj* 665
defensible *adj* 664
defensive *adj* 717
defer *v* 133
deference *n* 743, 928
deferential *adj* 457, 743, 928, 928
defer to *v* 928
defiance *n* 715
defiance *n* 742
defiant *adj* 715, 742
deficiency *n* 28, 34, 53, 304, 640, 651, 732
deficient *adj* 28, 34, 53, 304, 640, 651
deficit *n* 53
defile *v* 653

defiled *adj* 961
defilement *n* 653, 961
define *v* 233, 522
definite *adj* 79, 233, 246, 646, 474, 570
definition *n* 446, 522
definitive *adj* 467
deflect *v* 245, 279
deflection *n* 245, 291
deform *v* 241, 243
deformed *adj* 243
deformity *n* 241, 243, 846, 848
defraud *v* 545, 791, 923
defrost *v* 382
deft *adj* 698
defunct *adj* 2, 360
defy *v* 715, 742
degeneracy *n* 659
degenerate *n* 659; *adj* 659
degeneration *n* 659
degradation *n* 308, 659, 874
degrade *v* 308, 659, 879
degraded *adj* 207
degree *n* 26
degree *n* 58, 71
deification *n* 990, 991
deify *v* 990, 991
deity *n* 976
dejected *adj* 832
dejection *n* 837
dejection *n* 828, 859
delay *n* 133; *v* 133, 142, 706
delayed *adj* 133
delectability *n* 394, 829
delectable *adj* 394, 829
delectation *n* 827
delegate *n* 534, 758, 759; *v* 270, 755
delegation *n* 755, 758
delete *v* 552
deleterious *adj* 649, 657
deletion *n* 552
deliberate *v* 695; *adj* 174, 275, 383, 451, 685
deliberately *adv* 133, 600, 611, 620
deliberateness *n* 174, 275
delicacy *n* 160, 655, 850, 960
delicate *adj* 160, 203, 328, 329, 394, 428, 704, 829, 868, 960
delicate condition *n* 655
delicious *adj* 394, 829
delight *n* 377, 827, 829; *v* 829, 836
delightful *adj* 377, 829
delight in *v* 827
delineate *v* 554, 594
delineation *n* 554, 556, 594
deliquescence *n* 335
deliquescent *adj* 335
delirious *adj* 503, 825

delirium *n* 503, 825
delitescence *n* 447
deliver *v* 270, 580, 660, 672, 750, 784
deliverance *n* 672
deliverance *n* 660, 750, 834
delivery *n* 580, 784
dell *n* 252
delude *v* 545
deluge *n* 72, 348; *v* 337, 348, 641
delusion *n* 495, 503, 515, 545
delusive *adj* 545
delve *n* 252
demand *n* 601, 630, 741, 765, 812, 924; *v* 630, 741, 765, 812
demeanor *n* 448, 692, 852
demented *adj* 503
dementia *n* 503
demi- *adj* 91
demi-lune *adj* 245
demise *n* 360
demolish *v* 162
demolition *n* 162
demon *n* 980
demon *n* 969, 978
demonic *adj* 980
demonology *n* 980, 991
demonstrable *adj* 476, 478
demonstrate *v* 476, 478, 525
demonstrated *adj* 478
demonstration *n* 478
demonstration *n* 525
demonstrative *adj* 478
demure *n* 704; *v* 485, 603
demure *adj* 881
den *n* 189
dendrology *n* 369
denial *n* 536
denial *n* 764
denominate *v* 564
denotation *n* 516
denotative *adj* 550
denote *v* 516, 550
denounce *v* 908, 909
denouement *n* 65, 67
denseness *n* 202
density *n* 321
density *n* 202
dent *v* 252, 257
dented *adj* 252
denunciation *n* 908, 932
denunciatory *adj* 932
deny *v* 468, 536, 610, 708, 764
deny oneself *v* 955
deodorize *v* 512
depart *v* 66, 185, 293, 302, 360, 449
departed *adj* 2, 449

department *n* 51, 75
department store *n* 799
depart this life *v* 360
departure *n* 293
departure *n* 287, 360, 449, 623
departure from *n* 279
depend *v* 214
dependable *adj* 474, 664
dependence *n* 749
dependent *adj* 214, 749
depend upon *v* 154, 749
depict *v* 554, 556, 594
depiction *n* 554, 556, 594
deplane *v* 292
depletion *n* 640
deplorable *adj* 649, 830
deplore *v* 833, 839
deport *v* 270, 692
deportation *n* 270
deportment *n* 692
depose *v* 467, 535
deposit *n* 771
deposition *n* 467, 535
depository *n* 191, 802
depraved *adj* 945
depravity *n* 649, 659, 945
deprecate *v* 766
deprecation *n* 766
deprecation *n* 616, 932, 934
deprecatory *adj* 483, 786
depreciate *v* 36, 483, 934
depreciated *adj* 483
depreciating *adj* 483, 934
depreciation *n* 36, 483, 813, 815
depreciative *adj* 483
depress *v* 207, 252, 308
depressed *adj* 207, 308, 438, 837
depressing *adj* 383
depression *n* 308
depression *n* 207, 208, 252, 837
deprivation *n* 659, 776, 789
deprived of *adj* 776
deprive of *v* 38
deprive of color *v* 429
depth *n* 208
deputation *n* 755
deputy *n* 759
deputy *n* 634, 690
derange *v* 59, 61, 185
deranged *adj* 59, 503
derangement *n* 59, 185, 503
dereliction *n* 460, 732
dereliction of duty *n* 927
deride *v* 856, 929, 930
derision *n* 856, 929, 930
derisive *adj* 856, 929, 930
derisory *adj* 856
derivable from *adj* 154
derivation *n* 154, 155, 562

derivative *adj* 154
derived from *adj* 154
derive from *v* 155
derive pleasure from
  v 827
derogatory *adj* 934
descend *v* 217, 306, 310
descendant *n* 167
descending *n* 306;
  adj 217, 306
descent *n* 306
descent *n* 153
describe *v* 554, 594
description *n* 564
descriptive *adj* 554
descry *v* 441, 480a
desecrate *v* 679, 988
desecration *n* 679, 988
desert *n* 180, 344, 973;
  v 623, 624, 732, 757, 782
deserter *n* 607, 623
desertion *n* 624, 757, 782
deserve *v* 924
deserve consideration
  v 642
design *n* 22, 451, 516, 556,
  620, 626; *v* 451, 516, 556,
  620, 626
designate *v* 79, 550, 564
designation *n* 564, 877
designer *n* 559; 626
desirability *n* 646
desirable *adj* 646
desire *n* 865
desire *n* 600, 609, 858;
  v 602, 858, 865
desiring *adj* 865
desirous *adj* 602, 865
desist *v* 67, 142, 265
desolate *v* 162; *adj* 837
desolation *n* 162, 638, 828
despair *n* 828, 837, 859;
  v 828, 837, 859
despairing *adj* 859
desperate *adj* 173, 859
desperately *adv* 31
desperation *n* 825, 859
despicable *adj* 435, 930
despise *v* 715, 898, 930
despoil *v* 659
despond *v* 837, 859
despondency *n* 837, 859
despondent *adj* 837, 859
despot *n* 739
despotic *adj* 739, 964
despotism *n* 739
dessication *n* 340
destination *n* 67, 620
destine *v* 152
destined *adj* 152
destiny *n* 121, 152, 601,
  611, 621
destitute *adj* 804
destitution *n* 804
destroy *v* 2, 162, 619, 638,
  659, 679
destroyed *adj* 162

destroyer *n* 165
destroyer *n* 913
destroy oneself *v* 361
destruction *n* 162
destruction *n* 146, 173,
  619, 638
destructive *adj* 162, 638,
  649
desuetude *n* 614, 678
desultory *adj* 59, 70, 279,
  475
detach *v* 44, 47
detached *adj* 10, 47, 953
detachment *n* 44, 291, 953
detail *v* 79, 594
details *n* 32, 79
detain *v* 781
detect *v* 480a
detection *n* 480a
detective *n* 527
detention *n* 781
deter *v* 616
detergent *n* 652
deteriorate *v* 36, 185, 659
deteriorated *adj* 659
deterioration *n* 659
deterioration *n* 36, 283,
  655, 661, 732
determinate *adj* 474, 480,
  620
determination *n* 150, 278,
  480, 600, 604, 620, 480a,
  604a
determine *v* 79, 153, 278,
  480, 600, 604, 676, 967;
  480a
determined *adj* 474
deterrent *n* 706
detest *v* 867
detestable *adj* 649, 898
detestation *n* 898
detonate *v* 173
detonation *n* 406
detour *n* 245, 279, 629;
  v 629
detract *v* 483, 934
detracting *v* 934; *adj* 934
detraction *n* 934
detraction *n* 483
detractor *n* 936
detrain *v* 292
detriment *n* 659
detrimental *adj* 649
deuce *n* 89
devastate *v* 162
devastation *n* 162, 638
develop *v* 153, 161, 194,
  282, 313, 367
developing *adj* 35
development *n* 35, 144,
  154, 161, 194, 282, 313
developmental *adj* 35
deviant *adj* 15
deviate *v* 20a, 140, 245,
  279, 291, 629
deviating *adj* 15, 279
deviation *n* 279

deviation *n* 20a, 140, 245,
  291
device *n* 550, 626, 702
devil *n* 978
devil *n* 949, 980; *v* 392
devilish *adj* 978, 982
devise *v* 515, 626, 673
devoid *adj* 187
devoid of *adj* 777a
devolve *v* 783
devoted *adj* 897, 987
devotee *n* 987
devote oneself to *v* 676
devotion *n* 604, 682, 743,
  897, 928, 987
devour *v* 162, 298, 957
devout *adj* 987
devoutness *n* 987
dew *n* 339
dewy *adj* 339
dexterity *n* 698
dextral *adj* 238
dextrous *adj* 698
diabolic *adj* 978, 982
diabolical *adj* 649
diabolism *n* 978
diagnosis *n* 465
diagonal *adj* 217
diagram *n* 626
dialect *n* 560
dialectic *adj* 476, 560
dialectical *adj* 476
dialectician *n* 476
dialects *n* 476
dialog *n* 588
diameter *n* 202
diametrically opposite
  adj 237
diaphanous *adj* 425
diaphanousness *n* 425
diaphragm *n* 68
diary *n* 114, 551
dichotomy *n* 91
dictate *v* 741
dictatorial *adj* 739
dictatorship *n* 739
diction *n* 560, 569
dictionary *n* 86
dictum *n* 496, 741
didactic *adj* 537
die *n* 22; *v* 2, 67, 142, 360,
  659
die hard *v* 606
die out *v* 2, 142
differ *v* 15, 489, 713
difference *n* 15
difference *n* 18, 24, 28,
  291, 489, 713
different *adj* 15
differentia *n* 15
differentiate *v* 18, 79, 465
differentiation *n* 465
different time *n* 119
differ from *v* 14, 18
difficult *adj* 704
difficulties *n* 804
difficulty *n* 704
difficulty *n* 177, 533

diffidence n 881
diffident adj 881
diffuse v 73; adj 73, 573
diffused adj 186
diffuseness n 573
diffusion n 73, 186
diffusive adj 73, 573
dig v 208, 252, 259, 490, 827
digest n 596; v 384
digestible adj 299, 390
dig in v 298
digit n 84
dignified adj 873, 875, 878
dignity n 873, 875
digress v 279, 573, 629
digression n 279, 629
digressive adj 279, 573
dig to daylight v 260
dig up v 480a
dike n 198, 259, 350
dilapidate v 659
dilapidated adj 659
dilapidation n 162, 659
dilate v 35, 194, 322
dilation n 322
dilatory adj 133
dilemma n 476, 704
diligence n 682
diligent adj 682
dilly-dally v 133, 605, 683
dilly-dallying n 133
dilute v 160, 203, 337
diluted adj 203
dim v 421; adj 405, 422, 426, 447, 519
dimensions n 31, 192
diminish v 36, 38, 103, 174, 195, 834
diminished adj 34, 103
diminution n 36, 195, 638
diminution of number n 103
diminutive adj 32, 193
diminutiveness n 32, 193
dimness n 422
dimness n 343, 421
dimple n 252
dim-sighted adj 442, 443
dimsightedness n 443
dimwit n 493
dim-witted adj 254, 499
din n 404
dine v 298
dingdong n 407, 408
dingy adj 421, 422, 429, 431
dining n 298
dint n 252
dip n 217, 252, 300, 306, 308, 310; v 300, 310, 337
diplomat n 724
dipsomaniac n 959
dire adj 649, 735, 830
direct v 175, 278, 537, 600, 630, 692, 693, 741; adj 246, 278, 703

directing adj 693
direction n 278, 693
direction n 183, 537, 692, 697, 741
directive n 630; adj 692
direct line n 246
directly adv 132, 278
directness n 246
director n 694
director n 745
directory n 86
dirge n 363, 839
dirigible n 273
dirt n 342, 653
dirt cheap adj 815
dirty n 653; adj 653, 961
disability n 158
disable v 158
disabled adj 158
disadvantage n 619
disadvantageous adj 647
disagree v 24, 291, 489, 713
disagreeable adj 24, 830, 846, 867
disagreeing adj 24, 489
disagree with v 657
disallow v 761
disallowance n 761
disappear v 2, 4, 360, 449
disappearance n 449
disappearing adj 449
disappoint v 509, 732, 832
disappointed adj 509
disappointment n 509
disapprobation n 932
disapproval n 766, 932
disapprove v 766, 932
disapproving adj 932
disarm v 158
disarrange v 61
disarray n 59, 61
disaster n 619, 735
disastrous adj 619, 735, 830
disavow v 536; v 607
disavowal n 536, 607
disband v 44, 73
disbelief n 485
disbelief n 485, 487, 989
disbelieve v 485, 989
disburse v 809
disbursement n 809
discard v 297, 610, 678, 773, 782
discern v 441, 480a, 490, 498
discernible adj 446
discernibleness n 446
discerning adj 441, 459, 465, 490, 498, 868
discernment n 441, 465, 477, 480a, 490, 498, 868
discharge n 284, 295, 297,

299, 406, 750, 772, 807, 970; v 284, 295, 297, 692, 729, 750, 772, 807, 926, 927a, 970
discharge a function v 644
discharged adj 970
disciple n 492, 541
disciplinarian n 739
discipline n 58, 537, 972; v 537, 972
disclaim v 536; v 757, 764
disclaimer n 536, 764
disclose v 525, 527, 529, 531
disclosed adj 529
disclosure n 529
disclosure n 480a, 531, 985
discoloration n 429
discolored adj 429, 848
discomfort n 378, 828; v 828
discommodious adj 647
discompose v 61, 828
discomposure n 61, 828
disconcert v 61, 706, 832
disconcerted adj 509
disconnect v 44, 70
disconnected adj 10, 70
disconnectedness n 70
disconnection n 10, 44, 47
disconsolate adj 859
discontent n 832
discontent n 828
discontented adj 832
discontentment n 832
discontinuance n 142
discontinuation n 142
discontinue v 44, 70, 142, 265
discontinuity n 70
discontinuity n 44, 53
discontinuous adj 44, 70
discord n 414, 713
discord n 24, 59, 410, 720, 889
discordance n 489
discordant adj 24, 410, 414, 713
discount n 813
discount n 40a; v 813
discourage v 616
discouraged adj 837
discouragement n 616
discourse n 537, 582, 588, 595; v 537, 582
discourse with v 588
discourteous adj 895, 929
discourtesy n 895
discourtesy n 929
discover v 441, 462, 480a, 490, 529
discoverable adj 462
discovery n 480a
discovery n 462, 985
discredit n 874; v 485

dissension *n* 24, 489, 713, 720

dissent *n* 489

dissent *n* 485, 803, 984; *v* 291, 485, 489, 803, 708, 713

dissenter *n* 489, 984

dissenting *adj* 24, 489, 984

dissention *n* 720

dissertation *n* 595

dissever *v* 44

dissidence *n* 24, 713

dissident *n* 489; *adj* 489, 713, 764

dissimilar *adj* 18

dissimilarity *n* 18

dissimilarity *n* 15, 28

dissimilitude *n* 18

dissipate *v* 162, 638, 818

dissipation *n* 73, 638

dissociate *v* 44

dissociation *n* 10, 44

dissolution *n* 49, 182, 335, 360

dissolvable *adj* 335

dissolve *v* 2, 4, 49, 162, 335, 360, 449

dissonance *n* 24, 410, 414, 713

dissonant *adj* 24, 410, 414, 713

dissuade *v* 616

dissuasion *n* 616

dissuasive *adj* 616

dissyllable *n* 581

distance *n* 196

distance *n* 198, 200, 235

distanced *adj* 10

distant *adj* 196

distaste *n* 867

distasteful *adj* 830, 867

distend *v* 194

distention *n* 194

distill *v* 336

distillation *n* 336

distinct *adj* 402, 446, 518, 525, 570, 580

distinction *n* 15, 31, 465, 873, 875

distinctive *adj* 15

distinctive feature *n* 79

distinctness *n* 446, 570, 580

distinguish *v* 15, 441, 465

distinguished *adj* 206, 873

distinguishing *adj* 465

distort *v* 217, 243, 523, 555, 846

distorted *adj* 243

distortion *v* 243

distortion *n* 443, 544, 555, 846

distracted *adj* 503, 824

distraction *n* 825

distress *n* 735, 804, 828; *v* 828

distress signal *n* 669

distribute *v* 60, 73, 531, 786

distribution *n* 60, 73, 531, 786

distributive *adj* 786

district attorney *n* 968

distrust *n* 485; *v* 485, 487, 860

disturb *v* 61, 185, 315, 824, 830

disturbance *n* 59, 61, 315

disunion *n* 24, 44, 59, 905

disunite *v* 44, 713

disusage *n* 614

disuse *n* 614, 678

disuse *v* 614, 678

disused *adj* 678

ditch *n* 198, 259, 350

ditto *n* 21; *adv* 104

dive *n* 208, 310; *v* 310

diverge *v* 20a, 291

divergence *n* 291

divergence *n* 15, 18, 24, 73, 279

divergency *n* 20a

divergent *adj* 15, 24, 291

divers *adj* 15

diverse *adj* 15, 81

diversified *adj* 15, 16a, 18, 20a, 81, 440

diversify *v* 15, 18, 140, 440

diversion *n* 140, 279, 840

diversity *n* 15, 16a, 18, 81

divert *v* 279, 840

diverting *adj* 840

divest *v* 226, 789

divestment *n* 789

divest oneself *v* 782

divide *v* 44, 44, 51, 60, 73, 85, 91, 291, 778, 786

divided *adj* 51

divide into four parts *v* 97

divide into three parts *v* 94

divide in two *v* 91

divination *n* 511, 992

divine *n* 996; *v* 511, 514, 992; *adj* 976, 981, 983a

divinity *n* 976, 983

division *n* 44, 51, 60, 73, 75, 198, 291, 713, 786

divisive *adj* 713

divorce *n* 905

divorce *n* 44; *v* 44, 905

divorced *adj* 905

divulge *v* 529, 531

divulgence *n* 529, 531

do *v* 161, 170, 622, 639, 680, 729

do a good turn *v* 648

do as one likes *v* 748

do away with *v* 162, 297, 361

do a world of good *v* 648

do battle *v* 722

docile *adj* 725, 743, 926

docility *n* 725, 743

dock *n* 966

doctor *n* 662; *v* 544, 660, 662

doctrinal *adj* 983a

doctrine *n* 484, 537, 983

document *n* 551

dodge *v* 264, 279, 623

do *n* 374

doer *n* 680, 690

doff *v* 226

dog *n* 373

dogged *adj* 150, 640a, 606

doggedness *n* 150, 604a, 606

doggerel *n* 597

dogma *n* 484, 537, 983

dogmatic *adj* 535, 606, 737

dogmatism *n* 535, 606

dogmatist *n* 606

do good *v* 648

do harm *v* 649

doing *adj* 151

doings *n* 151

doldrums *n* 837

dole *n* 32, 640, 786

dole out *v* 60, 73, 784, 786

dolor *n* 378, 828

dolorous *adj* 378, 830

dolt *n* 493, 501

doltish *adj* 499

domain *n* 75, 181

dome *n* 250

domestic *n* 746; *adj* 188, 221, 370

domestic animals *n* 366

domesticate *v* 184, 370

domesticated *adj* 370

domestication *n* 370

domicile *n* 189

dominance *n* 175

dominant *adj* 175, 737

dominate *v* 175, 739

domination *n* 741

domineer *v* 739

domineering *adj* 739

dominion *n* 157, 737

don *n* 540

donate *v* 784

donation *n* 784

done *adj* 729

done away with *adj* 782

donee *n* 785

done with *adj* 678

donor *n* 784

do nothing *v* 169, 681, 683

doom *n* 152, 360, 421; *v* 152, 971

doomsday *n* 121

do one's duty *v* 926

door *n* 231, 232, 260, 627

doorway *n* 232, 260

do over *v* 144

do penance *v* 952

dull v 254, 381, 422;
  adj 160, 172, 254, 275,
  337, 376, 381, 422, 428,
  429, 491, 499, 575, 598,
  683, 841, 843, 901a
dullard n 493, 501
dulled *adj* 381
dullness n 843
dullness n 172, 254, 683,
  823, 841
dull understanding n 499
dull-witted *adj* 499
dumb *adj* 491, 581
dumb animal n 366
dumbness n 581
dumfound v 509, 581, 870
dumps n 837
dumpy *adj* 193, 201, 202
dun *adj* 429, 432
dunce n 493, 501
dunderhead n 501
dunderpate n 501
dungeon n 752
dunk v 310, 337
dunking n 310
duo n 415
dupe n 547
dupe n 486, 857; v 545
duplex *adj* 89
duplexity n 89
duplicate n 13, 21, 90;
  v 19, 90, 104; *adj* 19, 90,
  641
duplicated *adj* 90
duplication n 90
duplication n 19, 104
duplicitous *adj* 520, 702
duplicity n 520, 544, 702
durability n 110
durability n 112, 141, 150
durable *adj* 106, 110, 141,
  150
duration n 106, 200
duress n 744
during *adv* 106
dusk n 126, 421
duskiness n 421, 422
dusky *adj* 421
dust n 330, 362
dusty *adj* 330, 653
dutiful *adj* 743, 926
duty n 926
duty n 625, 743, 806, 928,
  963
duty bound *adj* 926
dwarf n 980; *adj* 193
dwarfish *adj* 193
dwell v 186, 188, 265
dweller n 188
dwelling n 189
dwindle v 36, 195, 732
dwindling n 36
dye n 428; v 428
dyed *adj* 428
dying n 360
dying day n 360
dynamic *adj* 171

E

each *adv* 79
each to each *adv* 79
each to his own *adv* 79
eager *adj* 602, 682
eagerness n 602, 682
eagle-eyed *adj* 441
ear n 418
earlier *adv* 116
earliness n 132
early *adj* 132; *adv* 121,
  132
earmark n 550
earn v 775
earnest *adj* 602, 642
earnestly *adv* 604
earnestness n 682
earnings n 775
ear-piercing *adj* 410
earshot n 197
ear-splitting *adj* 404
earth n 318, 342, 362
earthly *adj* 318, 342, 989
earthy *adj* 342
ease n 377, 578, 705, 748,
  827, 831, 834; v 705, 707,
  834
easily *adv* 705
easiness n 705
easy *adj* 275, 578, 685,
  705, 740
easy circumstance n 803
easy going *adj* 174, 740,
  826
eat v 298
eatable *adj* 299
eat away v 638
eating n 298
eating n 296
eavesdrop v 418
eavesdropper n 418, 455,
  527
ebb n 36; v 36, 195, 283,
  287, 659
ebb and flow n 314
ebbing n 36
ebon *adj* 431
ebony n 431
ebullience n 171
ebullient *adj* 171, 382, 824
ebullition n 171, 173, 315,
  825
eccentric *adj* 83, 499, 608
eccentricity n 83, 499, 503
ecclesiastic n 996
ecclesiastical n 995
echo n 21, 104; v 104, 277,
  402, 408
echoing n 408
eclipse n 421, 449; v 33,
  422
economical *adj* 817
economize v 817
economy n 817
economy n 58
ecstasy n 377, 827
ecstatic *adj* 377, 827, 829

ecumenical *adj* 78
eddy n 312, 348
edge n 231
edge n 233; v 231
edgewise *adv* 217
edging n 231
edible *adj* 299
edification n 537
edify v 537
edifying *adj* 537, 648
edition n 531
editor n 593, 805
educate v 537
educated *adj* 490, 498
education n 537, 673
educational *adj* 537
educational institution
  n 542
eel n 248
efface v 552
efface from the memory
  v 506
effacement n 552
effect n 154
effect n 65; v 153, 729, 731
effective *adj* 157, 175, 644
effects n 780
effectual *adj* 170, 644
effervesce v 173, 315, 353
effervescence n 171, 173,
  315, 353
effervescent *adj* 338, 353
efficacious *adj* 157, 170,
  644
efficacy n 157, 644
efficient *adj* 157, 170, 698
effigy n 21
effluence n 295
effluvium n 398
effort n 675, 680, 686
effulgence n 420
effulgent *adj* 420
effusion n 295, 297, 299
effusive *adj* 584
egalitarian *adj* 29, 78
egg n 153
egg-shaped *adj* 247, 249
ego n 5
egoism n 943
egotism n 878, 880, 943
egotistical *adj* 878, 880,
  943
egregiously *adv* 31
egress n 295
egress n 302
eight n 98
eject v 185, 297, 789, 893
ejected *adj* 893
ejection n 297
ejection n 185, 301, 893
eke out v 110
elaborate v 658
elaboration n 658
elapse v 109
elapsed *adj* 122
elastic *adj* 277, 324, 325

elasticity n 325
elasticity n 159, 277, 324
elated adj 838, 884
elbow n 244
elbow-grease n 331
elbowroom n 180
elder n 130; adj 128
elderly adj 124, 128
eldership n 128
eldest adj 128
elect v 609, 995
election n 609
electricity n 388
electric light n 423
electrify v 824
electrocute v 361
electrocution n 361
electronic music n 415
electronic sound
  reproduction n 402
elegance n 578
elegance n 577, 845, 850
elegant adj 578, 845
elegantly adv 850
elegy n 363, 839
element n 51, 56, 153, 211
elemental adj 42, 211
elementary adj 42
elements n 66
elephant n 192
elevate v 206, 235, 307
elevated adj 206, 307, 574
elevation n 307
elevation n 206, 574, 658
eleven n 98
elf n 979
elfin adj 980
elicit v 153, 301
eliminate v 38, 42, 55,
  103, 297, 299, 301, 610,
  893
eliminated adj 893
elimination n 42, 55, 103,
  297, 299, 301, 610, 893
elite n 648
ellipse n 247
elliptic adj 247
elliptical adj 247
elongate v 200
elongation n 196, 200
eloquence n 574, 582
eloquent adj 574
elsewhere adv 187
elucidate v 74, 518, 522
elucidation n 522
elude v 623, 671, 773
elusive adj 623, 773
elysian adj 981
emaciated adj 203
emaciation n 203
emanate v 295, 299
emanate from v 154
emanation n 295, 299, 398
emancipate v 672, 750
emancipation n 195, 672,
  750
emasculate v 158

emasculated adj 158
embalm v 363
embargo n 761
embark v 66, 267, 293
embarkation n 293
embark on v 676
embarrass v 704
embarrassed adj 434
embassy n 755
embed v 221
embedded adj 221, 229
embellish v 847
embellished adj 847
embellishment n 847
ember n 388
embezzle v 791
emblazon v 428, 882
emblem n 550, 747
emblematic adj 550
embody v 50, 54, 76, 82,
  316
embosomed adj 229
emboss v 251
embrace v 902; v 54, 76,
  902
embroider v 440, 549
embroidery n 549
embroil v 61
embryo n 153
embryology n 368
embryonic adj 66, 153,
  674
emend v 658
emendation n 658
emendatory adj 658
emerald adj 435
emerge v 295
emergence n 295
emergency n 8, 151, 704
emigrant n 268
eminence n 31, 33, 206,
  648, 873, 875
eminent adj 206, 873, 883
eminently adv 33
emissary n 534
emission n 297
emit sound v 402
emotion n 821
emotional adj 821
empathy n 821
emphasis n 535, 580, 642
emphasize v 535, 642
emphatic adj 535, 642
emphatically adv 31
employ v 677, 749; v 677,
  755
employable adj 677
employee n 746
employ figures of speech
  v 521
employment n 625
employ oneself v 625
empower v 157, 737, 755,
  760
emptiness n 2, 187, 209,
  452, 517, 640, 880

empty v 185, 297; adj 2, 4,
  187, 209, 298, 452
empty-headed adj 450a
empty vessel n 362
empty words n 517
emulate v 19, 648
enact v 599, 680, 692, 729,
  741, 963
enamored adj 897
encamp v 184
encampment n 184
encase v 223
enchant v 829, 992
enchanted adj 992
enchanting adj 897, 992
enchantment n 827, 829,
  991, 992
encircle v 76, 220, 227,
  247
enclose v 227, 232
enclosure n 232
enclosure n 229
encompass v 76, 227
encore adv 104
encounter n 276, 680, 716;
  v 151
encourage v 707, 836
encouraging adj 858
encroach v 303
encroachment n 303
encumber v 319, 704, 706
encumbrance n 706
end n 67
end n 65, 142, 152, 154,
  360, 620, 729; v 67, 142,
  360, 729
endanger v 665, 909
endangering adj 909
endear v 902
endearing adj 902
endearment n 902
endeavor n 675, 686;
  v 622, 675
ended adj 67
endemic adj 191
endless adj 102, 104, 112
endlessness n 105, 112
end of the day n 126
end of one's days v 360
endorse v 535, 769, 771,
  931
endorsement n 535
endow v 157
endowment n 698, 784
end result n 161
end to end adj 199
endurance n 112, 141,
  150, 826
endure v 1, 106, 110, 112,
  141, 151, 826
enduring adj 110, 141,
  150, 580, 826
endwise adv 212
enemy n 891

enemy n 708, 710, 726
energetic adj 157, 171,
  359

energetic activity *n* 680
energize *v* 171
energized *adj* 171
energy *n* 171
energy *n* 157, 159, 163, 359, 604, 680, 682, 686
enervate *v* 158, 160
enervation *n* 575
enfeeble *v* 160, 638
enfold *v* 229
enforce *v* 695, 744
enforcement *n* 744
enfranchise *v* 750
enfranchisement *n* 750, 760
engage *v* 132, 288, 615, 676, 768, 769
engage in *v* 622, 676
engage in a discussion *v* 588
engagement *n* 676, 680
engender *v* 161
engorge *v* 957
engrave *v* 259, 558
engrave in the mind *v* 505
engraver *n* 559
engraving *n* 558
engrossed in *adj* 451
enhance *v* 307, 658
enigmatic *adj* 519, 520
enjoin *v* 630, 695, 744
enjoy *v* 377, 394, 827
enjoyable *adj* 829
enjoyment *n* 827, 840
enjoy oneself *v* 827
enlarge *v* 31, 35, 35, 194, 573
enlargement *n* 35, 37, 194, 750
enlighten *v* 420, 527, 537
enlightened *adj* 490, 527
enlightenment *n* 490, 498, 527, 985
enlist *v* 615
enliven *v* 689, 836, 840
enmity *n* 889
enmity *n* 907
ennervation *n* 160
ennoble *v* 875
ennui *n* 688, 841
enormity *n* 102, 192
enormous *adj* 31, 192
enormously *adv* 31
enormousness *n* 31, 192
enough *n* 639; *adj* 639; *adv* 31
enplane *v* 293
enrapture *v* 824, 829
enrapturing *adj* 977
enravish *v* 829
enrich *v* 658
enroll *v* 551
ensconce *v* 528
ensconced *adj* 184
ensconcing *n* 528
ensemble *n* 416, 417

enslave *v* 749
enslavement *n* 749
ensnare *v* 545
ensue *v* 63, 151
ensuing *adj* 117
entangle *v* 43, 61, 219, 704
entangled *adj* 59
entanglement *n* 59, 219, 704
enter *v* 294, 551, 811
enter a protest *v* 766
enter into *v* 56, 768
enterprise *n* 622, 676
enterprising *adj* 861
entertain *v* 840
entertaining *adj* 840
entertainment *n* 840
enthral *v* 749
enthusiasm *n* 574, 602
enthusiast *n* 504
enthusiastic *adj* 825
enthymeme *n* 476
enticing *adj* 288
entire *adj* 50, 52, 729
entirely *adv* 31, 50
entirety *n* 50, 52
entitle *v* 564
entity *n* 1
entomb *v* 363
entombment *n* 363
entomology *n* 368
entrain *v* 293
entrance *n* 294; *v* 829, 992
entrancing *adj* 977
entrap *v* 545
entreat *v* 765
entreaty *n* 411, 765
entre é *n* 296
entrust *v* 784, 805
entry *n* 294, 296
entwine *v* 43, 248
enumerate *v* 85
enumeration *n* 85
enunciate *v* 580
enunciation *n* 580
envelope *n* 232
envious *adj* 435, 900, 920, 921
enviousness *n* 921
environ *v* 227
environment *n* 227
environs *n* 227
envision *v* 441
envy *n* 534
envy *n* 921
envy *n* 900, 920; *v* 921
eon *n* 108
ephemeral *adj* 111
ephemerality *n* 111
epicure *n* 945a, 957
epicurean *n* 945a; *adj* 954, 957
epicureanism *n* 954
epicurism *n* 954, 957
epigram *n* 496
epigrammatist *n* 844
epilog *n* 65

episode *n* 39, 70, 151
episodic *adj* 228
epistle *n* 592
epistolary *adj* 592
epithet *n* 564
epitome *n* 193, 596
epitomize *v* 201, 596
epoch *n* 106, 108
equal *n* 27; *v* 27; *adj* 13, 27, 30 216, 242
equality *n* 27
equality *n* 13
equalization *n* 30
equalize *v* 27, 30
equally *adv* 27
equal to *adj* 157
equate *v* 216
equation *n* 30, 216
equator *n* 68
equestrian *n* 268
equidistance *n* 68
equidistant *adj* 68
equilibrium *n* 27, 150
equip *v* 225, 673
equipment *n* 225, 633
equipoise *n* 27
equitable *adj* 246, 922
equitableness *n* 922
equitably *adv* 922
equity *n* 922
equivalence *n* 27
equivalent *n* 27, 30, 147; *adj* 12, 13, 27, 30, 216
equivocal *adj* 477, 520
equivocalness *n* 520
equivocate *v* 477, 520
equivocation *n* 477, 520, 544
era *n* 106, 108
eradicate *v* 103, 162, 301
eradication *n* 301
erase *v* 162, 331, 552
erased *adj* 552
erasure *n* 552
ere *adv* 116
Erebus *n* 982
erect *v* 161, 235, 307; *adj* 212, 246
erection *n* 161, 307
erectness *n* 212
ere now *adv* 122
ergo adv 155
erode *v* 638, 659
erosion *n* 659
err *v* 495, 945
errand *n* 755
errand boy *n* 534
errant *adj* 279
erratic *adj* 149, 279, 608
erroneous *adj* 4, 495, 544, 732, 923
error *n* 495
error *n* 538, 568, 984
erudite *adj* 490, 498, 539
erudition *n* 490, 498, 539
eruption *n* 173, 295
escape *n* 671

exclaim v 411
exclamation n 411
exclude v 55, 610, 893
excluded adj 57, 893
exclusion n 5, 7, 893
exclusion n 610
exclusive adj 55, 79
exclusive of adv 38
excrete v 299
excretion n 299
excruciating adj 982
exculpate v 970
exculpated adj 970
exculpation n 937, 970
exculpatory adj 937
excursion n 226, 302, 311
excursionist n 268
excuse n 617, 927a; v 617, 777a, 918, 927a
excused adj 927a
execrable adj 649
execrate v 898, 908
execration n 908
execute v 361, 416, 680, 692, 729, 772, 972
execution n 361, 680, 692, 729, 772
executioner n 165, 361, 690, 975
executive adj 692, 737
executor n 690
executrix n 690
exegesis n 522
exegetical adj 522
exemplar n 22
exemplary adj 82
exemplification n 82
exempt v 777a, 927a; adj 748, 927a
exempt from adj 777a
exemption n 777a, 927a
exercise n 170, 677, 680; v 677, 680
exert v 171, 677, 686
exert energy v 680
exert force v 288
exertion n 686
exertion n 171, 680, 682
exert oneself v 686
exhalation n 299, 398
exhale v 299
exhaust v 158, 638, 688, 841
exhausted adj 2, 158, 688, 841
exhaustion n 158, 638, 688, 841
exhaustive adj 52
exhibit n 467; v 525, 882
exhibition n 525
exhilarate v 836
exhilaration n 836
exhort v 695
exhortation n 695
exhumation n 363
exhume v 363
exigency n 8, 704

exigent adj 630
exiguity n 203
exile n 55, 185, 297, 893; v 55, 185, 297
exiled adj 893
exist v 1, 359
existence n 1
existence n 1, 359
existent adj 1
existing adj 118
exit n 293, 295, 449
exodus n 293
exonerate v 937, 970
exonerated adj 937, 970
exonerating adj 937
exoneration n 937, 970
exorbitant n 814, 954
exorbitant adj 31, 641, 814, 954
exorbitantly adv 31
exorcism n 993
exorcist n 994
exotic adj 10, 83
expand v 31, 35, 192, 194, 202, 322, 549, 573
expanded adj 194
expanse n 105, 180, 192
expansion n 194
expansion n 35, 180, 322
expansive adj 180, 194, 202
expatiate v 582
expect v 121, 451, 507, 510, 620, 858, 871
expectance n 871
expectancy n 507, 858, 871
expectant adj 507, 510, 858, 871
expectantly adv 507
expectation n 507
expectation n 121, 451, 472, 858, 871
expectations n 152
expected adj 871
expecting adj 871
expedience n 646
expediency n 646
expedient n 147; adj 646
expedite v 132, 684
expeditious adj 132, 274
expel v 185, 284, 297, 893
expend v 638, 677, 809
expenditure n 809
expenditure n 638
expense n 812
expenses n 809
expensive adj 814
expensiveness n 814
experience n 151
experienced adj 698
experiment n 463
experiment n 675; v 463, 675
experimental adj 463, 675
experimentally adv 675

experimentation n 463
experimenter n 463
experiment with v 140
expert n 700
expert n 500, 737, 832; adj 698
expertness n 698, 702
expiate v 952
expiating adj 952
expiation n 952
expiatory adj 952
expiration n 67, 360
expire v 67, 109, 360
expired adj 122
explain v 462, 478, 518, 522, 595
explainer n 524
explanation n 155, 478, 522, 537
explanation n 155, 478, 522, 537
explanatory adj 522
explicable adj 522
explicate v 522
explication n 522
explicit adj 518, 525, 570
explicitness n 518, 570
explode v 173
exploit n 680
exploration n 461
exploratory adj 461
exploring adj 461
explosion n 173, 404, 406, 825
explosive adj 173, 665
expose v 529; v 226, 260, 529
expose oneself to v 177
expose the error v 479
expose to danger v 665
exposition n 522, 525, 529, 595
expositor n 524
expository adj 522, 527
expostulate v 616, 766
expostulation n 616, 766
expostulatory adj 766
exposure n 448, 479, 529, 665
expound v 522, 537
expounder n 524
express v 516, 525, 527, 560, 566; adj 620
express by words v 560, 569
expression n 521, 525, 554, 560, 566, 985, 985
expressive adj 516, 518, 521, 569
expropriate v 789
expropriation n 789
expulsion n 185, 297, 893
expunge v 162, 552
expurgate v 652
expurgation n 652
exquisite adj 394, 650
exquisitely adv 31
extant adj 1

extemporaneous *adj* 612
extemporaneously
  adv 612
extempore *adv* 612
extemporize *v* 612, 874
extend *v* 35, 194, 200
extended *adj* 200, 202
extend to *v* 196, 200
extension *n* 35, 65, 180,
  194
extensive *adj* 31, 78, 180
extensively *adv* 180
extent *n* 26, 106, 180, 200,
  202, 233
extenuate *v* 469
extenuating *adj* 469
extenuating
  circumstances *n* 469
extenuation *n* 469
exterior *n* 220; *adj* 220
exteriority *n* 220
exterminate *v* 162
extermination *n* 301
external *adj* 6, 57, 220
externality *n* 57
externally *adv* 220
externals *n* 6
extinct *adj* 2, 122, 162, 360
extinction *n* 2, 162, 360,
  421, 552
extinguish *v* 162, 385, 421
extirpate *v* 301
extirpation *n* 301
extol *v* 883
extort *v* 814
extortion *n* 789
extra *adj* 37
extract *v* 301
extraction *n* 301
extracts *n* 596
extradite *v* 270
extradition *n* 270
extraneous *adj* 6, 10, 57,
  220
extraneousness *n* 57
extraneousness *n* 6
extraordinary *adj* 31, 83,
  870
extravagance *n* 497, 499,
  549, 814, 818, 954
extravagant *adj* 31, 497,
  499, 549, 641, 814, 818,
  853, 954
extravagant love *n* 991
extravagantly *adv* 31
extreme *n* 67; *adj* 31
extremely *adv* 31
extremity *n* 67
extricate *v* 301, 672, 705,
  750
extrication *n* 301, 672, 750
extrinsic *adj* 6, 57, 220
extrinsicality *n* 6
extrinsically *n* 57
extrinsically *adv* 6
exuberance *n* 573, 641
exuberant *adj* 573, 641

exude *v* 295
exultant *adj* 838, 884
eye *n* 247; *v* 441
eye for an eye *n* 30
eyeglasses *n* 445
eyeless *adj* 442
eyesight *n* 441
eyewitness *n* 444
eyot *n* 346

F

fable *n* 546
fabric *n* 7
fabricate *v* 161, 515, 544
fabrication *n* 161, 544,
  546
fabulous *adj* 2, 515, 546,
  549, 979
fabulous spirit *n* 979
facade *n* 220, 234
face *n* 220, 234, 448; *v* 223,
  224, 234
facet *n* 220
facetious *adj* 842
facetiousness *n* 842
face to face *adv* 237
facile *adj* 705
facilitate *v* 705, 707
facility *n* 705
facility *n* 157, 698, 748
facing *n* 223; *adj* 237
facsimile *n* 13, 21, 90
fact *n* 1, 151, 474, 494
faction *n* 712
factious *adj* 24
factory *n* 691
facts *n* 467, 527
factual *adj* 494
faculties *n* 450
faculty *n* 698
fad *n* 608
faddish *adj* 123
faddishness *n* 123
fade *v* 4, 111, 124, 160,
  287, 360, 422, 429, 449,
  659, 732
faded *adj* 659
fail *v* 160, 304, 360, 655,
  732, 773, 808, 927
failing *n* 732; *adj* 53, 128,
  927
failure *n* 732
failure *n* 304, 460, 509,
  735, 773, 808, 927
fail *adj* 602
faint *v* 158, 688; *adj* 32,
  160, 203, 405, 422, 429,
  430, 447, 688
faint-hearted *adj* 862
faint-heartedness *n* 862
faintly *adv* 32
faintness *n* 405
faintness *n* 575, 688
faint sound *n* 405
fair *n* 799; *adj* 174, 246,
  429, 430, 651, 829, 845,
  922, 942

fair game *n* 857
fairly *adv* 922
fairness *n* 174, 845, 922,
  942
fairy *n* 979
faith *n* 484, 858
faithful *adj* 17, 21, 494,
  772, 983a
faithfully *adv* 772
faithfulness *n* 772, 983a
faithless *adj* 544, 989
fake *n* 556; *v* 680; *adj* 19
fake god *n* 991
faker *n* 548
fall *n* 126, 162, 217, 283,
  306, 348, 360; *v* 162, 306,
  310, 360
fallacious *adj* 4, 477, 495,
  544, 545
fallacy *n* 4, 477, 495
fall again *v* 661
fall away *v* 195
fall back *v* 145, 283, 287,
  661
fall behind *v* 281, 283
fallibility *n* 475
fallible *adj* 475
fall in *v* 488
falling *n* 306; *adj* 217
falling back *v* 145, 287,
  661
falling-off *n* 36, 659
fall into a rut *v* 613
fall into a trap *v* 547
fall into raptures *v* 827
fall off *v* 36, 659, 732
fall on evil days *v* 735
fall on one's knees *v* 990
fall out *v* 151, 713
fallow *adj* 674
fall prey to *v* 749
fall short *v* 304, 651, 732
fall short of *v* 28, 34, 53,
  640, 730
fall through *v* 304
fall to *v* 151, 298, 670
fall to one *v* 785
fall to one's lot *v* 156
fall to pieces *v* 162
fall under *v* 76
false *adj* 19, 477, 495, 544,
  545, 546, 823
false coloration *n* 523
false expectation *n* 508
false god *n* 991
falsehood *n* 544
falsehood *n* 546
false impression *n* 495
falseness *n* 545
false statement *n* 477
falsification *n* 523, 544,
  555
falsify *v* 523, 544, 555
falter *v* 605
famed *adj* 883

fiber n 205
fibrous adj 205
fickle adj 149, 605, 608
fickleness n 605
fiction n 515, 544, 546, 598
fictional adj 598
fictitious adj 546
fidelity n 543, 772
fidget v 825
fidgetiness n 149, 682
fidgety adj 149, 682, 825
field n 344
field of battle n 728
fields n 344
fiend n 980
fiendish adj 980
fierce adj 173, 825
fiery adj 382, 684, 825
fiery furnace n 386
fifty n 98
fifty-fifty chance n 156
fifty-fifty split n 91
fight n 680; v 606, 720, 722
fighter n 726
fighting n 173, 722
figment n 515
figuration n 554
figurative adj 521, 554
figure n 84, 550, 812;
  v 240, 448, 554, 557
figured on adj 871
figure of speech n 521
figure of speech n 566
figures of beauty n 521
filament n 205
filch v 791
filcher n 792
file n 69, 86, 266, 330; v 38,
  60, 69, 195, 255, 330
file a claim v 969
filial adj 167
filiation n 11
filigree n 219
filing n 330
fill v 52, 186, 190, 224
filled in adj 527
fill in v 52
filling n 224
fill out v 194, 549
fill up v 52, 261
fill up the time v 106
film n 204, 427
filminess n 426
filmy adj 204, 329, 426
filth n 653
filthy adj 653
final adj 67
finale n 65, 67, 360, 729
final gasp n 360
finality n 67
finalize v 729
finally adv 67, 151
final stage n 67
final touch n 729
finance n 800, 811
financial adj 800
financier n 801, 811

fit for adj 698
fitful adj 70, 139, 149, 475,
  608
fitfully adv 139
fitfulness n 139, 475
fitness n 646
fit out v 225, 673
fits n 315
five, etc. n 98
five n 98
fivefold division n 99
fix n 704; v 43, 60, 150,
  184, 604, 660
fix a price v 812
fixed adj 5, 141, 150, 240,
  265, 474, 604, 613
fixed idea n 606
fixedness n 150
fixity n 150, 265
fix the time v 114
fizzle v 353, 409
fjord n 343
flabby adj 324
flaccid adj 160, 324, 326
flaccidity n 160, 324, 326,
  640
flag n 747; v 160, 275, 655,
  683, 688
flaky adj 204
flame n 382, 420, 423, 439,
  897; v 382, 897
flame-colored adj 439
flaming adj 434
flammable adj 384, 388
flank n 236; v 236
flanked adj 236
flanking adj 236
flap n 214; v 214, 315
flare n 420; v 173, 420
flare up v 420, 825
flash n 113, 420, 453, 612;
  v 113, 420
flash on v 505; v 112
flashy adj 428, 577, 851,
  882
flat n 344; adj 172, 207,
  213, 251, 337, 391, 395,
  598, 843
flat as a pancake adj 251
flatlands n 207
flatness n 251
flatness n 207, 213, 391,
  843
flatten v 213, 251, 255
flatter v 933
flatterer n 935
flattering adj 933
flattery n 933
flatulent adj 334, 338
flaunt v 882
flaunting adj 882
flavor n 390, 394; v 390
flavored adj 390
flavorful adj 390, 394
flavorfulness n 394
flavoring n 393
flavorless adj 395

foreign adj 10, 57, 220
foreign body n 57
foreign parts n 196
foreign substance n 57
fore-knowledge n 510
foreman n 694
foremost adj 33, 66, 234, 642
forenoon n 125
foreordain v 152
forerun v 62, 116, 280
forerunner n 84, 116, 534
foresee v 121, 507, 510, 511, 871
foreseen adj 507, 871
foreshadow v 909
foreshadowing adj 909
foresight n 510
forestall v 132
forestry n 371
foretell v 511
forethought n 510, 864
foretoken n 511; v 511
forever adv 16, 112
forewarn v 510, 668
foreword n 64
forfeit n 974; v 776
forfeiture n 776
for form's sake adv 82
forge n 386, 691
forge ahead v 282
forgery n 19, 21, 546
forget v 506
forgetful adj 506
forgetfulness n 506
forgive v 918
forgiveness n 918
forgiving adj 918
forgo v 624, 757, 782
for good adv 106, 141
for good and all adv 141
forgotten adj 122, 506
fork n 244; v 91, 244, 291
forked adj 244
for keeps adv 106
forking n 91, 291
fork out v 784
forlorn adj 859
form n 240
form n 7, 21, 54, 80, 329, 448, 569, 697, 998; v 54, 56, 60, 144, 161, 240, 557, 852
formal adj 80, 82, 240, 242, 383, 579
formal features n 567
formality n 240, 579
formal speech n 586
form an opinion v 480
formation n 161, 240
formative adj 127, 153, 161
formative years n 127
form a whole v 50
formed adj 820
former adj 62, 116, 122
formerly adv 122

former times n 122
formidable adj 704
form into a sphere v 249
formless adj 241
formlessness n 241
form part of v 56
forms n 567
formula n 80, 240, 626, 697
formulaic adj 80, 626
formulate v 963
forsake v 624, 732, 782
for sale adj 763, 794, 796
forswear v 624, 782
forsworn adj 782
forte n 698
forth adv 282
forthcoming adj 152
for the moment adv 111
for the most part adv 613
for the sake of conformity adv 82
for the time being adv 106
forthright adj 246, 946
forthwith adv 132
fortification n 717
fortify v 159, 717
fortitude n 826, 861
fortress n 666
fortuitous adj 134, 156, 621
fortunate adj 134, 734
fortune n 152, 156, 621, 734, 803
fortune-teller n 513
forum n 966
forward adj 234; adv 282
fossil fuel n 388
foster v 658
foul adj 401, 649, 653
foulness n 401
foul play n 619
foul smell n 401
found v 153, 215
foundation n 153, 211, 215, 673
founded on adj 211
founder n 164; v 732
foundling n 893
found wanting adj 651
fount n 153
fountain n 153
four n 95; adj 95, 96
four-flusher n 548
fourfold adj 95, 96
fourfold division n 97
fourth adj 96
fourthly adv 96
fourth part n 97
four times adv 96
fowls of the air n 366
foxy adj 702
fracas n 59

fractional part n 100a
fractious adj 713, 742
fracture n 44, 70
fragile adj 160, 203, 328
fragility n 160, 328
fragment n 32, 51
fragmentary adj 51
fragments n 596
fragrance n 400
fragrant adj 377, 400
frail adj 158, 160, 203, 328, 605, 651
frailty n 158, 160, 328, 575, 605
frame n 7, 231, 240, 329; v 161, 626, 852
frame of mind n 602
framework n 329
franchise n 748, 760; v 760
franchisement n 748
frangible adj 328
frank adj 246, 525, 543, 703
frankness n 543, 748
frantic adj 173, 503, 824
fraternal adj 712, 714
fraternity n 11, 709, 888
fraternize v 709, 714, 892
fratricide n 361
fraud 545, 548, 791
fraudulent adj 544
fraught adj 52
fraught with danger adj 665
fray n 331
freak n 156; v 608, 872
freaked adj 173
freakish adj 608
freckled adj 440, 848
free v 672, 705, 744, 750, 927a; adj 44, 600, 685, 748, 816
freed adj 748, 750, 927a
freedom n 748
freedom n 600, 672, 738, 760, 927a
freely adv 602, 748
free space n 180
free spirit n 748
free swinging n 214
freethinker n 989
freethinking n 989; adj 989
free time n 685
free will n 600
freeze v 376, 383, 385
freezer n 387
freezing adj 383
freight n 190
freighter n 271, 273
frenzied adj 173, 503
frenzy n 503, 825
frequency n 136
frequent adj 104, 136, 613
frequently adv 136

fresh *adj* 123, 428, 435, 505
freshen *v* 338, 689
freshness *n* 123
fresh wind *n* 349
fret *n* 828; *v* 378, 832
fretful *adj* 684
fretwork *n* 219
friability *n* 330
friction *n* 331
friction *n* 179, 719
fridge *n* 387
friend *n* 890
friend *n* 711, 912, 977
friendless *adj* 893
friendliness *n* 888, 897
friendly *adj* 707, 714, 721, 888, 892
friendship *n* 888
friendship *n* 714
fright *n* 860
frighten *v* 909
frightened *adj* 860
frightening *adj* 909
frightful *adj* 830
frightfully *adv* 31
frightfulness *n* 846
frigid *adj* 158, 383
frigidaire *n* 387
frigidity *n* 383
frills *n* 847
fringe *n* 231
frippery *n* 643, 851
frisk *n* 309; *v* 309
frisky *adj* 309, 682
fritter away time *v* 683
fritter one's money *v* 818
frivolity *n* 4, 209, 499
frivolous *adj* 4, 477, 499, 608, 643
frizz *v* 248
frizzle *v* 248, 258
from all points of the compass *adv* 180
from bad to worse *adv* 835
from beginning to end *adv* 52
from first to last *adv* 52
from head to foot *adv* 52
from pole to pole *adv* 180
from side to side *adv* 314
from the beginning *adv* 66
from the bottom of one's heart *adv* 821
from the four corners of the world *adv* 180
from this time *adv* 121
from time to time *adv* 136
from top to bottom *adv* 52
front *n* 234
front *n* 719; *v* 234; *adj* 234
frontage *n* 234
frontal *adj* 234
frontier *n* 233
fronting *adj* 237

frontispiece *n* 64, 234
front rank *n* 234
frost-bitten *adj* 383
frosted *adj* 426, 430
frostiness *n* 430
frosty *adj* 383
froth *n* 353; *v* 353
frothy *adj* 353
frown *v* 837, 900, 901a
frown upon *v* 932
frozen *adj* 381, 383, 385
fructification *n* 161
fructify *v* 168, 658, 734
frugal *adj* 817, 953
frugality *n* 817
fruit *n* 154, 367
fruitful *adj* 168
fruitfulness *n* 168
fruition *n* 161
fruitless *adj* 158, 645, 732
frustrate *v* 706
frustrated *adj* 732
frustration *n* 509
fry *v* 384
fuel *n* 388
fuel *v* 388
fuel oil *n* 388
fugitive *n* 268, 623; *adj* 623
fulfill *v* 52, 161, 168, 729, 772, 926
fulfilled *adj* 52
fulfillment *n* 161, 729, 731, 772
fulfill oneself *v* 731
full *adj* 31, 50, 52, 52, 404, 729
full-blown *adj* 194
full circle *n* 311
full-flavored *adj* 392, 394
full grown *adj* 131, 192, 194
fullness *n* 31, 52, 131
full of incident *adj* 151
full turn *n* 311
fully *adv* 31, 52
fulminate *v* 404
fulsome *adj* 401
fumble *v* 61, 699
fumbler *n* 701
fume *n* 398, 401; *v* 173, 382, 825, 900
fumigate *v* 652
fuming *adj* 434, 824
fun *n* 842
function *n* 170, 625, 926, 998; *v* 680, 746
functional *adj* 625, 644
functionary *n* 694, 758
fund *n* 636
fundamental *adj* 5, 211, 215
fundamentally *adv* 31
fundamental *adj* 5
fundamental part *n* 211
funds *n* 800
funeral *n* 363; *adj* 363
funeral rites *n* 363

funereal *adj* 363
fungus *n* 663
funish *v* 784
funnel *n* 350, 351
funny *adj* 853
funnyman *n* 844
fur *n* 223
furcation *n* 291
furious *adj* 173, 382, 825
furiously *adv* 31
furnace *n* 386
furnish *v* 637, 673
furor *n* 825
furrow *n* 259
furrow *v* 259
furrowed *adj* 259
further *adv* 37
furtherance *n* 707
furthermore *adv* 37
furtive *adj* 528
fury *n* 173, 825, 980
fuse *v* 43, 48, 384
fusion *n* 48, 384, 709
fuss *n* 315, 682; *v* 682, 825
fussy *adj* 682, 825, 868
fustian *n* 577
fustiness *n* 401
fusty *adj* 401
futile *adj* 158, 645
futility *n* 645
future *n* 117, 152; *adj* 121
future events *n* 152
futurism *n* 123

G

gab *v* 584
gad about *v* 266
gadding *n* 266
gadding about *n* 266
gag *v* 403, 581
gaggle *v* 412
gain *n* 618, 658, 775; *v* 775
gainful *adj* 775
gain ground *v* 282
gain knowledge *v* 539
gain on *v* 286
gainsay *v* 536, 708
gait *n* 264
galaxy *n* 318
gale *n* 349
gall *v* 378, 869
gallant *adj* 861, 894
gallantry *n* 861
gallimaufry *n* 41
gallop *v* 111
galvanism *n* 824
galvanize *v* 824
gamble *n* 156; *v* 621
gambler *n* 621
gambling *n* 156, 621
game *n* 366, 620, 857; *adj* 604, 604a
gamester *n* 621
gaming *n* 156
gander *n* 373
gang *n* 72, 712
gaol *n* 752

gaoler n 753
gap n 70, 196, 198, 260
gape v 198, 260, 455
gaping adj 208, 260
garb n 225; v 225
garble v 523, 583
garden n 371, 371
gardening n 371
garish adj 428, 851, 882
garland n 247
garner v 636
garrison n 717; v 664
garrote n 361; v 361
garroter n 361
garrulity n 584
garrulous adj 584
gas n 388; v 361
gaseity n 334
gaseous adj 334, 336
gaseousness n 334
gash n 198
gasification n 336
gasify v 336
gas lamp n 423
gasoline n 356, 388
gasp v 349, 655, 688
gassing n 361
gate n 232, 260
gateway n 232, 260, 627
gather v 72, 258, 775, 789
gathering n 72, 712
gathering place n 74
gather together v 290
gaudiness n 851
gaudy adj 428, 851, 882
gauge n 466
gauging n 466
gaunt adj 203
gauze n 424
gauziness n 425
gauzy adj 425
gawky adj 699
gay adj 829, 836
gaze n 441
gazette n 86
gear n 225
gelding n 373
gelid adj 383
gem n 648
genealogy n 69, 166
general adj 78, 613
generality n 78
generalization n 78
generalize v 78
generally adv 613
general public n 372, 876
generalship n 722
generate v 161, 168
generation n 11, 108, 161, 163
generative adj 153, 161, 168
generator n 164
generic adj 78
generosity n 784, 816, 906, 942

generous adj 784, 816, 906, 942
genesis n 66, 153, 161
genial adj 382, 602, 829, 888, 892
geniality n 602, 836
genius n 698, 700, 872
genius for n 698
genteel adj 852
gentility n 578, 852, 875, 894
gentle adj 174, 275, 405, 721, 740
gentleman n 373
gentlemanly adj 894
gentleness n 174, 740
gentlewoman n 374
genuflect v 308
genuflection n 308
genuine adj 494, 648, 922, 960
genuineness n 960
genus n 75
geography n 183
geology n 358
germ n 66, 153
germinate v 194, 367
gestation n 161
gesticulate v 550
gesticulation n 550
gesture n 550; v 550
get v 775, 789, 810
get across v 184
get along v 282, 736
get back v 790
get back to basics v 849
get better v 658
get between v 228
get closer to v 286
get close to v 286
get down v 306
get down to particulars v 79
get going v 66, 276, 284
get hold of v 775, 789
get into v 827
get into print v 531
get on v 282
get one's own way v 687
get over v 660
get ready v 673
get red in the face v 878
get rid of v 297, 776
get the scent of v 527
get through v 67
get to v 292
get to the heart of v 222
get under way v 293
get up v 305
get well v 660
ghost n 362, 980; 443
ghostlike adj 980
ghostly adj 976, 980
ghoul n 980
giant n 192
gibberish n 517

gibes n 856
giddy adj 499
gift n 698, 763, 775, 784
gigantic adj 31, 159, 192, 206
giggle n 838; v 838
gimmicky adj 643
gird v 43, 227
girdle n 232, 247
girl n 129, 374
girlfriend n 897
girlhood n 127
girlish adj 129
gist n 5, 516
give n 325; v 324, 325, 763, 784, 816
give a free rein v 738
give a hearing to v 418
give an account v 527
give and take v 148, 774, 794
give a new turn to v 140
give assent v 484
give assistance v 707
give a start to v 276
give audience to v 418
give away v 784
give back v 790
give birth to v 163, 359
give counsel v 695
give counsel to v 695
give credence to 484
give energy v 171
give entrance to v 296
give evidence v 467
give fight v 722
give help v 707
give in v 82, 360
give it a shot v 602
given adj 474, 514
give no quarter v 361
give notice v 668
given time n 134
given up adj 782
give offense v 830
give oneself airs v 878
give one's word v 768
give out v 732, 784
give out a smell v 398
give out sound v 402
give pleasure v 377
giver n 784
give rise to v 153
give satisfaction v 952
give security v 768, 771
give up v 624, 757, 782, - 790
give up hope v 859
give up the ghost v 360
give way v 160, 328
give way to v 681
giving n 784
glacial adj 383
glaciation n 385
gladden v 829, 836
gladdening adj 836
glade n 252

gladness n 827
gladsome adj 827, 829
glance n 441
glance around v 441
glare v 420, 441
glaring adj 428, 446
glaringly adv 31
glass n 389
glasses n 445
glassy adj 255, 420
glaze v 255
gleam v 420; v 420
glee n 827
gleeful adj 836
glen n 252
glib adj 584
glide v 264, 267
glider n 273
gliding n 267
glimmer v 420, 422, 446
glimmering n 420
glimpse n 441
glint v 420
glisten v 420
glitter v 420
gloat over v 377
globe n 249, 318
globe-trotter n 268
globular adj 249
globularity n 249
globule n 249
gloom n 837
gloominess n 422
gloomy adj 421, 422, 837, 901a
glorified adj 981
glorified spirit n 977
glorify v 883, 990, 991
glory n 420, 981
gloss n 255, 522; v 522
glossary n 562
gloss over v 458, 477
glossy adj 255, 420
glow v 382, 420, 574; v 382
glower v 900
glowing adj 382, 434, 574, 824
glue v 46
gluey adj 352
glut n 869; v 641, 869
glutinosity n 352
glutinous adj 327, 352
glutted adj 869
glutton n 957
gluttonous adj 957
gluttony n 957
gnarled adj 256
gnash v 900
gnaw v 298, 378
gnome n 980
go v 264, 293, 302, 449
go about v 218
go adrift v 279
go after v 117, 281, 622
goal n 67, 620
go along with v 709
go amiss v 732

go around v 247, 311
go ashore v 342
go astray v 279, 495
go away v 293, 302
go back v 287
go back to v 104
go bad v 653, 659
gobble v 957
gobble up v 957
go before v 116, 280
go berserk v 173
go-between n 534, 631, 724
go beyond v 303
go boating v 267
go by v 109
go by the rules v 82
god n 976, 979
goddess n 979
godhead n 976
godless adj 989
godliness n 987
godly adj 976, 987
go down v 306, 659
go downhill v 659, 735
godsend n 618
go forth v 293
go for the bait v 547
goggle-eyed adj 443
goggle eyes n 443
goggles n 445
go half way v 628
go halves v 91; v 778
go hand in hand with v 178
go hard with v 732
going n 264
going back n 145
going hungry n 956
going on adj 53, 151
go into hysterics v 825
gold n 435, 439
golden adj 435, 734
golden dreams n 515
golden mean n 29, 628, 736
golden opportunity n 134
golden rule n 697
golden years n 128
go mad v 503, 825
gone adj 2, 122, 360
gone bad adj 397, 653
gone by adj 122, 124
gone to waste adj 638
good n 618
good adj 52, 394, 618, 648, 922, 931, 944, 977
good behavior n 894
goodbye n 293
good chance n 472
good fellowship n 892
good fortune n 618, 731
good head n 502
good health n 654
good luck n 618, 621, 731
goodly adj 31
good man n 948

good manners n 894
goodness n 648
goodness n 618, 829, 922, 944
goods n 780, 798
good samaritan n 906
good taste n 578, 850
good will n 602, 888
gooey adj 396
go off v 173
go on v 106, 143
go on forever v 104, 112
go on vacation v 687
go out v 142
go over v 218
go over again v 104
go over the same ground v 104
go pit-a-pat v 315
gore n 260
gorge n 198; v 641, 869, 957
gorged adj 869
gorgeous adj 428, 845
gorgeousness n 845
gormandizing n 957; adj 957
go round about v 629
gory adj 361, 653
go shopping v 795
go side by side v 120
gossamer n 205
gossamery adj 329
gossip n 455, 532, 588; v 588
gossipy adj 588
go straight v 246, 628
go the way of all flesh v 360
go through v 151, 302
go to v 278
go to bed v 687
go to press v 591
go to seed v 659
go to sleep v 687
go to the dogs v 162, 735, 804
go to the law v 969
go to waste v 659
go to wrack and ruin v 162
gouge n 262; v 252
go up v 305
govern v 693, 737
governess n 753
government n 693
governor n 694, 753
go wild v 173
gown n 999
go wrong v 732
grab v 379
grace n 242, 578, 845, 850, 918, 987
graceful adj 578, 845
gracefulness n 242, 578, 845
graceless adj 579

gracious *adj* 894
graciously *adv* 602
graciousness *n* 894
gradation *n* 26, 58, 69
grade *n* 26, 58, 71, 217, 305, 306
grade crossing *n* 219
gradual *adj* 26, 69, 275, 685
gradually *adv* 26, 69, 275
graduate *v* 60, 69
graduation *n* 60
graft *v* 184, 300
grain *n* 5, 256, 329, 330
graininess *n* 330
grammar *n* 567
grammar *n* 542
grammar book *n* 567
grammarian *n* 567
grammatical *adj* 567
grand *adj* 574, 642, 882
grandchildren *n* 167
grandeur *n* 875
grandfather *n* 130, 166
grandiloquence *n* 577
grandiloquent *adj* 577
grandiose *adj* 577
grandmother *n* 130, 166
grandsire *n* 130, 166
grant *n* 784; *v*=529, 760, 762, 783, 784
grantee *n* 785
granter *n* 784
granular *adj* 330
granularity *n* 330
granulate *v* 330
granulation *n* 330
granule *n* 32
graphic *adj* 518
grapple with *v* 719
grasp *v* 518
grass *n* 367
grassland *n* 344
grassy *adj* 435
grate *v* 330, 378, 410, 414
grateful *adj* 916
grater *n* 330
gratification *n* 827
gratify *v* 829, 831
grating *n* 219, 410;
  adj 410, 414
gratitude *n* 916
gratuity *n* 784
grave *n* 363; *v* 558;
  adj 642, 739, 830
grave clothes *n* 363
gravestone *n* 363
graveyard *n* 363
gravitate *v* 306, 319
gravitate toward *v* 176
gravitation *n* 319
gravitational *adj* 288
gravity *n* 319
gravity *n* 288, 574, 642, 739
gray *n* 432

gray *n* 422; *adj* 128, 422, 428, 429, 432
graybeard *n* 130
gray hairs *n* 128
grayish *adj* 432
grayness *n* 422, 432
graze *v* 199
graze over *v* 379
grazing over *n* 379
grease *n* 355, 356; *v* 255, 332, 355
greasiness *n* 355
greasing *n* 332
greasy *adj* 355
great *adj* 31, 192
greaten *v* 35
greater *adj* 33
greatest *adj* 33
greatly *adv* 31
greatness *n* 31
greatness *n* 33, 192, 873
great waters *n* 341
greed *n* 957
greediness *n* 957
greedy *adj* 789, 819, 957
green *n* 435
green *adj* 123, 127, 435, 674
greenbacks *n* 800
greenhorn *n* 547, 701
greenish *adj* 435
greenish blue *adj* 438
greenness *n* 123, 435
greens *n* 367
gregarious *adj* 892
gregariousness *n* 892
gridiron *n* 219
grief *n* 833
grievance *n* 830
grieve *v* 828, 839
grieve at *v* 833
grievous *adj* 649, 830
grievously *adv* 31
grill *v* 384
grille *n* 219
grim *adj* 830
grimace *v* 243
grime *n* 653
grimy *adj* 653
grin *n* 838; *v* 838
grind *v* 195, 253, 330, 331, 410, 539
grinder *n* 330
grinding *n* 410
grindstone *n* 330
grip *n* 378
gripe *n* 378; *v* 378
grist *n* 637
gristly *adj* 327
grit *n* 327, 330
gritty *adj* 330, 604
grizzled *adj* 432
grizzly *adj* 432
groan *n* 839; *v* 411
groove *n* 259, 613; *v* 259
grope in the dark *v* 442
gross *adj* 653, 846, 961

grossness *n* 961
grouch *v* 900
ground *n* 181, 211, 215, 342, 467, 615; *v* 215
grounded on *adj* 211
groundless *adj* 4
grounds *n* 342, 344, 467
groundswell *n* 315
groundwork *n* 60, 64, 153, 211, 673
group *n* 72, 372, 416, 417, 712; *v* 60, 72
groupings *n* 60
grove *n* 252
grovel *v* 207, 275
groveling *n* 886; *adj* 207, 435, 886
grow *v* 35, 144, 194, 282, 367, 734
grow dim *v* 422
grow from *v* 154
growing *adj* 35
grow into *v* 144
grow old *v* 131
grow up *adj* 131
grown up *adj* 907, 921; *v* 819
growth *n* 35, 144, 161, 194, 250, 282, 365
grow up *v* 131
grudge *n* 907, 921; *v* 819
grudgingly *adv* 603
gruesome *adj* 846
gruff *adj* 254, 410
grumble *v* 407, 411, 832
grumbling *n* 407
grumpy *adj* 901a
grunt *v* 412
guarantee *n* 768, 771;
  v 768, 771
guard *n* 717, 753; *v* 664, 670, 717
guard against *v* 717
guarded *adj* 459, 585, 864
guardian *n* 664, 753, 977
guardian angel *n* 977
guardianship *n* 717
guarding *n* 670
guerilla *n* 361
guess *n* 514; *v* 514
guesswork *n* 514
guffaw *n* 838
guidance *n* 537, 692, 693, 695
guide *n* 524, 527, 540, 694;
  v 537, 692, 693
guidebook *n* 527
guiding *adj* 693
guile *n* 544, 702
guileless *adj* 703, 946
guilelessness *n* 946
guiling *n* 545
guillotine *v* 361
guilt *n* 947
guilt *n* 649, 961
guiltiness *n* 947
guiltless *adj* 946
guiltlessness *n* 946, 960

guilty *adj* 947, 961
guilty verdict *n* 971
guise *n* 448
gulf *n* 343
gull *n* 198, 343
gull *n* 486, 547; *v* 545
gulley *n* 259
gullibility *n* 486
gullible *adj* 486, 547
gully *n* 350
gulosity *n* 957
gulp *v* 298
gulp down *v* 298
gum *n* 356a
gummy *adj* 327, 352, 356a
gun down *v* 361
gunshot *n* 197
gurgle *v* 348, 353, 408
gurgling *n* 353
guru *n* 994
gush *n* 295, 348; *v* 295, 348, 584
gush out *v* 295
gust *n* 349; *v* 349
gusto *n* 390
gut *v* 162
guts *n* 221, 861
gutsy *adj* 861
gutter *n* 259, 350
guttural *adj* 410
guzzle *v* 957, 959
gymnasium *n* 728
gypsy *n* 268
gyration *n* 312

H

habit *n* 613
habit *n* 5, 820
habitat *n* 189
habitation *n* 189
habitation *n* 189
habitual *adj* 82, 104, 136, 613
habitually *adv* 136, 613
habituate *v* 613
hack *v* 44
hackneyed *adj* 598
hack up *v* 201
Hades *n* 982
haggard *adj* 203, 688
haggle *v* 794
hagiography *n* 983
hagiological *adj* 983
hail *v* 586
hair *n* 205
hair's breadth *n* 197
hairy *adj* 256
halcyon *adj* 721
hale *adj* 654
half a dozen *n* 98
half a hundred *n* 98
half and half *adj* 27, 41
half measures *n* 628
half-moon *n* 245
half-starved *adj* 956
halfway *adj* 68; *adv* 68
half-witted *adj* 499

hallowed *adj* 976
halo *n* 420
halt *n* 142, 685, 687; *v* 142, 160, 265, 275
halve *v* 91
halved *adj* 91
halving *n* 91
hammer *v* 104
hammered instruments *n* 417
hamper *n* 706
hamstring *n* 158
hand *n* 236, 372, 590, 590, 631; *v* 784
handbook *n* 527, 593
handful *n* 25, 32
handicap *n* 706
hand in hand *adv* 88
handle *n* 564; *v* 379, 677
handling *n* 379
hand of death *n* 360
hand over *v* 270, 783
hands *n* 269
handsome *adj* 845
handwriting *n* 590
handy *adj* 197, 673, 698
hang *n* 214, 361
hang a turn *v* 140
hang back *v* 683
hang by a thread *v* 665
hanging *n* 361; *adj* 214
hanging down *n* 214
hang in there *v* 604a
hang it up *v* 624
hangman *n* 975
hang over *v* 152
hang together *v* 46, 178
hap *n* 156; *v* 156
haphazard *adj* 139, 156
haphazardness *n* 139
hapless *adj* 735
happen *v* 1, 151
happening *n* 8, 151; *adj* 151
happily *adv* 827
happiness *n* 618, 827
happy *adj* 23, 134, 827, 836
happy-go-lucky *adj* 674
harangue *n* 537, 582; *v* 582
harass *v* 830
harbinger *n* 64, 512, 534
hard *adj* 159, 323, 376, 397, 704, 739, 830
hard and fast law *n* 80
hard as a rock *adj* 323
hard as nails *adj* 323
hard by *adv* 197
hard cash *n* 800
hard coat *n* 388
harden *v* 48, 159, 321, 323, 613
hardening *n* 321, 385
hard-featured *adj* 846
hard-hearted *adj* 914a
hard-heartedness *n* 914a

hardihood *n* 861
hardiness *n* 159
hardly *adv* 32, 137
hardly ever *adv* 137
hardness *n* 323
hardness of hearing *n* 419
hardness of heart *n* 951
hard of hearing *adj* 419
hardship *n* 735
hard task *n* 704
hard times *n* 735
hard to please *adj* 868
hard up *adj* 804
hardy *adj* 159, 654
harlequin *n* 501
harlot *n* 962
harm *n* 619; *v* 619, 649, 659, 828, 923
harmful *adj* 619, 649, 657, 663
harmfulness *n* 649
harmless *adj* 158
harmonious *adj* 23, 242, 413, 416, 428, 714
harmoniousness *n* 413
harmonious sounds *n* 415
harmonize *v* 23, 82, 413
harmonize with *v* 714
harmony *n* 23, 58, 242, 413, 415, 709, 714, 721, 888
harness *v* 43, 225
harping *n* 104; *adj* 104
harp on *v* 104
harpy *n* 980
harrow *v* 371, 830
harsh *adj* 410, 414, 579, 739, 830, 955
harshness *n* 410, 414, 739
hart *n* 373
harvest *n* 154, 618, 775
harvest time *n* 126
hash *n* 59
haste *n* 684
haste *n* 132, 863; *v* 274, 684
hasten *v* 132, 274, 310, 682, 684
hastily *adv* 132
hasty *adj* 684, 863
hatch *n* 260; *v* 161, 558, 626
hatchet man *n* 936
hate *n* 898
hate *n* 907; *v* 867, 898
hateful *adj* 849, 830, 898, 907
hating *adj* 898
hatred *n* 867, 889, 898, 907
hatred of mankind *n* 911
haughtiness *n* 878, 885
haughty *adj* 878, 885
haul *v* 190; *v* 190, 285
hauling *n* 285
haunt *n* 74, 189

haunted *adj* 980
haunt one's thoughts
  v 505
have *v* 777
have a bad name *v* 874
have a bad smell *v* 401
have a defect *v* 651
have affection for *v* 897
have a hand in *v* 153, 682,
  709
have a knack for *v* 698
have an acquaintance
  with *v* 888
have an odor *v* 398
have a perfume *v* 400
have a say *v* 175
have a short memory
  v 506
have a soft spot in one's
  heart *v* 822
have a temper *v* 901
have a true ring *v* 494
have charge of *v* 693
have confidence in *v* 484
have done with *v* 678
have enough *v* 639
have faith *v* 987
have faith in *v* 484, 858
have free play *v* 170
have had its day *v* 124
have in common *v* 778
have in hand *v* 777
have input *v* 175
have in sight *v* 441
have in store for *v* 152
have its seat in *v* 183
have leisure *v* 685
have no bearing upon
  v 10
have no chance *v* 471
have no connection with
  v 10
have no curiosity *v* 456
have no heart for *v* 866
have no idea *v* 491
have no interest in *v* 823
have no limits *v* 104
have no motive *v* 615a
have no odor *v* 399
have no pity for *v* 914a
have no preference
  v 609a
have no relation to *v* 10
have no taste for *v* 867
have nothing to do with
  v 10
have occasion for *v* 630
have one's act together
  v 502
have one's head in the
  clouds *v* 827
have precedence *v* 62
have priority *v* 280
have pull *adj* 288
have qualms *v* 485
have recourse to *v* 677
have scope *v* 748

have seen its day *v* 124
have the advantage *v* 28
have the lead *v* 208
have the means *v* 632
have the right *v* 924
have the virtue of *v* 944
have to do with *v* 9
have too high an opinion
  of oneself *v* 889
have to oneself *v* 777
have two meanings *v* 520
have words with *v* 713
having a right to *adj* 924
having no right to
  adj 925
havoc *n* 162
hawk *v* 763, 796
hawk *n* 386
hawker *n* 797
hazard *n* 156, 665; *v* 621,
  665
hazard a suggestion
  v 514
hazardous *adj* 665
haze *n* 353, 422
hazel *adj* 433
haziness *n* 422, 426, 447,
  475
hazy *adj* 353, 422, 426
head *n* 66, 353, 372, 450,
  564, 694, 745; *v* 62, 66,
  280; *adj* 210
head for the hills *v* 623
heading *n* 64, 66, 75, 280,
  564
headland *n* 250
headlines *n* 532
headlong *adj* 684, 863
head of the column *n* 234
headquarters *n* 74
heads or tails *n* 156
headstone *n* 363
headstrong *adj* 606
headway *n* 282
heal *v* 660, 662
healing *n* 660
health *n* 654
health *n* 159
healthful *adj* 654, 656
healthfulness *n* 656
healthiness *n* 656
healthy *adj* 654, 656
heap *n* 31, 72, 192
hear *v* 418
hear a cause *v* 967
hearer *n* 418
hearing *n* 418
hearing *adj* 418
hearsay *n* 532
hearse *n* 363
heart *n* 5, 68, 208, 221,
  222, 372, 574, 820
heartfelt *adj* 821
hearth *n* 386
heartless *adj* 383
heartsick *adj* 837
hearty *adj* 654, 836

heat *n* 382
heat *v* 382, 384
heated *adj* 382, 384
heater *n* 386
heath *n* 344
heathen *n* 984, 989
heating *n* 384
heave *v* 276, 284, 307
heaven *n* 981
heavenly *adj* 318, 829,
  976, 981
heavenly bodies *n* 318
heavenly kingdom *n* 981
heavenly spirit *n* 977
heavens *n* 180, 318
heaviness *n* 202, 319, 837,
  843
heavy *n* 202; *adj* 172, 194,
  319, 683
heavy as lead *adj* 319
heavy heart *n* 837
heavy news *n* 830
hebetude *n* 499
heckle *v* 830
hedge *n* 232
hedge in *v* 229
hedonist *n* 954a
heed *v* 457, 459, 864;
  v 418, 457, 928
heedful *adj* 451, 457, 459,
  864
heedfulness *n* 864
heeding *n* 418; *adj* 928
heedless *adj* 460, 506, 863
heedlessness *n* 458, 460,
  863
heel *n* 211; *v* 279
he him *n* 373
height *n* 206
height *n* 26, 125, 210, 307
heighten *v* 35, 206, 307,
  549, 835
heightening *n* 835
heinous *adj* 846
heir *n* 167
heirs *n* 121, 167
helicopter *n* 273
hell *n* 982
hellish *adj* 978, 982
helmsman *n* 269, 694
help *n* 644, 662, 707, 746,
  784, 834; *v* 215, 644, 707,
  746, 784, 834
helper *n* 707, 711, 746, 977
helpful *adj* 644, 707, 888
helpfulness *n* 644, 910
helpless *adj* 158
helplessness *n* 158
help oneself to *v* 789
helter skelter *adv* 59
hem *n* 231; *v* 43, 231, 258
hem and haw *v* 149, 583
hemi- *adj* 91
hem in *v* 227
hemisphere *n* 181
hemorrhage *n* 299
hen *n* 374

hence *adv* 155
henceforth *adv* 121
henchman *n* 746
her *n* 374
herald *n* 64, 534; v 116, 280
herb *n* 367
herbaceous *adj* 367
herbage *n* 367
herbal *adj* 367, 369
Herculean *adj* 159
herculean *adj* 686
herculean task *n* 704
herd *n* 876; v 72
here *adv* 186
hereabouts *adv* 183
here below *adv* 318
hereditary *adj* 5, 154
heredity *n* 167
heresy *n* 984
heretic *n* 487, 984
heretical *adj* 984
heretofore *adv* 122
herewith *adv* 88, 632
heritage *n* 11, 121, 122
hermetically sealed *adj* 261
hermit *n* 893, 955
hero *n* 948
heroic *adj* 861
heroism *n* 861
hero worship *n* 991
hesitancy *n* 485, 605
hesitant *adj* 485, 583, 603, 605
hesitate *v* 475, 485, 583, 603, 605
hesitating *adj* 485
hesitation *n* 485, 583, 603, 605
heterodox *adj* 984
heterodoxy *n* 984
heterogeneity *n* 10, 16a, 29
heterogeneous *adj* 10, 15, 41, 81
hew *v* 44, 240, 557
hiatus *n* 198
hibernal *adj* 383
hidden *adj* 447, 526, 528, 533, 571
hidden meaning *n* 526
hide *n* 223; *v* 442, 447, 528, 862, 893
hideous *adj* 830, 846
hiding *n* 528, 893
hiding place *n* 189, 530, 666
hie *v* 264, 274
hierarchical *adj* 995
hierarchy *n* 995
hieroglyph *n* 561
high *adj* 206, 410, 838, 959

high birth *n* 875
high-born *adj* 875
high caliber *n* 33
higher *adj* 33
highest *adj* 210
high-flown *adj* 577
high living *n* 954
highly seasoned *adj* 392
high-minded *adj* 878
highmindedness *n* 875
high note *n* 409
high price *n* 814
high-principled *adj* 939
high relief *n* 250
high seas *n* 341
high sounding *adj* 577, 882
high spirits *n* 836
high-strung *adj* 825
high time *n* 134
hike *n* 266
hill *n* 217, 250, 305, 306
hinder *v* 179, 233, 261, 275, 647, 704, 706, 708, 751, 761
hindmost *adj* 235
hindquarters *n* 235
hindrance *n* 706
hindrance *n* 177, 179
hinge *n* 43, 153
hinge upon *v* 154
hint *n* 505, 527, 550; *v* 505, 527
hip *adj* 563
hire *n* 812; *v* 788
hirsute *adj* 256
hiss *n* 409, 412
hissing *n* 409; *adj* 409
historian *n* 553
historiographer *n* 553
history *n* 122, 551
histrionic *adj* 599
hit *n* 276
hitch *n* 706; *v* 43, 315
hither *adv* 278
hitherto *adv* 122
hit on *v* 612
hit the bottle *v* 959
hit the road *v* 264, 266
hit upon *v* 480a
hive *n* 189, 691
hoard *n* 636
hoard away *v* 636
hoarse *adj* 405, 410
hoarseness *n* 405
hoary *adj* 124, 432
hoax *n* 545
hobble *n* 706; *v* 275
hobgoblin *n* 980
hobo *n* 268
hocus-pocus *n* 993
hodgepodge *n* 59
hoe *n* 371
hog *n* 957; *v* 957
hoist *v* 307
hold *n* 215; *v* 46, 54, 142,

151, 215, 265, 484, 751, 777, 781, 873
hold a conversation *v* 588
hold a course for *v* 278
hold back *v* 616, 623, 636, 819
holder *n* 191, 779
hold fast *v* 781
hold forth *v* 537
hold in disrespect *v* 929
holding *n* 777, 781
holding back *n* 603
hold on *v* 143
hold one's tongue *v* 403, 585
hold out *v* 763
hold to *v* 602
hold up *v* 143, 215, 235, 707
hole *n* 182, 189, 260, 351, 530
hole puncher *n* 262
holiday *n* 685, 687
holiness *n* 987
hollier *v* 404, 411
hollow *n* 208, 252; *v* 208, 252; *adj* 4, 252, 880
hollowed out *adj* 252
hollowness *n* 4, 880
hollows *n* 221
holm *n* 346
holocaust *n* 361
holy *adj* 976, 987
homage *n* 743, 926, 928, 990
home *n* 189; *adj* 221
homeless *adj* 185
homeliness *n* 576, 846, 849
homely *adj* 576, 846, 849, 876
homespun *adj* 329, 576
homestead *n* 189
homework *n* 673
homey *adj* 576
homicidal *adj* 361
homicide *n* 361
homily *n* 537
homogeneity *n* 9, 16, 42
homogeneous *adj* 16, 42
honest *adj* 246, 543, 703, 922, 939, 946, 960
honesty *n* 543, 703, 939, 946, 960
honey *n* 899
honeyed *adj* 396
honey-mouthed *adj* 933
honor *n* 733, 873, 877, 922, 928, 990; *v* 883, 928, 931
honorable *adj* 246, 543, 772, 875, 878, 939
honored *adj* 873
honorific *adj* 883, 990
honoring *n* 990
hoodwink *v* 442, 545
hook *n* 245; *v* 43, 789
hooked *adj* 244, 245

hoop n 247; v 411
hoot v 411
hop n 309; v 309
hope n 858
hope n 507; v 858
hope for v 507, 858
hopeless n 182
hopeful adj 472, 858
hopeless adj 645, 704, 859
hopelessness n 859
hopelessness n 471, 645, 837
horde n 72
horizon n 196, 213
horizontal adj 213, 251, 308
horizontality n 213
horizontally adv 213
horrible adj 649, 830
horribly adv 31
horrid adj 649, 830
horrified adj 860
horrify v 830
horrifying adj 982
horror n 860, 867, 898
horror-stricken adj 860
horseback riding n 266
horseman n 268
horsemanship n 266
horse-shoe n 645
horsewoman n 268
horticultural adj 369
horticulture n 371
hose n 348, 350
hospitable adj 816, 892
hospitality n 816
host n 72, 102
hostile adj 14, 24, 383, 708, 889, 907
hostilities n 173, 722
hostility n 708, 889
hot adj 382, 392, 434, 824
hot air n 517
hotchpotch n 41
hotheaded adj 825
hotness n 383
hot pink adj 434
hot-tempered adj 901
hourly adv 136
house n 184, 664
housebreak v 370
house-breaker n 792
housebroken adj 370
house of correction n 975
house of god n 1000
housing n 189
hover v 152, 206, 305
hover about v 264
hover around v 264
how adv 627
howbeit adv 30
however adv 30
howl n 411, 839; v 411, 412
howling n 412
hub n 222
hubbub n 315, 404, 411
huckster n 797
huddle n 72

hue n 428
hue and cry n 411, 669
hueless adj n
hug n 902; v 46
huge adj 31, 192, 206
hulky adj 192
hulky adj 192
hullabaloo n 411
hum n 405; v 405, 407, 412
human adj 372
human being n 372
human community n 372
humane adj 906
humaneness n 910
humanitarian n 910; adj 372, 910
humanitarianism n 910
humanities n 560
humanity n 372, 906
humankind n 372
human race n 372
human species n 372
humble adj 34, 725, 879, 881, 987
humbleness n 879
humbly adv 881
humbug n 548
humdrum adj 275, 598, 841
humid adj 337, 339
humidity n 339
humiliate v 879
humility n 879
humility n 881, 987
hummocky adj 250
humor n 5, 176, 602, 608, 820, 842; v 707, 760
humorist n 844
humorous adj 842
hump n 250
hunch n 250, 477
hundred n 98
hunger n 865
hungry adj 865, 956
hunt v 361
hunting n 361
hurdle n 309
hurl v 284
hurly-burly n 315
hurrah n 838
hurricane n 349
hurried adj 684, 825
hurry n 684; v 132, 274, 310, 684
hurt n 378, 619; v 378, 619, 649, 659, 828, 830
hurtful adj 619, 649, 830
hurtfulness n 649
hurtle v 276, 309
hurtle over v 309
husband n 903; v 636, 670, 817
husbandry n 371, 817
hush n 403; v 174, 265, 403
hushed adj 403
husky adj 405

hussy n 962
hustle n 682; v 276, 315, 682
hybrid n 41; adj 41
hydrous adj 337
hygienic adj 656
hyperbola n 245
hyperbole n 549
hyperbolic adj 549
hypercritical adj 868
hypercriticism n 868
hypertension n 315
hypocrisy n 988
hypocrite n 548, 988
hypocritical adj 544
hypothesis n 514
hypothetical adj 514
hysterical adj 173, 824, 825

I

ice v 385
ice box n 387
ice chest n 387
ice house n 387
iciness n 383
icing n 385
icon n 991
iconoclasm n 984
iconoclast n 165
iconoclastic adj 984
icthyology n 368
icy adj 383
idea n 453
idea n 451, 515, 516
ideal n 650; adj 2, 515, 977
ideality n 515
idealize v 515
ideational adj 453
ide'e fixe n 606
identical adj 13, 17
identically adv 13
identity n 13
identity n 17, 27
idiocy n 499
idiom n 521, 566
idiomatic adj 79, 521
idiosyncracy n 820
idiosyncrasies n 5
idiosyncrasy n 79, 83, 176
idiosyncratic adj 5
idiot n 493, 501, 501
idiotic adj 499
idle v 683; adj 661, 683
idleness n 681, 683
idler n 683
idle talk n 588
idol n 897, 899, 990
idolatrize v 991
idolatrous adj 991
idolatrousness n 991
idolatry n 991
idolatry n 897, 990
idolism n 991
idolization n 991
idolize v 897, 990, 991
idolizing n 990

idol-worship n 991
idol-worshiping adj 991
if adv 8
iffy adj 156
if it so happen adv 8
if so adv 8
if worst comes to worst
   adv 735
ignite v 384
ignoble adj 207, 851, 876
ignominious adj 874
ignominy n 874
ignoramus n 493
ignoramus n 501
ignorance n 491
ignorance n 442
ignorant adj 435, 442, 491
ignore v 460, 773
ill n 819; adj 649, 655
ill-advised adj 499
ill-behaved adj 895
ill-bred adj 851, 895
ill-breeding n 851, 895
ill-conceived adj 499
illegal adj 964
illegality n 964
illegitimacy n 925, 964
illegitimate adj 925, 964
ill-fashioned adj 243
ill-flavored adj 395
ill health n 655
ill-humored adj 901a
illiberal adj 32, 943
illiberality n 819, 943
illicit adj 964
illicitness n 964
illiteracy n 491
illiterate n 493; adj 491
ill-judged adj 499
ill-judging adj 481
ill-made adj 243
ill-mannered adj 851, 895
ill-natured adj 907
illness n 655
illogical adj 47, 477
illogically adv 477
ill-proportioned adj 243
ill-qualified adj 699
ill repute n 874
ill-tempered adj 945
ill-timed adj 135
ill treat v 739
ill-treatment n 649
illuminate v 420, 423, 428
illumination n 420
illumine v 420
ill-use v 649
illusion n 4, 443, 515, 545
illusory adj 4, 515, 545
illustrate v 82, 554
illustration n 82, 554
illustrative adj 82, 518,
   554
illustrious adj 883
ill will n 889, 907
ill wind n 649

image n 17, 21, 448, 521,
   556, 991; v 521
imagery n 521, 554
imaginable adj 470, 515
imaginary adj 4, 979
imagination n 515
imaginative adj 2, 515
imaginativeness n 515
imaginative writing
   n 598
imagine v 515
imagined adj 515
imagistic adj 521
imbecile n 493, 501;
   adj 499
imbecilic adj 499
imbecility n 499
imbecility n 450a, 497,
   499
imbibe v 296, 959
imbibition n 298
imbue v 41, 300, 537
imitate v 19, 680, 788
imitation n 19
imitation n 21, 554, 556;
   adj 19
imitative adj 17, 19, 554
immaculate adj 650, 652,
   946, 960
immaterial adj 4, 317, 643
immateriality n 317
immateriality n 643
immature adj 53, 123,
   127, 435, 651, 674
immaturity n 53, 123, 651
immeasurability n 105
immeasurably adv 31
immediate adj 132
immediately adv 113, 132
immemorial adj 124
immense adj 31, 104, 192
immensity n 31, 192
immerse v 300, 310, 337
immersed in adj 229
immersion n 300, 310
immigrant n 268
immigrate v 266
immigration n 266
imminent adj 152, 286
immobile adj 172
immobility n 141, 150,
   172, 265
immobilize v 265
immoderately adv 31
immodest adj 961
immodesty n 961
immoral adj 923, 940, 945
immorality n 923, 940,
   945
immortal adj 112
immortalize v 112
immovability n 141, 150,
   606
immovable adj 150, 606

immune adj 748, 927a
immune from adj 777a
immunity n 748, 777a,
   927a, 970
immutability n 141, 150
immutable adj 110, 150
imp n 980
impact n 276, 379
impair v 659, 848
impairment n 638, 659
impale v 260
impart v 784
impartial adj 246, 628,
   942
impartiality n 942
impart to v 527
impassable adj 261
impasse n 151
impassioned adj 383
impassioned adj 574, 821,
   825, 991
impassive adj 456, 823
impassivity n 823, 826
impatience n 825
impatient adj 825, 841
impeach v 938, 969
impeachment n 938
impeccability n 650
impeccable adj 650, 946
impecunious adj 804
impede v 179, 275, 706
impediment n 177, 706
impeding n 706
impel v 175, 264, 276, 284,
   744
impend v 121, 152, 909
impending adj 121, 152,
   286, 507, 909
impenetrability n 321,
   571
impenetrable adj 261,
   321, 323, 519, 571
impenetrable to light
   adj 426
impenitence n 951
impenitent adj 951
imperative adj 737, 926
imperceptibility n 447
imperceptible adj 193,
   447
imperceptibly adv 32
imperfect adj 34, 53, 304,
   640, 651, 658, 848, 961
imperfection n 651
imperfection n 28, 34, 53,
   304, 640, 945, 961
imperfectly adv 32
imperil v 665
imperishable adj 112
impermanence n 111
impermanent adj 111
impermeability n 321
impermeable adj 261, 321
impersonate v 19
impersonation n 19, 599
impertinence n 885, 929
impertinent adj 885, 929
imperturbability n 826

imperturbable n 823; adj 383, 826

impervious adj 261

impervious to light adj 426

impetuosity n 173, 825, 863

impetuous adj 173, 825, 863

impetus n 276, 284

impiety n 988

impiety n 989

impish adj 980

implacable adj 914a, 919

implant v 300

implantation n 300

implanted adj 5

implausibility n 473

implausible adj 473

implement n 633

implicit adj 526

implied adj 526

implore v 765

implosion n 276

imply v 467, 472, 516

impolite adj 895, 929

impoliteness n 929

import n 516, 642; v 296, 516, 642

importance n 642

importance n 31, 62, 175

important adj 31, 33, 175, 642

importation n 296, 300

importunate adj 765

importune v 765

impose v 741

imposing adj 642, 875, 878

impossibility n 471

impossible adj 471, 704

imposter n 548

imposture n 545

impotence n 158

impotence n 160, 169, 175a

impotent adj 158, 160, 175a

impractical adj 471, 647, 704

impracticality n 471, 647

imprecate v 908

imprecation n 908

impregnability n 664

impregnable adj 159, 664

impregnate v 168, 300

impress v 175, 375, 824

impressibility n 375, 822

impressible adj 324

impression n 375, 453, 591, 821

impressionable adj 822

impressive adj 574, 642

imprint n 569

imprison v 229

imprisoned adj 229, 751

improbability n 473

improbable adj 473

improbity n 940

impromptu adj 612; adv 612

improper adj 499, 568, 647, 923, 945

improper time n 135

impropriety n 568, 579, 647, 925

improve v 282, 648, 658

improved adj 658

improvement n 658

improvement n 282, 618

improvidence n 674

improvident adj 674, 818

improving adj 658

improvisation n 612

improvise v 416, 612, 674

imprudence n 863

imprudent adj 452, 460, 863

impudence n 885, 895, 929

impudent adj 885, 929

impugn v 716

impulse n 276, 612

impulse n 284, 601, 615, 744

impulsion n 284

impulsive adj 149, 612, 825, 863

impulsively adv 612

impulsiveness n 863

impunity n 777a, 927a, 970

impure adj 653, 961

impurity n 961

impurity n 653

imputation n 155, 938

imputative adj 938

impute v 938

impute to v 155

in a bad way adj 659, 735

in abeyance adv 172

inability n 158, 699

in a body adv 50

inabstinence n 954

inaccessible adj 196

in accord adj 714

in accordance with adj 23; adv 82

inaccuracy n 544

inaccurate adj 495, 568, 923

in a column adv 69

inaction n 681

inaction n 623, 683; adj 170, 680

inactive adj 172, 265, 681, 683

inactivity n 681

inactivity n 172, 681

in addition adv 37

inadequacy n 28, 34, 640, 645, 651

inadequate adj 28, 158, 640, 651

inadmissible adj 55

in advance adv 62, 234, 280

in adverse circumstances adj 735

in a fair way to adj 176

in a great measure adv 31

in a jiffy adv 113

in a line adv 69

in all aspects adv 52

in all creation adv 318

in all likelihood adv 472

in all probability adv 472

in a moment adv 113

in and out adv 248, 314

inane adj 497

inanimate adj 358

inanimate matter n 358

inanity n 4, 450a, 497, 517

in anticipation adv 132

inapplicable adj 10

inappreciable adj 32

inappropriateness n 647

inapt adj 699

inaptitude n 645

in a roundabout way adv 629

in arrear adj 806

inarticulate adj 583

inarticulateness n 583

inattention n 458

inattention n 452, 460, 866

inattentive adj 419, 452, 458, 460, 823, 866

inattentiveness n 458

inaudibility n 405, 419

inaudible adj 405

inaugural adj 66

inaugurate v 66

inauguration n 66

inauspicious adj 135, 909

in bad health adj 655

in bad taste adj 851

inbeing n 5

in black and white adj 531, 590

inborn adj 5, 221, 820

inbound adj 294

inbred adj 5

in broad daylight adv 525

incalculable adj 104

incalculably adv 31

incandescent adj 382

incantation n 993

incantory n 992

incapability n 158

incapable adj 158

incapacitate v 158

incapacitated adj 158

incapacity n 158, 499

incarcerate v 972

incarceration n 974

incase v 229; adv 8

in celebration adv 883

incendiary adj 162

informality n 83
informant n 527, 534
information n 527
information n 467, 490, 496, 532
informed adj 527
informer n 527, 532, 938
infraction n 83, 303, 742, 773, 927
infrequency n 137
infrequency n 103
infrequent adj 103, 137
infrequently adv 137
infringe v 303, 742, 773
infringement n 303
infringement n 83, 742, 773
in front adv 234, 280
in front of one's nose adj 446
in full sight adj 446
in full view adj 446
infuriate v 173
infuse v 41, 300, 537
infusion n 41, 300
in future adv 121
ingathering n 72
ingenious adj 698, 702
ingenuity n 698
ingenuous adj 703, 946
ingenuousness n 946
ingest v 296, 539
ingestion n 296, 298
in good taste adj 850
in good time adv 152
ingraft v 300
ingrained adj 5, 221, 820
ingrate n 917
ingratitude n 917
ingratitude n 917
ingredient n 51, 56, 211
ingress v 294
ingress n 302
inhabit v 184, 186, 188, 189
inhabitant n 188
inhabiting adj 186
inhale v 398
in hand adj 777
inharmonious adj 24, 414
inharmoniousness n 414
in harmony with adj 23
in harness adj 749
in health adj 654
inherence n 5
inherent adj 5, 221
inherited adj 5
in hiding adj 528
in high esteem adj 931
in honor of adv 883
inhumation n 363
inimical adj 708, 889
inimitable adj 20, 33, 648, 650
iniquitous adj 923, 945
iniquity n 923, 945
initial adj 66
initiate v 66, 296

initiation n 66, 296
initiative n 66
in its infancy adv 66
in its own sweet time adv 152
in its turn adv 58
inject v 300
injection n 296, 300
injudicious adj 499
injunction n 630, 695, 741, 761, 864
injure v 848
injure v 619, 649, 659, 828, 923
injured adj 659, 848
injurious adj 619, 649
injury n 173, 619, 649, 659, 665, 776
injustice n 173, 923
ink n 431
in keeping with adj 23; adv 82
inkling n 514, 527
inky adj 431
inlaid adj 221, 440
inlands n 342
inlay v 440
in league adj 709
in lieu of adv 147
inmate n 188
in moderation adv 174
inmost adj 221
in motion adj 264
in mourning adj 839
innate adj 5, 221
inner adj 221
inner coating n 224
inner man n 820
innermost adj 221
innermost recesses n 221
in part n 221
innocence n 946
innocence n 703, 944, 960
innocent adj 435, 703, 946, 960
in no respect adv 32
in no time adv 113
innovate v 140
innovation n 20a, 123, 140
innovative adj 140
innuendo n 527
in obedience to adv 743
inoculate v 300
inoculation n 300
inodorousness n 399
in one's birthday suit adj 226
in one's debt adj 916
in operation adj 170, 680
inoperative adj 158, 645
inopportune adj 135, 647
in opposition adj 708
in order adj 58; adv 58
inordinate adj 31, 641, 954

inordinately adv 31
inordinateness n 954
inorganic adj 358
inorganic matter n 358
in part adv 32, 51
in particular adv 79
in perfect condition adj 650
in place of adv 147
in plain English adv 576, 703
in plain sight adv 525
in plain terms adv 576
in play adj 170
in poor health adj 655
in possession of adj 777
in preparation adj 53
in presence of adv 186
in print adj 531, 532
in prison adj 754
in private adv 528
in progress adj 53
in prospect adj 121, 152, 620
in proximity adj 186
in pursuit of adj 622
input n 175
in question adv 454
in quest of adj 622
inquietude n 828
inquire v 461
inquirer n 461
inquiring n 461; adj 455, 461
inquiring mind n 455
inquiry n 461
inquiry n 539
inquisitive adj 455, 461
inquisitiveness n 455
inquisitor n 461, 739
inquisitorial adj 461, 739, 965
in rapport adj 413
in readiness adj 507
in reality adv 1
in relief adj 250
in reserve adj 636
in retaliation adv 718
inroad n 294
in rotation adv 138
insalubrious adj 657
insalubrity n 657
insane adj 173, 503
insanity n 503
inscrutable adj 519
in secret adv 528; adv 528
insect n 366
insecure adj 475, 665
insecurity n 475, 665
insensate adj 499
insensibility n 376, 823
insensibility n 866
insensible adj 376, 381, 506
insensitive adj 376, 823, 866
insensitiveness n 823, 866

intermediary n 534, 631;
adj 631
intermediate adj 29, 68,
631
intermedium n 631
interment n 363
interminable adj 104, 112,
200
intermission n 70, 106
intermittence n 138
intermittent adj 70, 138
intermittently adv 138
intern v 221
internal adj 5, 221
internally adv 221
interpenetrate v 228
interpenetration n 228
interpolate v 41, 228
interpolation n 41, 228,
300
interpose v 70, 228, 724
interposition n 37, 228,
724
interpret v 462, 522, 537
interpretable adj 522
interpretation n 522
interpretation n 155, 516
interpretative adj 522
interpreter n 524
interpreter n 513
interpretive adj 522
interregnum n 106, 142,
198
interrogate v 461
interrogation n 461
interrogative adj 461
interrupt v 70, 142, 198,
706
interrupted adj 70
interruption n 61, 70, 142,
198, 706
intersect v 219
intersection n 219
interspace n 198, 221
intersperse v 228
interspersion n 228
interstice n 198
intertwine v 41, 43, 219
intertwined adj 219
interval n 198
interval n 53, 70, 106, 196
intervene v 70, 198, 228,
631, 724
intervening adj 228
intervention n 228, 631,
724
interview n 588
interweave v 41, 43, 219
in the altogether adj 226
in the background
adv 235
in the blood adj 5
in the bud adj 66
in the buff adj 226
in the cards adj 152
in the course of adv 106

in the course of things
adv 151
in the event of adv 8
in the face of adv 715
in the first place adv 68
in the foreground adv 234
in the fourth place
adv 96
in the genes adj 5
in the headlines adj 532
in the interim adv 106
in the lead adv 234
in the long run adv 29,
152
in the main adv 50
in the matter of adv 9
in the meantime adv 106
in the middle adv 68
in the midst of adv 41
in the news adj 532
in the nick of time
adv 134
in the open air adv 338
in the open market
adj 763
in the rear adv 235, 281
in the same category
adj 9
in the thick of adv 228
in the third place adv 93
in the vanguard adv 280
in the wide open spaces
adv 338
in the wind adv 152
intimacy n 888
intimate n 890; v 527;
adj 197, 221, 888
intimately adv 43
in time adv 109, 152
intimidate v 909
intimidating adj 909
intimidation n 909
intolerable adj 830
intolerance n 606, 825
intolerant adj 606, 825
intonation n 402, 580
intone v 580
in top shape adj 654
in touch with adj 592
in tow adj 285
intoxicate v 824
intoxicated adj 959
intoxication n 824, 959
intractability n 606
intractable adj 606, 704
in trade adj 794
intrepid adj 861
intrepidity n 861
intricate adj 248, 704
intrigue n 626, 702; v 702
intriguer 626
intrinsic adj 5, 221
intrinsicality n 5
intrinsically adv 5
in triumph adv 731
introduce v 62, 228, 280,
296, 300

introduction n 64, 66, 296,
300
introductory adj 62, 64,
66, 116
intrude v 135, 228, 294
intrusion n 57, 135, 228,
294
intrusive adj 228, 706
intuit v 477
intuition n 477
intuition n 477
intuitive adj 477
intuitively adv 477
in turn adv 58, 138
intwine v 219
in two shakes (of a
lamb's tail) adv 113
inundate v 337, 348, 641
inundation n 348
in unison adj 413
inure v 613
inutile adj 645
inutility n 645
invade v 294, 716
invader n 718
in vain adv 732
invalidate v 158, 479, 536,
756
invalidation n 479, 536,
756
invaluable adj 648
invariability n 16, 141
invariable adj 5, 16, 110,
141, 150
invariably adv 16, 82
in various places adv 182
invasion n 294, 716
invent v 515, 698
invented adj 546
invention n 515, 546, 698
inventive adj 515, 698
inventiveness n 168, 698
inventor n 164
inventory n 86, 596, 811;
v 596
inverse n 237; adj 218,
237
inversely adv 218
inversion n 218
inversion n 14, 140, 145
invert v 14, 61, 218
inverted adj 59, 218
invest v 157, 755, 784
invested adj 225
investigate v 461
investigation n 461, 463,
595
investigator n 461
inveterate n 784
investment n 787
inveterate adj 124
invidious adj 830, 898
in view adj 507, 620
invigorate v 159, 171
invigorating adj 171, 656
invigoration n 159
invincible adj 159

judicious adj 174, 480, 498, 868, 967
judiciousness n 174, 868
juice v 354
juiced adj 959
juiceless adj 340
juicer n 959
juicy adj 333, 337, 339
jumble n 41, 59; v 41, 59, 61
jumbo jet n 273
jump n 305, 309; v 309, 310
junction n 43
junction n 41, 45, 48
juncture n 8, 43, 134
jungle n 59
junior adj 127
juridical adj 967
jurisdiction n 965
jurisdiction n 737
jurisdictive adj 965, 967
jurist n 967
juristic adj 967
juror n 967
just adj 246, 922
just as adv 17
just do v 639
just in time adv 134
justice n 922, 967
justification n 717, 737, 937
justified adj 937
justify v 717, 737, 937
just in time adv 134
justly adv 922
just now adv 123
jut out v 250
juvenile adj 127
juvenility n 123, 127
juxtapose v 464

K

kaleidoscope n 445
kaleidoscopic adj 440
kaput adj 503
karma n 152
keen adj 171, 253, 375, 868
keen blast n 349
keenness n 868
keep n 298; v 141, 143, 670, 751, 781, 883
keep accounts v 811
keep alive v 359
keep an account with v 805
keep apart v 44
keep away v 187
keep back v 678
keep clear of v 623
keep cold v 385
keep company with v 888
keep down v 751
keeper n 753
keep going v 143
keep hold v 150
keeping n 781

keeping out n 55
keeping secret n 528
keep in mind v 505
keep moving v 264, 682
keep on v 136, 143, 604a
keep on one's toes v 264
keep out v 55
keep out of sight v 528
keep pace with v 27, 120, 178
keep quiet v 265, 403, 585
keep safe v 717
keepsake n 505
keep secret v 528
keep silence v 585
keep the memory alive v 505
keep the peace v 721
keep up v 141, 143, 670
Kelly green adj 435
kelpie n 979
kempt adj 652
ken n 441
kernel n 68, 222
kerosene n 356, 388
kerosene lamp n 423
ketch n 273
key n 346, 428
keyhole n 260
khaki n 433; adj 433
kick n 276
kick up a row v 173
kid n 129
kill v 361
killer n 165
killing n 361
killing time n 681
kill time v 106, 683
kiln n 386
kind n 75, 569; adj 888, 906
kind-hearted adj 888, 906
kindheartedness n 906
kindle v 153, 171, 173, 384, 420, 824
kindliness n 897, 906
kindling n 388
kindly adj 888, 906
kindness n 897, 906
kindred n 11; adj 11
kinfolk n 11
kingdom of god n 981
kingdom of heaven n 981
kinsman n 11
kiss n 902
kith and kin n 11
knack n 698
knave n 941
knead v 324, 379
kneading n 379
knee n 244
knee-deep adj 209
kneel v 308, 886, 990
knell n 363
knife n 262
knife edge n 253
knit v 43, 259

knob n 249, 250
knock n 276; v 276, 406
knock down v 213
knot n 219, 321; v 219
knotted adj 59
know v 474, 484, 490, 527, 888
know how n 632
knowing adj 490
knowingly adv 620
knowledge n 490
knowledge n 498, 527, 698
knowledgeable adj 490, 698
known adj 490
know no bounds v 104
know-nothing n 493; v 491
knuckle n 244
kobold n 980
kohl-black adj 431
Koran n 986

L

label n 564; v 550, 564
labor n 680, 686, 704; v 680, 686
laboratory n 691
labored adj 579
laborer n 746
laborious adj 686, 704
laboriousness n 682
labyrinth n 59, 248
labyrinthine adj 248
lace n 219; v 43
lack n 804; v 34, 53, 304, 640, 804
lackadaisical adj 683
lack faith v 989
lack of adornment n 849
lack of affectation n 849
lack of bias n 942
lack of connection n 10
lack of decorum n 851
lack of discernment n 465a
lack of feeling n 376, 381
lack of interest n 456
lack of originality n 843
lack of practice n 614
lack of readiness n 603
lack of uniformity n 16a
laconic adj 572
lacquer n 356a; v 356a
lad n 129
ladle n 190
lade v 270
lading n 190
ladle v 270
lady n 374, 875
ladylove n 897
lag v 275, 281, 683
laggard n 683; adj 603, 683
lagoon n 343

laical *adj* 997
laid low *adj* 160
laid up *adj* 655
laim *v* 158
lair *n* 189
laity *n* 997
lake *n* 343
lake *n* 343
lamb *n* 129
lame *n* 53, 160, 651, 655
lame excuse *n* 617
lament *n* 411, 839; *v* 411,
  833, 839, 915
lamentable *adj* 649, 830,
  833, 839
lamentably *adv* 31
lamentation *n* 839
lamentation *n* 833, 915
lamenting *adj* 839
lamp *n* 423
lampoon *v* 856
lampooner *n* 844
lance *v* 260
lancet *n* 262
land *n* 342
land *n* 780; *v* 292, 342
landed *adj* 342
landing *n* 292
lands *n* 342
landscape *n* 448; *v* 371
landscaping *n* 371
language *n* 560
languid *adj* 160, 172, 275,
  405, 575, 683, 685
languish *v* 36, 160, 655,
  683
languor *n* 160, 172, 275,
  683, 688
lankness *n* 203
lanky *adj* 200, 203
lantern *n* 423
lap *n* 221, 311
lap of luxury *n* 377
lapse *n* 661, 776; *v* 109,
  122, 144, 659, 661
lapsed *adj* 122
lard *n* 356
large *adj* 31, 192, 202
largeness *n* 192
larger *adj* 194
largesse *n* 784
largesse *n* 784
lash *n* 975; *v* 43, 173, 972
lass *n* 129
lassitude *n* 688, 841
last *v* 1, 106, 110, 141,
  604a; *adj* 67, 122
last breath *n* 360
last forever *v* 112
lasting *adj* 106, 110, 141,
  150
lastingness *n* 110
last resort *n* 666
last stage *n* 67
last word *n* 67
late *adj* 122, 123, 133, 275,
  360; *adv* 133
lately *adv* 122, 123

latency *n* 526
latency *n* 172, 447
lateness *n* 133
latent *adj* 172, 526
latentness *n* 526
later *adj* 117; *adv* 117
lateral *adj* 236
laterality *n* 236
laterally *adv* 236
lather *n* 353; *v* 332, 353
lathering *n* 332
latitude *n* 180, 181, 202,
  748
latitude and longitude
  n 183
latter *adj* 122
lattice *n* 219
laud *v* 883, 990
laudatory *adj* 931
laugh *v* 838
laughable *adj* 853
laughing *adj* 838
laughing-stock *n* 857
laughingstock *n* 547
laughter *n* 838
launch *v* 273; *v* 66, 284
launch into *v* 676
launder *v* 652
laundress *n* 597
laureate *n* 597
laurel *n* 733
lavation *n* 652
lavender *adj* 437
lavish *v* 641, 784, 818;
  adj 641, 818
lavishness *n* 818
law *n* 80, 697, 963
lawful *adj* 246, 760, 922,
  963
lawfully *adv* 922
lawfulness *n* 922, 963
lawless *adj* 964
lawlessness *n* 964
lawsuit *n* 969
lawyer *n* 968
lax *adj* 47, 738, 773
laxative *n* 662
laxity *n* 738
laxity *n* 47, 495, 748, 773,
  989
laxness *n* 738, 773
lay *n* 413; *v* 184; *adj* 997
lay aside *v* 55
lay away *v* 636
lay bare *v* 260
lay claim to *v* 741
layer *n* 204
layer *v* 204
layered *adj* 204
lay groundwork *v* 626
lay in *v* 637
lay in a stock *v* 637
lay in a store *v* 637
lay in the grave *v* 363
lay in the ground *v* 363
lay it on thick *v* 933
layman *n* 997

lay oneself open to *v* 177,
  665
lay on thick *v* 641
lay open *v* 226, 260, 529
lay out *v* 363, 809
lay over *v* 133
lay siege *v* 716
lay stress on *v* 642
lay the foundations *v* 673
lay the groundwork *v* 60
lay to rest *v* 363
lay up *v* 678
lay waste *v* 162
laziness *n* 683
lazy *adj* 275, 683
lazy eye *n* 443
lead *n* 234; *v* 116, 176,
  615, 692, 693
lead estray *v* 545
leaden *adj* 422
leader *n* 64, 694, 745
leadership *n* 692, 693
leading *n* 280; *adj* 66
lead the way *v* 62, 66, 280
leaf *n* 204
leafage *n* 367
league *n* 712
leak *n* 198; *v* 295
leakage *n* 295
lean *v* 176, 217; *adj* 203
leaning *n* 176, 217, 602;
  adj 176
leanness *n* 203
lean on *v* 858
lean to *v* 602
leap *n* 309
leap *n* 305, 310; *v* 309, 310
leaping *adj* 309
leap with joy *v* 838
learn *v* 490, 527, 539
learn by heart *v* 505
learned *adj* 490, 498, 539
learned in the law
  adj 968
learner *n* 541
learner *n* 492
learning *n* 539
learning *n* 490, 498, 537
learn of *v* 480a
lease *n* 783; *v* 787, 788
leash *v* 43
leave *n* 760; *v* 44, 185, 293,
  302, 624, 782, 784
leave alone *v* 623
leaven *n* 320; *v* 320
leave no trace *v* 449, 552
leave off *v* 142, 678
leave out *v* 55
leaves *n* 367
leave-taking *n* 287, 293
leave undone *v* 730
leave unfinished *v* 730
leaving *n* 624
leavings *n* 40
lecher *n* 962
lecherous *adj* 961
lechery *n* 961

lecture n 537, 582; v 537, 582, 586
lecturer n 540
ledge n 215, 250
ledger n 86, 551, 811
lee 236
leer n 441; v 441
lee side n 236
leeway n 180
left n 238
left adj 40, 449, 782
left behind adj 782
left hand n 239
left-handed adj 239
leftover n 40; adj 40
left side n 239
legacy n 784
legal adj 760, 963, 967
legal action n 969
legal adviser n 968
legality n 963
legalize v 737, 963
legalized adj 760, 963
legal proceedings n 969
legal process n 969
legal profession n 968
legal separation n 905
legatee n 785
legation n 755
legislate v 693, 963
legislated adj 963
legitimacy n 963
legitimate adj 494, 760, 922, 963
legitimateness n 963
leguminous adj 367
leisure n 685
leisure adj 685
leisureliness n 275
leisurely adj 275, 685; adv 133, 275
lemon adj 435
lend v 787
lend an ear v 418
lender n 805
lending n 787
lend on security v 787
length n 200
lengthen v 110, 133, 200
lengthened adj 200
lengthiness n 200
lengthwise adv 200
lengthy adj 200, 573
lenience n 740
lenience n 174, 738
leniency n 740
lenient adj 174, 738, 740
lenity n 174
lens n 443, 445
leprechaun n 980
leprous adj 655
less adj 34; adv 34, 38
lessee n 779
lessen v 36, 174, 195, 834
lessening n 36, 195
lesser adj 34
lesson n 537, 668

let v 760, 782, 787
let alone v 678, 681, 730
let down v 308, 509
let down v 308, 509
let drop v 308, 529
let fall v 308, 527
let fly v 284
let go v 624, 782, 790
lethal adj 182, 360, 361
lethargic adj 683
lethargy n 683
let in partial light v 427
let out v 750
let slip v 529, 730, 776
let the opportunity slip
by v 135
let things take their
course v 681
levee n 72
level n 28, 27, 213, 251;
v 16, 27, 162, 213, 251,
255, 308; adj 16, 27, 207,
213, 251, 255
level at v 278
level-headed adj 502
level with v 543
leverage n 175
leviathan n 192
levity n 320
lewd adj 961
lewdness n 961
lexicography n 562
lexicon n 562
liability n 177
liability n 665, 806
liable adj 176, 177, 665,
806
liar n 548
liberal adj 784, 816, 906,
942
liberality n 816
liberality n 784, 906, 942
liberate v 44, 672, 748,
750, 970
liberated adj 750
liberation n 750
liberation n 871, 672
libertarian adj 760
libertine n 962
libertine n 954a
liberty n 685, 737, 748,
760, 780
librarian n 593
libretto n 593
licence n 738
license n 748, 760, 924;
v 760
licensed adj 924
licit adj 246, 963
lick the boots of v 886
lid n 223, 261, 263

lie n 544, 546; v 183, 213,
538, 544 546
lie around v 220
lie down v 213, 687
lie flat v 207, 213
lie idle v 681
lie in v 1
lie in wait for v 530
lie low v 207
lie still v 265
life n 359
life n 151, 171, 682
lifeblood n 5, 359
life-giving adj 168
lifeless adj 172, 360
lifelessness n 172
lifelike adj 17, 21
lifetime n 108
lift n 307, 309; adv 133
lift up v 235, 307
light n 420
light n 7; v 292, 384, 420,
423; adj 320, 322, 420,
430, 643
light bulb n 423
light-colored adj 429
lighten v 320, 420, 705
lightening n 420
light-fingered adj 791
light-footed adj 274
lightness n 320
light of day n 420
light on v 156
light up v 824
like v 394, 827, 897, 990;
adj 17, 216
like a shot adv 113
like a ton of bricks
adj 319
likelihood n 470, 472
likeliness n 472
likely adj 176, 177, 472
likeness n 17, 21, 216, 556
likening n 464
like two peas in a pod
n 17
likewise adv 37
liking n 602, 897
lilac adj 437
lily-liver n 862
lily-livered adj 435, 862
limb n 51
limber adj 324
limbo n 982
limit n 233
limit n 67, 71; v 195, 229,
233, 469, 761
limitation n 229, 469, 751
limited adj 103, 203, 233
limitless adj 104, 180
limitlessness n 104
limn v 556, 594
limp v 160, 275; adj 53,
158, 160, 324, 326
limpid adj 425
limpidity n 425

limpness n 326

line n 69, 278; v 224

lineage n 11, 69, 122, 166

lineal adj 166, 200

linear adj 69, 200, 246

lined adj 224, 440

line of march n 278

liner n 273

lines n 230, 448

linger v 133, 275

lingering adj 110

lingo n 560

lingual adj 560

linguist n 560

linguistic adj 560

liniment n 356

lining n 224

link n 45

link n 9, 43; v 9, 43, 45, 219

linkage n 43

link up v 43, 219

linseed oil n 356

lip n 231

lip-service n 933

liquefaction n 335

liquefaction n 333, 384

liquefy v 333, 335, 384

liquefying n 335

liquid n 337; adj 333, 337

liquidate v 807

liquidation n 807

liquid containers n 191

liquidity n 333

list n 86

list n 217, 596; v 551, 596

listen v 418

listener n 418

listening n 418

listing n 86

listless adj 683, 866

listlessness n 866

lists n 728

literal adj 561, 562

literally adv 19

literary adj 560

literature n 560, 590

litigant n 726, 969

litigation n 969

litigious adj 969

litter n 167; v 61

little adj 32, 193

little by little adv 26, 275

littleness n 193

littleness n 32, 201

little one n 129

live n 374; v 1, 141, 186, 188, 359; adj 359

live from hand to mouth v 804

livelihood n 803

liveliness n 515, 682, 829, 836

lively adj 309, 359, 375, 515, 574, 829, 836

live off v 298

live on v 298

livery n 225

livestock n 366

live through v 151

livid adj 431, 435

lividness n 431

living being n 364

living beings n 357

living thing n 366

load n 190, 319, 828; v 52, 190, 319, 641

loaf v 683

loafer n 683

loan n 787; v 787

loath adj 603, 867

loathe v 867, 898

loathing n 867, 898

loathsome adj 395, 830, 867, 898

local adj 183

locale n 182, 183

locality n 182, 183

locate v 183, 184

located adj 183, 184

locate oneself v 184

location n 184

location n 183

loch n 343

lock n 350; v 43

lock-up n 752

locomotion n 264

locomotive n 271

locution n 582

lodge v 184, 186

lodger n 188

lodging n 189

loft v 235

loftiness n 206, 574, 875

lofty adj 206, 574

log n 114, 388, 551

logic n 23, 476

logical adj 23, 476, 502

logician n 476

loiter v 133, 275, 683

loitering n 133

loll v 683

lone adj 87

long adj 200; adv 110

long ago adv 110, 122

long dozen n 98

longevity n 110, 128

long expected adj 507

long for v 858, 865

longhand n 590

longing n 858, 865

longitude n 200

longitudinal adj 200

longitudinally adv 200

long lost adj 776

long shot n 137

longstanding adj 110

long-winded adj 573

long-windedness n 573

look n 441, 448; v 441, 448, 457

look after oneself v 943

look ahead v 510

look askance v 443

look beyond v 510

look danger in the face v 861

looker-on n 444

look for v 461, 507

look forward v 121

look forward to v 507, 510

looking back adj 122

looking glass n 445

look into the future v 510

look like v 17

look on v 186, 444

lookout n 448

look out for v 507

look sharp v 682

look upon v 451

loom n 152, 446

looming adj 152

loon n 501

loop n 245, 247, 629

loophole n 671

loose v 44, 750; adj 44, 47, 279, 573, 575, 738, 748, 773

loosen v 47

looseness n 47, 573, 738, 748

loosening n 47, 738

loot n 793

lop n 371

loquacious adj 584

loquaciousness n 584

loquacity n 584

loquacity n 584

lord n 745, 875, 976

lore n 490, 537

lorgnette n 445

lose v 776

lose an opportunity v 135

lose color v 429

lose ground v 283

lose heart v 837

lose one's senses v 503

lose one's temper v 825

lose patience v 825

lose sight of v 506

loss n 776

loss n 40a, 449, 619, 638, 659, 732

loss of life n 360

lost adj 2, 449, 458, 732, 776

lost in thought adj 451

lost in wonder adj 870

lot n 25, 152, 621, 786

lottery n 156

loud adj 404

loudly adv 404

loudness n 404

loud noise n 404

lough n 343

lounge v 683

lounger n 683

lout n 501

lovable adj 897

love n 897

love *n* 865, 897, 899, 977;
  v 827, 928, 990
loveliness *n* 829, 845
lovely *adj* 242, 377, 597,
  829, 845, 977
lover *n* 897
lovesick *adj* 991
love token *n* 902
loving *adj* 897
low *v* 412; *adj* 32, 207, 405,
  438, 649, 874, 876, 879,
  930
low-born *adj* 876
lower *v* 207, 308, 879;
  adj 34
lowering *n* 308
lowland *n* 344
lowlands *n* 207
lowliness *n* 879
lowly *adj* 207, 879
low-lying *adj* 207
lowness *n* 207
low price *n* 815
low quality *n* 34
low relief *n* 250
low repute *n* 874
loyal *adj* 743
loyalty *n* 743
lubricate *v* 255, 332, 355
lubrication *n* 332
lubrication *n* 255, 355
lubricity *n* 255, 355
lucent *adj* 420
lucid *adj* 425, 502, 518,
  570, 849
lucidity *n* 420, 425, 502,
  518, 570, 578
Lucifer *n* 978
luck *n* 152, 156, 621, 731
lucky *adj* 134, 621, 734
ludicrous *adj* 853
lug *n* 285
lugubrious *adj* 837
lukewarm *adj* 382, 823,
  866
lull *n* 142, 265, 403, 683,
  685; *v* 174, 265
lull to sleep *v* 265
lumber *n* 275
luminary *n* 423
luminary *n* 500
luminosity *n* 420
luminous *adj* 420, 518
lump *n* 50, 51, 72, 192, 321
lumpish *adj* 192, 319
lump together *v* 72
lunacy *n* 503
lunar *adj* 245, 318
lunatic *n* 504; *adj* 503
lunch *n* 298
lunge *n* 276
lurch *n* 306; *v* 306
lure *v* 288
lurid *adj* 421, 422
lurk *v* 526
lurking *adj* 526
lurking place *n* 530

luscious *adj* 394, 396, 829
lush *n* 959; *v* 959; *adj* 337,
  365, 396
lust *n* 865
luster *n* 420
lust for *v* 865
lustful *adj* 865
lusthood *n* 159
lustrous *adj* 420
luxuriate *v* 377
luxuriate in *v* 827
luxurious *adj* 377, 829
luxuriousness *n* 377
luxury *n* 377, 827
lying *n* 544; *adj* 544
lying down *n* 213
lymph *n* 337

M

ma *n* 166
ma'am *n* 374
Machiavellian *adj* 702
machinery *n* 633
macrocosm *n* 318
mad *adj* 173, 503, 824, 825
madam *n* 374
madame *n* 374
mad as a hatter *adj* 503
madden *v* 173
madman *n* 504
madness *n* 503, 825
maelstrom *n* 312, 348, 867
magenta *adj* 437
magic *n* 992; *adj* 992
magical *adj* 992
magician *n* 994
magisterial *adj* 737
magistracy *n* 965
magistrate *n* 967
magnetic *adj* 288
magnetism *n* 288
magnetize *v* 288
magnificence *n* 845
magnificent *adj* 192, 845
magnify *v* 35, 194, 482,
  549, 990
magnifying glass *n* 445
magniloquence *n* 577
magniloquent *adj* 549,
  577
magnitude *n* 25, 31, 192
mahogany *adj* 433
maid *n* 129, 904; *adj* 66
maim *v* 158, 659
main *n* 341, 350
mainly *adv* 31
mainspring *n* 153, 615
mainstay *n* 866
maintain *v* 141, 143, 170,
  215, 535, 670, 717, 720,
  781, 937
maintain course *v* 143
maintenance *n* 141, 143,
  170, 670, 781, 803
majestic *adj* 882
majesty *n* 875
major *adj* 33

majority *n* 33, 100, 131
make *n* 240; *v* 54, 56, 144,
  161, 744, 852
make a choice *v* 609
make a circuit *v* 629
make a clean sweep of
  v 652
make a complete circle
  v 311
make a compromise
  v 628
make acquainted with
  v 527
make a fool of oneself
  v 853
make a fresh start *v* 66
make a generalization
  v 78
make allowance for *v* 469
make amends *v* 30, 952
make a mess of *v* 732
make a motion *v* 763
make an addition to *v* 37
make an end of *v* 67
make an exception *v* 469
make a noise *v* 402
make a pig of oneself
  v 957
make a place for *v* 184
make a point of *v* 604
make a pretext of *v* 617
make a resolution *v* 604
make a sign *v* 550
make a U-turn *v* 311
make believe *v* 546
make faces *v* 243
make for *v* 278
make free with *v* 789
make friends with *v* 888
make fun of *v* 856
make good *v* 660, 790
make grave *v* 835
make haste *v* 132, 682,
  684
make headlines *v* 532
make headway *v* 282
make known *v* 525, 527,
  529, 531
make light of *v* 483, 843
make little of *v* 483
make loose *v* 47
make manifest *v* 525
make merry *v* 840
make music *v* 415, 416
make news *v* 532
make nothing of *v* 871
make obeisance *v* 308
make one sick *v* 395
make one's way *v* 734
make out *v* 441
make over *v* 783
make payment *v* 807
make peace *v* 721, 723
make preparations *v* 673
make productive *v* 168
make progress *v* 282, 682
make provision *v* 637

make provision for *v* 673
make public *v* 531
make pungent *v* 392
make *n* 164
make ready *v* 673
make sail *v* 267
make serious *v* 835
makeshift *n* 147, 617
make solid *v* 150
make strides *v* 282
make sure *v* 150, 474
make terms *v* 769
make the best of *v* 826
make the mind a blank
  v 452
make time *v* 132
make-up *n* 54
make up for *v* 30
make use of *v* 677
make verses *v* 597
make war *v* 722
making verses *v* 597
maladroit *adj* 699
maladroitness *n* 699
malady *n* 655
malaise *n* 378, 828
malapropism *n* 565
malarkey *n* 477
malcontent *adj* 832
male *n* 373; *adj* 373
male animal *n* 373, 374
malediction *n* 908
malevolence *n* 907
malevolence *n* 649, 889
malevolent *adj* 649, 739,
  907, 919, 945
malformation *n* 243
malformed *adj* 243
malice *n* 907
malicious *adj* 898, 907,
  919, 945
maliciousness *n* 907
malign *v* 934; *adj* 649
malignant *adj* 919, 945
malignity *n* 649
mall *n* 799
malleability *n* 149, 324
malleable *adj* 82, 149, 324
maltreat *v* 649, 739, 830,
  923
mamma *n* 166
mammal *n* 366
mammoth *n* 192; *adj* 31
man *n* 373
man *n* 372
man about town *n* 854
man after one's own
  heart *n* 899
manage *v* 58, 692, 693
manageable *adj* 705
management *n* 692, 693,
  698
manager *n* 694
managerial *adj* 692
managing *adj* 693
mandate *n* 630, 741
maneuver *v* 702

manfully *adv* 604
mangle *v* 659
mangy *adj* 655
man-hater *n* 911
manhood *n* 131, 373
mania *n* 503
maniac *n* 504
maniacal *adj* 503
manifest *adj* 446, 525
manifestation *n* 525
manifestation *n* 446, 448
manifested *adj* 525
manifestly *adv* 525
manifold *adj* 15, 81, 102
manipulate *v* 379, 677,
  702
manipulation *n* 379
mankind *n* 372
mankind *n* 372
manliness *n* 604
manly *adj* 131, 373
man of learning *n* 500
mantle *n* 424
manual *n* 527
manufacture *n* 161; *v* 161
manuscript *n* 590
many *adj* 100, 102
many-colored *adj* 440
many-sided *adj* 81
map *n* 183, 527, 626
mar *v* 659, 848
marble *n* 249
marbled *adj* 440
march *n* 266
marches *n* 233
marching band *n* 417
march of time *n* 109
mare *n* 374
margin *n* 231
marine *adj* 341
marine blue *adj* 438
mariner *n* 269
mariner *n* 269
marital separation *n* 905
maritime *adj* 267, 341
mark *n* 26, 71, 550, 569,
  590, 620; *v* 450, 550, 642
marked *adj* 79
market *n* 799
market *v* 795
marketable *adj* 794, 796
marketplace *n* 799
market price *n* 812
mark the time *v* 114
mark time *v* 114, 265
maroon *adj* 434
marquee *n* 223
marriage *n* 903
marriage *n* 43
marriageable *adj* 131

married *adj* 903
married man *n* 903
married woman *n* 903
marrow *n* 5, 221
marry *v* 43, 48, 903
marsh *n* 345
marshal *v* 60
marshy *adj* 339, 345
mart *n* 799
martial *adj* 722
martyr *n* 955
marvel *n* 870, 872; *v* 870
marvelous *adj* 31, 870
marvelously *adv* 31
masculine *adj* 373
masculinity *n* 373
mash *v* 324, 352, 354
mask *n* 223, 424, 530;
  v 442, 528
masquerade *n* 530
mass *n* 25, 31, 50, 72, 102,
  192, 321
massacre *n* 361; *v* 361
massage *v* 379
massaging *n* 379
massive *adj* 192, 319, 321
massy *adj* 192
master *n* 745
master *n* 129, 540, 694,
  700, 779; *v* 518, 539, 731,
  749
masterful *adj* 731, 737
masterly *adj* 698
master mind *n* 500, 700,
  872
master of *adj* 777
masterpiece *n* 648, 650
master stroke *n* 650
mastery *n* 698, 731, 741
mastic *n* 356a
masticate *v* 298
mastication *n* 298
mat *n* 219; *v* 219
match *n* 17, 27; *v* 17, 23,
  27
matchless *adj* 33
mate *n* 17, 27, 711, 890,
  903
material *n* 316; *adj* 3, 316
material existence *n* 3
materialism *n* 316
materialist *n* 316
materialistic *adj* 3, 316
materiality *n* 316
materiality *n* 3
materialization *n* 525
materialize *v* 316, 525
materials *n* 635
materials *n* 316
maternal *adj* 166
maternity *n* 11, 166
mates *n* 269
matins *n* 125
matriarch *n* 130
matriarchal *adj* 166
matricide *n* 361
matriculation *n* 539

matrimony n 903
matrix n 22
matted adj 219
matter n 3, 316, 516, 591, 625; v 642
matter little n 1;
  adj 598, 703, 843
matter of fact n 1;
  adj 598, 703, 843
matter of factness n 703
matters n 151
matting n 219
mature v 144, 650, 658, 673; adj 673
mature years n 128
maturity n 124, 128, 131, 673
maul v 649
mausoleum n 363
mauve adj 437
maxim n 496
maxim n 537, 697
maximum n 210
maybe adv 470
maze n 248
mazy adj 248
meadow n 344
meager adj 32, 53, 103, 203, 575, 640, 643
meagerness n 203
mealy adj 330
mealy-mouthed adj 886
mean n 29
mean n 68, 628; v 451, 516, 620; adj 29, 32, 34, 68, 207, 435, 643, 649, 819, 851, 876, 886, 914a, 930, 943
meander v 248, 264, 266, 279, 573
meandering n 248
meaning n 516
meaning n 522, 620;
  adj 516
meaningful adj 516
meaningless adj 497, 517
meaninglessness n 517
meanness n 32, 34, 499, 886, 914a, 943
mean nothing v 517
means n 632
means n 627, 780, 803
means of access n 627
meantime adv 106
meanwhile adv 106
measurable adj 466
measure n 25, 26, 174, 413, 466, 786; v 106, 466
measured adj 174
measure for measure
  n 30
measureless adj 104
measurement n 466
measurement n 25
measure time v 114
meaty adj 354
mechanical adj 601, 633
medal n 733

meddlesome adj 455
meddlesomeness n 455
medial adj 68
median n 29; adj 68
meditate v 620, 631, 724
mediation n 724
mediation n 631, 766
mediator n 724
mediatory adj 724
medication n 662
medicinal adj 662
medicine n 662
medicine man n 994
mediocre adj 28, 29, 34, 598, 651, 736
mediocrity n 736
mediocrity n 28, 34
meditate v 451, 870
meditation n 451
meditative adj 451
medium n 29, 631, 994
medley n 41
meek adj 879
meekness n 879
meet v 23, 72, 199, 290, 772; adj 646
meeting n 43, 72, 199, 290, 680, 696
meetinghouse n 1000
meet up with v 151
meet with v 151
melancholy n 837;
  adj 830, 837
mélange n 41
melee n 59
meliorate v 174, 723
mellifluence n 413
mellifluous adj 413, 578
mellow v 144, 673;
  adj 128, 413, 428, 673, 721
melodic adj 413
melodious adj 377, 413, 580
melodiousness n 413
melody n 413
melody n 415
melt v 111, 144, 335, 384, 449
melt away v 4, 449
melting n 335, 384
member n 51, 56
membrane n 204
membranous adj 204
memento n 505
memento mori n 363
memorable adj 505
memorandum n 551
memorial n 505
memorialist n 553
memorialization n 883
memorize v 505, 539
memory n 505
memory n 122
menace n 667, 909; v 668, 909
menacing adj 909

menagerie n 72
mend v 658
mendacious adj 544
mendicant n 767
menial n 746
mental adj 450
mental balance n 502
mental cultivation n 539
mental excitation n 824
mental image n 515
mental suffering n 619
mention v 527
mentor n 540, 695
mephitic adj 401
mercantile adj 794
mercantilism n 794
mercenary adj 819
merchandise n 798
merchandise v 763, 796, 798
merchant n 797
merchant n 796
merchant ship n 273
merciful adj 740
merciless adj 914a
mercurial adj 149, 264
mercury n 389
mercy n 740, 914
mere n 343; adj 643
merely adv 32
merge v 48, 300
merge in v 56
merge into v 144
meridian n 125, 181
merit n 648, 944, 973
merit attention v 642
meritorious adj 931
mermaid n 979
merriment n 836
merry adj 829
merrymaking n 838
mesh n 219
mesmerist n 994
mesmerize v 992
mess n 59, 61, 162, 732
messenger n 534
messenger n 271, 527, 758
mess up v 59
messy adj 59
metallurgy n 358
metamorphose v 140
metamorphosis n 140
metaphor n 521
metaphorical adj 464
mete v 786
meteors n 318
mete out v 784
meter n 413
method n 627
method n 58, 60, 569, 626, 632, 692
methodical adj 58, 60, 692
methodically adv 58
methodological adj 626
methodology n 58
meticulous adj 459, 868
metrical adj 597

metrics *n* 597
mettle *n* 861
mew *v* 412
miasmic *adj* 401
microcosm *n* 193
microscope *n* 445
microscopic *adj* 32, 193
mid *adj* 68
mid-course *n* 628
midcourse *n* 68
midday *n* 125
middle *n* 68
middle *n* 29, 208, 222;
    adj 29,68, 222; *adv* 222
middle class *adj* 29
middle course *n* 628
middle ground *n* 68, 174
middlemost *adj* 222
middle of the road *n* 174
middle way *n* 628
midmost *adj* 68
midnight *n* 126
midnight *n* 421
mid-point *n* 29, 68
midriff *n* 68
midst *n* 68, 208, 222;
    adv 222
midsummer 125
midway *adj* 628; *adv* 68
mien *n* 448, 692
might *n* 31, 157, 159, 173
mightily *adv* 31
mighty *adj* 31, 157, 159,
    192, 192
migrate *v* 266
migration *n* 266
migratory *adj* 266
mild *adj* 174, 382, 391,
    721, 740
mildew *n* 653, 663
mildewed *adj* 659
mildness *n* 174, 740
militant *adj* 722
militarist *n* 726
military *adj* 722
military band *n* 417
milkiness *n* 427, 430
milk-white *adj* 430
milky *adj* 352, 427, 430
mill *n* 330, 691
millennium *n* 108, 121
millions *n* 372
mimic *v* 19, 554
mimicry *n* 19
mince *v* 275
mince steps *v* 275
mind *n* 450, 498, 842;
    v 602
mindblower *n* 137
mindful *adj* 451, 457
mindfulness *n* 457
mindful (of) *adj* 505
mindless *adj* 499
mine *n* 636; *v* 252, 280,
    659
mineral *adj* 358

mineral kingdom *n* 358
mineralogy *n* 358
mineral world *n* 358
mingle *v* 41
mingling *n* 41
miniature *adj* 32, 193
minimize *v* 483
minion *n* 899
minister *n* 631, 690, 694,
    996; *v* 631, 693
ministerial *adj* 995
ministering spirit *n* 977
ministration *n* 693
ministry *n* 995, 996
minor *n* 129; *adj* 32, 34
minority *n* 34, 127
minstrel *n* 416, 597
mint *n* 22, 691
minus *adj* 776; *adv* 38,
    777
minuscule *adj* 32
minute *adj* 32, 193
minutiae *n* 32
minx *n* 962
miracle *n* 872
miraculous *adj* 870
mirage 443
mire *n* 653
mirror *n* 445, 650; *v* 19;
    443
mirth *n* 836
mirthful *adj* 836
misanthrope *n* 165
misanthropic *adj* 911
misanthropy *n* 911
misapplication *n* 679
misapply *v* 523, 679
misapprehend *v* 495, 523
misapprehension *n* 481,
    495, 523
misappropriate *v* 679
misappropriation *n* 679
misbelieve *n* 984
misbelieving *adj* 984
miscalculate *v* 482, 495
miscalculation *n* 481,
    482, 508
miscall *v* 565
miscarriage *n* 732
miscarry *v* 732
miscellaneous *adj* 15, 41,
    465a
miscellaneousness *n* 78
miscellany *n* 41, 72, 78
mischief *n* 619
mischievous *adj* 649
miscomputation *n* 481
misconceive *v* 481, 495,
    523
misconception *n* 481, 495,
    523
misconjecture *v* 481
misconstruction *n* 523
misconstrue *v* 481, 523
miscreant *n* 949
misdate *n* 115; *v* 115
misdated *adj* 115

misdeed *n* 923
misdirect *v* 538
misdirection *n* 538
misemploy *v* 679
misemployment *n* 679
miser *n* 819
miserable *adj* 828, 837,
    930
miserably *adv* 31, 32
miserly *adj* 819
misery *n* 828
misfiguration *n* 555
misfortune *n* 619, 735, 830
misgiving *n* 485, 860
misguidance *n* 538
misguide *v* 538
mishap *n* 619, 732, 830
misinform *v* 538
misinformation *n* 538
misinstruct *v* 538
misinterpret *v* 481, 495,
    523
misinterpretation *n* 523
misinterpretation *n* 481,
    495
misjudge *v* 481, 495
misjudging *adj* 481
misjudgment *n* 481
misjudgment *n* 495
mislay *v* 61, 776
mislead *v* 477, 538, 545
misleading *adj* 520, 544,
    545
mismatch *n* 24; *v* 15
mismatched *adj* 24
misname *v* 565
misnamed *adj* 565
misnaming *n* 565
misnomer *n* 565
misogynist *n* 911
misogynist *n* 911
misplace *v* 61, 185
misplaced *adj* 115, 185
misplacement *n* 115, 185
misproportion *n* 241, 243
misread *v* 523
misreading *n* 523
misrepresent *v* 277, 477,
    523, 538, 544, 555
misrepresentation *n* 555
misrepresentation *n* 523,
    544
miss *n* 129, 374; *v* 776
misshape *v* 243
misshapen *adj* 241, 243
missing *adj* 187, 449
missing link *n* 53
mission *n* 755
missionary *n* 540
missive *n* 592
misspend *v* 638, 818
misstate *v* 523
miss the mark *v* 732
mist *n* 353, 422, 424, 427;
    v 353
mistake *n* 495, 523, 732;
    v 495, 523

mistaken *adj* 495, 544, 923
misteach *v* 538
misteaching *n* 538
mister *n* 373
misterm *v* 565
mistime *v* 135
mistimed *adj* 135
mistiness *n* 422, 426
mistreat *v* 830
mistress *n* 779
mistrust *n* 485; *v* 485
misty *adj* 353, 422, 426, 447
misunderstand *v* 481, 495, 523
misunderstanding *n* 495, 523, 713
misusage *n* 649, 679
misuse *n* 679
misuse *n* 638; *v* 638, 679
mite *n* 32
mitigate *v* 174, 469, 834
mitigating *adj* 469
mitigation *n* 174, 469, 834
mix *n* 41, 48; *v* 41, 48, 61
mixed *adj* 41
mixture *n* 41
mixture *n* 48
moan *n* 839; *v* 411
moaning *n* 411, 839
moat *n* 259, 350
mob *n* 72, 102
mobile *adj* 149, 264
mobility *n* 149, 264
mobilization *n* 264
mobilize *v* 264
mock *v* 19, 856, 929; *adj* 17, 19
mockery *n* 856
mocking *n* 19; *adj* 856
mode *n* 7, 569, 613, 852
model *n* 21, 22, 80, 240, 650, 948; *v* 144, 240, 557; *adj* 650
modeled after *adj* 19
modeled on *adj* 19
modeling *n* 557
model oneself on *v* 19
moderate *v* 174, 275, 723; *adj* 174, 275, 628, 736, 815, 881, 953
moderately *adv* 174
moderation *n* 174
moderation *n* 275, 736, 740, 826, 881, 953
moderator *n* 724, 967
modern *adj* 123
modernism *n* 123
modernity *n* 123
modernize *v* 123
modest *adj* 483, 879, 881, 960
modestly *adv* 881
modesty *n* 881
modesty *n* 483, 879, 960

modicum *n* 32
modification *n* 20a, 140, 469
modified *adj* 15, 20a
modify *v* 15, 20a, 140, 469
modish *adj* 852, 855
modulate *v* 140
modulation *n* 140, 413
module *n* 22, 273
moist *adj* 337, 339
moisten *v* 337, 339
moisture *n* 339
moisture *n* 339
mold *n* 7, 21, 22, 240, 329, 557, 653; *v* 144, 240, 557, 653, 852
moldable *adj* 324
molded *adj* 820
molder *v* 659
moldering *adj* 659
moldy *adj* 653, 659
molecule *n* 32
molest *v* 649, 716
molestation *n* 649
mollification *n* 324
mollify *v* 174, 324, 723
mollusk *n* 366
molten *adj* 384
mom *n* 166
moment *n* 113, 642
momentary *adj* 111, 113
momentous *adj* 642
momentousness *n* 642
monetary *adj* 800
money *n* 800
money *n* 803
moneybag *n* 802
money matters *n* 811
monolog *n* 589
monomania *n* 606
monomaniacal *adj* 606
monosyllable *n* 561
monotheism *n* 983
monotonous *adj* 16, 27, 104, 841
monotony *n* 16, 27, 104, 841
monsoon *n* 349
monster *n* 192, 949, 980
monstrosity *n* 192, 243, 872
monstrous *adj* 31, 192, 846
monstrously *adv* 31
monument *n* 363, 551
moo *v* 412
mood *n* 7, 176, 602, 820
moodiness *n* 901a
moods *n* 5
moody *adj* 901a
moon *n* 420, 423
moonbeam *n* 420

moor *n* 344; *v* 43
moored *adj* 184, 186
mooring *n* 184
mope *v* 837
moper *n* 683
moral *adj* 922, 944
moral imperative *n* 926
morality *n* 922, 944
moralize *v* 537
morals *n* 922
moral sensibility *n* 822
morass *n* 345
moratorium *n* 133
morbid *adj* 655
more *adv* 33, 37
more or less *adj* 25
moreover *adv* 37
more than one *adj* 100
morgue *n* 363
morn *n* 125
morning *n* 125
morning *n* 125
morningtide *n* 125
moron *n* 493, 501
morose *adj* 901a
moroseness *n* 901a
morphology *n* 368
morrow *n* 121
morsel *n* 32, 390
mortal *n* 372; *adj* 111, 361, 372
mortal coil *n* 362
mortality *n* 111, 360, 372
mortal remains *n* 362
mortar and pestle *n* 330
mortgage *n* 771, 787; *v* 771
mortification *n* 828, 830
mortify *v* 828, 830, 879
mortuary *adj* 363; *adj* 363
mosaic *adj* 81, 440
moss *n* 345
most *adv* 31
most likely *adv* 472
mote *n* 32, 451
moth-eaten *adj* 653, 659
mother *n* 166, 192
mother earth *n* 342
motherhood *n* 166
motherland *n* 189
motion *n* 264
motion *n* 550
motionless *adj* 172, 265, 683
motivate *v* 615, 744
motivation *n* 615
motive *n* 615
motive *n* 615
motive power *n* 264
mot juste *n* 496
motley *adj* 16a, 41, 81
motorboat *n* 273
motorcar *n* 272
motorcycle *n* 272
motoring *n* 266
motorscooter *n* 272
mottled *adj* 440
motto *n* 496, 566

mound n 192
mount v 206, 305
mountain n 192, 250
mourn for v 833
mournful adj 830, 839, 901a
mourn over v 839
mouth n 231, 343
mouthful n 25, 32
mouthpiece n 582
movable adj 264, 270
movableness n 264
move n 264, 270; v 175, 264, 266, 270, 302, 615, 763, 824
move away from v 287
move back v 287
moved adj 821, 914
movement n 264, 680, 682
move off v 293
move out v 293
move quickly v 274
mover n 164
move slowly v 275
move to the center v 29
move towards v 286
moving a 266, 680; adj 264
mow v 371
Mr. n 373
Ms. n 374
much adj 641; adv 31
much ado about nothing n 549
much the same adj 17, 27
muck n 653
muckraking n 529
mud n 345, 853
muddle n 59; v 61
muddle-headed adj 499
muddy adj 339, 345, 352, 519
muffle v 403, 408a, 590
muffled adj 405, 408a
muffled drums n 408a
muffler n 408a
muggy adj 339
mulish adj 606
mulishness n 606
mulling around n 681
multi-colored adj 440
multifarious adj 16a, 81
multifold adj 81
multiformity n 81
multiple adj 102
multiplication n 168
multiplicity n 102
multiply v 35, 85, 102, 163, 168
multiply by four v 96
multiplying by four n 96
multi-purpose adj 148
multitude n 102
multitude n 31, 72, 100, 876
multitudes n 372

multitudinous n 102; adj 102
mum n 581; adj 581, 585
mumble v 583
mumbling n 583
mumbo-jumbo n 993
mummify v 363
mummy n 166
munch v 298
mundane adj 318
munificence n 816, 910
munificent adj 816, 910
munitions n 727
murder n 361; v 361
murderer n 361
murderous adj 361
murk n 421
murkiness n 421
murky adj 421, 422, 426, 431
murmur n 405; v 348, 405
murmured adj 405
muscular adj 159
muse v 451
mushiness n 326
mushy adj 324, 339
musk n 415
musical adj 413, 415, 416, 597
musical instruments n 417
musicalness n 413
musician n 416
musing n 451
muster n 72; v 72, 85
mustiness n 401
musty adj 401, 653
mutability n 149
mutable adj 149
mutation n 140
mute n 408a; v 408a; adj 403, 581, 585
muted adj 405, 408a
muteness n 581
muteness n 403, 585
mutilate v 38, 241, 361, 659
mutilation n 38, 241
mutineer n 742
mutinous adj 742
mutinousness n 742
mutiny n 146, 742; v 742
mutter v 405, 583
muttering n 583
mutual adj 12, 148
mutuality n 12
muzzle v 158, 403, 581
myopia n 443
myopic adj 443
mysterious adj 208, 447, 519, 528, 533
mystery n 447, 533
mystify v 519

nadir n 211
naiad n 979
naive adj 435, 703, 946
naiveté n 703, 946
naked adj 226
nakedness n 226
name n 13, 562, 564, 569, 873, 877; v 564, 755
namely adv 522
namesake n 564
naming n 564
nannygoat n 374
nap n 256
naphtha n 356
napping adj 458
narrate v 594
narration n 594
narrative n 594
narrative prose n 598
narrow v 195, 203, 469; adj 32, 203
narrow escape n 671
narrowing n 469
narrow-minded adj 32, 499
narrow-mindedness n 32
narrowness n 203
narrowness n 203
nascent adj 66
nasty adj 395, 653
natal adj 66
nation n 188
national adj 372
native n 188; adj 188
nativity n 66
natural adj 501; adj 82, 494, 578, 703, 849
natural causes n 360
natural gas n 388
natural harbor n 343
natural history n 357
naturalist n 357
natural light n 423
natural philosophy n 316
natural world n 357
nature n 5, 80, 176, 318, 357, 820
naught n 4, 101
nauseate v 395, 830, 867
nauseating adj 401, 867, 898
nauseous adj 395, 401, 830
nautical adj 267
naval adj 267
navel n 222
navigable adj 267
navigate v 267
navigation n 267
navigator n 269
navy n 273; adj 438
near v 286; adj 17, 121, 186, 197, 199; adv 197
nearly adv 32
near miss n 671
nearness n 197
nearness n 9, 186, 286

N

nab v 789
nacreous adj 427, 440

near side n 239
nearsighted adj 443
nearsightedness n 443
near the mark adv 32
neat adj 58, 576, 578, 652, 849
neaten v 652
neatness n 652
nebbish n 547
nebula n 353
nebulosity n 353, 422
nebulous adj 422, 519
necessarily adv 154, 601
necessary adj 601, 630, 744
necessitate v 601, 630, 744
necessity n 601
necessity n 630, 744
neck and neck adv n 27
necklace n 247
necromancer n 513, 994
necromancy n 992
need n 630, 884, 804, 865; v 630, 640
needful adj 601, 630
neediness n 804
needle n 253, 262
needless adj 641
needy adj 804
negate v 536
negation n 536
negation n 468
negative n 22; adj 14, 84, 489, 536
neglect n 460
neglect n 730, 732, 773, 927; v 53, 460, 678, 730, 773, 927
neglected adj 460
neglectful adj 460
neglecting adj 460
negligence n 460, 773
negligent adj 460, 738, 773, 927
negotiate v 724, 769, 794
negotiation n 724, 769, 774, 794
negotiator n 724
neigh v 412
neighbor n 197
neighbor v 197
neighborhood n 197, 227
neighboring adj 197
neighborly adj 707, 888, 892
nemesis n 919
neologic adj 563
neological adj 563
neologism n 563
neologist n 563
neology n 563
neophyte n 541

nest n 189
nestle v 186
net n 219; v 219
nethermost adj 211
netting n 219
nettle n 663
network n 219
neutral adj 29, 609a, 628
neutrality n 29, 609a, 628
neutrality n 29, 609a, 628
neutralization n 179
neutralize v 30, 179
neutral tint n 429, 432
never adv 107
never-ending adj 104, 112
nevermore adv 107
nevertheless adv 30
never to be forgotten adj 505
new adj 18, 123, 146, 435
new birth n 660
newborn adj 129
newfangled adj 83, 123, 140
new-fangled expression n 563
newfangledness n 123
newly adv 123
newness n 123
news n 532
news n 498, 527
newsmonger n 527, 532, 534
newsstory n 532
New Testament n 986
next adj 63; adv 117
next generation n 127
next world n 152
nibble v 298
nice adj 394, 829, 868
nice distinction n 15
nicety n 465, 868
niche n 182, 221, 244
nick n 257; v 257
nickname n 564, 565; v 564
nick of time n 134
niggard n 819
niggardly adj 819
niggling adj 643
nigh adj 197; adv 197
night n 421
nightfall n 126
nihilist n 165
nil n 4
nimble adj 274, 498, 842
nincompoop n 501
nine n 98
ninny n 501
nip n 392; v 385
nip in the bud v 361
nipping adj 383
nipple n 250
nippy adj 392
nirvana n 981
nit-picking adj 477

nobility n 875
nobility n 33
noble adj 31, 875, 878
nobody n 101
no choice n 609a
nocturnal adj 421
node n 250
no doubt adv 474
nodular adj 250
nodulation n 256
nodule n 250
noise n 402, 404, 414
noiseless adj 403
noisily adv 404
noisome adj 401, 657
noisy adj 404
nomad n 268
nomadic adj 264, 266
nomadism n 266
nom de guerre n 565
nom de plume n 565
nomenclature n 564
nominal adj 564
nominate v 755
nomination n 755
nominee n 758
no more adj 360
no more than adv 32
nonadhesion n 47
nonadhesive adj 47
nonappearance n 187
nonattendance n 187
nonbeliever n 485, 487, 989
nonchoice adj 47
noncompletion n 730
noncompletion n 53, 304
noncompliance n 742, 773
noncompliant adj 764
nonconforming adj 984
nonconformist n 489, 984; adj 489, 984
nonconformity n 16a, 24, 79, 83, 489, 984
none n 101
nonentity n 2
nonessential adj 57, 643
nonetheless adv 30
nonexistence n 2
nonexistent adj 2, 187
nonexpectant adj 508
nonexpectation n 508
nonextension n 180a
nonfulfillment n 730
nonfunctional adj 674
nonimitation n 20
noninterference n 748
nonlinear adj 245
nonobservance n 83, 742, 927
nonobservant adj 773
nonpayment n 808
nonperformance n 730, 732, 927
nonplus n 704
nonpreparation n 674

nonrational *adj* 450a
non-relation *n* 10
nonresidence *n* 187
nonresistance *n* 725
nonresonance *n* 408a
nonresonant *adj* 408a
nonsense *n* 497, 517
nonsensical *adj* 477, 497, 499, 517, 853
non sequitur *n* 497
nontranslucent *adj* 426
nontransparency *n* 426
nontransparent *adj* 426
noodle *n* 450
noon *n* 125
noon *n* 125
noonday *n* 125
noontide *n* 125
noontime *n* 125
normal *adj* 5, 29, 82, 736
normalcy *n* 80
normality *n* 502
normal state *n* 80
nose *n* 250
not a bit *adv* 32
notable *adj* 31, 642
notably *adv* 31
not act *v* 681
not a jot *adv* 32
notary *n* 553
not at all *adv* 32
not a whit *adv* 32
not bad *adj* 651
not beat around the bush *v* 576
not be good for *v* 657
not be surprised *v* 871
not care *v* 823
notch *n* 257
notch *n* 244; *v* 257
notched *adj* 257
not come up to *v* 28, 34
not come up to snuff *v* 34
not complete *v* 730
not conversant *adj* 699
not curved *adj* 246
not cut it *v* 640
not discriminate *v* 465a
not do *v* 640, 681
not enough *adj* 640
notes *n* 802
noteworthy *adj* 31
not exist *v* 2
not expect *v* 508
not germane *adj* 57
not get involved *v* 623
not give an inch *v* 604
not have *v* 777a
not have much of a chance *v* 473
not hear *v* 419
not here *adj* 187
nothing *n* 4, 101, 643
nothingness *n* 2, 4

notice *n* 457, 668; *v* 450, 457, 480a, 928
notification *n* 527
notify *v* 668
no time *n* 107
not in *adj* 187
not included in *adj* 55
not in sight *adj* 447
not in the least *adv* 32
not in use *adj* 678
notion *n* 451, 453, 515
not licensed *adj* 925
not many *adj* 103
not matter *v* 643
not often *adv* 137
not pass muster *v* 34, 651
not pay *v* 808
not pertinent *adj* 10
not possible *adj* 471
not present *adj* 187, 187
not quite *adv* 32
not reach *v* 304
not see *v* 442
not smell *v* 399
not sorry *adj* 951
not straight *adj* 243
not suffice *v* 640
not the same *adj* 15
not think *v* 452
not true *adj* 243
not use *v* 678
not well *adj* 655
not with it *adj* 246
notwithstanding *adv* 30
nourishment *n* 298, 359
novel *n* 593; *adj* 18, 123
novelty *n* 18, 123
novice *n* 541, 701
now *adv* 118
nowadays *adv* 118
now and then *adv* 136
no way *adv* 471
noway *adv* 32
nowhere *adv* 187
nowise *adv* 32
now or never *adv* 134
noxious *adj* 649, 657
nozzle *n* 250
nuance *n* 15
nub *n* 68, 222
nubile *adj* 131
nuclear power *n* 388
nucleus *n* 68, 153, 222
nude *adj* 226
nudity *n* 226
nuisance *n* 619, 663, 830, 975
null and void *adj* 756
nullification *n* 536, 756
nullify *v* 2, 30, 179, 536, 756
nullity *n* 4
numb *v* 376; *adj* 376, 381
number *n* 84
number *v* 85
number among *v* 76
numbering *n* 85

numberless *adj* 104
numbers *n* 102
numbing *adj* 383
numbness *n* 381
numbness *n* 376
numerable *adj* 85
numeral *n* 84; *adj* 84, 85
numeration *n* 85
numerical *adj* 85
numerous *adj* 100, 102
numskull *n* 493, 501
nuptials *n* 903
nurse *n* 753; *v* 662
nursery *n* 127
nursling *n* 129
nurture *v* 235, 673
nut *n* 504
nutbrown *adj* 433
nutriment *n* 298, 359
nutrition *n* 298
nutritious *adj* 299, 656
nutritive *adj* 299
nuts *adj* 503
nutshell *n* 32

O

oaf *n* 501
oath *n* 535, 768
obduracy *n* 606, 951
obdurate *adj* 600, 951
obedience *n* 743
obedience *n* 725, 749, 772
obedient *adj* 725, 743, 772, 926
obediently *adv* 743
obeisance *n* 308
obese *adj* 192, 194
obesity *n* 192
obey *v* 725, 743, 772
obey the rules *v* 82
obfuscate *v* 528
obfuscation *n* 528
object *n* 3, 316, 453, 516, 620
objection *n* 704
objectionable *adj* 846
objective *n* 453; *adj* 6
object to *v* 932
obligate *v* 630
obligation *n* 177, 601, 768, 806, 926, 963
obligations *n* 770
obligatory *adj* 744, 926
oblige *adj* 707, 744, 770
obliged *adj* 177, 916, 926
obliging *adj* 894, 906
oblique *adj* 217
obliquely *adv* 217
obliquity *n* 217
obliquity *n* 243
obliterate *v* 2, 552
obliterated *adj* 552
obliteration *n* 552
obliteration *n* 2
obliteration of the past *n* 506
oblivion *n* 506

oblivious *adj* 506
obloquy *n* 874
obnoxious *adj* 830, 898
obscene *adj* 961
obscenity *n* 961
obscuration *n* 421
obscure *v* 421, 422, 528;
  adj 208, 421, 426, 447,
  519, 571, 704, 876
obscure meaning *n* 526
obscuring *n* 528
obscurity *n* 571
obscurity *n* 208, 421, 431,
  447, 475, 519, 526
obsequies *n* 363
obsequious *adj* 886
obsequiousness *n* 743,
  886
observance *n* 772
observance *n* 82, 613, 743,
  883, 983a, 998
observant *adj* 457, 772
observation *n* 453, 457
observe *v* 441, 457, 772,
  883, 926
observer *n* 444
obsolete *adj* 122, 124
obstacle *n* 177, 704, 706
obstinacy *n* 606
obstinacy *n* 141, 150, 327,
  603, 604, 704, 742
obstinate *adj* 150, 327,
  499, 604, 606, 719, 742
obstreperous *adj* 173, 404
obstruct *v* 261, 275, 706,
  708, 761
obstruction *n* 261, 706
obstructive *adj* 706
obstruct the passage of
  light *v* 426
obtain *v* 775, 795
obtrude *v* 228
obtrusive *adj* 706
obtuse *adj* 254, 376, 499
obtuse angle *n* 244
obtuseness *n* 254, 376,
  843
obverse *adj* 218
obvious *adj* 446, 474, 518,
  525
occasion *n* 8, 134, 615;
  v 153
occasional *adj* 103, 137
occasionally *adv* 136
occultism *n* 992
occupancy *n* 186, 777
occupant *n* 188, 779
occupation *n* 186, 625
occupy *v* 186, 777
occupying *adj* 186
occur *v* 1, 151
occurrence *n* 151
ocean *n* 341
ocean-going *adj* 267
oceanic *adj* 341
oceanographic *adj* 341
ocher *adj* 435

ochre *adj* 433
octet *n* 415
ocular *adj* 441
odd *adj* 40, 83, 87, 870
oddity *n* 83, 503, 857
odds *n* 28, 156, 713
odds and ends *n* 40
odious *adj* 830, 898
odium *n* 898, 932
odor *n* 398
odoriferous *adj* 398, 400
odorific *adj* 400
odorless *adj* 399
odorlessness *n* 399
odorous *adj* 398
oeuvre *n* 161
of age *adj* 131
of a piece *adj* 16, 17
of every description
  adj 81
off *adj* 187
off and on *adv* 138
offend *v* 289, 830
offend against the law
  v 964
offended *adj* 900
offense *n* 718, 830
offensive *adj* 395, 401,
  653, 716, 830, 846, 867,
  898
offensive smell *n* 401
offer *v* 763
offer *v* 763
offer congratulations
  v 896
offer counsel *v* 695
offer for sale *v* 796
offering *n* 763, 784
offer pleasure *v* 829
offer prayers *v* 990
offhand *adv* 132, 612
office *n* 170, 625, 799
official *n* 694; *adj* 625,
  737, 983a
offing *n* 196
off one's guard *adj* 508
off-set *n* 30; *v* 30, 179
offshoot *n* 39, 51, 65, 154
offside *n* 238
offspring *n* 154, 167
of late *adv* 122, 123
of little account *adj* 643
of long standing *adj* 124
of necessity *adv* 601, 630
of no account *adj* 643
of old *adv* 122
of one accord *adj* 488
of one mind *adj* 178
of one's own accord
  adv 600
of other times *adj* 124
of small importance
  adj 643
oft *adv* 136
often *adv* 104, 136

oftentimes *adv* 136
of the same mind *adj* 488
oft-repeated *adj* 136
of various kinds *adj* 16a
of vital importance
  adj 642
of yore *adv* 122
ogle *v* 441
ogre *n* 980
oil *n* 356
oil *n* 355; *v* 255, 332, 355
oil burner *n* 386
oiliness *n* 355
oiling *n* 332
oil lamp *n* 423
oily *adj* 255, 355
oink *n* 412
ointment *n* 355, 356, 662
old *adj* 124, 128, 130
old age *n* 124, 128
older *adj* 128
old-fashioned *adj* 124
old hand *n* 700
old lady *n* 186, 903
old maid *n* 904
old man *n* 130, 166, 903
oldness *n* 124
old soldier *n* 700
Old Testament *n* 986
old woman *n* 130
oleaginous *adj* 355
olive *adj* 435
olive oil *n* 356
omen *n* 512
omen *n* 668
ominous *adj* 665, 668, 909
omission *n* 53, 55, 460,
  732, 773, 893
omit *v* 55, 460, 773
omitted *adj* 893
omnipotence *n* 157, 976
omnipotent *adj* 104, 157
omnipresence *n* 186, 976
omnipresent *adj* 186
on *adv* 125, 282
on a bed of roses *adv* 377
on account of *adv* 155
on a large scale *adv* 31
on a level with *adj* 27
on a line with *adv* 278
on all sides *adv* 227
on a moment's notice
  adv 113
on an equal footing with
  adj 27
on a par with *adj* 27
on bended knee *adv* 879
once and for all *adv* 67
once more *adv* 90, 104
on compulsion *adv* 744
on condition *adv* 770
on dry land *adv* 342
one *n* 372; *adj* 13, 52, 87,
  729
one and the same *adj* 27
one by one *adv* 44
on edge *adv* 507

one in a million *n* 648
on end *adv* 212
oneness *n* 87
one of a kind *adj* 20
onerous *adj* 649, 706, 830
oneself *n* 13
one's own *n* 11
one's own flesh and
blood *n* 11
one step at a time
adv 275
on every side *adv* 227
one way or another
adv 627
on fire *adj* 382
on foot *adj* 179
ongoing *adj* 53
on land *adv* 342
onlooker *n* 444
only *adv* 32
only just *adv* 32
only so far *adv* 233
on no account *adv* 32
on no occasion *adv* 107
on one's back *adv* 213
one's honor *n* 768
on one side *adv* 237, 239
on one's own time
adv 133
on one's toes *adj* 507
on purpose *adv* 620
onset *n* 66, 716
on sight *adv* 441
onslaught *n* 718
on target *adj* 494
on tenterhooks *adj* 507
on that occasion *adv* 119
on the average *adv* 29
on the ball *adj* 498
on the brink of *adv* 121
on the dot *adv* 132
on the eve of *adv* 121
on the face of it *adv* 448
on the face of the earth
adv 180, 318
on the go *adv* 264
on the horizon *adj* 152,
507
on the horns of a
dilemma *n* 476
on the instant *adv* 132
on the march *adv* 264
on the move *adv* 264
on the offensive *adv* 716
on the other hand *adv* 30
on the point of *adv* 121
on the road *adv* 264, 266
on the road to *adv* 278
on the safe side *adj* 664
on the sly *adv* 528
on the spot *adv* 132, 134
on the spur of the
moment *adv* 113, 132,
134
on the wagon *adj* 958
on the wane *adj* 36

on the watch *adj* 457;
adv 507
on the whole *adv* 50
on time *adj* 132; *adv* 132
ontology *n* 1
on trial *adv* 675
onus *n* 926
onward *adv* 282
ooze *v* 295, 348
oozing *n* 295
oozy *adj* 352
opacity *n* 426
opacity *n* 353
opalescence *n* 427
opalescent *adj* 427
opaline *adj* 430, 440
opaque *adj* 422, 426
opaqueness *n* 426
ope *v* 260
open *v* 66, 194, 198, 260,
525; *adj* 177, 260, 338,
525, 543, 665, 703
open air *n* 338
open-eyed *adj* 507
open field *n* 134
opening *n* 260
opening *n* 66, 198, 260
open into *v* 348
openly *adv* 525
openness *n* 525, 703, 748
open space(s) *n* 180
open to the view *v* 446
opera *n* 599
opera glasses *n* 445
operahouse *n* 599
operatic *v* 161, 170, 680
operatic *adj* 415, 416
operation *n* 170, 680
operation *adj* 170, 680
operator *n* 690
ophthalmia *n* 443
opine *v* 454
opinion *n* 451, 453, 480,
484, 537, 695, 821
opponent *n* 710
opponent *n* 726, 891
opportune *adj* 134, 646
opportunely *adv* 134
opportuneness *n* 134
opportunism *n* 646
opportunist *n* 935
opportunity *n* 134
oppose *v* 14, 179, 237, 536,
708, 719
opposed *adj* 14
opposer *n* 726
opposing *n* 708; *adj* 14,
237, 489
opposite *n* 237; *adj* 14,
218, 237
oppositeness *n* 14
opposite poles *n* 237
opposite side *n* 237
opposition *n* 237, 708
opposition *n* 14, 24, 218,
489, 710, 719, 720, 726
opposition *n* 179

oppress *v* 649, 739, 823
oppression *n* 649, 739
oppressive *adj* 382, 421,
649, 739, 830
oppressor *n* 739, 913
opprobrious *adj* 874
oppugnance *n* 719
opt for the mean *v* 774
optic *adj* 441
optical instruments *n* 445
optics *n* 420, 441
optimism *n* 482
optimistic *adj* 858
option *n* 600, 609
optional *adj* 600, 609
opulence *n* 803
opus *n* 590, 593
oracle *n* 513
oracle *n* 500
oracular *adj* 511
oral *adj* 580, 582
oral communication
n 588
orange *n* 439
orange *adj* 439
orangish *adj* 439
orangy *adj* 439
oration *n* 582
orator *n* 582
oratory *n* 582
orb *n* 181, 247
orbit *n* 247
orchestra *n* 416, 417
orchestral *adj* 415
orchestral music *n* 415
orchid *adj* 437
ordain *v* 741, 755, 963, 995
ordained *adj* 996
ordeal *n* 722, 828
order *n* 58
order *n* 63, 75, 242, 630,
693, 697, 721, 741, 963;
v 58, 630, 652, 673, 693,
741
ordered *adj* 60, 242
ordering *n* 60
orderliness *n* 58, 652
orderly *adj* 58, 60
order of succession *n* 63
ordinance *n* 741
ordinariness *n* 736
ordinary *adj* 82, 598, 613,
643, 651, 736
ordinary condition *n* 80
oread *n* 979
organic *adj* 357
organic chemistry *n* 357
organic remains *n* 357
organisms *n* 357
organization *n* 60, 161,
329, 626
organizational *adj* 329,
626
organize *v* 60, 161, 626
organized *adj* 58
organizer *n* 626
orgasm *n* 173, 377

orgasmic adj 173, 377
orifice n 260
origin n 66, 153
original n 22, 590, 857;
adj 20, 79, 83, 153, 515,
614
originality n 18, 20, 83,
123, 168, 515
originate v 66, 153, 515
originate from v 154
originate in v 154
origination n 153
originator n 164
ornament n 577, 847
ornament v 577, 847
ornamental adj 847
ornamentation n 847
ornamented adj 577, 847
ornate adj 577, 847
ornateness n 577
ornithology n 368
orthodox adj 82, 983a
orthodoxy n 983a
orthography n 561
oscillate v 148, 314
oscillating adj 149, 314
oscillation n 314
oscillation n 138, 149, 605
ossification n 323
ossify n 323
ostensible adj 448, 617
ostensibly adv 448, 617
ostentation n 882
ostentatious adj 855, 882
ostracism n 893
ostracized adj 893
other adj 15
other side of the coin
n 235
other time n 119
otherworldly adj 317
oust v 297, 789
out adj 187; adv 220
out and out adv 52
outbound adj 295
outbreak n 66, 153, 295,
713
outburst n 173, 295, 825
outcast n 893
outcome n 63, 65, 154
outcry n 404, 411
outdated adj 124
outdo v 33, 303
outer adj 220
outer edges n 233
outer space n 180
outfit n 225; v 225, 727
outflank v 236
outgoing adj 295
outgrow v 194
outgrowth n 65, 154
outing n 266
out in the open adv 338
outlandish adj 10, 83, 853
outlast v 110
outlawed adj 964
outlay n 809

outlet n 260
outline n 230
outline n 240, 448, 596;
v 230
outlined adj 446
outlive v 110, 141
outlook n 441, 446
outlying adj 196, 220
outmoded adj 124
outnumber n 102
out of all proportion
adv 31
out of commission
adj 659
out of danger adj 664
out of date adj 124
out of debt adj 807
out of doors adv 338
out-of-fashion adj 124
out of focus adj 447
out of its element adj 185
out of joint adj 24
out of mind adj 506
out of one's depth
adv 208
out of order adj 59, 651,
674, 923
out of place adj 59, 115,
185
out of practice adj 699
out of proportion adj 241;
adv 641
out of shape adj 243
out of sight adj 447
out of sorts adj 655
out of step adj 24
out-of-style adj 124
out of the frying pan and
into the fire adv 835
out-of-the-way adj 10, 196
out of tune adj 24, 414,
651
out of view adj 447
out of work adj 681
outpost n 196
outpouring n 295
outrage n 173, 619, 649
outrageous adj 31, 853
outrageousness n 853
outrank v 33
outride v 303
outrigger n 215
outright adv 52
outrival v 33
outrun v 303
outset n 66, 293
outside n 220; adj 220
outsider n 448
outside time n 107
outskirts n 196, 227
outspoken adj 703
outspread adj 202
outstretched adj 200, 202
outstrip v 33, 303
outward adj 220, 295
outwards adv 220
outweigh v 33, 175

outwit v 545
oval n 247; adj 247
oven n 386
over adj 40, 67; adv 33,
122, 220, 237
overabound n 641
over again adv 90, 104
over against adv 237
over and above adj 641;
adv 33, 37, 641
over and done with
adv 67
over and over adv 104
overbearing adj 878, 885
over-blown adj 882
overburden v 649
overcast v 421; adj 421,
422, 901a
overcharge n 814; v 577,
814
overcome v 731
over-confident adj 878
overdo v 641
overdose n 641; v 641
overdraw v 555
overdue adj 115, 133
overeat v 957
over-eating n 957
overestimate v 481, 482,
549
overestimated adj 482
overestimation n 482
overflow n 641; v 348, 641
overgrown adj 192, 194
overhang v 206
overhanging adj 206
overhear v 418
overlay v 223, 356a
overload v 641
overlook v 458, 460, 693
overlying adj 206
overly sensitive adj 641
overmatch v 28
overmuch adj 641;
adv 641
over one's head adv 208,
641
overpower v 744
overpowering adj 824
overpraise v 482, 933
overprize v 482
overrate v 482
overrated adj 482
overreach v 303
over-refined adj 477
override v 175
overripe adj 128
overrun v 194, 303, 641
overseer n 694
overshoot v 303
oversight n 495
oversimplification n 78
overspread v 223
overstate v 549
overstatement n 549
overstep v 303
overtask v 679

passing time n 109
pass into v 144
passion n 173, 382, 820, 821, 824, 825, 865, 897
passionate adj 382, 574, 821, 825, 897
passive adj 172, 681, 725
passiveness n 172
passivity n 172, 681, 725
pass judgment v 480
pass muster v 648
pass off v 151
pass on v 360
pass out v 449
pass out of v 295
pass over v 55
pass sentence v 966
pass sentence upon v 480
pass through v 302
pass time v 106
past adj 122
past cure adj 659
paste n 354; v 46
past hope adj 659
pastiche n 41
pastime n 840
pastiness n 352
pastor n 996
pastoral adj 995
past recollection adj 506
past time n 122
pasturage n 344
pasture n 344
pasty adj 354, 391
pat n 276; v 276; adj 23
patch up v 660
patchwork n 41; adj 16a
pate n 450
patent adj 474, 525
paternal adj 166
paternity n 11, 166
path n 260, 278, 302
pathetic adj 830
pathless adj 261
patience n 826
patriarch n 130
patriarchal adj 166
patrician adj 875
patriot n 910
patrol n 664, 668
patron n 795, 890, 912, 977
patronage n 175, 707
patronize v 136
patter v 407
pattern n 22, 240, 650
pattern after v 19
paucity n 32, 103, 640
pauperism n 804
pause n 70, 142, 198, 265, 685, 687; v 70, 142, 265, 681, 687
paw v 379
pawn n 771; v 771, 787, 788
pawning n 788
pay n 973; v 784, 807, 973

pay attention v 457
pay in full v 807
paymaster n 801
payment n 807
payment n 809
pay no attention to v 458
pay out v 809
pea n 249
peace n 721
peace n 265, 403, 714
peaceable adj 721
peaceful adj 174, 265, 685, 721, 826
peacefulness n 174, 721
peacemaker n 724
peace offering n 723
pea-green adj 435
peak n 206, 210
peaked adj 253
peal n 404; v 404, 407
peal of bells n 407
peal of laughter n 838
pearliness n 427
pearly adj 427, 428, 430, 440
pear-shaped adj 249
peasantry n 876
peat n 388
peck at v 298
peculiar adj 5, 79, 83, 870
peculiarities n 5
peculiarity n 83, 550
peculiarly adv 31, 33
pecuniary adj 800
pedagogic adj 537
pedagogical adj 537
pedagogies n 537
pedagogy n 537
pedant n 492
pedantic adj 577
peddler n 797
pedestal n 211
pedestrian n 268; adj 598
pedigree n 69
peek n 441; v 441
peel n 204, 223; v 204, 226
peep n 441; v 441
peephole n 260
peeping adj 455
peep of day n 125
peep up v 446
peer n 27; v 441
peevish adj 684, 901a
peg n 250
pellet n 249
pellucid adj 425, 570
pelt v 276
pen n 232, 752; v 590
penalize v 972, 974
penalized v 974; adj 972
penalizing adj 972
penalty n 974
penalty n 972
penance n 974
penchant n 177, 602
pencil n 556
pendant n 214

pendent adj 214
pendulous adj 214
pendulum n 314
penetrate v 294, 302
penetrating adj 480, 498
penetration n 294, 302, 441, 480, 498
penitence n 950
penitence n 833
penitent n 950; adj 833, 950
penitential adj 950
penitentiary n 752
penmanship n 590
pen name n 565
penniless adj 804
pennywise adj 819
pensioner n 785
pensive adj 451
pent up adj 751
penumbra n 421
penurious adj 819
penury n 804
people n 188, 372, 997; v 102
people the world v 163
pep n 171
pepper n 393; v 392
peppery adj 392
peradventure adv 470
perambulate v 264
perambulation n 266
perceivability n 446
perceivable adj 446
perceive v 375, 441, 490
perceptibility n 446
perceptible adj 446
perception n 418, 441, 453, 490
perceptive adj 375, 465, 490, 842
perch n 189; v 184, 186
perchance adv 156, 470
percolation n 295
percussion n 417
perdition n 162
peregrination n 266
peremptory adj 737, 739
perennial adj 112
perfect n 650, 729; adj 31, 52, 104, 648, 650, 729, 960
perfection n 650
perfection n 52, 648, 729, 960
perfectly adv 729
perfidious adj 544
perforate v 260
perforated adj 260
perforation n 260
perforator n 262
perform v 161, 170, 415, 416, 599, 644, 680, 772, 926
performable adj 470
performance n 161, 599, 680, 729, 772

perform a rite v 998
performer n 416, 599, 690
performing n 680
perfume n 400; v 400
perfumed adj 400
perfunctory adj 53, 640
perhaps adv 470
peril n 665
perilous adj 475, 665
perimeter n 230
period n 108
period n 71, 106, 138, 198, 200
periodic adj 70, 138
periodical adj 138
periodically adv 138
periodicity n 138
peripatetic adj 266
periphery n 230
perish v 2, 162, 360, 659
perishable adj 111
permanence n 141
permanence n 16, 110, 150
permanent adj 106, 110, 141, 150, 613
permanently adv 141
permeable adj 260
permeate v 186, 228, 302
permeation n 186, 228, 302
permissible adj 760
permission n 760
permission n 737, 762
permissive adj 760
permit n 737, 755, 760; v 737, 748, 760, 762
permitted adj 760
permutation n 140, 148
pernicious adj 649, 663
perpendicular adj 212, 246
perpendicularity n 212
perpetrate v 680
perpetrator n 690
perpetual adj 104, 110, 112, 136, 143, 150
perpetually adv 112, 136
perpetuate v 112, 143
perpetuation n 143
perpetuity n 112
perpetuity n 105
perplex v 475, 519, 704, 830
perplexed adj 59
perplexity n 59
persecute v 649, 830
persecution n 649
perseverance n 604a
perseverance n 143, 150, 604, 682
persevere v 604a, 682
persevering adj 604a
persicuity n 518
persist v 106, 110, 141, 143, 604a, 606, 682

persistence n 110, 141, 143, 604a, 606
persistent adj 141, 143, 604a, 606
person n 3, 372
personage n 372
personal adj 5, 79, 372
personality n 5, 13, 79
personate v 19, 554, 599
personify v 554
personnel n 58
persons n 372
perspective n 183, 441, 448
perspicacious adj 480, 498, 868
perspicacity n 441, 480, 868
perspicuity n 570
perspicuous adj 570
perspiration n 299, 339
perspire v 299, 339
persuade v 175, 615, 895
persuasion n 175, 484, 695
persuasive adj 615, 695
pertain to v 9
pertinacious adj 150, 606
pertinacity n 150, 606
pertinent adj 23
perturb v 61, 824
perturbation n 61, 315, 824
peruse v 539
pervade v 186
pervasion n 186
pervasive adj 186
pervasiveness n 186
perverse adj 606, 704, 901a
perversion n 477, 523, 538
perversity n 606
pervert v 477, 523, 538
pessimism n 483, 859
pessimist n 165
pessimistic adj 483, 837
pest n 975
pester n 830
pestilence n 649
pestilential adj 657
pet n 899
petite adj 32
petition n 765, 990; v 765, 990
petitioner n 767
petrification n 321, 323
petrify v 321, 323
petroleum n 356, 388
pettifogging adj 477
pettiness n 32
petty adj 32, 643
petulant adj 684, 901
phantasm n 443, 515
phantom n 4
phase n 7, 8, 71, 448
phenomenon n 151, 448, 872

philanthropic adj 784, 906, 910
philanthropist n 910
philanthropy n 910
philanthropy n 784, 906, 910
philology n 562
philosopher n 500
phonetic adj 561
phonetics n 402, 561
phonology n 402
phony n 548; adj 19, 544
phosphorescence n 423
phosphorescent adj 420, 423
photoengraving n 558
photography n 420
phrase n 566
phrase n 521; v 566
phraseology n 560, 566, 569
physical adj 3, 173, 316
physical elements n 316
physical gratification n 377
physical insensibility n 381
physicality n 316
physical science n 316
physician n 662
physicist n 316
physics n 316
physiognomy n 448
physiology n 357
physique n 364
phytology n 369
pick n 609, 648; v 609
picket v 43
pickings n 793
pickle n 7; v 392, 670
pick of the litter n 648
pickup n 274
picky adj 465
pictorial adj 556
pictorialization n 558
picture n 448, 556; v 554, 594
picture gallery n 556
picturesque adj 556, 845
piddle v 683
piddling adj 643
piebald adj 440
piece n 51
piecemeal adv 51
pieces n 596
piece together v 43
pied adj 440
pierce v 260, 378, 385, 649
piercer n 262
pierce the ears v 404
piercing adj 404, 410, 498
pietist n 987
pietistic adj 987
piety n 987
pig n 857
pigeon n 547
pigeonhole n 182
piggish adj 957

piggishness n 957

pig-headed adj 606

pigment n 428

pigmy adj 193

pile n 72, 256

pile on v 641

pile up v 37

pilfer v 791

pilferer n 792

pilgrim n 268

pilgrimage n 266, 676

pill n 249

pilot n 269, 694; v 693

pimple n 250

pin n 253, 262, 263; v 43, 45

pince-nez n 445

pinch n 8, 704; v 195, 378, 385, 819

pinched adj 203

pinch hit v 147

pine n 655

pinhole n 260

pink n 434

pinnacle n 206, 210

pioneer n 64

pious adj 987

pipe n 350

piquancy n 392, 394

piquant adj 392

pique n 900

piratical adj 791

pirouette n 312

pit n 208, 252, 363

pitapat n 407

pitch n 26, 210, 356a, 402, 413, 431; v 284, 306, 314

pitch black adj 421, 431

pitchy adj 431

piteous adj 830

piteously adv 31

pitfall n 667

pitfall n 530

pith n 5, 221

pithiness n 572

pithy adj 572, 574

pitiable adj 649, 830

pitiful adj 643, 649

pitiless adj 914a

pitilessness n 914a

pit one against another v 464

pittance n 640

pitted adj 848

pity n 914

pity n 821; v 914

pitying adj 914

pivot n 43, 153, 222; v 312

pivotal adj 222

pixie n 979

placate v 723

place n 182

place n 8, 58, 71, 183, 184; v 60, 184

place a bet v 621

place before v 62

placed adj 184

place in the record v 551

place of business n 799

place of departure n 293

place of learning n 542

place of worship n 1000

place side by side v 464

place together v 72

placid adj 721, 826

placidity n 826

plagiarism n 19

plague n 649, 663, 828, 975; v 828, 830

plaid adj 440

plain n 344

plain adj 16, 246, 446, 474, 518, 525, 570, 576, 703, 849, 879

plainly adv 525

plainness n 576

plainness n 570, 703, 849

plainsong n 413

plain-speaking n 518, 570, 703

plain spoken adj 525, 703

plaint n 411

plaintiff n 938

plaintive adj 839

plait n 219, 258; v 219, 258

plan n 626

plan n 60, 453, 673, 692; v 60, 620, 626, 673

plane n 213, 251; v 255, 267, 273; adj 213, 251

planets n 318

planning n 60

plant v 184, 300, 371

plant life n 357, 365, 367

plastered adj 959

plastic adj 324

plasticity n 324

plat v 219

plate n 22, 251; v 204

plateau n 344

plate engraving n 558

platitude n 517

platter n 204, 251

plausibility n 472

plausible adj 472

play n 170, 175, 180, 599; v 170, 416, 554, 599, 680, 840

played out adj 87

player n 416, 599

play false v 544, 940

play for v 621

playful adj 840, 842

playhouse n 599, 728

playing n 840

playing field n 728

play of colors n 440

play on words n 520

play second fiddle to v 749

playwright n 599

playwriter n 599

playwriting n 599

plea n 617

plea n 411

plead v 617, 765, 968

pleader n 968

pleading n 717

pleadings n 969

pleasant adj 829, 836, 840, 842

pleasantness n 829

pleasantry n 842

please v 829

pleasing adj 413, 850

pleasing sounds n 413

pleasing combination n 413

pleasing sounds n 415

pleasurable adj 377, 829

pleasurableness n 829

pleasure n 377

pleasure n 827

pleasure n 377, 600, 840

pleasure-seeker n 954a

pleat n 258; v 258

plebeian adj 851, 878

pledge n 177, 768, 771; v 768, 788

pledged adj 768

pledging n 788

plenty n 639

plethora n 641

pliability n 324

pliable adj 324

pliancy n 324, 705, 725

pliant adj 324, 705

plight n 7, 8

plod v 275, 682

plot n 626; v 626

plough v 371

plow n 259, 371

plowed adj 959

pluck n 150, 604, 604a, 861; v 789

plucked instruments n 417

pluck out v 301

plug n 261, 263; v 261

plugging n 261

plug up one's ears v 419

plumb adj 212

plum-colored adj 437

plump adj 192

plumpness n 192

plunder n 793

plunge n 310

plunge n 300; v 208, 300, 310, 337, 863

plunge into v 676

plural adj 100

plurality n 100

plus adv 37

ply n 258; v 677

pock n 250

pocket n 789

poesy n 597

poet n 597

poetaster n 597
poetic adj 521, 597
poetical adj 597
poetic device n 521
poeticize v 597
poetics n 521, 597
poetry n 597
poetry n 590
poignancy n 392
poignant adj 516
point n 8, 26, 32, 71, 180a,
  182, 253, 620; v 253, 278
point-blank adj 703;
  adv 278, 576
pointed adj 201, 253, 516,
  518
pointedly adv 31, 620
pointedness n 253
pointer n 550
point of departure n 293
point of view n 441
point out v 525
points of the compass
  n 278
point to v 155, 472, 516,
  638
point toward v 278
poison n 659, 663
poisonous adj 649, 657,
  663
polar adj 210, 383
polarity n 89, 179, 218,
  237
pole n 222
polemic n 726
polemicist n 476
poles apart adv 237
policy n 626, 692
polish n 255, 578, 850;
  v 255, 331
polished adj 255, 578, 850,
  852
polite adj 383, 457, 852,
  879, 894, 928
politeness n 457, 894
polite society n 852
politic adj 498, 702
poll n 85; v 85
pollute n 653, 659
poltroon n 862
poltroonery n 862
polyglot adj 560
polyp n 250
polyphony n 413
polysyllabic n 561
pommel n 249
pomp n 882
pompous adj 482, 577, 882
pompousness n 882
pond n 343
ponder v 451, 870
pondering n 451
ponderous adj 319, 579
pool n 343, 709; v 709
poor adj 34, 477, 575, 640,
  643, 736, 804, 828, 879
poorer adj 34

poorly adj 655
poorly timed adj 135
poorness n 34, 640
poor substitute adj 651
pop n 166, 406
pop off v 360
populace n 72, 876
popular adj 415
popular music n 415
populate v 102
population n 188, 372
populous adj 72, 102
pop up v 446
porch n 231, 260
pore over v 539
porous adj 260
port n 239
portable adj 270
portal n 231, 260
portend v 511, 668, 909
portent n 511, 512, 668,
  909
portentous adj 511, 668
porter n 271;532
portion n 51, 100a, 786
portion out v 786
portly adj 192
portrait n 21
portraiture n 554
portray v 554, 594
portrayal n 594
pose n 183; v 475, 704, 855
position n 8, 71, 183, 625
positive adj 1, 31, 84, 246,
  474, 484, 535
possess v 777
possessed adj 503
possessed of adj 777
possessing adj 777
possession n 777
possession n 780
possessions n 780
possessive adj 777
possess oneself of v 789
possessor n 779
possess the means v 632
possibility n 470
possibility n 2, 156
possible adj 2, 177, 470,
  515
possibly adv 470
post n 183; v 184, 274, 811
post bail v 771
post card n 592
postdate v 115
posterior n 235; adj 117,
  235
posteriority n 117
posteriority n 63
posterity n 67
posterity n 121
posthaste adv 274
posthumous adj 117
postman n 271
post meridian n 126
post mortem
  examination n 363

postpone v 133
postponement n 133
postscript n 65
postulant n 767
postulate n 476, 514;
  v 476
posture n 8, 183, 240
potable adj 298
pot-bellied adj 194
potency n 157, 159
potent adj 157, 159, 171,
  175
potential n 2; adj 2, 470,
  526
potentiality n 470, 526
potion n 298
potpourri n 41
potted adj 959
potting n 557
pound n 232; v 330
pour v 333, 348
pour forth v 584
pour in v 294
pour out v 295, 348
pour out v 295
pout v 900, 901a
poverty n 804
poverty-stricken adj 804
powder n 330
powdery adj 330
power n 157
power n 159, 171, 175,
  404, 574, 737, 741, 965;
  v 388
powerful adj 157, 159,
  171, 175, 404, 574
powerfully adv 31, 157
powerless adj 158, 160
powerlessness n 158,
  175a
practicability n 705
practicable adj 644, 705
practical adj 170, 470,
  644, 692
practicality n 470
practically adv 5
practice n 613, 692; v 677
practiced adj 698
practice law v 968
practice sorcery v 992
practitioner n 690
pragmatism n 646
prairie n 344
praise v 883, 931, 990
praised adj 931
praiseworthy adj 931
prance n 315
prank n 608
prate v 584, 588
prattle n 582, 584, 588
pray n 990
prayer n 411, 765, 990
preacher n 540, 996
preamble n 64
precarious adj 111, 475,
  665
precariousness n 665

precaution n 510, 664, 673
precautionary adj 673
precede v 62, 116, 280
precedence n 62, 280
precedence n 116
precedent n 22, 64, 80, 813, 969; adj 62
preceding adj 62, 116
precept n 697
precept n 630
precincts n 227
precious adj 31, 814
precipice n 212, 306, 667
precipitancy n 684
precipitate v 684; adj 132, 684, 863
precipitately adv 132
precipitation n 132, 684
precipitous adj 217, 306
pré cis n 596; v 596
precise adj 494, 518
precision n 80, 494, 518
preclude v 761
precluded adj 893
preclusion n 893
precocious adj 132
precocity n 132
precursor n 64
precursor n 62, 116, 280, 534
precursory adj 64, 116
predatory adj 789, 791
predecessor n 64, 116
predeliberation n 611
predestination n 611
predestine v 152, 611
predetermination n 611
predetermine v 611
predicament n 8, 183, 704
predicate v 514
predict v 507, 510, 511
prediction n 511
prediction n 668
predilection n 177, 609
predisposed adj 820
predisposition n 176, 820
predominance n 33, 175
predominant adj 175, 737
predominate v 33, 175
pre-eminence n 33, 206
pre-eminent adj 33, 206
pre-eminently adv 31, 33
pre-engage v 132
pre-existence n 116
pre-existent adj 116
preface n 64; v 62
prefatory adj 62, 64
prefer v 609
preference n 62, 609
preferential adj 609
prefix n 64; v 62
prehistoric adj 124
prelacy n 995
preliminary adj 62, 64, 673
prelude n 64, 66

premature adj 132, 135, 674
prematurely adv 132
prematurity n 132
premeditate v 611
premeditation n 611
premises n 476
premium n 973
premonition n 668
premonitory adj 511, 668
preordain v 152
preparation n 673
preparation n 60, 64, 537
preparative adj 673
preparatory adj 62, 673
prepare v 60, 537, 673
prepared adj 507, 673, 698
prepare for v 507, 673
prepare for battle v 727
prepatory adj 673
preponderance n 33, 175
preponderant adj 737
preposterous adj 497, 549, 853
preposterously adv 31
prepubescence n 131
prerequisite n 630
prerogative n 924
presage n 511, 668; v 116, 511, 909
presbyopia n 443
prescience n 510
prescient adj 510
prescribe v 693, 695, 741
prescribed adj 474, 924
prescript n 697
prescription n 613, 697, 924
prescriptive adj 124, 613, 983a
presence n 186
presence n 1, 448
present n 784; v 448, 763, 784; adj 118, 186
presentation n 784
present events n 151
presentiment n 477
present itself v 446
presently adv 132
present the music v 416
present time n 118
present to the view v 448
preservation n 670
preservation n 141, 664, 717, 781
preservative adj 670
preserve v 141, 143, 664, 670, 717, 781
preserved adj 670
preserver n 664
president n 694
press n 72; v 255, 319
press forward v 684
press in v 300
pressing adj 642
press into service v 677

press on v 622, 684
press onward v 282
pressure n 175, 319, 642, 735
presto adv 113
presumable adj 472
presumably adv 472
presume v 484, 514, 858, 878, 885
presumption n 507, 514, 878, 925
presumptive adj 514
presumptuous adj 863, 878, 885
presuppose v 514
pretend v 544, 546, 617, 855
pretender n 548, 925
pretense n 617, 855, 882
pretension n 577, 855, 882
pretentious adj 482, 855, 882, 884
pretentiousness n 882
pretext n 617
pretty adj 845; adv 31
pretty well adv 31, 32
prevail v 78, 175
prevailing adj 78, 983a
prevail upon v 615
prevalence n 33, 78, 175, 613
prevalent adj 1, 78, 175, 613
prevaricate v 520, 544
prevarication n 520, 544
prevent v 706, 708, 761
preventing n 706
prevention n 761
preventive adj 761
previous adj 116
previously adv 116
prevision n 510
prey n 620
price n 812
price v 812
priceless adj 33, 648, 814
prick n 253; v 260, 378, 380
pricking n 380
prickle n 253
prickly adj 253, 256
prick up one's ears v 418
pride n 878
pride n 880
priest n 904, 996
priesthood n 995, 996
priestly adj 995
prig n 854
priggish adj 868
prim adj 868
primal adj 66, 153
primary adj 153, 642
primary color n 428
prime n 125, 648; v 537, 673; adj 84, 642, 648
prime mover n 153, 976
prime of day n 125

primer n 542, 567
primeval adj 124
primitive adj 124
primordial adj 124
princely adj 816
prince of darkness n 978
principal n 694; adj 642
principally adv 33
principle n 5, 80, 153, 211, 537, 615
print n 591; v 531, 558, 590, 591
printed adj 591
printer n 591
printing n 591
prior adj 62, 116
priority n 62, 116, 280
prior to adv 116
prism n 428, 445
prismatic adj 428, 440
prison n 752
prison n 975
prisoner n 754
pristine adj 122
privacy n 893
private adj 79, 221, 528, 533, 893
privately adv 881
privation n 776, 804
privilege n 748, 924, 927a
privileged adj 924, 927a
privy adj 528
privy to adv 490
prize n 618, 733, 793, 973; v 991
probability n 472
probability n 156
probable adj 472, 858
probably adv 472
probationary adj 675
probative adj 463, 478
probe n 262
probity n 939
probity n 543, 944
problem n 533, 704
problematical adj 59, 475
procedural adj 80, 626, 692
procedure n 80, 463, 626, 627, 680, 692, 998
proceed v 109, 282, 302
proceed from v 154
proceeding n 151, 282; adj 53
proceeds n 775
proceed with v 692
process n 627, 692
procession n 69, 266
proclaim v 531, 883
proclamation n 531, 985
proclivity n 176, 686, 820
procrastinate v 133
procrastination n 133, 683
procreate v 161, 168
procreation n 161, 168
procreative adj 168

procreator n 166
procure v 775, 795
procurement n 775
prod v 276
prodigal n 818; adj 638, 818
prodigality n 818
prodigality n 638
prodigal son n 950
prodigious adj 31
prodigy n 872
prodigy n 700
produce v 775, 798; v 153, 161, 168
produce a good effect v 648
produce nothing v 169
producer n 164
producer n 153
product n 84, 154, 161, 798
production n 153
production n 153
productive adj 153, 161, 168, 644
productiveness n 168
productiveness n 644
productivity n 168
proem n 64
profanation n 679
profane v 679, 988
profaneness n 988
profanity n 988
profession n 535, 625, 768
professional n 700; adj 625
professor n 540
proffer v 763
proficiency n 698, 731
proficient adj 698, 731
profile n 230, 236, 448; v 230
profit n 618, 775; v 618, 648, 775
profitability n 646
profitable adj 644, 646, 648, 775, 810
profit by v 677
profitless adj 645
profligacy n 818
profligate n 962; adj 818, 945
profound adj 31, 208, 498
profundity n 208, 875
profuse adj 102, 573, 641, 818
profuseness n 573, 641, 818
profusion n 102, 641, 818
progenitor n 166
progeny n 167
prognosticate v 507, 511, 909
prognostication n 511, 909
progress n 144, 264, 282, 731; v 282, 658, 731

progression n 282
progression n 58, 69
progressive adj 69, 282, 658
prohibit v 761, 893
prohibited adj 893, 964
prohibition n 761
prohibition n 55, 893
prohibitive adj 761
project n 620, 626; v 250, 284, 620, 626
projection n 250, 284
proletarian adj 876
proletariat n 876
prolific adj 161, 168
prolix adj 573
prolog n 64
prolong v 35, 110, 133, 143, 200
prolongation n 110, 133, 143
prolonged adj 110
promenade n 266
prominence n 206, 250, 307, 642
prominent adj 206, 250, 642
prominently adv 31, 33
promiscuous adj 41
promise n 768
promise n 771; v 676, 768, 769, 771
promised adj 768
promises n 770
promising adj 858
promissory adj 768, 769
promissory note n 771
promontory n 250
promote v 176, 658, 707
prompt v 505, 615; adj 132, 682
promptitude n 132, 684
promptness n 684
promulgate v 531
promulgation n 531
prone adj 207, 213, 820
proneness n 176, 207, 213
pronounce v 535, 580, 582, 586
pronouncement n 531, 535
proof n 463, 467, 478, 591
proofreader n 591
prop n 215; v 707
propagandist n 540
propagate v 161, 531
propagation n 168, 531
propel v 264, 284
propensity n 176, 177, 602, 820
proper adj 79, 494, 578, 646, 868, 881, 922
proper name n 564
proper time n 134
property n 780
prophecy n 511

punished v 974; adj 972
punishing adj 972
punishment n 972
punishment n 974, 975
punitive adj 972
punster n 844
punt v 267
puny adj 193
pupil n 492, 541
puppet n 547
purblind adj 442, 443
purblindness n 443
purchase n 795
purchase n 775; v 795
purchaser n 795
purchasing n 795
pure adj 42, 494, 576, 578, 652, 881, 944, 946, 960, 977
purely adv 32
purgation n 652
purgative n 652
purge n 297, 652, 952
purification n 42, 652
purify v 42, 652
purist n 578
puritan n 955
puritanical adj 955
puritanism n 955
purity n 960
purity n 42, 578, 652, 944, 946
purlieus n 227
purloin n 791
purple n 437, 625
purple adj 437
purplish adj 437
purport v 516; n 516
purpose n 451, 516, 800, 615, 620; v 451, 516, 620
purposeful adj 604
purposely adv 620
purr v 412
purring n 412
purse n 802
purser n 801
pursuance n 622
pursue v 143, 286, 281, 622
pursuit n 622
pursuit n 461, 622
pursuit of knowledge n 539
purvey v 637
purveyance n 637
purveying n 637
push n 276, 284; v 276, 284, 682
push ahead v 682
push aside v 297
push away v 297
push back v 289
push on v 684
pusillanimous adj 862
pustule n 250
put v 184
put about v 311

put an end to v 67
put an end to oneself v 361
put aside v 55, 636, 678
put away v 528
put down v 856
put forth v 514
put forward v 763
put in v 300
put in motion v 284
put in order v 660
put in the place of v 147
put into operation v 677
put into shape v 60
put into words v 566
put off v 133, 226
put on airs v 855
put on a pedestal v 991
put one's trust on v 484
put on sale v 813
put on the brakes v 275
put on the stage v 599
put on trial v 969
put out v 385, 421
put out of order v 59
put out to sea v 293
put pen to paper v 590
putrefaction n 49, 653
putrefy v 653
putrid adj 401, 653
put right v 246, 662
put straight v 246
putter v 683
put things in order v 652
put to death v 361
put to flight v 717
put together v 43
put to sea v 267
put to the sword v 361
put to use v 677
putty n 356a
put up v 161, 235, 636
put up to v 615
put up with v 151, 826
puzzle v 475
puzzlement n 870
puzzling adj 519

Q

quack n 548
quadrilateral adj 95
quadripartite adj 97
quadripartition n 97
quadrisection v 97
quadruped n 366
quadruple adj 96
quadruplicate v 96
quadruplication n 96
quadrupling n 96
quaff v 298
quaggy adj 345
quagmire n 345, 653
quail n 392
quaint adj 83
quake n 314, 315, 383
qualification n 469

qualification n 140, 536, 698, 813
qualified adj 469, 698
qualify v 140, 174, 469
qualifying adj 469
qualities n 820
quality n 5, 33, 176, 550, 780, 875, 944
qualm n 485, 603
quandary n 704
quantitative adj 25
quantity n 25
quantity n 31, 72, 102
quarrel n 713, 720; v 24, 713
quarrelsome adj 713, 720
quarry n 620
quarter n 95, 97, 181, 236, 740; v 97, 184
quartered adj 97
quartering n 97
quarter of a hundred n 96
quarters n 189
quartet n 95, 415, 416
quasi adv 17
quaternity n 95
quaver n 315, 407, 406; v 314, 315
queer adj 83
queer fish n 857
quell v 265
query n 461; v 461
quest n 622, 676
quester n 268
question n 333, 533; v 461, 475, 870, 989
questionable adj 473, 475, 485, 520
questionableness n 473, 475, 520
questioning n 461, 539; adj 461
quibble n 520; v 477
quibbling adj 477
quick adj 111, 274, 498, 682, 684, 698, 842
quick as lightning adj 274
quicken v 132, 170, 173, 274, 359, 684, 824
quickly adv 132
quickness n 132, 274, 684
quicksand n 667
quick-tempered adj 901
quick to fly off the handle v 842
quick-witted adj 842
quiddity n 477
quid pro quo n 30
quiescence n 150, 172, 265, 403, 526, 683
quiescent adj 172, 265, 403
quiet n 174, 403, 721;

rear rank n 235
rearward adv 235
reason n 450, 498, 502, 615; v 450, 498
reasonable adj 174, 472, 498, 502, 736, 815
reasonable chance n 472
reasonableness n 174; 498
reasoner n 476
reason falsely v 477
reasoning n 476
reasoning v 476
reasons n 476
reason why n 155
reassuring adj 858
rebate n 813; v 813
rebel n 165, 489; v 146, 719, 742
rebellion n 146, 719, 742
rebellious adj 146, 715, 742
rebelliousness n 715, 742
reborn adj 660
rebound n 145, 277; v 145, 277
rebuff n 277, 289, 764; v 289, 610, 764
rebuild v 660
rebuilding n 660
rebut v 462, 468, 536
rebuttal n 468, 536
recalcitrance n 715
recalcitrant adj 715, 719, 742, 764
recall v 451, 505
recant v 536, 607
recantation n 607
recantation n 536
recapitulate v 104
recapitulation n 104
recast v 140, 146, 626
recede v 283, 287
receipt n 810
receipt n 771, 807
receive v 76, 296, 775, 785, 789, 810
receive an impression v 821
received adj 490, 785
receive pleasure v 377
receiver n 191, 785, 801
receive the call v 996
receiving 785
receiving adj 785
recent adj 122, 123, 435
recentness n 123
receptacle n 191
reception n 296
reception n 76, 292, 785
recess n 198, 244, 530, 687
recesses n 221
recession n 287
recession n 283, 659
recipient n 785
reciprocal adj 12, 148, 718

reciprocally adv 12
reciprocate v 12, 148
reciprocation n 12, 148, 718
reciprocity n 12, 148, 718
recision n 756
recital n 594
recitation n 582
recite v 85, 594
reckless adj 884, 863
recklessness n 460, 863
reckon v 85, 480, 873
reckoning n 85, 466, 507, 807, 811, 973
reclaim v 660, 952
reclamation n 660, 952
reclination n 213
recline v 213, 687
recluse n 893, 955
recognition n 505, 733
recognizable adj 446
recognize v 441
recognized adj 490
recoil n 277
recoil n 145, 283, 287, 603, 623; v 145, 179, 277, 287, 325, 603, 623
recollect v 451, 505
recollection n 505
recommend v 695
recommendation n 695
recompense n 973; v 30, 807, 973
reconcilable adj 23
reconcile v 723, 831
reconcile oneself to v 826
reconciliation n 723
recondition v 662
reconstitute v 660
reconstruct v 660
reconstruction n 660
reconversion n 660
record n 551
record n 86, 527, 594; v 60, 551
reorder n 53
recount v 594
recounting n 594
recoup v 660, 790
recouperative adj 790
recourse n 677
recover v 660, 789, 790
recovery n 660, 789, 790
recovery of strength n 689
recreant adj 544, 862
recreation n 840
recrimination n 718
rectification n 660
rectify v 246, 658
rectilinear adj 246
rectitude n 922, 939, 944
recumbency n 213
recuperate adj 660
recur v 104, 136, 138
recure v 660

recurrence n 104, 136
recurrent adj 70, 104, 138
recurring adj 104, 136, 138
recur to v 677
recurve v 245
recusancy n 984
recusant adj 984
red n 434
red adj 434
red and yellow n 439
red as a lobster adj 434
red as beet adj 434
redden v 434
reddish adj 434
redeem v 30, 147, 660, 672, 790, 952
redemption n 660, 672, 952
redemptive adj 790, 952
redesign v 140
red-faced adj 434
red-hot adj 824
redneck n 887
redness n 434
redolence n 398, 400
redolent adj 398, 400
redouble v 35, 90
redress n 660, 662, 973; v 660, 662
reduce v 38, 103, 195, 201, 308, 638, 813
reduced adj 34, 103, 201
reduce to v 144
reduce to a square v 95
reducible adj 38
reductio ad absurdum n 476
reduction n 36, 103, 144, 195, 201, 813
reduction to power n 330
redundance n 641
redundance n 104
redundancy n 573
redundant adj 104, 641
reduplicate v 90
reduplication n 90
re-echo v 408
reed instruments n 417
reef n 346
reefs n 667
reek v 401, 653
reeking adj 382, 401
reeky adj 653
reel v 314, 315
reestablish v 660
reestablishment n 660
refashion v 163
referable adj 155
referable to adj 9
referee n 967; v 174
reference n 9, 467
reference to n 155
referential adj 467
refer to v 9, 155, 695
refine v 477, 652, 658

remodel v 140, 144, 146
remonstrance n 616, 766
remonstrate v 616, 766
remonstrative adj 766
remorse n 833, 950
remorseful adj 950
remorseless adj 945
remote adj 10, 196
remote cause n 153
remoteness n 196
remote past n 122
removable adj 38
removal n 38, 185, 270, 287, 293, 301
remove v 196; v 2, 38, 185, 270, 301, 682
removed adj 196
remunerate v 30, 807, 973
remuneration n 973
remunerative adj 775, 810, 973
renaissance n 660
renascence n 660
renascent adj 163, 660
rend v 44
render v 144, 784, 790
render blunt v 254
render certain v 474
render concave v 252
render curved v 245
render few v 103
render general v 78
render horizontal v 213
render insensible v 376
render intelligible v 518
render invisible v 447
render oblique v 217
render powerless v 158
render sensible v 375
render straight v 246
render uncertain v 475
render unintelligible v 519
rendezvous n 74
renegade n 607
renew v 90, 123, 163, 660, 689
renewal n 90, 163, 660
renounce v 536, 607, 610, 624, 757, 764, 782
renovate v 123, 163, 660
renovated adj 123
renovation n 123, 163, 660
renown n 31, 873
renowned adj 873, 883
rent n 44, 198, 260; v 788
renunciation n 607, 610, 624, 757, 764, 782
reorganize v 144, 660
repair n 658, 660, 689; v 658, 660, 662, 689, 790, 952
reparation n 30, 660, 790, 952, 973
reparatory adj 973
repartee n 842

repay v 718

repeal n 756; v 756
repeat v 90, 104, 136
repeated adj 104
repeatedly adv 104, 136
repel v 289, 610, 616, 717, 719, 764, 830, 867
repellant adj 830
repellent adj 289, 719, 867
repelling adj 289
repent v 833, 950, 952
repentance n 833, 950
repentant adj 950
repenting adj 950
repercussion n 145
repetition n 104
repetition n 17, 90, 136, 143, 641
repetitious adj 104, 641
repetitive adj 104
repine v 832
replace v 63, 147, 660
replacement n 147, 634, 660
replenish v 52, 637
replete adj 52, 641
repletion n 641, 869
replica n 13, 19, 21
reply n 462; v 462
reported adj 527
reporter n 527, 532, 534
repose n 687
repose v 265, 681; v 265, 685, 687
reposing adj 687
repository n 191
reprehensible adj 649, 923, 945
represent v 147, 550, 554, 556, 594, 759
representation n 554
representation n 17, 19, 21, 550, 556, 594, 599, 626
representative n 147, 524, 534, 690, 758, 759; adj 17, 550, 554
representing adj 17
repress v 179, 751, 826
repression n 179, 751
repressive adj 751
reprieve n 133, 671, 672, 918; v 672, 918
reprint n 21
reprisal n 148, 718, 789, 919
reproach v 932
reproachful adj 932
reproduce v 19, 104, 163, 168, 660
reproduction n 163
reproduction n 13, 19, 21, 104, 660
reproductive adj 163
reproof n 972

reprove v 932, 972
reprover n 936
reptile n 366
repudiate v 55, 489, 536, 610, 764
repudiation n 55, 536, 610, 764, 808
repugnance n 867, 898
repugnant adj 867, 898
repulse n 145, 277, 289, 764; v 289, 719, 764
repulsed adj 893
repulsion n 289
repulsion n 719
repulsive adj 289, 395, 719, 830, 846, 867, 898
reputable adj 246, 873
reputation n 873
repute n 873
reputed adj 873
request n 765
request v 741, 865; v 630, 765, 865
require v 601, 630, 640, 741, 744, 765, 812
requirement n 630
requirement n 601, 741
requisite v 601, 630; adj 601, 630
requisition n 630, 741
requital n 30, 148, 718, 919, 973
requite v 148, 718, 919, 973
rescind v 44, 756, 764
rescue n 672, 707; v 660, 670, 672, 707
research n 461, 463
resemblance n 13, 17, 216
resemble v 17, 197
resembling adj 17
resent v 900, 907, 919, 920
resentful adj 900, 907, 919, 920
resentment n 900
resentment n 907, 920
reservation n 528
reserve n 528, 585, 836; v 636, 678, 781
reserved adj 383, 528, 585, 901a
reservoir n 191, 343, 636
reside v 188
residence n 189
resident n 188; adj 186
residual adj 40
residue n 40
residuum n 40
resign v 624, 725, 757, 782
resignation n 757
resignation n 624, 725, 782, 826, 831
resigned adj 826, 831
resign oneself to v 826
resilience n 325
resiliency n 325
resilient adj 325

reverse n 235, 237; v 145,
218; adj 14, 218, 237
reversion n 145
reversion n 218
revert v 14, 104, 145, 283,
287
reverting n 145
review n 595
reviewer n 480, 595
revile v 988
reviler n 936
revise v 658
revision n 658
revival n 163, 660, 689
revive v 163, 359, 660, 689
revivification n 163, 660
revivify v 159, 163, 660
revocation n 607, 756
revoke v 536, 607, 756, 764
revolt n 146; v 146, 289,
719, 742, 830
revolting adj 846, 898
revolution n 146
revolution n 138, 140, 218,
312
revolutionary adj 146, 742
revolutionize v 146
revolve v 138, 312
revolving adj 312
revulsion n 145, 146, 218,
277
reward n 973
reward n 733; v 973
rewarded adj 973
rewarding adj 973
rhapsodic adj 497
rhapsodist n 598, 597
rhapsody n 497
rhetoric n 517, 577, 582
rhetorical adj 577
rhetorical flourish n 577
rhetorician n 582
rheumy adj 337
rhyme v 597
rhymeless adj 598
rhymer n 597
rhymes n 597
rhyme with v 17
rhyming n 597
rhythm n 104, 138, 413
rhythm n 413
rhythmic adj 104, 138,
597
rhythmical adj 138
rib n 215
ribald adj 961
ribaldry n 961
ribbed adj 259
rich adj 394, 413, 428, 577,
734, 803
riches n 803
richly adv 31
richness n 573
rickety adj 160
ricochet n 145, 277; v 277
riddle n 520; v 260
ride n 226

rider n 39, 268
ride roughshod over
v 885
ride the waves v 267
ridge n 250, 346
ridicule n 856
ridicule v 856, 929
ridiculous adj 497, 499
ridiculousness n 853
rid of adj 776
rife adj 78, 175
rifler n 792
rift n 44, 198, 260
rig n 272
rigging n 225
right n 780, 924, 965;
v 246, 658, 662; adj 494,
922, 944
right ahead adv 234
right and left adv 180,
227
right angle n 244
righteous adj 944, 977
righteously adv 922
righteous man n 967
rightful adj 494, 922
rightfully adv 922
right hand n 238
right-handed adj 238
rightly adv 922
right now n 118
right on adj 494
right side n 238
rigid adj 82, 150, 240, 323,
704, 739, 955
rigidity n 141, 323, 739
rigorous adj 739, 955
rigorousness n 739
rig out v 225
rill n 348
rim n 231
rimple n 258; v 258
rind n 223
ring n 247, 408, 712, 726;
v 408
ringing n 408; adj 413
ring in the ear v 408
ring in the ears v 404
riot n 59, 173; v 173
rioter n 742
riotous adj 59, 173, 742
ripe adj 128, 673
ripe age n 128
ripen v 144, 650, 658, 673
ripeness n 124, 131, 673
ripen into v 144
ripe old age n 128
rip open v 260
rip out v 301
ripple n 258, 314, 315, 348;
v 258, 314
rise n 35, 217, 282, 305;
v 35, 146, 305, 734
rise above v 31

rise from v 154
rise up v 146, 206, 719
rising n 146, 305;
adj 217, 305
rising ground n 217
risk n 665; v 621, 665
risky adj 665
rite n 998
rites n 990
ritualistic adj 998
ritualize v 883
rival n 710, 726; v 648, 720
rivalry n 720
rive v 44
river n 348
river n 348
rivet v 43, 824
rivulet n 348
road n 278, 302, 627
road to ruin n 162
roam v 266
roan adj 433
roar n 404, 408, 411;
v 173, 404, 411, 412, 838
roaring n 404
roast v 384
rob v 791
robber n 792
robbery n 791
robe n 999; v 225
robust adj 159, 654, 836
robust health n 654
rock n 342, 415
rock and roll band n 416
rocks n 667
rod n 215, 975
roe n 374
rogue n 941
role n 625
roll n 407
roll n 86, 248, 249, 312,
408; v 248, 255, 264, 314,
348, 407
roll call n 85
roller n 249
rolling pin n 249
rolling seas n 348
roll into a ball v 249
roll on v 264
romance n 515
romantic adj 504; adj 515
romp v 173
roof n 223
rookie n 701
room n 180
roomy adj 180
roost n 189; v 186
root n 153; v 184
rooted adj 124, 184
root out v 301
ropy adj 205
rosin n 356a; v 356a
rosy adj 434
rot n 49, 653; v 49, 653,
659
rotary adj 312
rotate v 312

rotating *adj* 312
rotation *n* 312
rotation *n* 138, 145
rotten *adj* 160, 401, 649, 653, 659
rottenness *n* 659
rotund *adj* 249
rotundity *n* 249
rotundity *n* 247
roué *n* 962
rough *adj* 16a, 173, 241, 254, 256, 329, 397, 410, 674
roughen *v* 256
rough-hewn *adj* 256
rough it *v* 686
roughness *n* 256
roughness *n* 254
rough seas *n* 348
rough up *v* 256
round *n* 69, 138; *v* 245, 247, 249; *adj* 247, 249, 254
roundabout *adj* 279, 311, 573, 629; *adv* 279
roundabout way *n* 629
round and round
  adv 138, 248
rounded *adj* 245, 247, 254
rounded inward *adj* 252
roundness *n* 247, 249
round number *n* 84
round the edge *v* 254
rouse *v* 175, 615, 824
rouse oneself *v* 682
rousing *adj* 171
route *n* 302, 627
routine *n* 18, 58, 80, 138, 613; *adj* 16, 138
rout out *v* 652
rove *v* 266, 279
rover *n* 268
roving *adj* 266; *adj* 266
row *n* 59, 69; *v* 267
rowdy *n* 887
royalty *n* 875
rpm *n* 138
rub *v* 255, 331, 379
rubadub *n* 407
rubbery *adj* 325
rubbing *n* 331, 379
rubbish *n* 643
rub out *v* 331, 552
ruby *adj* 434
ruckus *n* 59
ruddy *adj* 434
rude *adj* 173, 241, 579, 851, 885, 895, 929
rudeness *n* 885, 895, 929
rudimental *adj* 66, 674
rudiments *n* 66
rue *v* 833, 950
rueful *adj* 830, 833
ruffian *n* 887
ruffle *v* 258; *v* 59, 256, 258, 824

rugged *adj* 241, 256
ruin *n* 162, 619, 638;
  v 162, 619
ruinous *adj* 162, 619, 663, 830
ruins *n* 40
rule *n* 80, 157, 175, 240, 466, 537, 613, 693, 737, 741; *v* 157, 480, 693, 737, 749
rulebook *n* 567
ruler *n* 737, 745
rules of language *n* 567
ruling passion *n* 820
rumble *n* 408; *v* 59, 407
rumbling *n* 407
ruminate *v* 450, 451
rumor *n* 532
rump *n* 235
rumple *v* 256, 258
rumus *n* 59
run *n* 264; 109, 264, 274, 333, 348
run abreast *v* 27
run against *v* 276
run amuck *v* 173
runaway *n* 623
run away *v* 287, 671
run counter to *v* 179
run down *v* 649, 934;
  adj 124
run for one's life *v* 623
run headlong *v* 173
run into *v* 276
run into trouble *v* 665
run its course *v* 67, 109, 122
runner *n* 271, 534
running water *n* 348
run off at the mouth
  v 584
run on and on *v* 573
run out *v* 67
run over *v* 641
run parallel *v* 178
run riot *v* 173, 641
run smoothly *v* 705
run the eye over *v* 441
run the fingers over *v* 379
run the risk of *v* 177
run through *v* 186, 361
run up against *v* 179
run up bills *v* 808
run wild *v* 173, 825
rupture *n* 44, 713, 720;
  v 44
ruse *n* 545
rush *n* 72, 274, 310, 348, 684; *v* 173, 274, 310, 684
russet *adj* 433
rust *v* 659; *adj* 433
rustic *adj* 876
rustle *v* 409
rusty *adj* 659, 683, 699
rut *n* 259, 613
ruthless *adj* 739, 914a

S

Sabbath *n* 687
sable *adj* 431
saboteur *n* 361
saccharine *adj* 396
saccharinity *n* 396
sacred *adj* 976, 987
sacrilege *n* 988
sacrilegist *n* 988
sacrosanct *adj* 976
sad *adj* 649, 837
sadden *v* 830
sadly *adv* 31
sadness *n* 837
safe *n* 802; *adj* 664, 670
safe and sound *adj* 664
safecracker *n* 792
safeguard *n* 664, 666, 670, 717; *v* 670, 717
safekeeping *n* 664, 670
safety *n* 664
safety valve *n* 664
saffron *adj* 435
sag *v* 245
sagacious *adj* 498, 842, 868
sagacity *n* 480, 498, 698, 842
sage *n* 500
sage *n* 492, 872; *adj* 498
sail *n* 267; *v* 267
sailboat *n* 273
sailing *n* 267; *adj* 267
sailor *n* 269
saint *n* 948
saintly *adj* 987
salable *adj* 796
salad oil *n* 356
sale *n* 796
sale *n* 783, 813
salesman *n* 797
saleswoman *n* 797
salient *adj* 250, 642
sallow *adj* 429, 430, 435
sally *n* 716; *v* 293
salmon *adj* 434
salt *n* 393; *v* 392
salt and pepper *n* 432;
  adj 440
salt of the earth *n* 648, 948
salt water *n* 341
salty *adj* 392
salubrious *adj* 656
salubrity *n* 656
salutary *adj* 644, 648, 656
salutation *n* 896
salute *n* 896; *v* 586, 836, 896
salvation *n* 670, 672
salve *n* 356
salvo *n* 406
sameness *n* 13, 16, 17, 104
sample *n* 82
sanctify *v* 987
sanctimoniousness *n* 988

sanctimony n 988
sanction n 737, 760, 924, 931; v 737, 760, 931
sanctioned adj 924
sanctity n 987
sanctuary n 666
sand n 330, 687; v 255
sand bar n 209
sanded adj 255
sandiness n 330
sandpaper v 255
sandy adj 330
sane adj 246, 502
sanguine adj 831, 858
sanitary adj 656
sanity n 502
sans adv 187
sap n 5, 501; v 162, 659
sapience n 498
sapient adj 498
sapless adj 340
sapphire adj 438
sappy adj 333, 499
sarcastic adj 856
sarcophagous n 363
sash n 247
Satan n 978
satanic adj 978, 982
satanism n 978
sate v 869
satiate v 376, 829, 869
satiated adj 869
satiety n 869
satire n 856
satirist n 844, 936
satirize v 856
satisfaction n 772, 807, 827, 831, 952
satisfactory adj 639
satisfied adj 474, 484, 831
satisfy v 462, 639, 746, 772, 807, 829, 831, 952
saturate v 52, 339, 869
saturated adj 52
saturation n 869
satyr n 980
sauce n 393
saunter n 266; v 266, 275
sauté v 384
savage adj 173
savant n 492
save v 672, 817; adv 38, 83
saving n 817
savoir faire n 698, 852
savor n 390; v 390, 394
savoriness n 394
savory adj 390, 394
saw n 257; v 44
say n 175; v 535, 560, 582
saying n 496
say nothing v 517, 585
say what comes to mind
    v 612
scabrous adj 256
scaffolding n 673
scald v 384

scale n 69, 71, 204, 466;
    v 305
scale the heights v 305
scallop n 257; v 257
scalpel n 262
scaly adj 204
scamper v 274
scan v 441
scant adj 32, 137, 640
scantiness n 103, 203
scanty adj 32, 103
scarce adj 32, 103, 137, 640
scarcely adv 32, 137
scarcity n 32, 103, 640
scared adj 862
scarify v 257
scarlet adj 434
scatter v 61, 73, 291
scattered adj 73
scene n 448
scenery n 448
scent n 398, 550; v 398, 400
scented adj 400
scentless adj 399
scepter n 747
schedule n 86
scheme n 626; v 626
schemer n 626
schism n 713, 984
schismatic adj 984
scholar n 492
scholar n 541
scholarly adj 539
scholarship n 490, 539
scholastic adj 537, 539, 542
school n 542
school v 537
schoolbook n 542
schoolboy n 129
schooled adj 498
schoolgirl n 129
schooling n 537
schoolmaster n 540
schooner n 273
science n 490
science of existence n 1
science of light n 420
science of living beings
    n 357
science of matter n 316
science of sound n 402
science of the mineral
    kingdom n 358
scintilla n 32, 420
scintillate v 420
scintillating adj 842
scintillation n 420
scion n 167
scoff v 929, 988
scoff at v 856
scoffer n 988
scoffing n 856, 988
scold v 972
scoop n 262; v 252

scoop out v 252
scope n 26, 180, 748
scorch v 384
scorched adj 384
score n 98, 259, 805, 806, 811; v 259
scores n 102
scorn n 930; v 715, 929, 930
scornful adj 929, 930
scotch v 659
scot free adj 748
scoundrel n 941, 949
scour v 331, 652
scourge n 975
scourge v 663, 972
scour the country v 266
scout n 664, 668
scowl v 900, 901a
scraggly adj 256
scramble n 59, 684; v 684
scrap n 32
scrape n 704, 732; v 38, 195, 255, 330, 331
scratch n 257, 259; v 257, 331, 380, 590, 649
scraiching n 380; adj 410
scratchy adj 380
scrawl v 590
scrawny adj 203
scream n 411, 669; v 404, 410, 411, 839
screech v 411, 412
screeching n 412; adj 414
screen n 223, 424, 530, 717; v 424, 442, 528, 664, 717
screening n 528
screw n 243; v 43, 243
screw up the eyes v 443
scribble v 590
scribe n 553, 590
scrimp v 819
script n 590, 593
scriptural adj 983a
Scriptures n 985, 986
scrivener n 590
Scrooge n 819
scrub v 331, 652
scruple n 485
scrupulous adj 246, 459, 543, 603, 772, 868, 939
scrupulousness n 603
scrutinize v 457
scrutinizing adj 461
scrutiny n 457, 461
scull v 267
sculpt v 557
sculptor n 559
sculpture n 557
scum of the earth n 949
scurrilous adj 934
scurry v 684
scuttle v 162
scuttlebutt n 532
sea n 341
sea dog n 269

seafaring adj 267
seafaring man n 269
sea-girt adj 346
seagoing adj 267, 341
sea-green adj 435
seal n 22; v 261, 550
sealing n 261
sealing wax n 356a
seam n 43; v 259
sea-maid n 979
seaman n 269
sear v 384
search n 461, 539, 622; v 461
season n 106, 106; v 41, 392, 393, 613, 673
seasonable adj 134
seasoned adj 392
seasoning n 41, 393
seat n 184
seat of activity n 691
secession n 624
seclude v 55, 87
secluded adj 893
seclude oneself v 893
seclusion n 893
seclusion n 55
second n 113, 759; v 707 adj 90
secondary adj 32, 34, 651
secondary color n 428
second hand adj 19
second-rate adj 34, 651
second-story man n 792
second thoughts n 65
second to none n 648
secrecy n 528, 893
secret n 533
secret adj 221, 526, 528, 533
secretary n 553, 590
secrete v 299, 528
secretion n 299, 528
secretive adj 528, 533
secretiveness n 528
secretly adv 528
secret place n 530
sect n 75
section n 51, 75
sectional adj 51
secular adj 997
secularize v 997
secure v 43, 132, 664, 717, 768, 775, 781; adj 43, 150, 484, 664
secure an objective v 731
securities n 802
security n 771
security n 664, 717, 721
sedate adj 826
seducer n 962
seduction n 829
seductive adj 288, 615, 829
see v 441, 457, 480a;484
seed n 32, 153; v 371
see double v 443

seedy adj 160, 659, 804
see fit v 600
seeing that adv 8
seek v 461, 622
seeker n 268, 767
seek refuge v 666
seem v 448
seeming n 448; adj 448
seemingly adv 448
seemliness n 845
seemly adj 845
see one's future v 510
seer n 130, 504, 513
seesaw adv 314
seethe v 382
see the light v 359
seething adj 824
see-through adj 425
segment n 51, 100a
segregate v 44, 55
segregated adj 44
segregation n 44, 55
seize v 789
seize the day v 134
seize the opportunity v 134, 682
seize the time v 134
seizure n 789
seldom adv 137
select v 609; adj 648
selection n 609
self n 13; adj 13
self-abnegation n 955
self-admiration n 880
self-assurance n 878
self-assured adj 878
self-centered adj 943
self-command n 604
self-complacency n 880
self-complacent adj 880
self-contradictory adj 497
self-control n 600, 604, 953
self-controlled adj 953
self-deception n 486
self-delusion n 486
self-denial n 604, 955
self-denying adj 955
self-depreciation n 483
self-esteem n 878, 880
self-glorification n 880
self-importance n 878
self-indulgence n 954
self-indulgent adj 943, 954
self-interest n 943
self-interested adj 943
selfish adj 32, 819, 943
selfishness n 943
selfishness n 32, 819
self-love n 880, 943
self-luminous adj 423
self-mortifying adj 955
self-mortification n 955
self-possessed adj 502
self-possession n 604, 826
self-reliance n 604
self-respect n 878

self-restrained adj 953
self-restraint n 604, 826, 953
selfsame adj 13
self-satisfied adj 878
self-seeking n 943; adj 943
self-styled adj 565
sell v 796, 798
seller n 796, 797
sell for v 812
selling n 796
semblance n 17, 19, 21, 216, 882
semi- adj 91
semi-circular adj 245
semifluid adj 352
semiliquid adj 352
semiliquidity n 352
seminary n 542
semiology n 550
semiopaque adj 427
semipellucid adj 427
semitransparency n 427
semitransparent adj 427
send v 270
send a letter v 592
send off v 284
semblance n 17, 19, 21, 216, 882
senile adj 124, 128, 158
senility n 124, 128, 158, 160, 659
seniority n 128
sensation n 375, 379, 390
sensational adj 824
sensations of touch n 380
sense v 450, 498, 502, 516, 842
senseless adj 376, 497, 499, 517
senselessness n 517
sense of duty n 926
sensibility n 375, 822
sensibility n 821
sensible adj 316, 375, 498, 502
sensical adj 450
sensitive adj 375, 597, 821, 822
sensitiveness n 375, 822
sensitivity n 821, 901
sensitize v 375
sensual adj 377, 829
sensual delight n 377
sensualist n 954a
sensualist n 962
sensuality n 377, 829
sensuous adj 375, 377
sensuousness n 377
sentence n 972
sententious adj 577
sentient adj 375
sentiment n 453, 821
sentimental adj 822
sentimentalism n 822
sentimentality n 821, 822
sentinel n 444, 664, 668
sentry n 668

since the occasion
presents itself *adv* 134
sinewy *adj* 159
sinful *adj* 923, 945, 961
sinfully *adv* 923
sing *v* 416, 597, 838
singe *v* 384
singer *n* 416
singing *n* 412; *adj* 413
single *adj* 42, 87
singlehanded *adj* 87
singleness *n* 87
single out *v* 79
singly *adv* 87
sing out *v* 411
singular *adj* 79, 83, 87
singularity *n* 79, 87
singularly *adv* 83
sinister *adj* 663, 909
sinistral *adj* 239
sink *n* 162, 208, 306, 348,
360, 659, 688, 732, 735,
837
sink back *v* 661
sinking *n* 306
sink into oblivion *v* 506
sinless *adj* 946
sinner *n* 949, 988
sinning *adj* 945, 961
sinuosity *n* 248
sip *n* 296, 390
siphon *n* 350
sir *n* 373
sire *n* 168
siren *n* 669, 980
sisterhood *n* 11, 72, 995
Sisyphean *adj* 686
site *n* 183
sit in judgment *v* 965
situate *v* 183, 184
situated *adj* 183
situation *n* 183
situation *n* 7, 8, 151, 182,
184
situations *n* 527
six *n* 98
six and half a
dozen of another *n* 628;
adj 27
sizable *adj* 192
size *n* 192
size *n* 25, 31, 200
skeletal *adj* 203
skeleton *n* 40, 362
skeleton in the closet
n 649, 830
skeptic *n* 485, 487, 984,
989
skeptical *adj* 485, 487,
984, 989
skepticism *n* 485, 487,
984, 989
sketch *n* 594, 626; *v* 230,
556
sketcher *n* 559

sketchy *adj* 53, 730
skill *n* 698
skill *n* 79, 702, 731
skilled *adj* 698
skillful *adj* 698, 702
skillfully *adv* 698
skillfulness *n* 698, 702
skin *n* 220, 223
skin-deep *adj* 209
skinflint *n* 819
skinniness *n* 203
skinny *adj* 203
skip *n* 198; *v* 309, 838
skipper *n* 269
skirt *n* 231; *v* 231, 236
skirting *n* 231; *adj* 236
skulk *v* 862
skull *n* 450
sky *n* 318, 338
skyscraping *adj* 206
slab *n* 204, 251
slack *adj* 47, 160, 172,
275, 603, 674, 683, 738
slacken *v* 47, 275, 687
slackness *n* 275, 738
slake *v* 174, 829
slam *n* 276; *v* 276
slander *n* 908, 934; *v* 908,
934
slanderer *n* 936
slanderous *adj* 934
slang *n* 579; *adj* 563
slangy *adj* 560
slant *n* 217; *v* 217
slantwise *adv* 217
slap *n* 276; *v* 276
slash *v* 44
slaughter *n* 361; *v* 361
slaughtering *n* 361
slavery *n* 749, 886
slavish *adj* 886
slavishness *n* 886
slayer *n* 361
sleek *v* 255; *adj* 255
sleep *n* 687
sleeping *adj* 172, 265
sleeping car *n* 272
slender *adj* 32, 203, 643
slenderize *v* 203
slenderness *n* 32, 203
slice *n* 204; *v* 44, 204
slick *adj* 355
slide *v* 109, 264, 306
slight *v* 450, 483, 927;
adj 432, 209, 322, 575,
643, 736
slightly *adv* 32
slightness *n* 4, 32, 203
slim *v* 203; *adj* 203
slime *n* 653
slimness *n* 203
slimy *adj* 352, 355, 653
sling *n* 284
slink away *v* 623
slip *n* 32, 306, 495, 568,
732; *v* 109, 306, 495, 623
slip back *v* 661

slipperiness *n* 665
slippery *adj* 255, 355, 607,
665
slippery ground *n* 667
slippery memory *n* 506
slip-shod *adj* 575
slit *n* 44, 198, 259, 260;
v 44
sliver *n* 32
slobber over *v* 933
sloop *n* 273
slope *n* 217, 306; *v* 217
sloping *adj* 217, 306
sloppy *adj* 345, 575
slot *n* 260
sloth *n* 133, 172, 275, 683
slothful *adj* 681, 683
slothfulness *n* 681
slouch *v* 307, 217, 275, 683
slough *n* 345
slovenliness *n* 653
slovenly *adj* 59, 575, 653
slow *v* 275, 420; *adj* 133,
172, 275, 603, 683, 685,
843, 901a
slowly *adv* 133, 275
slowness *n* 275
slowness *n* 133, 603
sluggard *n* 683
sluggish *adj* 172, 275, 683,
901a
sluggishness *n* 275, 683,
901a
sluice *n* 350
slumber *n* 687
slumberer *n* 683
slump *n* 306
slur one's words *v* 583
slushy *adj* 352
slut *n* 962
sluttish *adj* 653
sly *adj* 702
slyness *n* 702
smack *n* 32, 276, 390;
v 390
smack the lips *v* 390
small *adj* 32, 193
small change *n* 800
smallness 32
smallness *n* 193
small number *n* 103
small quantity *n* 32, 103
small talk *n* 588
smart *n* 378, 828; *v* 378;
adj 682, 698
smarts *n* 450, 498
smash *v* 162
smatch *n* 390; *v* 390
smear *v* 653
smell *n* 398, 400; *v* 398,
401
smell bad *v* 401
smell of *v* 398
smell rotten *v* 401
smell sweet *v* 400
smelly *adj* 398
smile *n* 838; *v* 838

smirch v 431, 653
smirk n 838; v 838
smite v 649
smitten adj 897
smoggy adj 426
smoke v 382, 392
smoking adj 382
smoky adj 426
smolder v 382, 526
smoldering adj 172
smooth v 16, 174, 255, 705, 723; adj 174, 213, 251, 255, 705
smoothly adv 705
smoothness n 255
smoothness n 255
smoothness n 251, 705
smooth-tongued adj 933
smother v 361, 581
smudge v 653
smug adj 878
smut n 653, 961; v 431
smutch v 431
smutty adj 653,961
snag n 667
snaggy adj 253
snake n 248
snake in the grass n 548, 649, 667
snaky adj 248
snap n 406
snap v 277; v 44, 328, 406
snap back v 277
snappish adj 901
snap up v 789
snare n 530, 545, 667
snarl v 412, 900
snatch n 32; v 789
sneak n 941; v 275, 623, 862, 886
sneak off v 623
sneer n 858; v 929
sneer at v 856
sneeze v 409
sniff v 398
snip v 44
snippet n 32
sniveling adj 886
snobbish adj 878
snort v 412
snout n 250
snow-white adj 430
snowy adj 430
snuff v 398
snuff out v 421
snug adj 261, 664
soak v 337, 339, 959
soak up v 340
soap n 356
soar v 31, 206, 267, 303, 305
sob n 839; v 411, 839
sobbing n 411
sober v 174; adj 174, 246, 502, 826, 953
sobriety n 953
sobriety n 502, 953
sobriquet n 565

so-called adj 565
sociability n 894
sociable adj 892
sociableness n 892
social adj 372, 892
social interaction n 892
social intercourse n 892
socialism n 778
socialist n 778; adj 778
socialistic adj 778
sociality n 892
society n 188, 372, 852
society of men n 372
sodden v 339; adj 337
soft adj 255, 324, 345, 403, 405, 413, 499
soft as butter adj 324
soft coal n 388
soften v 174, 324
softening n 324
softness n 324
softness n 160, 326
soggy adj 337, 339
soi-disant adj 565
soil n 181, 342; v 653
soiled adj 653
sojourn v 186
solace n 834
solar adj 318
solar energy n 388
solar system n 180, 318
solder v 43, 46
soldier n 726, 948
sole n 211; adj 87
solecism n 568
solecism n 579
solecize v 568
solemn adj 403, 642, 882
solemnity n 642
solemnization n 883
solemnize v 883
solicit v 765, 865
solicitation n 411, 765
solicitor n 767, 968
solicitous adj 411, 765, 860, 920
solicitude n 459, 828, 860
solid adj 16, 52, 150, 202, 321, 323
solid body n 321
solidification n 321, 385
solidify v 46, 48, 321
solidity n 150, 321
solidness n 321
soliloquize v 582, 589
soliloquy n 589
solipsism n 943
solipsistic adj 943
solitary adj 87, 893
solitude n 893
solo n 415; adj 87; v 416
soloist n 416
solubility n 333
soluble adj 333, 335, 462, 662
solubleness n 335

solution n 462, 522, 662
solve v 462, 662
solvency n 803
solvent adj 335, 807
somatic adj 316
somber adj 431, 901a
some adj 25, 100; adv 32
somebody n 372
someone n 372
somersault n 218
something like adj 17
some time ago adv 122
sometimes adv 136
somewhere adv 182
somewhere about adv 32
son n 167
sonata n 415
song n 415, 415
sonneteer n 597
sonority n 402
sonorous adj 402, 404, 577
sonorousness n 402, 408
soon adv 111, 121, 132
sooner or later adv 121
soothe v 723, 834
soothing adj 834
soothsayer n 513, 994
soothsaying n 511
sooty adj 431, 653
sop v 339
sophism n 477
sophist n 477, 548
sophistical adj 477
sophistry n 477
sophistry n 538
soporific adj 683
sorcerer n 994
sorcerer n 513
sorcery n 992
sordid adj 32, 207, 435
sordidness n 32
sore n 378, 830; adj 378, 830
sorely adv 31
soreness n 378
sore subject n 830
sorority n 11
sorrel adj 433
sorrow n 833
sorrowful adj 828, 839
sorrow over v 839
sorry adj 643, 828, 833, 950
sorry sight n 830
sort n 75; v 60
sortie n 716
sorting n 60
SOS n 669
so-so adj 32, 643, 651
sot n 959; v 959
so to speak adv 17
sotted adj 959
sough n 350
soul n 5, 359, 372, 820
soul-stirring adj 821, 824
sound n 402
sound n 343; v 208, 402;

adj 50, 150, 246, 498, 650, 654, 664, 670, 983a
sound dead *v* 408a
sounding *adj* 402
soundings *n* 208
soundless *adj* 208, 403
soundness *n* 150, 502, 654, 983a
sound the alarm *v* 669
sound vibrations *n* 402
soupçon *n* 32
sour *v* 397; *adj* 392, 395, 397, 410, 901a
source *n* 66, 153
sourness 397
sourness *n* 392, 395
souse *v* 310, 337
souvenir *n* 505
sovereign *n* 737; *adj* 737
sovereignty *n* 157
sow *n* 374; *v* 73, 371
sow the seeds of *v* 153

space *n* 180
space *n* 106, 198, 318
space heater *n* 386
spaceman *n* 269
spaceship *n* 273
space station *n* 273
spacious *adj* 180, 192
span *n* 106, 180, 196, 200; *v* 43, 45
spare *v* 678, 784; *adj* 40, 636, 641, 685
spare no effort *v* 686
spare no expense *v* 816
spare time *n* 685
sparing *adj* 953
spark *n* 382, 420, 423
sparkle *v* 420
sparkling *adj* 574, 836, 842
sparse *adj* 32, 73, 103, 640
sparseness *n* 32, 103
spasm *n* 146, 173, 315, 378
spasmodic *adj* 70, 139, 173
speak *v* 580, 582
speak directly *v* 576
speaker *n* 524, 582
speaking of *adv* 134
speak in low tones *v* 405
speak one's mind *v* 703
speak plainly *v* 576
speak prettily *v* 521
speak softly *v* 405
speak the truth *v* 543
speak to *v* 586
spear *n* 262; *v* 260, 361
special *n* 79; *adj* 20, 79, 474
special committee *n* 755
specialist *n* 700
speciality *n* 79
specialize *v* 79
specially *adv* 79
specialty *n* 79

species *n* 75
specific *n* 662; *adj* 79
specify *v* 79, 564
specimen *n* 82
specious *adj* 477, 545
speciousness *n* 477
speck *n* 32, 848
speckle *v* 440
speckled *adj* 440
spectacle *n* 448, 872
spectacles *n* 445
spectator *n* 444
specter *n* 980; 443
spectral *adj* 2, 4, 980
spectroscope *n* 428
spectrum *n* 428
speculate *v* 155, 514, 621, 675, 870
speculation *n* 156, 451, 621, 675
speculative *adj* 514, 621, 675

speech *n* 582
speech *n* 560, 586
speech impediment *n* 583
speechless *adj* 403, 581, 583
speechlessness *n* 403, 590
speed *n* 264, 274, 684; *v* 274, 682, 684
speedily *adv* 132
speediness *n* 132
speed up *v* 274
speedy *adj* 274, 684
spell *n* 993
spell *n* 106, 198, 992; *v* 561, 707
spell-bound *adj* 870
spelling *n* 561
spend *v* 638, 809
spend freely *v* 816
spendthrift *adj* 638, 818
spend time *v* 106
spent *adj* 158, 160, 688
spew *v* 297
sphere *n* 26, 181, 249, 318; *v* 249
spherical *adj* 249
sphericity *n* 249
spheroid *n* 249
spice *n* 41, 393; *v* 392
spiced *adj* 392
spick and span *adj* 123
spicy *adj* 392, 400
spigot *n* 263
spike *n* 253, 263; *v* 260
spiked *adj* 253
spiky *adj* 253
spill *v* 348
spin *n* 266; *v* 312
spin a melody *v* 416
spin around *v* 312
spindly *adj* 203
spine *n* 253
spineless *adj* 862
spinelessness *n* 172
spinning *n* 312

spin out *v* 200
spinster *n* 904
spiny *adj* 253
spiral *n* 248, 311; *adj* 248
spirit *n* 5, 171, 359, 516, 574, 682, 709, 820, 861, 977, 980
spirited *adj* 171, 574, 836, 861
spiritual *adj* 2, 317, 976, 977
spiritualism *n* 992
spirituality *n* 317
spit *v* 300
spite *n* 907
spiteful *adj* 898, 907, 919, 945
spitefulness *n* 907
splash *n* 348; *v* 337, 348, 653
splendid *adj* 420
splendor *n* 420, 845, 882
splice *v* 43, 219
splint *n* 215
splinter *n* 32; *v* 44, 328
splintery *adj* 328
split *n* 44, 713; *v* 44, 91, 293, 328, 713, 838
split down the middle *v* 91
split hairs *v* 868
split one's sides *v* 838
split the difference *v* 29
split the differences *v* 774
split the eardrums *v* 404, 419
split up *v* 778, 905; *adj* 51, 905
spoil *v* 397, 659
spoilage *n* 659
spoliation *n* 638
spoiled *adj* 397
spoiled child *n* 899
spoiler *n* 165
spoils *n* 793
spokesman *n* 524, 534, 582
sponge *n* 339, 340
sponginess *n* 354
sponsor *v* 771
sponsorship *n* 771
spontaneous *adj* 612
spook *n* 980
spoonful *n* 25, 32
sporadic *adj* 103, 137, 139
sport *v* 840
spot *n* 182, 848, 874; *v* 653, 848
spotless *adj* 650, 652, 946, 960
spotlessness *n* 946
spotted *adj* 440
spottiness *n* 440
spotty *adj* 440
spouse *n* 903
spout *n* 348, 350; *v* 295, 348, 582

sprawl v 200, 213, 306
spray n 353
spread n 180, 291; v 73, 194, 291, 531; adj 73
spreading n 73, 194
spread out v 35, 194
spread the sails v 267
spread to v 196
sprightliness n 829
sprightly adj 829, 836
spring n 153, 159, 309, 325, 348; v 274, 309, 325
spring back v 277, 325
spring from v 154
springiness n 325
springtime n 125
spring up v 367
springy adj 309, 325
sprinkle v 73, 337
sprinkling n 32, 41
sprite n 979, 980
sprout v 35, 194, 367
spruce adj 652
spry adj 682
spun-out adj 110
spur n 250, 253, 615; v 615
spurious adj 544
spurn v 764, 866
spurning n 764
spurt n 274, 348, 612, 684; v 348
sputter v 348, 583
spy n 444, 455; v 441, 455
spyglass n 445
spying n 455; adj 455
squabble n 713, 720; v 713
squad n 72
squadron n 72
squalid adj 653, 846
squall n 349
squalor n 653
squander v 162, 638, 679, 818
squanderer n 818
squandering n 818
square n 857; v 30, 95, 660; adj 246
square accounts v 807
square one n 66
square-rigger n 273
square with v 23
squash v 162, 195, 352, 354, 409
squashy adj 345
squat v 188; adj 193, 201, 202, 207
squawking adj 410
squeak v 411, 412
squeal v 411
squeeze v 195, 348, 354
squeeze out v 301
squeezing n 195, 301
squelch v 162
squint v 443; v 443
squirt n 348
squishy adj 324
stab v 260, 361, 649

stability n 150
stability n 16, 110, 141
stabilization n 150
stabilize v 150
stable adj 110, 141, 150, 265
staff n 215, 896, 747
staff of life n 359
stag n 373
stage n 26, 71, 106, 204, 728
stage business n 599
stage name n 565
stage-play n 599
stagey adj 855
stagger v 275, 314, 315, 508, 824, 870
stagnant adj 265, 901a
stagnate v 265
stagnation n 265
stagy adj 599
staid adj 826
stain n 428, 874; v 428, 653, 848, 874
stained n 961
stainless adj 652
stake n 621, 771; v 621
stale adj 124, 659
stalk n 215
stall v 133
stallion n 373
stalwart adj 192
stamina n 159, 604a
stammer v 583
stammering n 583
stamp n 7, 22; v 240, 550
stamp out v 162, 385
stand n 71, 211, 719; v 106, 110, 141, 719
stand a chance v 177, 470
stand aloof v 681
standard n 22, 26, 80, 466, 650; adj 29, 82, 650
standardization n 16
standardize v 58
stand as an example v 82
stand as opposites v 237
stand at the head v 66
stand by v 186
stand condemned v 971
stand convicted v 754
stand erect v 212
stand fast v 141, 265
stand firm v 150, 265, 604
stand for v 147, 550, 759, 771
stand immobile v 265
stand in front v 234
standing n 8, 26, 71, 110, 183, 873
stand next to v 197
stand one in good stead v 644
stand out v 250
standpoint n 183, 441
stand still v 265

stand straight and tall
v 212
stand the test v 648
stand to reason v 474
stand up v 719
stand upright v 212
stand up straight v 212
staple commodity n 798
staples n 635
starboard n 238
starchy adj 352
stare n 441; v 455, 870
stark adj 31
stark-naked adj 226
stars n 423
start n 66, 293; v 66, 151, 276, 284, 293, 309, 870
start again v 66
start fresh v 652
starting point n 66, 293
startle v 508, 824, 870
startled adj 870
startling n 508, 870
start over v 66
start up v 250, 446
starvation n 956
starve v 385, 804, 819, 955, 956
starved adj 956
starving adj 956
starving oneself n 956
stash n 636; v 636
state n 7
state n 188; v 516, 535
stated adj 474
statelessness n 875
stately adj 875, 878
statement n 535, 594, 811
station n 26, 71, 183; v 184
stationary adj 265
statistical adj 85
statistics n 85
statuary n 557
statue n 557, 963, 991
statuette n 557
stature n 206
status n 7, 8, 71
statute n 697, 963
staunch adj 150, 604a
stave in v 252
stay n 133, 215, 685; v 1, 133, 141, 142, 186, 265
stay away v 187
stay in the background
v 881
stay together v 46
stead n 644
steadfast adj 150, 604, 604a
steadfastness n 150, 604a
steadiness n 138, 150
steady adj 80, 138, 150, 604a
steal v 275, 789, 791
steal a march on v 132
steal away v 623, 671
steal from v 788

stealing n 791
stealing n 788
stealthily adv 528
stealthy adj 528, 702
steam n 353; v 267, 336, 353
steamer n 273
steaming n 336
steam press v 255
steam up v 353
steamy adj 353
steel v 159
steep v 337; adj 217, 306
steepness n 217
steer n 373; v 693
steerage n 693
steer a middle course v 628
steer clear of v 279, 623
steer for v 278
steersman n 269
stench n 401
stencil n 21
stenography n 590
stentorian adj 404, 411
step n 71, 264
step by step adv 26, 58, 69, 275
step in v 724
steppe n 344
stereoscope n 445
sterile adj 158, 169
sterility n 169
stern adj 604, 739, 955
sternness n 739
stew v 382, 384
steward n 801; v 693
stewardship n 693
stewed adj 959
stewed to the gills adj 959
stick n 215, 975; v 46, 260
stick fast v 150, 265
stick in v 300
stickiness n 46, 352, 396
stick it out v 604a
stick out v 250
stick to v 143
stick to an idea v 606
stick up v 250
sticky adj 46, 327, 352, 396
stiff adj 240, 579, 739
stiff breeze n 349
stiffen v 323
stiffness n 246, 579
stifle v 361, 403
stifled adj 405
stifling adj 382
stiletto n 282
still v 174, 403, 723; adj 174, 265, 403; adv 30
still-born adj 732
stillness n 265, 403
stilted adj 307, 577, 855
stilts n 215

stimulate v 171, 173, 382, 615, 689, 824, 829
stimulating adj 171
stimulation n 824
stimulus n 615
sting v 378, 380, 663
stinginess n 819, 943
stinging n 380; adj 392
stingy adj 819, 943
stink n 401; v 401, 653
stinking adj 401
stinky adj 401
stint v 819
stipple v 558
stipulate v 769, 770
stipulations n 770
stir n 264, 315, 682, 752;
v 264, 315, 375, 382, 824
stir about v 682
stirring adj 151, 505
stir up v 173, 824
stitch n 43, 378, 828; v 43
stock n 11, 25, 635, 636, 637, 798; v 637; adj 598, 613
stocks n 802
stock-still adj 265
stockyard n 232
stoical adj 383, 826
stoicism n 826
stoke v 388
stolen away adj 671
stolen goods n 793
stolid adj 499, 843
stolidity n 499
stomach n 826
stone-blind adj 442
stone-deaf adj 419
stone's throw n 197
stony adj 914a
stoop v 217, 306, 886
stop n 133, 142, 360; v 67, 70, 142, 261, 265, 403
stopcock n 263
stopgap n 147
stoppage n 142, 261, 706
stop payment v 808
stopper n 263
stopping n 142, 263, 706
stop short v 142, 265
stop up v 261
stopwatch n 114
storage n 636
storage areas n 191
store n 636
store v 31, 637, 798, 799;
v 72, 636, 837, 670
store up v 636
storing n 636
storm n 315, 348, 349;
v 173, 349, 716
stormy adj 173, 349
story n 204, 546, 593
storyteller n 548
stout adj 159, 192
stout-hearted adj 861

stoutness n 159
stove n 386
stow away v 528
strabismus n 443
straggle v 279
straggler n 268
straggling adj 59
straight n 857; adj 212, 246, 278, 807, 958;
adv 132, 278
straighten v 246
straighten out v 60
straightforward adj 543, 703, 849; adv 278
straight line n 246
straightness n 246
straightway adv 132
strain n 402, 413, 415, 666; v 42, 686, 688
strait n 704
strait-laced adj 739
straitness n 203
straits n 343, 804
strand n 205, 342
strange adj 10, 83, 519, 870
strangely adv 31
strangle v 158, 361
strangulation n 361
strap n 975; v 43
strapper n 192
strapping adj 159
stratagem n 545, 626, 702
strategic adj 626
strategical adj 692
strategist n 626
strategy n 692, 722
stratified adj 204
stratosphere n 338
stratum n 204, 213
straw-colored adj 435
stray v 279; adj 73, 279
streak n 259, 420; v 440
streaked adj 440
streakiness n 440
stream n 347
stream n 346, 347, 348, 420; v 72, 264, 333, 348, 349
streamy adj 348
street-walker n 962
strength n 159
strength n 25, 26, 31, 157, 171, 327, 364, 739
strengthen v 157, 159, 171, 689
strengthening n 159
strength of mind n 604
strenuous adj 682
stress n 580, 642, 686
stretch n 180; v 194, 200, 325
stretch out v 200
stretch the meaning v 523
stretch to v 196, 200
strew v 73

sucking n 296
suction n 296
sudden adj 111, 113, 132, 508
sudden impulse n 278
suddenly adv 113, 132, 508
suddenness n 111, 113, 508
sudden thought n 612
suds n 353
sue v 765, 969
suet n 356
suffer v 378, 655, 760, 826, 828
sufferance n 760, 826
suffer a relapse v 661
suffering n 378, 828, 982
suffice v 639
sufficiency n 639
sufficiency n 31, 803
sufficient adj 31, 639
sufficiently adv 639
suffix n 39, 65
suffocate v 361, 641
suffocating adj 382, 401
suffocation n 361
suffuse v 41
suffusion n 41
sugar v 396
sugariness n 396
sugary adj 396
suggest v 505, 514, 527, 695
suggestion n 505, 514, 526, 527, 695, 993
suggestive adj 514, 695
suicidal adj 361
suicide n 361, 361
suit n 225, 765, 969; v 23, 646, 852
suitability n 134, 646
suitable adj 134, 646, 850, 922
suitable time n 134
suite n 69
suiting adj 413
suitor n 767, 897, 969
suit the occasion v 134, 646
sulk v 901a
sulky adj 901a
sullenness n 901a
sullied adj 961
sully v 653, 848
sultry adj 382
sum n 50, 84, 800; v 37, 85
summarily adv 132, 572
summarize v 596
summary n 572, 596
summer n 125
summertime n 125
summit n 210
summit n 206, 650
summon v 969
summons n 969
summon up v 505

sumptuous adj 882
sun n 420, 423
sunbeam n 420
sundown n 126
sundry adj 102
sunglasses n 424
sunk adj 208
sunken adj 252
sunken rocks n 667
sunk into oblivion adj 506
sunny adj 382, 420, 829, 836
sunrise n 125, 420
sunset n 126
sunshade n 223, 424
sunshine n 420
sunup n 125
sup v 298
superabound v 641
superabundance n 641
superabundant adj 641
superannuation n 124, 128
supercilious adj 878
superciliousness n 878
superficial adj 209, 220, 491
superficiality n 209
superficies n 220
superfluity n 40, 641
superfluous adj 40, 57, 641
superfluousness n 57
superhuman adj 976
superimpose v 223
superintendent n 694
superior adj 33, 642, 648
superiority n 33
superiority n 28, 62, 648, 650
superlative adj 33, 648
superlatively adv 31, 33
supernal adj 210, 981
supernatural adj 976, 980
supersaturate v 641
supersede v 147, 678
superstition n 486
superstitious adj 486
supervise v 692, 693
supervision n 693
supervisor n 694
supervisory adj 693
supination n 213
supine adj 207, 213, 683
supping n 298
supplant v 147
supplanting n 147
supple adj 324
supplement n 37, 39, 65; v 37
supplemental adj 37
supplementary adj 37
suppliant n 767, 990
supplicant n 767
supplicate v 765, 990
supplication n 765, 990

supplies n 635, 800
supply n 636, 637; v 637, 784
supplying n 637
support n 215
support v 153, 666, 670, 707, 937; v 170, 215, 670, 707, 737, 834, 937
supported adj 215, 937
supporter n 215, 707, 890, 912
supporting adj 215
supportive adj 707
suppose v 451, 514
supposing adj 469
supposition n 514
supposition n 453, 515
suppress v 581, 751
suppressed adj 528
suppression n 162, 528, 751
suppressive adj 751
supremacy n 33, 737
supreme adj 31, 33, 210, 737
supreme being n 976
supremely adv 31, 33
sure adj 246, 474, 484, 664
sure enough adv 474
surely n 664, 771
surf n 348, 353
surface n 220, 329
surfeit n 641, 869; v 869
surfeited adj 869
surge n 348; v 72
surgeon n 662
surly adj 901a
surmise v 510, 514
surmount v 206, 303, 305, 731
surname n 564
surpass v 33, 303
surpassingly adv 33
surplice n 999
surplus n 40, 641
surprise n 137, 508, 870; v 508, 702
surprised adj 508, 870
surprisingly adv 31
surrender v 624, 725, 782; v 624, 725, 782
surreptitious adj 528
surrogate n 759
surround v 227, 229
surrounding adj 227
surroundings n 7, 227
survey n 441, 466, 596; v 441, 466, 596
surveyor n 694
survival n 110
survive v 1, 40, 110, 141
surviving adj 40
susceptibility n 176, 177, 821, 822
susceptible adj 375, 822
suspect v 485, 487, 514
suspend v 133, 142, 214

take down v 308
take effect v 170
take fire v 384
take flight v 623
take for granted v 514
take from v 38, 789
take heart v 861
take hold v 46
take ill v 655
take in v 54, 518, 545, 785
take in hand v 676
take into account v 469
take into consideration v 469
take in tow v 285
take it easy v 683
take its course v 151
take liberties v 885
take no interest in v 456, 866
take no note of time v 115
take oar v 267
take off v 19, 226, 267, 293, 813
take offense v 900
take off like a shot v 274
take off the point v 279
take one's chances v 156
take one's leave v 293
take one's time v 685
take orders v 996
take out v 301
take over v 775
take pains v 686
take pen in hand v 590
take place v 1, 151, 151
take pleasure in v 827
take possession of v 775
take precautions v 664
take precedence v 33, 62, 280
take refuge v 666
take root v 184, 613
take shelter v 666
take sick v 655
take soundings v 208
take steps v 673
take the average v 29
take the bull by the horns v 861
take the first step v 66
take the initiative v 66
take the lead v 66, 280
take the place of v 147
take the pledge v 958
take time v 133
take to the altar v 903
take to the skies v 267
take up v 307, 676, 677
take up one's abode v 189
take upon oneself v 676
take up quarters v 184
take up the pen v 590
take what's offered v 607
take wing v 266, 267
taking n 789

taking nourishment n 298
tale n 546, 549
talebearer n 532
talent n 79, 698
talents n 698
talismanic adj 992
talk n 582, 588; v 582
talk a mile a minute v 584
talkative adj 582, 584
talkativeness n 584
talk big v 577, 884
talker n 584
talk fancy v 577
talk it over v 588
talk nonsense v 497
talk together v 588
talk to oneself v 589
tall adj 200, 206
tallness n 206
tallow n 356
tall tale n 546
tally n 86, 805; v 23, 85
tallying n 85
tame v 174, 370, 749;
   adj 172, 370, 575, 725
taming n 370
tamper with v 140
tan adj 433
tang n 390, 392, 394
tangerine adj 439
tangibility n 3
tangible adj 3, 316
tangle n 61, 219
tangled adj 59
tanked adj 959
tanker n 273
tantalize v 509
tantamount adj 27
tap n 263, 276; v 260, 276, 406
taper n 423; v 203
tapering adj 253
taper to a point v 253
tapping n 407
tar n 358a
tardiness n 133, 275
tardy adj 133, 275
target n 620
tarn n 343
tarnish n 874; v 429, 653, 848, 874
tarnished adj 874
tarpaulin n 223
tarry v 110, 133
tarrying n 133
tart adj 397
tartness n 397
task n 676, 704; v 677, 688
taskmaster n 694, 739
taste n 390, 850
taste v 394, 465, 480, 578;
   v 298, 390, 394
taste bad v 395
tasteful adj 465, 578, 850
tastefully adv 850

taste good v 394
taste great v 394
tasteless adj 337, 391, 395, 579
tastelessness n 391
tastelessness n 395, 579
tastiness n 394
tasty adj 377, 390, 394
tattle v 588
tattler n 532
tattoo v 440
taunt v 856
taunts n 856
taut adj 43
tautological adj 104
tautology n 104
tawdriness n 851
tawdry adj 643, 851
tawny adj 433, 435
tax n 677, 688
teach v 537, 673
teacher n 540
teacher n 753
teaching n 537
teaching n 537
team-work n 709
tear v 44, 173, 274
tearful adj 839
tear out v 301
tears n 411
tear to pieces v 44
tear up v 162
teasing n 377
teat n 250
technicality n 697
technique n 627
tedious adj 275, 841, 843
tedium n 688, 841
teem v 168
teeming adj 72, 102, 168
teem with v 102
teenage adj 131
teenage years n 131
teeter v 160, 275, 315
teetering adj 160
teetotaler n 953, 958
teetotalism n 958
telescope n 445
telethermometer n 389
tell v 85, 467, 527, 529, 594
teller n 801
telling n 594; adj 642
temper n 5, 7, 323, 820;
   v 174, 323, 324
temperament n 5, 176, 820
temperamental adj 901
temperance n 953
temperance n 174
temperate adj 174, 736, 953
temperateness n 174
temperature n 382
tempered adj 820
tempest n 173, 315, 349, 825
tempest in a teacup n 549

tempestuous adj 349
temple n 1000
temporal adj 111, 997
temporarily adv 111
temporary adj 111
tempt v 615, 675
temptation n 615
tempter n 978
tempt fate v 621
tempt fortune v 675
ten n 98
tenable adj 664
tenacious adj 46, 150, 327, 604, 604a
tenacity n 327
tenacity n 150, 604, 604a
tenancy n 777
tenant n 188, 779; v 186
tend v 176, 278, 472
tendencies n 5
tendency n 176
tendency n 177, 278, 472, 613
tender n 763; v 763;
   adj 324, 378, 428, 597, 740, 821, 822, 897, 906
tender age n 127
tender-hearted adj 906
tenderness n 378, 821, 822, 897, 906
tender years n 127
tending adj 176
tendril n 205, 248
tend toward v 278
tenet n 451, 484, 537, 983
tenor n 7, 26, 278, 516
tensile adj 325
tension n 159
tent n 223
tentative adj 675
tenuity n 322
tenuous adj 322
tenure n 777
tepid adj 382
tergiversation n 607
term n 71
term n 106, 108, 198, 200, 233, 562; v 564
terminal adj 67, 233
terminate v 67, 142, 729
termination n 67, 142, 233, 261, 729
terminology n 560, 562
terminus n 233
terms n 476, 770
terrain n 342
terrestrial adj 318, 342
terrible adj 846, 860
terribly adv 31
terrified adj 860
territorial adj 181, 342
territory n 181, 965
terror n 860
terror-stricken adj 860
terse adj 572
terseness n 572
tertiary adj 92

test n 463; v 463
testify v 467, 535
testimony n 467
testy adj 684, 901
te'te-a'te'te n 588
tether v 43
tetrad n 95
text n 22, 542, 591
textbook n 542
texture n 256, 329
textured adj 256
thank v 916
thankful adj 916
thankfulness n 916
thankless adj 917
thanklessness n 917
thanks n 916
that being the case adv 8
thatch n 223
that is to say adv 522
thaw v 335, 382, 384
thawing n 335
the all-merciful n 976
the all-powerful n 976
the almighty n 976
theater n 599, 728
theatrical adj 599, 855, 882
theatricals n 599
the cloth n 996
the common people n 876
the converse n 14
the drama n 599
the eternal n 976
the future n 121
the infinite n 976
the inverse n 14
theism n 983
the latest thing n 123
the lead n 62, 280
the like n 17
the lower classes n 876
thematic adj 454
theme n 413, 454, 595
then adv 119
thence adv 155
theologian n 983
theological adj 983
theologics n 983
theologue n 983
theology n 983
the open n 338
the opposite n 14
theorem n 514
theoretical adj 514
theorize v 155, 514
theory n 155, 453, 514
theosophical adj 983
theosophy n 983
the past n 122
the present day n 118
the present juncture n 118
therapeutic adj 662
there adv 186
thereabouts adv 32, 183

thereafter adv 117
thereby adv 631
therefore adv 155
thereupon adv 117
the reverse n 14
therewith adv 88, 632
thermometer n 389
thermometograph n 389
thermoscope n 389
thermostat n 389
the same n 13
thesaurus n 86,562
thesis n 454, 514, 595
thespian n 599
the stage n 599
the theater n 599
the time being n 118
the times n 118, 151
The Vedas n 986
the void n 180
the whole time adv 106
the word n 532
the world n 151
thick n 202; adj 102, 321, 332, 376, 426, 491
thick as a brick adj 499
thicken v 202, 321, 352
thickening n 321
thickness n 202
thickness n 202
thicket n 202
thick-skinned adj 823
thick-skulled adj 499
thief n 792
thieve v 791
thievery n 791
thievish adj 791
thimbleful n 32
thin v 38, 103, 203, 322;
   adj 4, 32, 203, 322, 337, 640
thing n 3, 316
thing mixed n 41
thing of the past n 124
things n 151
thing signified n 516
think v 451, 870, 484
think back upon v 505
thinker n 492, 500
think fit v 600
thinking n 451
think no more of v 506
think out loud v 589
think up v 66, 515
thinness n 203, 322
thinness n 4, 32, 203, 425
thin out v 38
third n 94; adj 93
thirdly adv 93
third part n 94
thirst n 865
thirst for knowledge n 455
thirsty adj 865
thirteen n 98
thistly adj 253
thither adv 278

thorn n 253, 663
thorn in the side n 663, 830
thorny adj 253
thorough adj 52, 459, 729
thoroughfare n 302
thoroughgoing adj 52
thoroughly adv 52, 729
thoroughness n 52, 729
though adv 30
thought n 451
thought n 453, 515
thoughtful adj 451, 457, 459, 498
thoughtless adj 452, 458, 480, 499, 674, 684, 863
thoughtlessness n 452, 863
thousand n 98
thrall n 749
thralldom n 749
thread n 205; v 69, 302
threadbare adj 659
threadlike adj 203, 205
thread n 909
threaten v 121, 152, 665, 668, 716, 909
threatening adj 909
three n 92; adj 92
threefold adj 92, 93
threefold division n 94
three times adv 93
threnody n 839
threshold n 231
thrice adv 93
thrift n 817
thriftiness n 817
thrifty adj 817
thrill n 151, 824; v 377, 380
thrilling adj 821, 824
thrive v 734
throb n 315, 378; v 314, 315
throbbing adj 315
throe n 146, 173, 315, 378, 828
throng n 72, 102, 975; v 72, 828
throttle v 158, 261, 361
through adv 631
through-and-through adj 729
throughout adv 52, 106
through the agency of adv 170
throw n 284; v 284
throw aside v 678
throw away v 610
throw in v 228
throw in one's lot with v 709
throw in the towel v 624
throw off one's guard v 508
throw of the dice n 156
throw open v 260
throw out v 55, 297, 638

throw out of gear v 61
throw out of whack v 61
throw up v 297
thrust n 276, 284; v 276
thrust in v 300

thud n 406, 408a; v 408a
thug n 361
thumb n 379
thump n 276, 408a; v 276, 408a
thumper n 192
thumping adj 192
thunder n 404, 406; v 173, 404
thundering adj 192, 404
thunderousness n 404
thus adv 8
thus far adv 233
thus far and no further adv 233
thwack n 276; v 276
thwart v 706, 708
thwarted adj 732
tick v 407
ticket n 550
tickle the palate v 390, 394
tickle the tastebuds v 390
tickling n 380
ticklish adj 380, 704
tidal adj 348
tide n 348
tides n 341
tidiness n 652
tidings n 498, 532
tidy adj 58, 652
tidy up v 652
tie n 9, 11, 27, 45, 771; v 9, 43, 45, 770
tied adj 926
tier n 69, 204
tiered adj 204
ties of blood n 11
tie the hands v 158
tie the knot v 903
tie up v 342
tie up in knots v 158
tiff n 713
tight adj 43, 46; adj 261, 572, 819, 959
tighten v 572
tightness n 572
till n 802; v 371; adv 106
tillage n 371
till the soil v 371
tilt n 217, 306; v 217, 244, 306
tilted adj 217
tilt over v 218
tilt up v 307
timber n 413
timbre n 408
time n 106
time n 108; v 106
time-honored adj 124
time immemorial n 122
timeless adj 112

timelessness n 112
timeliness n 134, 684
timely adj 106, 132, 134
timeout n 106
timepiece n 114
timeserving adj 607
timetable n 114
time to come n 121
timeworn adj 124, 659
timid adj 605, 862, 881
timidity n 605, 862, 881
timorous adj 862, 881
tincture n 41, 428; v 41
tinge n 32, 41, 428; v 41, 428
tingle n 378, 380
tininess n 32, 193
tinsel n 851
tint n 26, 428; v 428
tinted adj 428
tintinnabulation n 408
tiny adj 32, 193
tippler n 959
tipsy adj 959
tiptop adj 210, 648
tirade n 582
tire v 688, 841, 869
tired adj 688, 841, 869
tiredness n 688
tired to death adj 688
tiresome adj 841
tissue n 329
tit for tat n 30
titillation n 377, 380
title n 877
title n 584, 747, 771
titled adj 875, 877
title page n 66
titter n 838; v 838
titular adj 564
to a certain degree adv 32
toady n 886, 935; v 886
to a large extent adv 31
to all appearance adv 448
to all intents and purposes adv 27, 52
to and fro adv 314
to arms adv 722
to a small extent adv 32
toast n 384
to blame adj 947
to boot adv 37
to come adj 121, 152
to crown all adv 33
tocsin n 669
toddler n 129
together adj 46, 502; adv 120
togetherness n 709, 714
together with adv 37, 88
togs n 225
toil n 686; v 682, 686
token n 505, 550
tolerable adj 32, 651, 736
tolerableness n 736

transporter n 271
transporting adj 977
transposal n 218
transpose v 148, 185, 218, 270
transposition n 140, 148, 185, 218, 270
transverse adj 217, 219
trap n 530, 545, 667
trappings n 225
trash n 643
trashy adj 209, 575, 643
travail n 686
travel n 266; v 266
traveler n 268
traveling adj 264, 266
traverse v 266, 302
travesty n 21, 523; v 19, 523
trawler n 273
treacherous adj 544
treachery n 545
tread n 264
tread down v 749
tread upon v 649
treasure n 648; v 991
treasurer n 801
treasury n 802
treat v 595, 829
treatise n 593, 595
treatment n 662
treat well v 906
treaty n 23, 721, 769
treble n 93; adj 93
trebly adv 93
tree n 367
trellis n 219
tremble v 149, 160, 315, 383
tremendously adv 31
tremor n 315
tremulous adj 149, 315
trench n 259
trenchant adj 171, 253, 572, 574, 642
trend n 176, 278, 516
trendiness n 123
trendy adj 123
trepidation n 860
trespass n 303; v 303, 945
trestle n 215
triad n 92
trial n 463, 675, 686, 828, 830, 969
triality n 92
tribe n 72, 75
tribunal n 966
tributary n 348; adj 784
trice n 113
trick n 545; v 545
trickle n 348; v 295, 348
trickly adj 348
tricky adj 545, 702
trifle n 32, 451, 643; v 499
trifling n 499, 643; adj 4, 32, 477, 499, 643, 880

triform adj 92
trill v 407
trim n 258, 240; v 27, 231; adj 652
trimming n 231
trinity n 92
trio n 92, 415, 416
trip n 266, 302, 306; v 306, 309
tripartition n 94
triple v 93; adj 93
triplet n 92
triplicate adj 93
triplication n 93
triplicity n 93
tripling n 93
triply adv 93
trip the light fantastic toe n 309
trip up v 495
trisect v 94
trisection n 94
trite adj 496, 598, 613
triumph n 731, 733, 838; v 731, 838
triumphant adj 731, 838, 884
trivial adj 32, 209, 499, 517, 643, 880
triviality n 32, 209, 643, 736, 880
troll n 980
trollop n 962
troop n 72
trophy n 733
tropical adj 382
troubadour n 597
trouble n 59, 686, 704, 735, 828, 830; v 61, 828, 830
troublemaker n 913
trouble oneself about v 682
troublesome adj 59, 704, 830
trough n 252, 259, 350
trove n 480a
truant n 623
truce n 142, 721, 723
truck n 271, 272; v 264
trudge v 275
true adj 1, 17, 246, 246, 494, 543, 648, 772, 922, 604
true faith n 983a
truelove n 897
true to life adj 17
truism n 496
truistic adj 496
truly adv 31
trump card n 731
trumped up adj 546
trumpery n 643
truncate v 201, 241
truncation n 241
trunk n 50
truss n 215

trust n 484, 507, 805, 858; v 858
trusted adj 484
trustee n 758, 801
trusting adj 484, 486, 547
trustworthy adj 474, 484, 543, 664
trusty adj 474
truth n 494
truth n 1, 474, 543, 922, 983a
truthful adj 494, 543
truthfulness n 543
try v 463, 480, 675, 677
try a case v 967
trying adj 841
tube n 350, 351
tubed instruments n 417
tuck n 258; v 258
tuck in v 300
tug n 285; v 285
tugboat n 273
tumble n 306; v 162, 306, 315
tumid adj 194
tumult n 59, 315, 825
tumultuous adj 59, 173, 404, 825
tundra n 344
tune v 413, 415; v 413
tuned out adj 452
tuneful adj 413, 597
tunefulness n 413
tuneless adj 414
tune out v 452
tunnel n 350; v 252, 260
turbulence n 173, 315
turbulent adj 59, 173, 825
turf n 388
turgid adj 194, 577, 579
turgidity n 579
turkey n 493
turmoil n 59, 173, 315
turn n 7, 134, 138, 140, 176, 245, 311, 621, 698; v 49, 140, 245, 248, 279, 311, 312
turn about v 218
turn a circle v 311
turn a deaf ear to v 419
turn and turn about adv 148
turn around v 311
turn aside v 140, 279, 616
turn away v 297
turn away from v 623
turn back v 145, 283
turncoat n 607
turn color v 434, 435
turn down v 764
turned n 397
turned off adj 452
turning n 311
turning point n 8, 67, 134, 145, 153, 210, 233
turn into v 144
turn off the brain v 452

turn of speech n 566
turn of the tide n 145, 218
turn one's hand to v 625
turn on the juice v 274
turn out v 151, 297
turn over v 218, 270, 784
turn pale v 429
turn tail v 623
turn the scale n 28
turn the stomach v 395
turn the tide n 28, 145
turn to dust v 360
turn to profit v 775
turn topsy-turvy v 61, 218
turn up n 151, 156, 446
turn upside down v 14, 61
turquoise adj 438
tutelage n 537, 539, 749
tutor n 540, 753; v 537
tutorship n 537
twaddle n 584
twain adj 89
twang n 402, 408
tweak v 378
twelve n 98
twenty n 98
twenty-five n 98
twerp n 493
twice adv 90
twilight n 421
twin n 17; adj 17, 88, 89,
90
twine v 219, 248
twine round v 227
twinge n 378, 828; v 378
twinkle v 113, 422
twinkling n 113
twins n 89
twirl n 248; v 248, 311, 312
twist n 243, 248, 503; v 43,
219, 243, 248, 279, 311
twisted adj 248
twister n 315, 349
twist the meaning v 523
twit v 856
twitch n 378; v 378
twitter n 315; v 315, 412
two n 89; adj 89
two-faced adj 544
twofold division n 91
two or more n 100
two-sided adj 89
type n 5, 17, 22, 75, 550,
591; v 240
typical adj 82, 550
typify v 550
typographical adj 591
typography n 591
tyrannical adj 739
tyrannize v 739
tyrant n 739

U

ubiquity n 186
ubiquitous adj 186
ugliness n 846
ugliness n 243

ugly adj 846
ukase n 741
ulterior adj 121
ulterior motive n 615
ultimate adj 67
ultimately adv 117, 121,
133
ululation n 412
umbra n 421
umbrage n 900
umbrageous adj 421, 422
umbrella n 223, 424
umpire n 967; v 174
unable adj 158, 699
unaccompanied adj 87
unaccountable adj 964
unaccustomed adj 614
unachievable adj 471
unacquaintance n 491
unadorned adj 576, 849
unadulterated adj 42, 960
unadvisable adj 647
unaffected adj 578, 823,
849
unallied adj 10
unalterability n 141
unalterable adj 150
unanimity n 23, 709
unanimously adv 709,
714
unanswerable adj 964
unanticipated adj 508
unapplied adj 678
unapproachable adj 196
unappropriate adj 923
unartificial adj 703
unassailable adj 664
unassuming adj 849, 879,
881
unassured adj 475
unattested adj 951
unattached adj 44
unattended adj 87
unattended to adj 460
unauthorized adj 925,
964
unavailing adj 645
unavoidability n 601
unavoidable adj 601, 744
unavoidableness n 601
unaware adj 508, 823
unawareness n 491
unbearable adj 830
unbegotten adj 2
unbeliever n 485
unbelieving adj 485, 487,
989
unbend v 246, 687
unbent adj 246
unbiased adj 942
unblemished adj 650
unborn adj 2
unbound adj 748, 927a
unbridled adj 748
unbroken adj 50, 69, 729
uncanny adj 980
uncanonical adj 984

uncared for adj 460
uncaring adj 823
unceasing adj 104, 112
uncertain adj 139, 475,
485, 520, 605, 704
uncertainty n 475
uncertainty n 111, 139,
485, 519, 520, 605
unchained adj 748
unchangeable adj 5, 150
unchangeableness n 150
unchanged adj 16, 141
unchanging adj 16, 141,
150
unchartered adj 964
unchaste adj 961
unchecked adj 748
uncivil adj 895, 911, 929
uncivilized adj 876
unclad adj 226
unclean adj 653, 961
uncleanness n 653
uncleanness n 961
unclear adj 426
unclose v 260
unclosed adj 260
unclouded adj 420
uncolored adj 429
uncomfortable adj 378,
828
uncommon adj 83, 137
uncommon adv 31
uncommunicative
adj 528, 585
uncommunicativeness
n 585
uncompleted adj 53
uncompliant adj 742
uncomplicate v 849
uncompromising adj 604
unconceived adj 2
unconcern n 456, 458, 866
unconcerned adj 866
unconditional adj 52, 748
unconfined adj 748
unconformable adj 748
unconformity n 83
uncongenial adj 24
unconnected adj 10, 44,
70
unconquerable adj 159
unconscious adj 823
unconsciousness n 376,
491
unconsolidated adj 47
unconstitutional adj 964
unconstrained adj 748
uncontaminated adj 960
uncontrite adj 951
uncontrollability n 606
uncontrollable adj 173,
606, 825
uncontrolled adj 748, 825
unconventional adj 83
unconventionality n 83
uncopied adj 20
uncorroborative adj 468

uncorrupted adj 960
uncouth adj 579
uncover v 228, 260, 480a, 529
uncovered adj 260
uncovering n 529
uncreated adj 2
uncuriosity n 455
unctuosity n 355
unctuous adj 355
unctuousness n 355
uncurbed adj 748
uncurl v 246
uncurved adj 246
uncustomary adj 83
undated adj 115
undecided adj 475
undefiled adj 960
undefined adj 447
undeniable adj 474
undependability n 475
undependable adj 475
under adv 34, 207
under adv 228, 260, 480a, 529
under a cloud adj 735
underage adj 127
under consideration adv 454
under control adj 749
undercover adj 528
undercurrent n 526
undercut v 179
underdeveloped adj 193
underestimate v 481, 483
underestimated adj 483
underestimating adj 483
underestimation n 483
underfoot adv 207
undergo v 151
undergo pain v 378
underground adv 207
underlie v 207, 526
underline v 550, 642
undermine v 179, 659
undermost adj 211
underneath adv 207
under obligation adj 926
under one's nose adj 446
under one's very nose adv 715
under protest adv 603
underrate v 483
under restraint adj 751
underscore v 550, 642
undersized adj 193
understand v 450, 490, 498, 518, 522
understandable adj 518
understanding n 23, 450, 480, 490, 498, 714, 822, 842; adj 498, 822
understand one another v 714
understudy n 211
understood adj 634
undertake v 622, 625, 676, 768
undertaking n 676

undertaking n 620, 622, 625, 768
under the circumstances adv 8
under the conditions adv 8
under the head of adv 9
under the pretense of adv 617
under the stars adv 338
under the sun adv 180, 318
under the weather adj 655
undertone n 405
undervaluation n 483
undervalue v 483
under way adv 264
underwrite v 768, 771
undesirability n 647
undesirable adj 830
undetermined adj 475
undeviating adj 278
undevout adj 989
undiminished adj 50
undirected adj 279
undiscerning adj 442
undiscriminating adj 465a
undisturbed adj 265
undiversified adj 16
undivided adj 50, 52
undo v 145, 162, 179
undone adj 732
undoubtedly adv 474
undraped adj 226
undress n 226
undress v 226
undressed adj 226
undulate v 248, 314
undulating adj 248
undulation n 248, 314
undulatory adj 314
undutiful adj 927
unearth v 363, 480a
unearthly adj 317, 976, 980, 981
uneasiness n 828, 832
uneasy adj 828, 832
uneducated adj 491
unembellished adj 849
unemotional adj 383
unemployed adj 678
unendurable adj 830, 982
unenlightened adj 491
unenlightenment n 491
unentitled adj 925
unequal adj 15, 28
unequaled adj 18, 33
unequivocal adj 31, 246, 570
unequivocally adv 31
unessential adj 643
unestablished adj 185
uneven adj 16a, 28, 243, 256

unevenness n 16a, 28
uneventful adj 643
unexciting adj 174
unexpected adj 132, 508
unexpectedly adv 132, 508
unfaded adj 428
unfading adj 112
unfailing adj 474
unfaithful adj 544
unfashioned adj 241
unfathomable adj 208, 519
unfathomed space n 208
unfathomed adj 208
unfavorable adj 135, 708, 735
unfeasibility n 471
unfeasible adj 471, 704
unfed adj 956
unfeeling adj 381, 383
unfetter v 750
unfettered adj 748
unfinished adj 53, 730
unfit adj 158, 647, 699, 923
unfitness n 647
unfitted adj 158
unfixed adj 149, 475
unfocused adj 447
unfold v 246, 313
unfolding n 313
unforeseen adj 508
unforeseen occurrence n 508
unforgettable adj 505
unforgiving adj 919
unforgotten adj 505
unformed adj 241
unfortunate adj 135, 735
unfounded adj 546
unfriendliness n 889
unfriendly adj 708, 889
unfrozen adj 382
unfruitful adj 169
unfruitfulness n 169, 645
unfulfillment n 509
unfurl v 313
ungenerous adj 32, 819
ungentlemanly adj 895
ungodliness n 989
ungodly adj 989
ungovernable adj 173, 825
ungoverned adj 748
ungraceful adj 579
ungracious adj 895
ungrammatical adj 568
ungrammatical usage n 568
ungrateful adj 917
ungrounded adj 4
unguarded adj 460
unguent n 356
unhallowed adj 989
unhandy adj 699

unhappy adj 828, 837
unharmonious adj 410
unhealthiness n 657
unhealthy adj 655, 657
unheard of adj 137, 508
unheeded adj 460
unheedful adj 452
unheeding adj 419, 458
unhewn adj 674
unhindered adj 748
unhinge v 61
unhinged adj 173, 503
unhip adj 246
unholy adj 989
unhoused adj 185
unhurried adj 275
unhurt adj 670
unification n 48, 87
unified adj 46, 48
uniform v 225; adj 16, 42, 58, 80, 242
uniformity n 16
uniformity n 17, 23, 58, 80, 87, 150, 242
uniformly adv 16, 82
uniforms n 225
unimaginable adj 471
unimaginative adj 598, 843
unimitated adj 20
unimpaired adj 50, 670
unimpeachable adj 474
unimportance n 643
unimportant n 32, 175a
unimportant adj 32, 34, 643, 736
unimpressionable adj 823
unimproved adj 659
uninfluential adj 175a
uninformed adj 491
uninjured adj 670
uninquiring adj 456
uninquisitive adj 456
uninstructed adj 491
unintellectual adj 450a
unintelligent adj 450a
unintelligibility n 519
unintelligibility n 533, 571
unintelligible adj 519, 571
unintentional adj 621
unintentionally adv 621
uninterested adj 456, 841
uninteresting adj 843
uninterrupted adj 69, 112, 143
unintoxicated adj 958
union n 23, 43, 46, 48, 178, 709, 714, 903
unique adj 18, 20, 79, 83, 87, 870
uniqueness n 18, 20, 123
unison n 87, 714
unite v 41, 43, 48, 72, 87, 178, 290, 709, 712
united adj 46, 903

uniting n 37
unity n 87
unity n 13, 23, 50, 52, 714
universal adj 78
universality n 78
universalize v 78
universe n 180, 318
university n 542
unjust adj 923
unkempt adj 653
unknown n 233; adj 533
unlawful adj 964
unlawfulness n 923, 964
unlearn v 506
unlearnedness n 491
unless adv 8, 83
unlettered adj 491
unlicensed adj 964
unlike adj 15, 18
unlikelihood n 473
unlikely adj 473
unlikeness n 18
unlimited adj 31, 104, 180, 748
unlimited space n 180
unload v 185
unlooked for adj 508
unlovely adj 846
unlucky adj 135, 735
unmake v 145
unman v 158
unmanageable adj 704
unmarked adj 447
unmarried adj 904
unmarried man n 904
unmarried woman n 904
unmask v 529, 529
unmatched adj 15, 18, 20
unmeaningness n 517
unmelodious adj 414
unmerciful adj 914a
unmindful adj 452, 458, 460, 917
unmindfulness n 458
unmistakable adj 525
unmitigated adj 52
unmixed adj 42, 960
unmoved adj 265, 823
unmoving adj 172
unmusical adj 410, 414
unmuzzled adj 748
unnatural adj 83, 855
unnaturalness n 855
unnecessary adj 641
unnerve v 158, 160
unnerved adj 160
unnoticed adj 460
unobservant adj 458
unobserved adj 460
unobstructed adj 748
unobtainable adj 471
unobtrusive adj 881
unoccupied adj 452
unopened adj 261
unorthodox adj 984
unorthodoxy n 984
unostentatious adj 881

unpaid adj 806
unpalatable adj 395, 830
unparalleled adj 20, 33
unperceptive adj 376
unperformable adj 471
unpersuasive adj 175a
unpierced adj 261
unplaced adj 185
unpleasant adj 395, 830, 846
unpoetic adj 598
unpointed adj 254
unpolished adj 256
unprecedented adj 18, 137
unpredictability n 139
unpredictable adj 139, 475
unprejudiced adj 942
unprepared adj 674
unpreparedness n 674
unpretentious adj 849, 879, 881
unprized adj 483
unproductive adj 169
unproductiveness n 169
unprofitable adj 169, 647
unprofitableness n 169
unpropitious adj 135·
unprosperous adj 735
unpunctual adj 133, 135
unqualified adj 52, 158
unquestionable adj 474
unquestionableness n 474
unquestioned adj 474
unquiet adj 264
unrational adj 450a
unravel v 60, 246, 522, 705
unreadiness n 674
unready adj 674
unreal adj 2, 317, 515
unreasonable adj 471, 497, 499, 608, 814
unrecorded adj 552
unrefined adj 851
unreflective adj 452
unrelated adj 10
unreliability n 475
unreliable adj 149, 475
unremedial adj 859
unremembered adj 506
unrepentant adj 951
unrepented adj 951
unrepenting adj 951
unreserved adj 525
unresponsive adj 376, 383
unresponsiveness n 376
unrest n 149, 264
unrestricted adj 748
unrevealed adj 533
unrightful adj 925
unrightfulness n 925
unripe adj 123, 674
unrivaled adj 33
unroll v 313

unruffled adj 174, 265, 826

unruliness n 742

unruly adj 606, 742

unsafe adj 475, 665

unsavoriness n 395

unsavoriness n 391, 392

unsavory adj 392, 395, 874

unscoured adj 653

unscriptural adj 984

unscrupulous adj 940

unseasonable adj 135

unseasonableness n 135

unseasoned adj 435

unseeing adj 442

unseemly adj 647, 846

unseen adj 447

unselfish adj 906, 942

unselfishness n 906, 942

unserviceable adj 645

unsettle v 61, 185

unsettled adj 149, 185, 475, 503

unshackled adj 748

unshaped adj 241

unshapely adj 241

unsharpened adj 254

unsightliness n 846

unsightly adj 846

unskilled adj 699

unskillful adj 699

unskillfulness n 699

unsmelling adj 399

unsmooth adj 256

unsophisticated adj 946

unsought adj 766

unsound adj 203, 477, 651, 655

unsoundness n 657

unspiritual adj 316, 989

unstable adj 149, 333, 475, 605, 665

unstained adj 960

unsteady adj 149, 475, 665

unstrung adj 160

unsubmissive adj 742

unsubstantial adj 2, 4, 203, 317, 322, 515

unsubstantiality n 4

unsuccessful adj 732

unsuccessfully adv 732

unsuccessfulness n 732

unsuitability n 647

unsuitable adj 135, 647

unsuitable time n 135

unsuited adj 135

unsullied adj 652, 960

unsupportable adj 830

unsupportive adj 468

unsure adj 475, 485

unsurpassed adj 31, 33

unsusceptible adj 376, 826

unsuspecting adj 486, 547

unsuspicious adj 703

unswerving adj 278

unsymmetrical adj 243

unsympathetic adj 383

unsystematic adj 59

untainted adj 946, 960

untaught adj 491, 675

untenable adj 4, 477

untested adj 123

unthankful adj 917

unthankfulness n 917

unthinking adj 452

unthriftiness n 818

unthrifty adj 818

untidiness n 59

untidy adj 59, 653

until adv 106

untimeliness n 135

untimely adj 135

untouchable adj 317

untoward adj 135

untried adj 123

untrue adj 495, 544, 545, 546, 923

untrustworthy adj 545

untrustworthy memory n 506

untruth n 546

untruth n 544

untruthful adj 544

untruthfulness n 544, 545

untutored adj 491

unusable adj 645

unused adj 40, 678

unusual adj 83, 137, 614

unusually adv 31

unutterable adj 519

unvalued adj 483

unvanquished adj 748

unvaried adj 16

unvarnished adj 576

unvarying adj 16, 143, 150

unveil v 529

unventilated adj 261

unvulnerable adj 112

unwarned adj 508

unwarranted adj 925, 964

unwary adj 460, 863

unwavering adj 150

unwelcome adj 830

unwell adj 655

unwholesome adj 657, 663

unwieldy adj 192, 319, 704

unwilling adj 603

unwillingly adv 603

unwillingness n 603

unwillingness n 704

unwind v 313

unwise adj 499

unwittingly adv 621

unworkable adj 647

unworldliness n 703

unworldly adj 703

unworthy adj 874

unworthy of consideration adj 643

unworthy of notice adj 643

up and down adv 314

Upanishads n 986

upgrowth n 305

upheaval n 307

uphill adj 217

uphold v 143, 670, 707, 717, 937

uplift v 307

upon one's oath adj 768

uppermost adj 210

upraise v 307

uprear v 307

upright adj 212, 246, 922, 939, 944, 946, 960

uprightness n 922, 939, 944, 946, 960

uprising n 146

uproar n 59, 173, 404

uproarious adj 404

uproot v 301

ups and downs n 314

upset n 308; v 162, 218, 308; adj 824

upshot n 154, 480, 729

upside down adj 218

upstairs n 450

up to adj 157; adv 106

up to a point adv 26

up-to-date adj 123

up to the mark adj 27, 639

up to this time adv 122

upturn n 218

upwards of adv 100

urbane adj 894

urchin n 980

urge v 173, 276, 684

urgency n 642, 684

urgent adj 630, 642

urging n 695

urinate v 299

urination n 299

urn n 363

usage n 567, 613, 677, 998

use n 677

use n 644; v 677, 788

used up adj 158, 659

useful adj 176, 618, 631, 644, 677

usefulness n 644, 677

useless adj 169, 499, 643, 645, 647, 732, 880

uselessness n 645

use the occasion v 134

use up v 677

usher n 296

usher v 296

usher in v 62, 66, 280

usual adj 82, 613

usurer n 805, 819

usurious adj 819

usurp v 789

usurper n 925

utensil n 633

utilitarian *adj* 677
utility *n* 644
utility *n* 646, 677
utilization *n* 677
utilize *v* 677
utmost *adj* 33
utter *v* 580, 582; *adj* 31
utterance *n* 580, 985
utterly *adv* 52
uttermost *adj* 31

V

vacancy *n* 187, 209, 499
vacancy of mind *n* 452
vacant *adj* 4, 187, 209,
  452, 499
vacate *v* 185, 293
vacation *n* 685, 687
vacationer *n* 268
vacillate *v* 149, 314, 605
vacillating *adj* 149
vacillation *n* 149, 314,
  485, 605
vacuity *n* 187, 452
vacuous *adj* 4, 187, 209
vacuum *n* 187
vagabond *n* 268
vagabondism *n* 266
vagary *n* 608
vagrant *n* 268; *adj* 266
vague *adj* 475, 477, 517,
  571
vagueness *n* 475, 519, 571
vain *adj* 158, 645, 878, 880
vain expectation *n* 509
vainglorious *adj* 884, 880
vainglory *n* 878
vale *n* 252
valediction *n* 293
valid *adj* 157
validity *n* 157
valley *n* 252, 259
valor *n* 861
valorous *adj* 861
valuable *adj* 644, 648
valuation *n* 466, 812
value *n* 644, 648, 812, 815;
  v 466, 480, 642, 931
valueless *adj* 645
value received *n* 810
valve *n* 263, 350
vampire *n* 980
van *n* 280
vanguard *n* 234, 280
vanish *v* 4, 111, 360, 449
vanished *adj* 449
vanishing point *n* 193
vanity *n* 880
vanity *n* 878
vantage ground *n* 175
vapid *adj* 337, 391, 575,
  843
vapor *n* 353
vaporization *n* 336
vaporize *v* 336
vaporous *adj* 334, 336
vaporousness *n* 334

vapory *adj* 336
variability *n* 475
variable *adj* 140, 149, 475
variance *n* 15, 24, 291,
  713
variant *adj* 15
variation *n* 20a
variation *n* 15, 83, 140
varied *adj* 15, 16a, 20a
variegate *v* 440
variegation *n* 440
variegated *adj* 41, 440
variety *n* 75, 81
various *adj* 15, 102
varnish *n* 223, 356a;
  v 356a
vary *v* 15, 18, 20a, 140,
  149, 291, 314
vast *adj* 31, 104, 180, 192
vastness *n* 31, 105
vault *n* 245, 309, 318, 363,
  802; *v* 309
vaulted *adj* 245
vaunt *v* 884
veer *v* 140, 279
vegetable *adj* 367
vegetable *adj* 367
vegetable kingdom *n* 367
vegetable life *n* 365
vegetable oil *n* 356
vegetable physiology
  n 369
vegetal *adj* 367
vegetarian *n* 953
vegetate *v* 367
vegetation *n* 365
vegetative *adj* 365, 367
vehemence *n* 173, 825
vehement *adj* 173, 382,
  574, 825
vehicle *n* 272
vehicle *n* 271, 631
veil *n* 424, 530; *v* 424, 528
veiled *adj* 447, 526
veiling *n* 528
vein *n* 176, 205, 602
veined *adj* 440
velocity *n* 274
velocity *n* 264
velvety *adj* 255, 256
venal *adj* 211, 819
venality *n* 819
vend *v* 796
vendible *adj* 796
vendition *n* 796
vendor *n* 796
veneer *n* 223; *v* 204, 223
venerable *adj* 124, 128,
  928
venerate *v* 860, 928, 987
veneration *n* 860, 928, 987
vengeance *n* 718, 919
vengeful *adj* 718, 919
vengefulness *n* 919
venom *n* 663, 907
venomous *adj* 649, 657,
  663, 907

vent *n* 260, 351
ventilate *v* 338, 349, 652
ventilation *n* 338
venture *n* 621, 675, 676;
  v 621, 665, 675, 861
venturesome *adj* 621, 675
veracious *adj* 494, 543
veracity *n* 543
veracity *n* 494
verbal *adj* 562
verbal interchange *n* 588
verbiage *n* 573
verbose *adj* 573, 584, 641
verbosity *n* 573, 584, 641
verdant *adj* 367, 435
verdict *n* 480, 969
verdure *n* 367, 435
verdurous *adj* 435
verge *n* 231, 233; *v* 176,
  278
verification *n* 478
verify *v* 478
veritable *adj* 494
verity *n* 494
vermilion *adj* 434
vernacular *n* 560; *adj* 560
versatile *adj* 149
versatility *n* 149
verse *n* 590, 597
versification *n* 597
versifier *n* 597
versify *v* 597
versus *adv* 708
vertex *n* 210
vertical *adj* 212, 246
verticality *n* 212
vertically *adv* 212
verve *n* 159, 515, 574
very *adv* 31
very best *adj* 648
very much *adv* 31
vespers *n* 126
vessel *n* 191, 273
vestal virgin *n* 960
vestige *n* 551
vestments *n* 999
veteran *n* 130
veteran *n* 700
veterinary science *n* 370
veto *n* 761
vex *v* 828, 830
vexation *n* 828, 830, 835
vexatious *adj* 830, 901a
vibes *n* 314
vibrate *v* 314
vibration *n* 138, 314, 408
vibrato *n* 408
vice *n* 945
vice *n* 649, 923
vice versa *adv* 148
vicinity *n* 186, 197
vicious *adj* 907, 945
vicissitude *n* 111, 149
victimize *v* 649
victorious *adj* 731
victory *n* 731
vie *v* 648, 720

wolf in sheep's clothing n 667
woman n 374
woman n 372
woman-hater n 911
womanhood n 131, 374
womanly adj 131, 374
womb n 208, 221
wonder n 870
wonder n 508, 872; v 870
wonderful adj 870
wonderfully adv 31
wondrous adj 870
wont n 613, 613
wood n 388
woodwinds n 417
wooer n 897
woolly adj 256, 329
word n 562
word n 768
word coiner n 563
word for word adv 19
wordiness n 573
wording n 569
Word of God n 985
word-play n 520
words n 713
words of wisdom n 496
wordy adj 573, 584
work n 170, 590, 593, 680,
  686; v 170, 677, 680, 686
workable adj 644
workaday adj 625
workbook n 542
worked up adj 900
worker n 680, 690, 746
work hard v 686
work in v 228
working n 170, 680
working toward adj 176
workmanship n 161
works n 161
workshop n 691
work the land v 371
work well v 705
wordly adj 318, 989
worldwide adj 78, 180
worm n 248, 366
worm-eaten adj 659
worm one's way v 275
worn adj 160, 659
worn out adj 158, 659, 688
worrisome adj 830
worry n 828; v 828, 830
worse adj 835
worsen v 835
worsening n 835

worshiping adj 990
worth n 644, 648, 812
worthiness n 33
worthless adj 643, 645,
  647
worthlessness n 645
worthwhile adj 646
worthy adj 246
wound n 830; v 659, 830
woven adj 219
wrack n 162; v 378
wraith n 980
wrangle n 720; v 476, 713,
  720
wrangler n 476
wrap n 223, 225
wrapped adj 223
wrapper n 232
wrapping n 191
wrappings n 223
wrap up v 67, 223
wrath n 900
wrathful adj 900
wreak v 739
wreath n 247
wreathe n 219
wreck n 162; v 162
wrecker n 165
wrench n 301; v 44, 285,
  301
wrest v 243
wretch n 949
wretched adj 649, 828
wretchedly adv 32
wretchedness n 735
wriggle v 315
wring n 248, 378
wring from v 301
wrinkle n 258; v 248, 258,
  259
wrinkled adj 128
writ n 590, 969
write v 569, 590
write down v 590
write prose v 598
writer n 590, 593
write to v 592
writhe v 243, 315, 378
writing n 590
writing n 593, 598
written adj 590
wrong n 923
wrong n 173, 619; v 649,
  923; adj 481, 495, 544,
  649, 923, 945
wrongdoer n 913, 949
wrongheaded adj 481
wrongly adv 923
wrong side out adj 218
wrought up adj 824

Y

yacht n 273

yachting n 267
yank n 285; v 285
yap v 412
yard n 232
yarn n 549
yawl n 273
yawn v 260, 688
yawning n 688; adj 208,
  260
year n 106, 108
year after year adv 104
yearning n 276, 865, 897
years n 128
years ago adv 122
yeast n 320, 353
yell n 411; v 411
yell out v 411
yellow n 436
yellow v 435; adj 435
yellowish adj 435
yellow streak n 862
yelp v 410, 412
yesterday n 122
yesteryear n 122
yet adv 30, 106, 116, 122
yield v 82, 324, 360, 488,
  624, 725, 762, 782, 812
yielding n 624, 725, 782
yoke n 749; v 43, 89
yon adj 196
yonder adj 196
young adj 123, 127, 129,
  435
younger adj 127
youngster n 129
young years n 127
youth n 127
youth n 123, 129

Z

zany n 501
zeal n 171, 382, 604, 682,
  821
zealot n 606
zealotry n 606
zealous adj 171, 606, 682
zenith n 206, 210
zephyr n 349
zero n 101
zero n 4
zest n 394
zigzag n 279; adj 279,
  629; adv 314
zip n 101; v 409
zipping n 409
zone n 181, 204, 247
zonkers adj 503
zonko adj 503
zoography n 368
zoological adj 366, 368
zoologist n 357
zoology n 368
zoology n 357